I0605583

MAKING SENSE OF SLAVERY

MAKING SENSE OF SLAVERY

AMERICA'S LONG RECKONING, FROM THE FOUNDING ERA TO TODAY

SCOTT SPILLMAN

BASIC BOOKS
New York

Basic Books
Hachette Book Group
1290 Avenue of the Americas, New York, NY 10104
www.basicbooks.com

Printed in the United States of America

First Edition: March 2025

Published by Basic Books, an imprint of Hachette Book Group, Inc. The Basic Books name and logo is a trademark of the Hachette Book Group.

Print book interior design by Amy Quinn.

Library of Congress Cataloging-in-Publication Data

Names: Spillman, Scott, author.
Title: Making sense of slavery : America's long reckoning, from the founding era to today / Scott Spillman.
Description: First edition. | New York : Basic Books, 2025. | Includes bibliographical references and index.
Identifiers: LCCN 2024043749 | ISBN 9781541602090 (hardcover) | ISBN 9781541602106 (ebook)
Subjects: LCSH: Slavery—United States—Historiography. | Slavery—United States—History—Study and teaching.
Classification: LCC E441 .S74 2025 | DDC 306.3/620973—dc23/eng/20241203
LC record available at https://lccn.loc.gov/2024043749

ISBNs: 9781541602090 (hardcover), 9781541602106 (ebook)

LSC-C

Printing 1, 2024

For my mother
Carolyn Spillman

and in memory of my father
David Spillman II
(1949–2018)

Indeed my kind friend the object of Slavery is still an object worthy the deepest consideration, of a philosophic mind.

—Anthony Benezet to Benjamin Franklin (1783)

CONTENTS

PREFACE

THIS BOOK IS NOT ABOUT SLAVERY. IT IS, INSTEAD, ABOUT HOW AMERicans have made sense of slavery: how they have researched and written about it, how they have justified and criticized it, how they have struggled with the paradox of its existence in a country that professes its devotion to principles of liberty and equality, and how they have wrestled with its enduring legacies.

We sometimes think of this process of reckoning with slavery as new. It is not. Slavery first became a major problem in American life around the time of the Revolution, and Americans have wrestled with it ever since—not to mention all the other related issues, such as race and labor, agriculture and industry, culture and conquest, opportunity and inequality. Not only has thought about the subject of slavery reflected the changing contours of American intellectual life, but in many cases it has also shaped those contours as founding figures in various scholarly disciplines—Francis Lieber in political science, Herbert Baxter Adams in history, Franz Boas in anthropology, Robert Park in sociology—saw slavery and its consequences as central problems that their fields would have to puzzle out in order to prove their worth.

The study of slavery matters because it affects not only how we think about the past but also how we draw the boundaries of social and political possibility in the present and for the future. Yet we tend to take the existence of scholarship about slavery for granted. We rarely wonder when American studies of slavery began, why they became embedded in the research university, and how they have influenced our understanding of history, politics, and society over the past 250 years. That is one of the points of this book: that the study of slavery itself has a history, that the nature of its development and the shape of its arguments were influenced by intellectual logic as well as institutional setting, political climate, social situation, and personal quirks. Ideas are always soaked in the circumstances of their creation even as they sometimes, somehow, transcend them. Intellectual life is not the dry stuff of stereotype but has a drama of its own.

Just what does it mean to study slavery? By "study," I have meant making arguments based on evidence. But what is evidence? And who has the authority to make those determinations? These are precisely the kinds of questions that the study of slavery has raised from the start. In part because a large number of the people involved—namely, the enslaved—were kept forcibly illiterate and there was never any truth commission after emancipation (the concept did not exist at the time), there is a limit to what we can know for sure about how it functioned. This leaves a lot of room for imagination and interpretation. The special problems involved in the study of slavery have revealed where the normal practices of scholarship begin to break down, but in addition to exposing those boundaries the study of slavery has also tested them, stretched them, and forced historians (and scholars in other fields) to add new tools to their belts. Scholars have sometimes dropped tools, too, and lost those older ways of seeing the world.

The study of slavery is enormous. The most comprehensive database of worldwide slavery scholarship now has tens of thousands of entries. More than a thousand new books and articles are published every year. I have not tried to cover everything; I have tried to tell a story about the most important debates, not write an encyclopedia.

Before we begin, it is worth saying a few words about the nature of those debates. First, the language. It can be unpleasant, often offensive, occasionally obscene. I have chosen to reproduce it in full because I believe that it is valuable to see exactly how people in the past were thinking, right down to the specific texture of the terms they used.

Second, the characters. They are mostly scholars and other intellectuals, people who spent their lives studying and writing about the world. This is not to say that other people didn't have ideas, only that their ideas have not traditionally carried the same authority as those of scholars who had a specific social and cultural imprimatur. Before the late nineteenth century, such scholars tended to be gentleman amateurs; after that, they became attached to the new institution of the research university. For a long time, these people were overwhelmingly wealthy, white, and male. A steady stream of intellectuals who didn't check all those boxes also entered the debate, but it was only in the second half of the twentieth century that they gained more equal access to funding and research, professorships and publications. How that change affected the scholarly conversation about slavery is one of the stories of this book.

Finally, the content. The tradition of Western intellectual engagement with slavery goes back more than two thousand years, to the time when Plato and Aristotle first formulated theories about who should be slaves and what role slavery played in society. Modern scholarship about slavery arrived on the scene much later, after many of the major arguments for and against slavery had already taken shape, and indeed part of the work of slavery scholarship has always been to subject old ideas to fresh analysis in the light of new evidence.

But this is not a linear story of evidence accumulated and knowledge gained, culminating in the enlightened and entirely correct academics who bestride the Earth today. Like all history, intellectual history is not neat. It doubles back and circles around, a little like a committee meeting or a political debate. People are always butting in and raising old questions, leading to a whole new round of discussion on some topic that you thought or hoped had been settled. But it is never settled. Evidence keeps getting reused, arguments rehashed, ideas recycled. Subtle variations in the statement of a problem or in the circumstances of its reception can make it resonate in new ways, and that is what we will be tracking. The Revolution, racial ideology, emancipation, industrialization, segregation, the civil rights movement—all have shaped how Americans have seen slavery and what they have wanted to get out of it. The history of slavery studies is itself a history of American politics, society, and thought.

Slavery also raises deep and profound questions that drill to the core of the human condition but can never truly be solved. These kinds of questions don't go away; they just get raised anew in each generation. This is doubly true of slavery because it raises questions about not just the human condition but also the nature of America and of American history, the kind that we as Americans grapple with constantly as part of the ongoing project of defining our identity.

Indeed, one reason that the study of slavery has often circled around the same questions is precisely that the questions are so hard and the stakes are so high, potentially implicating many of the ideas and institutions that make up our modern world. Are the traditional methods of scholarly objectivity sufficient for the study of slavery, or are they inadequate, impossible, even undesirable? Did capitalism kill slavery, or does slavery lie at capitalism's dark heart? Should we see slavery as an example of Americans struggling to live up to our stated principles, or might its existence suggest that those principles were rotten from the start?

These are just some of the questions that recur throughout the history of slavery studies. One way to begin to answer them is through an account of how others have tried.

MAKING SENSE OF SLAVERY

PROLOGUE
KNOWLEDGE IS POWER

THE STUDY OF SLAVERY IN AMERICA STARTED IN A SPECIFIC TIME AND place: in Philadelphia during the decades after 1750. Before that moment, slavery had not been the subject of much scholarly inquiry. It had no place in the colonial college curriculum, and it generated little public debate that might have driven people to seek new evidence or arguments. The practice of slavery had existed throughout the European colonies in the New World since around 1500, and although slavery itself (the ownership of individuals) and even serfdom (the permanent attachment of peasants to a plot of land) had largely died out in the heart of Europe over the previous centuries, such practices had survived on the margins and could be connected to a long history of enslavement going back to medieval Mediterranean merchants, Arab traders, and ancient Greeks and Romans. Through all those millennia, there had never been a mass movement in opposition to the institution, just a series of scattered critiques and revolts.

Around 1750, however, there was a fundamental shift in human moral perception, at least in Europe and the Americas, such that old justifications of slavery as divinely or naturally ordained no longer held the same sway. A growing ethic of benevolence and the rise of evangelical Christianity helped shift attitudes, making it possible to see enslaved Africans as equals worthy of empathy and compassion. New travel accounts from across the globe confronted Europeans with vivid depictions of human cultural and physical difference. Enlightenment philosophy undermined traditional justifications for domination while articulating new doctrines of individual liberty and natural equality.[1] It was only in this context that it began to make sense to "study" slavery in something like the way we mean today.

The first person to do it in America was Anthony Benezet. A beloved schoolteacher and librarian, Benezet lived in a brick house near the center of Philadelphia, and he had connections throughout the community, including to influential local leaders such as Benjamin Franklin. "Who could have lived a month in Philadelphia without knowing Anthony Benezet!" a French diplomat later wrote, adding, "Benezet has intelligence, wit, and fire, and if I may express it, he carries his love of humanity to the point of madness."[2]

Benezet poured all those qualities—intelligence, wit, fire, love of humanity, a touch of madness—into a campaign against slavery. Often considered one of the most important early abolitionists because of the way he expanded the movement's influence and reach, Benezet was perhaps most distinctive in the way he tried to persuade others. His key insight was that, if read in the right way, accounts of the slave trade could become powerful evidence against slavery, allowing him to show "how by various perfidious, and cruel Methods, the unhappy Negroes are inslaved."[3] The collection and proper interpretation of evidence, he saw, could serve the cause by convincing people that slavery was wrong.

Benezet soon realized that accounts of West African society could be useful as well. Even hostile depictions revealed the existence of African government, administration, agriculture, and trade—which could open another line of attack on the slave trade. Showing Africans as fundamentally the same as Europeans might help disprove the notion that they were savages who benefited from enslavement. He sketched this theme in a series of pamphlets, culminating in 1771 in *Some Historical Account of Guinea*, which soon became one of the most influential studies of slavery ever written.

Benezet's research galvanized isolated antislavery sentiment into a transatlantic movement. Yet it also called forth a vigorous response. Those in favor of slavery now had to articulate the principles on which slavery was based and provide, for the first time, specific evidence to support their case. It was in the space between these two positions—and in the effort to define what counted as facts, how those facts would be assessed, and what implications they had—that the study of slavery took shape.

IN COMPARISON WITH CONTEMPORARY INTELLECTUAL LIFE, WHICH OPERates through well-established structures such as universities and journals and publishing houses, the world of early modern scholarship was amorphous. A bare handful of colleges dotted the long coast of the thirteen British mainland colonies. Their mission was to pass down a curriculum derived largely from Christianity and the classics, not to produce new knowledge. When scholarship was conducted, it was done by gentleman amateurs and shared—when it was shared—via letters and locally published pamphlets.

But what the early modern scholarly world may have lacked in formal structure, it made up for in the lively flow of people and ideas around the Atlantic. Anthony Benezet was himself a product of this cosmopolitan intellectual world. Born in France to a prosperous family of Huguenots, he may have turned to antislavery activism later in life partly because his family was the target of religious persecution. They fled France for a brief stay in Rotterdam and a longer one in London before eventually landing in Philadelphia in the early 1730s, when Benezet was eighteen. He could read French, English, German, and Dutch.[4]

It was probably in Philadelphia that Benezet became a Quaker. Soon he married Joyce Marriott, the daughter of a prominent Quaker family. Many Quakers, including Benezet's father, became successful merchants, but Benezet did not. "I find being much amongst the buyers and sellers a snare to me . . . ," he wrote. "I had rather be otherwise employed."[5] So he quit and became a schoolteacher—first in Germantown, a few miles north of the city, then back in Philadelphia at the Penn Charter School.

By this time, the 1740s, Benezet was beginning to take on more responsibilities within the Quaker community. First he was asked to evaluate young men who wanted to get married—to make sure their minds and morals were right. Soon he became an overseer in the Philadelphia Monthly Meeting, and then an elder. He was charged with investigating when members were accused of improprieties such as adultery, drunkenness, or business fraud, and he was tasked with writing petitions and letters to colonial leaders about issues of special concern to Quakers, such as theatrical productions (against) and fast days (also against). He was gaining moral authority within the Quaker community, but he was also learning how to persuade powerful people outside it.

And he was developing important ties to the local Black community. At the time, Philadelphia had a total of around fifteen thousand residents. Roughly three thousand of them were Black, and some eight hundred of those were enslaved. Benezet encountered them out on the street—indeed, even just across the street. "A Parcel of likely Negroes . . . ," said one ad, "may be seen at a Free Negroe Woman, in Chester Street, opposite to Mr. Anthony Benezet."[6]

Benezet recognized that Black people were part of the brotherhood of mankind, as he would have put it, and he became convinced that they deserved the same education and opportunities as anyone else. Starting in 1750, he invited free Black children to his house to teach them the same things he taught his white pupils: reading, writing, and arithmetic. He did this quietly, in the evenings, so as not to cause any controversy, and he discovered that it was exactly how he wanted to spend his time. "I know of no station in life I should prefere before it," he later told Benjamin Franklin.[7] He kept it up for two decades, until he had enough support to start the official Friends School for Black People—to which he eventually left most of his own money and books.

Benezet stood at the confluence of two great streams of thought that prepared the ground for both the antislavery movement and the study of slavery. These were the radical strand of Protestant Christianity that had emerged a century earlier, during the English civil wars, and Enlightenment philosophy, the culmination of a centuries-long movement in Europe that changed the grounds for understanding the world from Providence and tradition to nature and history.

The radically egalitarian Protestant dissenters who had emerged in the seventeenth century held that God was not a fixed good but a revolutionary force, one that collapsed moral gradations into clear dichotomies and that flattened social hierarchies into equality before the Lord. Their belief in the power of Christian love was so strong, their faith in individual conscience so complete, that they proved unwilling to compromise with the existence of darkness, evil, and enslavement. Their names—Diggers, Levellers, Puritans, Seekers—suggest something of the fervor of their faith, a flame that burned with such pure white heat that it often burned itself right out. The Quakers were also one of these groups—perhaps the only one to strike a sustainable balance between radical purity and worldly compromise. It was a balance that managed to keep the group from dying out, but also from going slack.[8]

Quakers believed that all souls shared an inner light that made them equal before God, and they believed in the power of each individual's inner light to illuminate the difference between good and evil. Slavery placed tremendous stress on these ideas—ideas of equality and brotherhood and freedom—and it was the kind of stress that some Quakers felt duty bound not just to articulate but to act on. One radical Quaker, Benjamin Lay, started writing strident abolitionist pamphlets in 1729, two years before the Benezet family arrived from Britain. A few decades later, John Woolman, a much quieter Quaker soul, traveled through the southern colonies and took notes on what he saw. When he returned to Philadelphia, he drafted an antislavery pamphlet—then put it away, concerned about the effects it might have. Benezet made sure it saw the light of day.[9]

In 1752, Benezet joined the Overseers of the Press for the Philadelphia Yearly Meeting of Friends, which was charged with reviewing publications by church members to ensure that they conformed to Quaker doctrines. Two years later, Benezet helped bring Woolman's pamphlet, called *Some Considerations on the Keeping of Negroes*, to press. He also drafted a letter imploring his fellow Quakers to stop participating in the slave trade. "Now, dear Friends," the letter read, "if we continually bear in mind the royal law *of doing to others as we would be done by*, we shall never think of bereaving our fellow creatures of that valuable blessing, liberty, nor endure to grow rich by their bondage." Benezet also reminded his readers of an important piece of Mosaic law, Exodus 21:16, which reads, "*He that stealeth a man and selleth him, or if he be found in his hand, he shall surely be put to death.*" Published and read aloud in worship meetings, the letter made slavery a prominent subject among the Society of Friends.[10]

After he saw the letter and Woolman's pamphlet through publication in 1754, Benezet's antislavery activity stalled at the start of the Seven Years' War, the largest colonial conflict to that time, which dominated most of the next decade. But the war stimulated the Pennsylvania slave trade by causing a shortage of white laborers. At the same time, stories of British colonists being taken captive by Indians and sold into slavery started circulating. By the end of the 1750s, Benezet could no longer avoid discussing the connections he saw between slavery and the war—which he, as a pacifist Quaker, opposed. He pushed the Philadelphia meeting to declare in 1758 that members must free their slaves. He also got a subsidy from the Overseers of the Press to reprint a letter that the London Yearly Meeting had issued against the slave trade. Benezet began to draft an introduction to place at the start of the letter.[11]

By this time, Benezet's thinking on slavery had evolved to include Enlightenment thinkers—who, not unlike evangelical Protestants, tended to look to human nature to discover truths that could challenge traditional authority. Most important was the French political philosopher Montesquieu, whose 1748 book *The Spirit of the Laws* immediately became one of the most influential works of the Enlightenment, especially in Britain and America. "The state of slavery is, in its own nature, bad," Montesquieu declared. "It is neither useful to the master nor to the slave." It made masters into tyrants and stripped slaves of any virtuous motivations; it was based on nothing but prejudice and contempt.

But Montesquieu's inquiry fed into a nascent pro-slavery position when it turned toward what he called "the true origin of the right of slavery." Montesquieu claimed that a country's laws should be adapted "to the people for whom they are framed." This placed a new premium on understanding a country's particular conditions—its soil, climate, people, and so on. In that spirit, Montesquieu said that slavery found its true origin in warm climates, the kind of places "where the excess of heat enervates the body, and renders men so slothful and dispirited that nothing but the fear of chastisement can oblige them to perform any laborious duty." Although Montesquieu maintained that "all men are born equal," he conceded that in warm places slavery might be rational: "reconcileable to reason," he said, or even "founded on natural reason." Eventually he dropped reason and sidled right up to nature, concluding that "natural slavery . . . is to be limited to some particular parts of the world."[12]

Montesquieu stated more clearly than any other major philosopher at the time that slavery was a problem. If people were by nature free, as most Enlightenment philosophers maintained, then slavery needed to be either ended or somehow explained.[13] He also showed that the problem of slavery could be analyzed and debated, and even rationalized or defended, on the basis of empirical evidence.

Soon other Enlightenment thinkers were following up on Montesquieu's example. The Scottish philosophers David Hume and Robert Wallace modeled a new kind of scholarly social scientific inquiry in the 1750s as they argued about the relationship among slavery, population, and social progress. Hume said that slavery was uniquely cruel and led to more misery, less productivity, and fewer people than free labor. Wallace countered that slavery resulted in greater care for the poor because masters had a vested interest in keeping their slaves healthy and productive. Their debate prefigured nearly all later arguments about slavery, in which scholars sought new evidence and data to support theories about history and society that depended largely on slavery's purported effects on measures such as population, poverty, production, and profit.

Evangelical religion and Enlightenment philosophy provided the framework for Benezet to turn against slavery. Their shared emphasis on individual experience also helped him see that convincing people of his views would require bringing them as close to personal encounters as he could—by presenting them with eyewitness evidence. But where would he get that evidence? Benezet lived in a society that practiced slavery; he probably would have seen slaves every day in the streets, or he could have traveled a short distance to Virginia to see large-scale plantation slavery in person. Yet his attacks usually focused not on slavery itself but on the African slave trade, which he saw as the ultimate source of the evil. Unable to travel to Africa himself, at least not easily, he turned to a growing genre of travel narratives and trader accounts that had developed over the previous few hundred years of European exploration and empire building.

As Britain became more heavily involved in the African slave trade after the 1670s, British publishers began to put out more accounts of West Africa, many of them written by slave traders or naval officers who had helped protect the trade. During these decades, Britain also began to tighten its control over a previously motley collection of overseas colonies where slavery was becoming an important labor source; accounts of them also followed. By this time, the travel genre had pushed beyond narrowly practical information into a form marked by curiosity and close observation of the local landscape, flora, and fauna as well as the people, customs, and government. In the eighteenth century, a flood of multivolume travel compendiums such as Awnsham and John Churchill's *Collection* (first published in 1704 but expanded in 1732 and again in 1747) and Thomas Astley's *New General Collection of Voyages and Travels* (1745–47) made it even easier to compare different accounts to confirm which observations were true. As Enlightenment philosophers used the accounts to ground their generalizations about progress and politics, this wealth of information spurred the start of what we now call the social sciences.[14]

The travel collections were large, expensive books, but Benezet may have had access to them through the Library Company of Philadelphia, where his younger brother was a member, as well as from the Loganian Library, where he served as librarian, and the Friends' Library, which he operated out of his own house. At a certain point it occurred to him that the accounts of European travelers and traders provided him with eyewitness evidence from Africa. "By these," he explained, "we shall see that in order to get Slaves, the Europeans settled at the Factories in Africa, encourage Wars, and promote the Practice of stealing Men, Women and Children, which they readily purchase without any Regard to Justice, Equity or any of the tender Ties of Nature." He began to mine the recent Churchill and Astley collections for evidence—especially Astley, which became his major source of information thanks to its large second volume, devoted entirely to West Africa. Benezet lined up lengthy, damning statements from Willem Bosman of the Dutch African Company, Jean Barbot of the French Royal African Company, and

French trader André Brüe. He even did some sleuthing of his own, seeking out the unpublished journal of a Philadelphia surgeon who had served as a slave doctor during a two-year trading voyage to Guinea.[15]

Although Benezet initially intended this evidence for his introduction to the London Yearly Meeting's 1758 letter against the slave trade, his research eventually grew to the size of a short pamphlet in its own right. Published in 1759 as *Observations on the Inslaving, Importing and Purchasing of Negroes*, it marked the first time anyone had deployed eyewitness evidence to show "the Truth" about the slave trade. And it soon proved popular enough to merit a second edition.[16]

NOT CONTENT TO ARGUE ONLY AGAINST THE SLAVE TRADE, BENEZET GATHered additional evidence to examine African society as a whole. Within three years, he published *A Short Account of That Part of Africa, Inhabited by the Negroes*. In the expanded second edition, it was roughly six times as long as his first pamphlet and included eight times as many quotations from the Astley collection. Benezet documented these sources with footnotes—far from a standard practice at the time, but one he continued in later works. Although most of the writers he cited depicted Africa as a place of barbarous customs, internecine warfare, and savage slavery, Benezet built on his experience with Philadelphia's free Black community to read these jaundiced accounts against the grain. He showed that far from being a benevolent enterprise intended to redeem captive Africans for Christianity, the slave trade actually provoked wars intended specifically to generate slaves. He drew out selective details to demonstrate "that the *Negroes* are generally sensible, humane and sociable, and that their Capacity is as good, and as capable of Improvement, as that of the White People."[17]

A year after Benezet published *A Short Account*, Britain won the Seven Years' War. It gained a sprawling empire as well as a mountain of debt. Parliament embarked on an ambitious program of imperial reform, which soon provoked protests in the North American colonies. Benezet took advantage of the imperial dispute, and especially the rising colonial rhetoric of rights and liberties, to launch a new attack on the slave trade. Published in 1766,

A Caution and Warning to Great Britain and Her Colonies examined the conditions of colonial slavery and the details of imperial trade in a new light. As more economic and demographic data were becoming available, Benezet used his merchant's education and his experience teaching math to dig into new kinds of quantitative sources. Using the *Liverpool Memorandum Book*, a trade publication for merchants, he was able to tally the number of ships that left Liverpool for Guinea and the number of slaves that each one carried across the Atlantic. He came up with a total of more than thirty thousand slaves per year, then extrapolated across Britain's other major slaving ports, Bristol and London, to estimate that British ships transported at least a hundred thousand people from Africa annually. Accounts of the slave trade suggested that at least one-tenth of those people died in transit and another one-quarter died soon after starting to work in the colonies (a process known as "seasoning"). That yielded a minimum of thirty thousand people, Benezet figured, who were "truly and properly speaking, murdered every year." "Britons boast themselves to be a generous, humane people . . . ," he wrote, "but is this a true character whilst that barbarous, savage slave trade, with all its attendant horrors, receives countenance and protection from the legislature, whereby so many thousand lives are yearly sacrificed?" Benezet distributed the pamphlet widely, including to the archbishop of Canterbury.[18]

Soon Benezet was at work on a full history of Guinea and the slave trade. "As time has given an opportunity of a farther insight in the progress and consequence thereof," he told a friend, "it appeared proper to make some additions, in order to set the Origine & Nature of the Trade &c in a more regular order, than had yet been done." The result, *Some Historical Account of Guinea*, was published in 1771. He hoped it would serve as a resource for other antislavery activists, and it even included an index.[19]

The key difference from Benezet's previous pamphlets was the new book's broader scope, including not just arguments against slavery but also a detailed history of the parts of Africa where American slaves originated. Benezet's decade of research on the subject showed. In addition to his usual supply of eighteenth-century traveler and trader accounts, he now drew from older writings about Africa, such as the twelfth-century *Geographica Nubiensis*, as well as some of the earliest English travelers' accounts, compiled in the seventeenth century. Using these, Benezet was able to describe the lay of the land (a good climate, with plenty of food and water) as well as the temperament of the natives ("affable and easily overcome with reason": basically Quakers) and the judicial structure of kingdoms such as the Kongo, where "the king appoints a judge in every particular division, to hear and determine disputes and civil causes."

All this could constitute propaganda of its own, of course. But as before, Benezet was pleased to have garnered his information from hostile, prejudiced sources, which he thought helped insulate his arguments from attack. "They cannot but allow the Negroes to be posessed of some good qualities," he declared, "though they contrive as much as possible to cast a shade over them."[20]

Benezet used his sources to reconstruct the history of slavery and the slave trade from the first Portuguese trading post at Elmina (in what is now Ghana) in the 1480s. Early Portuguese enslavement of peaceful Africans arose, he claimed, "solely from an inordinate desire of gain." And the system of modern slavery that developed from there was markedly different, he believed, from the "reasonable servitude" that had existed in the ancient societies of Europe and Asia. He deployed commercial data from the *Liverpool Memorandum* and historical evidence from accounts of the Caribbean colonies to demonstrate that inhuman punishments and crushing workloads resulted in widespread infertility and death among the enslaved. He concluded by using British West Indian histories to show that, despite slaveholder claims to the contrary, the annual massacre of enslaved African workers was not even necessary: whites had worked the islands successfully in the early years of settlement.[21] He could prove that slavery was the result of greed and sloth, not necessity or inevitability. The only right thing to do was to end it.

After publishing *Some Historical Account*, Benezet began casting about for strategies to turn his study of slavery into political action. By that time, thanks to his own pamphlets as well as insistent colonial assertions about rights and liberties in the face of their own enslavement to British tyranny, a growing number of his fellow American colonists were coming around to his view. In Philadelphia, antislavery sentiment was building in a city where about a quarter of households held slaves. "Anthony Benezet stood alone a few years ago in opposing Negro slavery in Philadelphia," wrote one of his young followers, with just a little exaggeration, "and now 3/4 of the province as well as the city cry out against it."[22]

By the end of 1772, Benezet had come up with a plan. He would organize a petition to the Pennsylvania General Assembly, requesting that body to send its own petition asking Parliament and the king to end the slave trade. At the same time, Benezet recruited his young doctor, Benjamin Rush, to write a pamphlet "to lay the weight of the matter briefly before the members of the session, and other active members of the government, in this and neighboring provinces," as Benezet put it.[23]

Rush had proved to be an easy convert to the abolitionist cause. He dated his antislavery commitments back to 1766, when, as a twenty-year-old on his way to medical school at Edinburgh, he was horrified to see slave ships floating in the Liverpool harbor. Returning to Philadelphia a few years later, he joined the faculty of the College of Philadelphia's recently established medical school, where he became the first colonial professor of chemistry. He read Benezet's work and donated to the African Free School, which had recently grown out of the evening instruction that Benezet had been providing for two decades.[24]

When Benezet first asked Rush to write on slavery, Rush demurred; not only did he consider himself somewhat ignorant on the subject, but he also owned a slave. Eventually he agreed, on the condition that he could publish the pamphlet anonymously: he didn't want any blowback to affect his medical practice. He then dashed off his brief *Address to the Inhabitants of the British Settlements, on the Slavery of the Negroes in America* in a matter of hours, summarizing the main arguments against slavery to convince people to support Benezet's proposal. He started by stating that Africans were equal to Europeans "when we allow for the diversity of temper and genius which is occasioned by climate." Then he delved into slavery's position in Scripture, showing that Jews were not supposed to hold their own people in servitude for more than seven years and that the substance of every sermon Jesus gave went against the spirit of slavery. He concluded with an account of the evils of slavery as it existed in the Americas, including a litany of "arbitrary punishments" suffered by slaves in the sugar islands of the West Indies.[25]

Rush's pamphlet quickly sold more than a thousand copies; excerpts appeared in local newspapers, and the pamphlet itself was reprinted in New York and Boston. In Pennsylvania the General Assembly didn't agree to petition Parliament, but it did double the import tax on slaves—making it so high, Benezet thought, that it would effectively end importation. The act soon inspired similar laws in a handful of other colonies from Massachusetts to Delaware (although in some cases they were overturned by royal governors).[26]

Antislavery activists such as Benezet and Rush had faith that if they made the facts available, people could not help coming over to their side. But as the antislavery movement grew in power and began to influence policy, it also began to provoke a response. Supporters of slavery had a lot invested in the institution, financially and otherwise, and they would not let the new wave of attacks go unanswered. They responded by starting to gather their own facts and their own data, so the question eventually returned to the realm of interpretation—but now grounded, on both sides, in new kinds of evidence.

Rush's pamphlet, for instance, provoked one Richard Nisbet, a West Indian who had moved to Philadelphia, to compose a reply called *Slavery Not Forbidden by Scripture*. After pointing to passages in Exodus and Leviticus that said Jews were allowed to enslave heathens for life, he condemned as "blasphemous" all efforts to portray Jesus's teachings as antislavery because Jesus never said a word against slavery in the ancient Roman Empire. Then Nisbet moved to the specifics of West Indian slavery. Based on his own experience, he believed it was clear that Rush had never been to the Caribbean and had no clue how slavery operated there. "His information must have been received from an obscure writer, unworthy of credit . . . ," Nisbet charged. "For my part, I never knew a single instance of such shocking barbarities, and every West-Indian with whom I have conversed on the subject, has made the same declaration." Nisbet told of happy slaves who worked no harder than the average peasant and were relatively carefree. "I trust to facts, and the goodness of my cause," he declared, "rather than elegant language and flowery declamation."[27]

By now, Rush's authorship of the *Address* had leaked. He had been right to worry: when his name got out, he lost half his business. Having been challenged on the matter of facts, he churned out a response that he considered his *Vindication*. Almost certainly influenced by Benezet, he cited numerous West Indian sources, including Hans Sloane's *Natural History of Jamaica* and Edward Bancroft's *Natural History of Guiana*, to support his contention that Caribbean slavery was especially cruel. "The authorities upon which I have rested all my Facts," he concluded, "cannot be contradicted."[28]

After Benezet, it was possible to debate slavery as never before. In the summer of 1773, not long after Rush's first pamphlet helped convince people to support Benezet's petition, two students at Harvard's commencement held a formal debate on the question "Whether the slavery, to which Africans are in this province, by the permission of law, subjected, be agreeable to the law of nature?" Both sides presented an array of evidence, including Benezet's *Some Historical Account of Guinea*.[29] Debates like the one at Harvard could exist now because Benezet had shifted the terrain from private conscience to public policy, and from principles to facts. He had made slavery a subject to be studied.

Benezet had also begun building a transatlantic network to share antislavery information and strategy, particularly in Britain, where abolitionist pioneers adopted his methods of study and argumentation.[30] Benezet's work thus became the foundation for a broad antislavery movement that swept across the Atlantic world, a movement that eventually led to the Haitian Revolution, the end of British involvement in the slave trade, and abolition in the British West Indies. But that is, for the most part, another story. In America the Revolution was about to shake slavery to its core while also giving people greater power over their own institutions. It was in this environment that the study of slavery became a way not only to evaluate proposals to end the practice or curtail the trade but also to probe the meaning and purpose of the new nation itself.

PART I

ARGUMENT

1

NATIONAL IDENTITY

THE BIRTH OF THE ABOLITIONIST MOVEMENT SPARKED BY ANTHONY Benezet coincided almost exactly with the birth of a new nation. The world's first abolitionist organization, the Society for the Relief of Free Negroes Unlawfully Held in Bondage, was established on April 14, 1775, in Philadelphia, with Benezet at its head. It went dormant almost immediately because of the war that started five days later at Lexington and Concord, but it would return in 1784, on the far side of independence, to a landscape profoundly changed by abolitionism.[1]

During the war, Benezet saw a clear connection between the fate of slavery and the promise of the new republic. He thought his fellow Americans simply needed to follow through on what they were already saying. "Nothing can more clearly and positively militate against the slavery of the Negroes," he wrote in 1778, "than the several declarations lately published with so great an appearance of solemnity through all the colonies," by which he meant the Declaration of Independence and the Virginia Declaration of Rights. "When this unjust and cruel treatment of the Negroes is considered and brought to the test of the above declarations," he wrote at the end of the war, "will it not appear wonderfully inconsistent, and a matter of astonishment to the whole world, that an alteration of conduct towards them has not yet taken place, preparatory to a general abolition of slavery on the continent[?]" Crucially, the success of the Revolution in establishing a republic meant the decision was now in the hands of Americans themselves, not distant monarchs and ministers. "Hence," he added, "it becomes a matter of the utmost weight to the Americans, in a peculiar manner, duly to consider how far they can justify a conduct so abhorrent from these sacred truths."[2] Benezet died in 1784, so he did not live to see how far Americans ended up going to justify that conduct.

Although the rights rhetoric and wartime turmoil of the Revolution helped spur the world's first constitutional ban on slavery, in Vermont, as well as gradual emancipation acts in many northern states, including Pennsylvania, slavery would soon spread throughout the Old Southwest. Southern slave owners contested successfully for political and economic control of the country, and whole new branches of anthropology, law, and sociology sprouted up to support their claims to power. All this ultimately culminated in the formation of a breakaway republic, based explicitly on racial slavery, which had to be violently crushed in the Civil War.

It took decades for these forces to come to fruition. But the outlines of the conflict were already being sketched in the first generation after the Revolution as some of the earliest American historians tried to figure out how slavery fit into the story of the new United States. One of these historians, David Ramsay, had been on the edge of Benezet's abolitionist circle in the early 1770s. He was a student and protégé of Benjamin Rush at the College of Philadelphia during the period when Rush served as Benezet's personal physician, drafting antislavery pamphlets at Benezet's behest even as they cost him half his business. After Ramsay received his Bachelor of Physic degree in 1773, Rush enthusiastically recommended him for a position in South Carolina, citing his memory, principles, and morals.

Ramsay got the job and moved to Charleston. He started out skeptical of slavery and initially kept some distance from the slaveholding aristocracy. But over the next four decades in South Carolina—until his untimely death in 1815, when a tailor shot him in the back after Ramsay testified (accurately, it turned out) that the man was insane—he gradually accommodated himself to slavery. He grew to accept the institution, eventually marrying the daughter of a prominent slave trader and becoming a slave owner himself. He also became the most influential historian of the young United States. At a time when the future of slavery in America remained an open question, his historical works helped establish a framework for understanding the place of slavery—and eventually finding a place for slavery—in the new nation.[3]

The trajectory Ramsay traveled was not uncommon. In the generation from the 1770s to the early 1800s, the first abolitionist movement was remarkably successful: it enacted emancipation laws everywhere north of the Mason-Dixon Line, ended the African slave trade, and even pushed for the rights of free Blacks. But as hallucinatory visions of societal breakdown and slave violence emerged from revolutions in France and St. Domingue while slavery spread rapidly and profitably across the Old Southwest, many southerners—even former abolitionists like Ramsay—became increasingly comfortable articulating a vision of American society in which slavery played a vital social and economic role.

RAMSAY WAS THE YOUNGEST SON OF A FARMING FAMILY IN A SMALL TOWN on the Susquehanna River. His oldest brother attended the relatively new College of New Jersey (now Princeton), which was acquiring a reputation for elevating farmers' sons into the professions of law, medicine, and the ministry. Ramsay soon followed him there. Standing out for his prodigious memory and precocious intellect, he completed all the classical texts normally assigned in grammar school by the time he was twelve. He was considered too young to start college—at the time, the median age for a Princeton freshman was seventeen—so he spent a gap year as a teacher before enrolling in 1762. He qualified for the junior class but decided to start as a sophomore because he was still just thirteen years old.[4]

By that time, Princeton had already become a vital institution for forging American identity. Founded in 1746 as the fourth college in British North America, Princeton grew quickly and soon boasted the most broadly representative student population of all the colonial colleges, attracting boys from up and down the coast. The effect was to dissolve distinctions into a common culture. It is no coincidence that multiple Princetonians played a prominent role in the new nation: James Madison and Aaron Burr were Princeton graduates, as were numerous future members of the Continental Congress, the House of Representatives, and the Senate.[5]

Colonial colleges like Princeton were different from the modern research universities we know today. They existed not to expand knowledge through new research but to pass down the wisdom of revered texts. Princeton's original entrance exam required prospective students "to render Virgil and [Cicero's] Orations into English . . . and to be so well acquainted with the Greek as to render any part of the four Evangelists in that language into Latin or English." The goal was to foster religion and morality as the foundation of social and political order.

The colonial curriculum reflected that goal. In contrast to today's system of majors, electives, and distribution requirements, the classical curriculum of the colonial colleges provided a clear, well-trod path. Rhetoric, logic, mathematics, and classical languages provided the foundation. Benjamin Rush, who graduated from Princeton in 1760, later recalled that a good memory made it easy to succeed under such a curriculum, which involved what now seems like endless hours of Greek and Latin recitations. Students also studied geography and natural philosophy to gain a greater understanding of God's creation. Finally, as seniors, they took a capstone course in moral philosophy, usually taught by the college president, which attempted to present a holistic vision of the unity of religious faith, natural science, and (at least after the 1770s) republican politics.[6]

This curriculum provided little space where slavery might be discussed, analyzed, or evaluated. Students would surely read about ancient slavery as they droned through their recitations, but the primary emphasis of those exercises lay squarely on ancient languages, not ancient life. Subjects that we might consider a natural site for the study of slavery—history, economics, sociology, and other social sciences—either received scant attention, as in the case of history, or did not yet really exist. These fields, which started in embryonic form during the Enlightenment, were still being born, and it would be another fifty years before they entered the curriculum.[7]

If students didn't confront slavery in the classroom, they did encounter it around the quad. When Ramsay arrived in the early 1760s, Princeton's president had at least seven slaves. When students like Ramsay came to take their entrance examination, it's probable that their Princeton experience started with an enslaved person greeting them at the door.[8]

AFTER GRADUATING IN SEPTEMBER 1765, RAMSAY WENT BACK TO WORK AS a teacher for several years, this time at schools in Maryland and northern Virginia. In 1770, at age twenty-one, he quit teaching and enrolled at the College of Philadelphia's school of medicine. It was there that he met Benjamin Rush, who would become his mentor and eventually secure him a job in Charleston.

Arriving in South Carolina in the spring of 1774, Ramsay encountered a society very different from the Mid-Atlantic farms and towns of his youth. Even compared to what he had experienced during his years teaching in Maryland and northern Virginia, Charleston was a different world, an aristocracy of race and class in which more than half the population was enslaved. Free whites were a minority, and an even smaller oligarchy of wealthy planters and merchants controlled local politics and society.

Ramsay was an outsider. He had no patron or family connections, and he was Presbyterian, not Episcopalian like the city's leaders. He stood out because he didn't like dueling, which occurred with remarkable frequency among the city's doctors, and because he opposed slavery—a serious problem in a city run by wealthy slaveholders. Ramsay disapproved of slavery so strongly that he took it into account even when looking for a wife. He reported to Rush that "a very encouraging circumstance" about one prospective bride, the daughter of a Charleston merchant, was that "her fortune does not consist in negroes, but is reducible to an annuity from the rent of houses and interest of money."[9] He was perfectly frank about desiring a woman from a wealthy family, but he hoped that this wealth would have forms other than human flesh.

Nevertheless, Ramsay rose quickly in Charleston society—aided initially, perhaps, by his marriage to the merchant's daughter. After she died suddenly in the summer of 1776, however, Ramsay lost the prospect of her large inheritance and threw himself into the war with Britain. He served as surgeon in a local militia, operated a public niter works for colonial defense, and was elected to a seat in the new state assembly. One friend later described him as "a flaming Whig and Patriot." On July 4, 1778, he delivered one of the first public orations to celebrate Independence Day. "I am confident that the cause of America is the cause of Human Nature," he declared, "and that it will extend its influence to thousands who will never see it, and procure them a mitigation of the cruelties and oppressions imposed by their arbitrary task-masters."[10]

At the end of 1778, when British forces invaded Georgia, Ramsay and other South Carolinians came to see slavery in a new light as slaves fled to British lines by the thousands, imperiling economic production while also sparking fears of insurrection. Ramsay hoped that slaveholders would see that slavery made certain areas of South Carolina more vulnerable to attack by concentrating Black slaves at the expense of white settlement. "The invasion of the enemy will teach people experimentally the folly of accumulating negroes," he told Rush, "& will point out the superior policy of encouraging the settlement of poor white people."

When the British besieged and ultimately captured Charleston in early 1780, Ramsay was arrested and deported to a prisoner-of-war camp in St. Augustine. There, already convinced that the colonies would win their independence, he decided that he would write a history of his home state's experience in the war. Freed in the summer of 1781, he made his way back to Charleston and resumed his political career, gaining a seat in the state's delegation to the Confederation Congress. In Philadelphia he was able to conduct his research with the help of the secretary of Congress, who provided access to his well-organized files. After a quick revision when the Treaty of Paris officially ended the war, Ramsay published his *History of the Revolution of South-Carolina* in 1785, making it the first account of the war to appear in print.[11]

Perhaps because of his own observations in Charleston, Ramsay portrayed slavery primarily as a potential military danger. South Carolinians, he noted, "were not ignorant that their slaves might be worked upon, by the insidious offer of freedom, to slay their masters in the peaceful hour of domestick security." In his account, wily Black people sometimes used secret knowledge to aid the enemy: American forces were routed and lost Savannah after a Black man led British troops to "a private path through the swamp." Later, twenty-five Americans were killed or taken prisoner when "a negro-slave, for a sum of money, conducted the British from Goose creek, in the night, through unfrequented paths."[12]

More often, though, Ramsay focused on how the British stole slaves or used what he described as false offers of freedom to attract slaves to their lines. The slaves came in for some criticism—"The hapless Africans, allured with hopes of freedom, forsook their owners," and so on—but Ramsay's main targets lay elsewhere. He accused the British of luring slaves to their side and then leaving them to be consumed by miserable diseases without any medical care. "Their dead bodies, as they lay exposed in the woods, were devoured by beasts and birds," he wrote of one such episode, "and to this day the island is strewed with their bones." It sometimes sounded as if Ramsay was saying that slaves, in seeking freedom, only found worse masters. Yet he also criticized South Carolina slaveholders because many of them, fearing the confiscation of their slaves, cowardly sided with the British. Slavery, it turned out, posed a military danger not only because slaves might fight for their own freedom but also because slaveholders feared poverty more than dishonor or death.[13]

Still, Ramsay acknowledged that the loss of enslaved property was real. He touched on the convoluted, ultimately failed negotiations to return escaped slaves at the end of the war, noting that "the inhabitants [of Georgia] lost upwards of four thousand, each of whom was worth, on an average, about two hundred and fifty Spanish dollars." In South Carolina, he reported, some twenty-five thousand slaves died or escaped. For years afterward, the loss continued to affect the state's economy and politics. "Our negroes were carried away & our plantations laid waste," he explained to John Adams. "700,000 sterling of our present debt has been contracted since the peace to replace the negroes destroyed or taken away during the war."[14]

Ramsay concluded his *History of the Revolution of South-Carolina* on an optimistic note. "The blessings of peace were diffused among the people," he wrote, "and nothing is now wanting but the smiles of Heaven, and their own good conduct, to make them a great and a happy republick." In private, however, he seemed less sure, perhaps in part because he was serving in the Confederation Congress and could see political dysfunction up close. As in his *History*, he identified slavery as a source of vice in the new republic, but it was only one of several. "We have neither honesty nor knowledge enough for republican governments," he confided to Rush in 1786. "During the war we thought the termination of that would end all our troubles. It is now ended three years & our public situation as bad as ever."[15]

When Ramsay shipped his *History of the Revolution of South-Carolina* to John Adams and Thomas Jefferson at the end of 1785, fishing for their approval, both men replied that the book was a good first step toward a general history of the Revolution. Ramsay promptly made that his next project. It turned out that serving in a moribund government gave him plenty of time to read through historical records in the office of the congressional secretary. By the summer of 1786, he had finished researching the colonial period and analyzing what he called "the predisposing causes of the revolution."[16]

But then the project stalled. The most important reason for Ramsay's delay was the Constitutional Convention, which he hoped would correct the problems he saw with the country. A strong nationalist, Ramsay supported the new Constitution that emerged in the fall of 1787, and he served in the South Carolina convention that ratified it by a large margin the following spring. He then completed his *History of the American Revolution*, with the Constitution as its culmination, and published it in 1789 to coincide with the start of the new government. It was immediately hailed as the best book on the subject and is often credited with launching a new American historical consciousness.[17]

Ramsay never mentioned slavery in his brief account of the Constitution. This silence was not the same as ignorance. As a prominent local politician, he was well aware of the convention's compromises over slavery—and of the consternation they provoked among people in Charleston. He knew, for example, of the role that South Carolina's delegates played in imposing a delay on any federal ban of the Atlantic slave trade, and of the way they worked with their New England counterparts to push the date to 1808 in the final draft. He also reported to Rush that local opponents of the Constitution harped on the injustice of the potential ban. "They contend that it is a matter of domestic police," he wrote a few weeks before the state convention, "& that they should be allowed to import them forever."[18] But none of these negotiations and conflicts made it into Ramsay's *History*, where he focused instead on praising the Constitution's improvements over the Articles of Confederation.

Ramsay may not have seen slavery as integral to the Revolutionary War or the Constitution. But what about earlier periods in American history? Ramsay believed that the most important part of his book was its opening section on the growth of the colonies. "If I was sufficiently informed," he told Rush, "I would devote half or even whole of the first volume to a recapitulation of the history of the colonies from their settlement to the year 1761." He believed the subject would "afford a large field for Philosophical & political observations." But he didn't have the data he needed to flesh it out: "calculations of the numbers of people & of the imports & exports of the provinces in different periods so as to trace their gradual rise from a wilderness to a cultivated country."[19]

That lack of information restricted Ramsay to a relatively short treatment of colonial history, but even so, he found space there to discuss slavery in a more sustained and critical way than had nearly any other American historian to that point. In general, he focused on slavery's deleterious effects on white society. He described slavery as deadly to "Industry, temperance, and abstinence" because of the way it fostered "early, excessive, and enervating indulgences." The result was that the southern colonies remained "far inferior to their neighbours in strength, population, industry, and aggregate wealth." Ramsay wanted to make sure that people got the point: "This inferiority increased or diminished, with the number of Slaves in each Province, contrasted with the number of freemen."

Ramsay suggested that it didn't have to be this way. "From imagined necessity," he wrote, "founded on the natural state of the country, domestic slavery seemed to be forced on the Southern provinces." There were heavy qualifications in that formulation: "imagined necessity," "seemed to be forced." He acknowledged the arguments about climate, land, and labor that were usually deployed to justify or excuse the existence of slavery in

America, but his phrasing distanced him from the claims and questioned their truth.[20]

Still, all this amounted to only a few pages of analysis. Even that was more than many other early histories managed. There were several overlapping reasons for this neglect. Perhaps most fundamentally, history at the time tended to focus on politics and war, long seen as the main realms of human action and distinction. This bias may have been especially pronounced in America immediately after the Revolution, an event which proved beyond any doubt that politics and war could change the world. Slavery, on the other hand, was a form of labor, which is to say that it partook of the endless, monotonous, seemingly changeless cycle of life rather than the purposeful, dynamic action of the public realm. Not coincidentally, any discussions of slavery that did occur in early American histories often came in volumes dedicated not to chronological narratives of events but to static descriptions of natural history and social customs. Americans would soon reconceive of labor as a noble pursuit rather than necessary drudgery, a shift with dramatic effects on attitudes toward slavery in both scholarship and society. But that transformation was still in its early stages in the first years after the Revolution.

In the meantime, slave labor, like all other forms of labor, was seen as essentially private, not public, and slaves, like all laborers, were defined in part by their incapacity for citizenship and their inability to distinguish themselves through public action. In the case of Black slaves, this attitude toward labor mapped neatly onto nascent notions of biological racial difference. As a result, many historians, even some who supported abolition, did not regard Black Americans, free or enslaved, as part of the political community. They generally portrayed the Revolution and even the colonial history that preceded it as a narrowly English or European story. Passages on demography often noted only the various European immigrants who had settled in a given state or region, not the indigenous inhabitants or African imports.

Just as important, history, like most intellectual productions in the early republic, was largely a northern phenomenon, and slavery played a far less important role in the North than it did in the South. These things were not unrelated. The North was dotted by bustling cities, churches, and colleges, while the slave-based agriculture of the South led to more dispersed settlements lacking the density and educated middle classes usually necessary for a vibrant intellectual culture. It's telling that Ramsay, despite being based in South Carolina, received his major honors from northern institutions: an honorary degree from Yale as well as membership in the Massachusetts Historical Society, the American Philosophical Society (based in Pennsylvania), and the American Antiquarian Society (based in Massachusetts).[21] Nevertheless, Ramsay remained based in Charleston, and he gradually learned to make accommodations to the local environment.

RAMSAY WROTE THE COLONIAL SECTION OF HIS *HISTORY OF THE AMERICAN Revolution* in 1786. That spring, he had the relationship between slavery and the environment very much on his mind. He told Rush that he thought "the vices of [South Carolina] are more chargeable on slavery than on the climate." After all, he added, "Paradise was in the same latitude. Spain was formerly a fine country. So was Egypt. Warm weather is favorable to Longevity. By the act of heaven it was the original seat of man."[22]

Less than a month later, perhaps in the course of his research, he read Thomas Jefferson's *Notes on the State of Virginia*, which Jefferson had composed in the early 1780s and printed in a small run in Paris, where he was serving as minister to France, in 1785. At the time, Ramsay was corresponding regularly with Jefferson, who was arranging for the French publication of Ramsay's *History of the Revolution of South-Carolina*. Ramsay was pleased to read Jefferson's reflections in the *Notes* on slavery's dangerous moral effects, but he flinched at Jefferson's assertion that Black slaves' inferiority to free whites derived more from innate biological characteristics than from education and circumstance. Jefferson was reluctant to come down too firmly on the side of nature over nurture because he knew that he was dealing largely with anecdotes and isolated incidents. "To justify a general conclusion, requires many observations," he reminded his readers (and also himself). And those observations—"to our reproach," he noted—were embarrassingly few. Even though Africans had lived and worked as slaves in America for more than 150 years, he lamented, "they have never yet been viewed by us as subjects of natural history." Still, from the available evidence he believed it was not slavery, but race—"not their condition then, but nature"—that could best explain the apparent inferiority of Black slaves in America.[23]

Ramsay was provoked to respond. "I admire your generous indignation at slavery," he told Jefferson, "but think you have depressed the negroes too low." He went on to explain his view that environment played a stronger role than Jefferson allowed:

> I believe all mankind to be originally the same & only diversified by accidental circumstances. I flatter myself that in a few centuries the negroes will lose their black color. I think now they are less black in Jersey than Carolina. Their [lips] less thick—their noses less flat. The state of society has an influence not less than climate. Our back country people are as much savage as the Cherokees.[24]

Although Ramsay assumed that whites were the default for both skin color and civilization, he asserted that all humans were fundamentally the same and could be assimilated socially and even physically without much trouble. This was not an eccentric view at the time. During the 1770s and 1780s, the colonial conflict with Britain pushed many Americans to embrace the belief that differences between people derived more from external circumstances (i.e., the environment) than from innate nature. Many white Americans traced their ancestry to Britain, grew up under British colonial governments, aspired to British ideas of culture and civilization, and appealed to British concepts of rights and liberty. Yet they had somehow developed irreconcilable differences with their British fellow subjects and felt that they had become a separate people. The only factor that seemed to adequately explain these developments was the different environment in which Americans lived. This explanation preserved the fundamental connection between America and Britain (as well as between America and the rest of humanity), drawing upon a shared Christian and Enlightenment commitment to a common human core while also asserting that America represented something new and different in the world.[25]

For some Americans, this idea, known as environmentalism, merged with Revolutionary arguments about rights to provide a fertile field for challenging the system of race-based slavery that existed throughout the colonies. From an environmentalist perspective, Black Americans were not innately different from white Americans. Despite surface differences, each group had the same human core and was thus entitled to the same rights of liberty and equality. Black Americans simply needed education and uplift, according to this view, to undo the degrading effects of slavery.[26]

But this environmentalist notion of racial difference as something easily overcome was also contested in the late eighteenth century. Alongside the Enlightenment belief in the unity of man ran a parallel impulse to divide and to classify, to separate and to identify. The growth of race-based slavery in the eighteenth century made it newly important to determine whether race was a temporary adaptation to climate or a permanent physical and moral feature. The Bible seemed to indicate that all humans derived from a single pair, Adam and Eve. Yet in race, as in other realms, the investigation of human affairs was slowly shedding its religious jacket. In the 1730s, the Swedish botanist and zoologist Carl Linnaeus published a classification system for the world's plants and animals. He included humans under "Mammalia" and further divided them into several varieties, including African, European, Asiatic, and American. Starting in the 1770s, his categories were further refined by the German naturalist Johann Friedrich Blumenbach, who based his distinctions on physiological characteristics such as skull, hair, and skin color. Some Enlightenment speculators began to assert that "there are different species of men as well as of dogs," as the Scottish philosopher Lord Kames memorably put it.[27] Jefferson, in his *Notes on the State of Virginia*, did not go quite that far, but he clearly saw racial difference as rooted in biology, not environment.

Around the time Ramsay read and responded to Jefferson's *Notes*, in the spring of 1786, he happened to share a coach across New Jersey with two friends and relatives.[28] One of his companions was his father-in-law, John Witherspoon. Originally a Scottish minister, Witherspoon had come to America when Benjamin Rush helped convince him to accept the presidency of Princeton in 1768. He brought with him a commitment to Scottish commonsense philosophy, which emphasized the harmony between revealed religion and natural science, the idea being that sensory observations of the world could reveal the universal truths of God's creation. Under Witherspoon, students no longer simply memorized the classics. Moral philosophy became the heart of the curriculum, including at least some insights from new social sciences such as economics, sociology, and anthropology.[29]

On their coach journey across New Jersey, Ramsay and Witherspoon were joined by Samuel Stanhope Smith—another member of the extended Witherspoon clan. One of Witherspoon's earliest and best students at Princeton, Smith had gone on to become a college trustee, marry Witherspoon's eldest daughter, and join him on the faculty as a professor of moral philosophy. A convert to commonsense philosophy, he believed that moral laws could be derived from the experience of human nature. If those moral laws were to be truly universal, however, then human nature needed to be universal as well. Thus, Smith believed deeply in the common origin of all human beings.[30]

It's not surprising, then, that during their coach ride in the spring of 1786, Ramsay, Smith, and Witherspoon would have discussed the possible causes of racial difference. Ramsay and Smith surely saw the similarity of each other's environmentalist ideas. Ramsay soon arranged for Smith to get a precious manuscript copy of Jefferson's *Notes*, which had not yet been published in America, and he also secured Smith an invitation to deliver an oration before the American Philosophical Society in early 1787. In Smith's talk, published later that year as *An Essay on the Causes of the Variety of Complexion and Figure in the Human Species*, he deployed environmentalism to defend the biblical account of the unity of mankind. "The minutest causes, acting constantly, and long continued, will necessarily create great and conspicuous differences among mankind," he claimed. A tan was a small example of how the larger process worked: "The face or the hand, exposed uncovered during an intire summer, contracts a colour of the darkest brown." The African's darker hue, he thought, was nothing more than a permanent tan, or "an universal freckle."[31]

Like Ramsay and many other environmentalists at the time, Smith saw "environment" as including not only climate but also society. A more advanced civilization, he thought, could ameliorate the effects of climate on the human body. He used an example drawn from slavery. Field slaves, living by themselves in poor conditions, naturally retained more African customs, he claimed. Domestic slaves, on the other hand, were better fed and enjoyed closer interactions with whites—circumstances that were reflected, according to Smith, in physical changes such as a moderate mouth and lips, raised nose, and sparkling eyes (all stereotypically "white" features) after a generation or two. Some might see in those features a cause somewhat closer to hand than climate or society, but Smith did not—at least not in print. But he did regard the changes as an argument for emancipation: "If they were perfectly free, enjoyed property, and were admitted to a liberal participation of the society, rank and privileges of their masters, they would change their African peculiarities much faster." Yet his obvious disdain for African characteristics and celebration of white ones could also, potentially, cut the other way, providing support for one of the most common arguments in favor of slavery and the slave trade: the idea that Africans improved by exposure to white civilization, even under slavery.[32]

Few of these ideas were original to Smith, but he put them together in a way that won him acclaim for defending Christian doctrine through commonsense principles. His *Essay* was soon reprinted in Edinburgh and London. Along with the publication of London and Philadelphia editions of Jefferson's *Notes* around the same time, it sparked a flurry of discussion about slavery, race, and the environment during the next two decades.[33]

In addition to Ramsay, the second major source of American historical consciousness during the early years of the republic was a New England minister named Jeremy Belknap. During the Revolution, Belknap was serving in Dover, New Hampshire, where he was a prominent supporter of independence. Inspired by Thomas Prince, a Puritan historian and minister who prized primary sources, Belknap began to send out questionnaires and travel the state in search of documents. He published the first volume of his *History of New-Hampshire* in 1784. It was the first state history published after the war, helping to inspire a wave of others.

But soon Belknap tired of isolated Dover and returned to his hometown of Boston, where he led the Long Lane Church and became a leading figure in civic and cultural life.

In Boston, one of the seats of the Revolution, Belknap became convinced of the need for a historical society to preserve the records of the new republic. The ratification of the Constitution soon pushed the issue from his mind; the state ratifying convention was held at his church in early 1788, and his notes are now an important source for what went on. Within eighteen months, though, Belknap was pursuing the project again, and in 1791, he helped establish the Massachusetts Historical Society, the first such institution in the country, with his own collection as the seed of its library. He became the group's corresponding secretary, arranging for the election of members from across the country (including Ramsay) and sending out circulars asking for manuscripts, pamphlets, and information. In South Carolina, Ramsay arranged to print one of Belknap's circulars in the state's largest newspaper, and he also helped get the state legislature to send "every official printed paper" to Belknap's society.[34]

At the same time, Belknap was finishing the second and third volumes of his *History of New-Hampshire.* In Belknap's book, as in other early state histories, slavery was generally regarded as an embarrassment incompatible with the new republic. The only sustained discussion of the subject came in the third volume, a compilation of notes on the state's geography, natural history, economy, and society. "Slavery is not prohibited by any express law," Belknap explained in a chapter on "Constitution, Laws, Revenue and Militia." He noted that there was an ongoing dispute about whether the "born equally free and independent" clause of the New Hampshire constitution freed all the state's slaves, as a similar clause in the Massachusetts constitution had been interpreted, or only those born after the constitution was adopted.[35]

Three years later, Belknap received a letter that raised new questions for him about exactly how slavery and abolition in the North had played out. The letter came from St. George Tucker, a Virginia judge and law professor who was trying to advance the abolitionist cause in his own commonwealth. Tucker's first marriage had brought him three plantations and more than a hundred slaves, and his second marriage, in 1791, only added to his holdings. But like many slaveholders in the wake of the Revolution, he believed that slavery was incompatible with a republic based on principles of freedom and equality. For a while, with many Tidewater families deeply in debt, it seemed possible that slavery would simply wither away. Yet by the 1790s, with the Constitution's three-fifths clause granting political power to slave states and the Haitian Revolution provoking white fears of free Blacks, Tucker worried that the moment for action was passing. He started to sketch a proposal for gradual abolition in Virginia. Notably, out of all the enlightened Virginia slaveholders, including Jefferson, who wrung their hands about the wrongs of slavery, Tucker was the only one who put forward a practical plan to end it.[36]

Tucker embarked on the most ambitious program of research about slavery in America since Anthony Benezet. He had two goals: to document the development of slavery in Virginia and to understand how abolition had happened in the North in order to apply those lessons farther south. For Virginia, he tried to find information in early histories of the colony but ended up frustrated. "Our historian Mr. Stith mentions the arrival of a Dutch-ship here with twenty Slaves in the year 1620. This is the only notice of the subject in his Book," he complained. Even that bit of information was wrong (the true date was 1619), an error that seems to have been introduced by Robert Beverley in his *History and Present State of Virginia* (1705), repeated by William Stith in 1747, and then copied far and wide.[37] That example illustrates the problems historians confronted when exploring the murky depths of the colonial past. Even the inadequate old histories that did exist were exceedingly rare. Tucker had seen only a single copy of Beverley's history, "and that many years ago," while his copy of Stith suffered from a mutilated preface and some missing pages.[38]

Faced with these problems, Tucker based his own history of slavery on two other sources of information. One of those was old laws—he may have been the first American to realize that old laws about slavery provided good evidence about the institution's origins and development. He tracked down Virginia's earliest slave laws, passed in the 1660s, and analyzed their alterations up through the 1780s as a way of tracing the history of slavery in the state.[39] Nearly a century later, many of the first academic studies of slavery would adopt the same technique.

But Tucker knew he still needed more information, particularly regarding the process of peaceful abolition in the North, so in early 1795, he reached out to a few northern correspondents for help. One of them was Belknap. Tucker sent him a list of eleven queries: on the introduction of slaves in Massachusetts, the extent of the slave trade there, the state of slavery when it was at its height, the mode of its abolition, and the conditions of the emancipated Blacks.[40]

Tucker's queries must have made Belknap realize that he didn't have much solid information about the history of slavery in Massachusetts because it launched him on a monthslong project to find out more. Characteristically, in addition to conducting his own research, he also printed about forty copies of Tucker's queries and circulated them to prominent Bostonians, including a few free Blacks.

Belknap compiled all the answers he received along with his own research, sending a copy to Tucker and also publishing the information in the *Collections of the Massachusetts Historical Society*. He laid out the origins of slavery in Massachusetts in the 1630s and 1640s, the colony's role in the slave trade, and the growth of slavery to its peak in the mid-eighteenth century, when there was roughly one slave for every forty whites. His most important answer came in the query on abolition, where he concluded, "The general answer is, that slavery hath been abolished here by *publick opinion*; which began to be established about thirty years ago." Tying the rise of antislavery sentiment to the start of Revolution-era discussions of rights, he showed that by the 1770s, Massachusetts juries were always coming down "in favour of liberty" when they decided slaves' suits for freedom. By 1780, when the state constitution was ratified, its "free and equal" clause was, according to Belknap, "understood by the people at large . . . to establish the liberation of the negroes on a general principle." A court case a few years later fixed that reading as the correct one, and slavery came to an end. This account, which yoked abolition to the Revolution and assigned responsibility to the people at large, helped burnish the state's sense of itself as the special home of Revolutionary freedom, and in later decades allowed its citizens to feel absolved of any complicity with the slave South. Belknap's emphasis on public opinion also held out the elusive promise that the problem of slavery could be solved without political conflict.[41]

With Belknap's responses in hand, Tucker sketched a proposal by which all women born after the act and their descendants would become free after serving their owner until adulthood. In a letter to Belknap, he performed extensive calculations to show that the plan would end slavery in about a century. Modern historians estimate that it would have taken even longer, but that was precisely the goal: a slow transition to a new economy and society.[42]

Tucker packaged his proposal with an account of slavery stretching back to ancient times, based on his own research and what he'd learned about northern abolition, and presented the whole thing to the state legislature for consideration. It was tabled, which Tucker found disappointing but not surprising. In fact, he embodied as well as anyone the difficulty of extricating oneself from slavery. He sold off several of his family's plantations and encouraged his sons to get professional training so they wouldn't be dependent on slave labor, but most of his family's wealth and status remained tied to slaves. A few days after sending his abolition proposal to the statehouse in the fall of 1796, he contacted a Petersburg trader to sell four of his slaves, a mother and three daughters. It took months to find a buyer, and when he finally sold the women, in March 1797, it was for less than he'd hoped. When his daughter married a few years later, he gave her six slaves as a wedding gift.[43]

Those years around 1800 marked a turning point for white Virginians' attitudes toward slavery. The institution became more entrenched as it spread to new territories across the Appalachians. Already in the 1790s, Tucker had worried about the possible effects of this process. In contrast to contemporaries like Jefferson, who believed (or maybe just hoped) that diffusion across a larger territory would dilute slavery's power and lead to its decline, Tucker saw that allowing slavery to spread west would render emancipation efforts in eastern states like Virginia essentially meaningless. Slaves would continue to multiply, making nationwide abolition practically impossible. As he ruefully put it, "The continual migrations from this State to the

Western Country, if Slavery be not there prohibited will render this calculation infinitely too large." By the time Jefferson, as president, completed the Louisiana Purchase in 1803, Tucker was calling abolition a "Utopian idea" and "a mere visionary project."[44]

ONCE CHALLENGED AS INCOMPATIBLE WITH REVOLUTIONARY PRINCIPLES, slavery received new rationalizations that placed it on a stronger footing going forward. Nascent notions of inherent racial differences displaced the environmentalist emphasis on malleability, with Black people placed at the bottom of the racial hierarchy, outside the realm of rational citizenship. Whites portrayed themselves as protectors in an increasingly paternalistic vision of slavery as a benevolent institution necessary for the survival and education of Black people who would not otherwise be able to support themselves. This "domestication" of slavery ameliorated some aspects of the institution—by bringing slaves into the family circle, respecting the formation of slave families, and encouraging Christianity—but it did so precisely as a way of meeting and defeating the challenge posed by the Revolution.[45]

The later lives of both Tucker and Ramsay illustrate these shifting ideas about slavery and interpretations of the Revolution. Ramsay's own attitude toward slavery changed around the time the Constitution was written and ratified. Following the untimely death of his second wife, he married once more—this time into a wealthy slaveholding family, the Laurenses. The union brought Ramsay into the Revolutionary elite: the family patriarch, Henry Laurens, had been a president of the Continental Congress and a delegate to the peace negotiations in Paris.[46]

With the Constitution in place, Ramsay put himself up for election to the House of Representatives in the fall of 1788. The race was considered a three-way toss-up heading into the final days, but accusations that Ramsay was an abolitionist—that he did not have South Carolina's "*true political interests*" at heart—helped kill his chances. Ramsay issued "A Calm Reply," in which he tried to distance himself from abolitionism, but nothing in the exchange redounded to his benefit, and he finished a distant third. Bitter with disappointment, Ramsay mounted a campaign to deny his victorious opponent a seat in Congress on the ground that he was not a citizen of the United States because he had been in Britain while the Revolution took place. Ramsay's petition was defeated overwhelmingly in the House of Representatives, but it was indicative of a broader impulse to impose stricter boundaries on the political community (regarding British people as well as Black people) at the moment of the republic's birth.[47]

Marriage into a major slaveholding family and political defeat because of his abolitionist reputation quickened Ramsay's changing attitudes about slavery. His environmentalism shifted from a critique of slavery to a justification of it. "The negroes are here & in a state of slavery," he wrote at the end of 1788. "Experience proves that they who have been born & grown up in slavery are incapable of the blessings of freedom. Emancipation therefore would be ruinous both to masters & slaves."[48]

Over the next few years, Ramsay retreated from active participation in politics. He also didn't write any new histories. But then his finances collapsed. Houses burned, lands proved unproductive, a hurricane hit, and twenty-five thousand dollars were sunk into a canal that he described as "publicly beneficial, but . . . privately ruinous." Things got so bad that he resumed writing history as a way to raise money (never a good plan). His new projects were designed to be completed quickly and to sell well, and they were often copied from other authors or his own earlier works. Nevertheless, they are revealing. He retained some of his ambivalent statements about slavery, particularly regarding its baleful effects on white society, yet his overall emphasis changed. One small detail is telling. Twenty years earlier, Ramsay had written the following: "From imagined necessity, founded on the natural state of the country, domestic slavery seemed to be forced on the Southern provinces." Repeating the same passage in a new draft, he silently dropped his claim of "imagined necessity," taking him a long way toward conceding that slavery was necessary in the South—in fact and not only in imagination.[49]

Several hundred miles to the north, Tucker traveled a similar journey. In 1804, he was appointed to the Virginia Supreme Court. Two years later, he heard a case about an enslaved family that had sued for freedom, claiming they were descended from a free Indian woman. In a lower court, Tucker's mentor, George Wythe, declared the family free. In a controversial move, Wythe also used the case to push for a Massachusetts-style abolition, claiming that the first article of Virginia's Declaration of Rights—"all men are by nature equally free and independent"—meant, as in Massachusetts, that all the state's slaves were now free.

Hearing the case on appeal, Tucker agreed with Wythe about the specific family in question but didn't buy the broader argument about abolition. Although he'd been sympathetic to the abolitionist cause a decade earlier, times had changed, and even then his goal had always been an extremely gradual emancipation, not a sudden abolition that abrogated property rights and didn't have the force of public opinion behind it. Notably, he drew on what he called "the natural history of the human species" to argue that there was a nearly ineradicable distinction between the races. Moreover, Tucker added, Wythe had no legislative history to back up his position. Evidence indicated that the Declaration of Rights had been "notoriously framed with a cautious eye to this subject, and was meant to embrace the case of free citizens, or aliens only." He appealed to the Revolution to seal his case. Enslaved Blacks remained "in the same state of bondage that they were in at the revolution, in which they had no *concern*, *agency* or *interest*." Not only had the Revolution been achieved by and for whites, according to this logic, but Revolutionary ideals of liberty and equality were also self-evidently not applicable to Black slaves.

Tucker's fellow justices agreed. They confirmed Wythe's logic in freeing the family in the case at hand but firmly rejected it regarding "native Africans and their descendants, who have been and are now held as slaves by the citizens of this state."[50] Slavery would not be ending in Virginia anytime soon.

Over the next two decades, Tucker continued his retreat from challenges to slavery. At one point he went so far as to stop his stepson's plan to free his own slaves, arguing that the "poor ignorant Creatures" wouldn't be able to support themselves on their own. In addition to questioning Black Americans' equality and capacity for liberty, Tucker also became suspicious of any attempts to restrict slavery's spread. Southern interests increasingly trumped Revolutionary ideals. Sometime around 1820, during a protracted political crisis over the expansion of slavery that was prompted by Missouri's petition for statehood, Tucker dug up his old *Dissertation on Slavery*, then about twenty-five years old, and drafted an eight-page "Supplement" with new details about his notion that free Blacks might migrate west of the Mississippi River. Then he stuck it back in a drawer. He told himself that he still saw the plan as a rational way to end slavery, something that he believed he still desired. Yet now he also believed that Congress had no right to exclude slavery from western territories, and he cast slavery's expansion as a boon to American agricultural interests, not an obstacle to emancipation. For Tucker, as for the rest of the South in the generation after the Revolution, those beliefs won out.[51]

2

LAND AND LABOR

THE MISSOURI CRISIS OF 1819–21 SIGNALED THE START OF A NEW era. It was, Jefferson famously remarked, "like a fire bell in the night."[1] As congressmen and local committees debated the extension of slavery across the Mississippi River, Americans suddenly got a clearer sense of slavery's place in their country's past and present. Slavery, particularly the expansion of slavery, came to be accepted as the primary source of American political conflict, a position it retained for the next forty-five years.

By that time, the late 1810s, slavery was no longer under siege in the South. Revolutionary concerns with liberty, equality, and republican virtue had largely given way to a new emphasis on the order and stability that sustained commerce. Slavery was on the march, particularly after the United States acquired more than twenty-three million acres at the conclusion of the Creek War in 1814 and asserted its sovereignty across the Old Southwest, soon to become the heart of the Deep South. Slaveholders and prospective slaveholders poured into the region, spurring the development of an internal slave trade that tied the southeastern coast to the cotton kingdom.[2]

The Missouri Crisis also signaled a shift in the way that slavery was studied in the United States. As the country grew and its economy evolved, the relatively new science of political economy seemed to hold the key to understanding the complex relationship of slavery to problems of land and labor. The economy was not yet evaluated primarily through profits and productivity, but on the question of whether it produced the independent citizens that the republic needed to survive, and whether slavery was a help or a hindrance.

As slavery spread across the South and wage labor developed in the North, the main touchstone for nineteenth-century Americans concerned about their country's social and economic development was the English economist Thomas Malthus. His *Essay on the Principle of Population* had first appeared in 1798, when the prospects for free workers in Europe appeared bleak. Malthus sought some principle to explain why modern wageworkers toiled in such misery. The primary problem he saw was that people reproduced faster than they could produce more food. The result was that in times of plenty, population growth easily outpaced the increase in food production. More people meant less food for each, and higher-priced food for the few who could afford it. A period of misery for the poor was sure to follow, with the population stagnating or declining as people starved and refrained from having children. Once the population got back in balance with food production, according to Malthus, the same cycle of growth followed by misery was sure to begin again.[3]

Already in 1804, Thomas Jefferson praised Malthus's essay as "a work of sound logic," one that seemed to prove that his own cherished ideal of yeoman farmers was socially and morally superior to commerce and industry.[4] But, as became evident during the Missouri Crisis, Malthus's simple proposition could support widely divergent conclusions.

During the Missouri debates in Congress, no fewer than three representatives invoked Malthus by name on the floor of the House. Virginia representative George Tucker—a relative of St. George Tucker—used Malthusian theory as the basis for a lengthy analysis of slavery's future in the United States. To Tucker's mind, Malthus proved that slavery would eventually end. "As soon as our population has overspread the whole habitable parts of our territory," Tucker explained, "and brought our waste lands into cultivation, human labor will begin to decline in value." Malthus's Europe was an example of a place where this process had already happened—slavery no longer existed because the price of labor had sunk so low that it just barely sustained life. In America as well, Tucker explained, labor would eventually become so cheap that slavery would no longer make economic sense: "The self-interest of individuals will bust the bonds of the slave."

For Tucker, the crucial question was not whether emancipation would happen but what the proportion of Blacks to whites would be when it did. His calculations indicated that the United States would have some twenty-four million slaves when it hit the population density that would lower the cost of labor to the point where emancipation made economic sense. Would it be better, he asked, for those future free Blacks to be concentrated in a small area where they would form the majority, or spread over a much larger area where they would remain a minority? This was why Missouri mattered. Tucker wanted to ensure that free Blacks would be in the minority, and that was why he believed that slavery should be allowed to expand.

About a week after Tucker spoke, Representative Charles Kinsey of New Jersey invoked Malthus to make a slightly different point that also supported the expansion of slavery. "Drawing the cordon of restriction around the present slaveholding States . . . will not ameliorate the condition of the slave," Kinsey warned on the floor of the House. "It appears more like putting in practice the abominable doctrines of Malthus, of reducing their numbers by curtailing their means of subsistence." Crowded in the South, he believed, their population would grow until some began to starve.[5]

Kinsey served on the conference committee that helped broker a compromise, and soon after his speech the votes were tallied: Missouri would be allowed into the Union with slavery, but in the future slavery would be prohibited anywhere else north of the state's southern border. The South added a slave state, the North confirmed the principle that Congress could regulate slavery in the territories, and both sides got a bit of what they wanted most: the prospect of free land where their preferred form of labor could expand.

Yet not everyone was happy with the compromise, or sanguine about its future. "This is a reprieve only, not a final sentence," Jefferson wrote. "A geographical line, coinciding with a marked principle, moral and political, once conceived and held up to the angry passions of men, will never be obliterated; and every new irritation will mark it deeper and deeper."[6]

The man who would become the most prominent and influential American historian of the nineteenth century missed the Missouri Crisis. Instead of seeing firsthand that slavery stood at the center of American debates over land and labor, George Bancroft was getting a different kind of education across the Atlantic Ocean. This was another effect of the end of the War of 1812: after a period of relative isolation from European intellectual life, Americans began to travel abroad in larger numbers after 1815, and a handful of especially ambitious young men like Bancroft started to attend German universities for postgraduate education.

In the nineteenth century, German universities occupied the position that American universities have now held since roughly the middle of the twentieth: they were acknowledged leaders in nearly every field; they were home to the best laboratories, the biggest libraries, and the most highly regarded professors; they were magnets for foreign students seeking skills, knowledge, and prestige. Berlin, Heidelberg, and Göttingen had the stature that schools like Harvard, Yale, and Stanford have assumed today. At the time, American colleges remained committed, as they had been during David Ramsay's days at Princeton, to a classical curriculum focused almost obsessively on language rather than content. Daily classroom exercises consisted primarily of the recitation and translation of classical excerpts. A few college textbooks, such as Alexander Adam's *Roman Antiquities*, tried to provide a more comprehensive survey of ancient society by collecting disparate facts under topical headings.[7] Yet little that we would consider the study of slavery came up in the classical curriculum, even though ancient Greece and Rome were full of slaves.

The German research seminar was designed to ask the questions and to investigate the topics that American colleges did not. In 1817, Edward Everett became the first American to get a German PhD, and he wrote back to Harvard's president, John Kirkland, recommending that another Harvard man follow in his shoes. Kirkland selected Bancroft, a young scholarship student with a reputation for staying in his lane. Bancroft was planning to become a minister, like his father, and had stuck around Cambridge after graduation to study for an MA in theology. Kirkland hoped that high-class German scholarship would mold him into "an accomplished philologian and biblical critic."[8]

Bancroft crammed some German and sailed for Europe in June 1818, still a few months shy of his eighteenth birthday. On registration day at Göttingen, he arrived early enough to scribble his name on the second line in the matriculation book. He maintained the same diligence in his classwork, waking at five most mornings to prepare for a full day of lectures in Latin, Greek, Syriac, biblical exegesis, and ethnography. But soon his interests began to shift. The catalyst was probably a course with the pioneering historian Arnold Heeren, who taught that politics, society, and culture were all organic expressions of a nation's character. This struck Bancroft as a new way of approaching the past. "It is wonderful to see how a learned man can look back upon antiquity, how intimately he can commune with her, how he rests upon her bosom as upon the bosom of a friend," he wrote to a Harvard mentor, Andrews Norton. He was even learning to appreciate the rigors of historical research: "It is admirable to see with what calmness and patience every author is read, every manuscript collected, every work perused, which can be useful, be it dull or interesting, the work of genius or stupidity; to see how most trifling coins and medals, the ruins of art and even the decay of nature is made to bear upon the investigated subject."[9]

After two years at Göttingen, Bancroft had done enough to get his doctorate. He completed his exams and performed a public defense of nine theses, four from Heeren on ancient Greek history and five to satisfy another professor's interest in literary minutiae. Degree secured, he departed for Berlin to spend more time with some of the celebrities of German academic culture. He enjoyed Homer with Friedrich August Wolf and Greek history with August Böckh, but philosophy with Hegel, he confided, was a "display of unintelligible words."[10]

Bancroft was getting a crash course in the cutting edge of classical scholarship, which had been reinvented in Berlin in the 1810s.

Alterthumswissenschaft—literally, "the science of antiquity"—was the German word for it. Friedrich Wolf's studies of the Homeric age were among the first to shift from a narrow emphasis on texts to a broader interest in society. Wolf's colleague Barthold Niebuhr revolutionized the field of Roman history by reading political and legal documents for their broader social and economic significance, and August Böckh applied Niebuhr's approach to ancient Greece. In 1817, Böckh completed the first study of the ancient Greek economy—a subject that, for Böckh, necessarily involved a study of Greek slavery. "In every thing where labour was necessary," he explained, "the actual work was performed by slaves." So along with wages and taxes, Böckh investigated the slave population and even the profits of slave labor—which he figured must have been quite high, for owners had to invest significant sums to buy slaves, and "the proprietor lost unless both capital and interest were replaced before their death."[11]

For Bancroft, Böckh's work represented the sort of wide-ranging classical scholarship that he hoped to transplant to American soil when he returned to Boston in 1822. But he overplayed his hand. His friends and former supporters were dismayed to see an arrogant and foppish scholar who was pretentiously dropping German, French, and Italian phrases into casual conversation. His mentor Andrews Norton told him not to visit again, Ralph Waldo Emerson reported that Bancroft had "sadly disappointed great expectations," and students at Harvard, where he got a position teaching Greek, ridiculed him by standing under his window at night chanting, "Thus we do in Germany!"[12]

To be sure, Bancroft did want Harvard to become more like a German university. At the most basic level, he hoped to replace Alexander Adam's stale *Roman Antiquities* with his own translations of Heeren's *Reflections on the Politics of Ancient Greece* and *History of the States of Antiquity*, giving students a much broader view of ancient society, with slavery an integral part of the story. But Bancroft's translations didn't displace Adam in the curriculum, and larger reforms went nowhere. When Bancroft hinted to President Kirkland that the school could use a history professor, he was rebuffed. Frustrated, Bancroft left and started a boarding school based on European educational ideas.[13] Not for another decade, until he entered public life as a historian and a politician in the 1830s, would he finally be forced to confront the question of slavery's place in America's past and present.

BANCROFT'S EFFORTS AT EDUCATIONAL REFORM MAY HAVE STALLED, BUT THEY represented the leading edge of a broader movement as new methods of social scientific analysis gradually entered the country and its colleges. Beneath a stolid facade of Christianity and classicism, foundations were slowly shifting, opening the way for professors to bring slavery into the classroom.

One such professor was Thomas Cooper. Born in England, he'd attended Oxford without taking a degree and then become a prominent political liberal. In 1787, as the British campaign against the slave trade was getting under way, he contributed a pamphlet to the cause. He later prepared an edition of Thomas Paine's *The Rights of Man* for the Manchester Constitutional Society and gave a talk to the Paris Jacobin club in 1792. He fled France after getting on the wrong side of Robespierre, then fled England as well when it stepped up repression of radicals. He landed in Pennsylvania. Drawn to Jeffersonian republicanism, he was jailed for six months under the Sedition Act for criticizing the Adams administration. Eventually, he settled down and started to teach chemistry, first at Dickinson College and then at the University of Pennsylvania. He also developed a reputation as an economist; by 1810, Jefferson believed that his articles on the subject were "the best . . . which have been written in this country." Cooper visited Jefferson at Monticello to help plan the University of Virginia, which was intended to train students in practical subjects, including political economy. Jefferson even tapped Cooper for a professorship, but the appointment was blocked because of Cooper's disdain for the clergy and for the doctrine of transubstantiation.[14]

Instead, he headed to South Carolina College. Once there, Cooper pushed the college to train its students in new subjects that might yield some concrete benefit to society. He started with chemistry and other natural science fields. In 1825, he added political economy. When he published his lectures the following year, they became one of the first American political economy texts.[15]

The addition of political economy and other social scientific fields was decisive in opening the way to an examination of slavery as it actually existed. At South Carolina, for example, Cooper performed detailed calculations for his students regarding slave labor. One key fact about slaves, Cooper said, was that they were less efficient than free laborers. He was building on an old idea that had been stated most influentially by Adam Smith, the founding father of political economy, in *The Wealth of Nations* (1776). There, Smith argued that slave labor was inherently less efficient than free labor because slaves had no incentive to work hard or to invent labor-saving machines (because they would not be saving themselves any time or effort). "The experience of all ages and nations, I believe, demonstrates that the work done by slaves, though it appears to cost only their maintenance, is in the end the dearest of any," Smith wrote.[16]

Cooper applied Smith's ideas about the inefficiency of slave labor to the South. If a slave did only two-thirds of the work of a free white worker, he reckoned, and cost about forty dollars per year in food, clothing, and medicine, then a slave's production would cover his costs for only six years of his life—the period of peak productivity from fifteen to twenty-one. Before and after that brief window, Cooper found, the slave would be a burden on his owner's bottom line.

Yet Cooper, now long removed from his early radicalism, owned slaves himself, and many planters in the South and the Caribbean had grown extraordinarily rich from slave labor. How to explain this seeming contradiction? As political economists examined the question more closely, they began to see that the profitability of slavery depended on many variables, including the type of work (agricultural or industrial), the item or crop produced, the scale of the enterprise, the number of slaves employed, and the time frame under consideration. For his part, Cooper believed that Black slavery in the South was an exception to the economic orthodoxy for reasons of race and climate. Hot southern summers prevented white Europeans from working, he asserted, and Black people would not work voluntarily. In the heat and humidity of South Carolina and Georgia, he told his slave-owning students, "I doubt if the rich lands *could* [be] cultivated without slave labour."[17] In general, he believed that slave labor was less efficient than free labor, but in the South the extra costs were a necessity because harsh conditions made cultivation impossible otherwise. As Montesquieu might have said, it was unnatural in theory but not unreasonable in practice.

Despite his scholarly arguments in favor of slavery, Cooper got himself into trouble with South Carolina's slaveholding elites. His materialism did not endear him to the Presbyterian segment of the planter aristocracy. In 1831, the state legislature ordered the college trustees to investigate his conduct after learning that he had given lectures on the errors of the Old Testament. He defended himself at an open meeting of the trustees, noting that his positions differed little from those of a luminary like Jefferson. He had tried to avoid controversy, he explained, but he found it hard to keep up with new taboos. "If I am to avoid unpopular and offensive opinions, which change their character and costume almost every year," he declared, "give me, if you please, under the authority of the Board, an index expergatorius for the year; furnish me with a chart of my annual voyage, so that I may avoid the rocks, and shoals, and breakers of what is called heterodoxy." The audience broke into applause several times and had to be silenced by the president of the board.[18]

Cooper managed to clear his own name but not that of the college. Enrollment declined 25 percent by 1833, when he resigned the presidency. But he remained on the faculty as a chemistry professor, and the state's clergy continued to call for a boycott. By the end of 1834, enrollment had dropped to only fifty-two. The trustees fired the whole faculty and decided to start again with a clean slate.[19]

At the same time, the teaching of political economy and its application to slavery took the College of William & Mary on the opposite trajectory. In part, this was because the school's economics teacher, Thomas Dew, could never be accused of atheism. Dew had first encountered political economy as a student at William & Mary in the 1810s. By the time he returned as a professor, in 1826, the school was in dire straits, plagued by low enrollments and a failed plan to move to Richmond. Dew brought it back from the brink. His hugely influential defense of slavery, published in 1832, earned him the college presidency and prompted a flood of enrollments as William

& Mary became perhaps the most prominent intellectual outpost of the pro-slavery movement.[20]

Dew's defense of slavery arrived as the answer to one long-term problem and one short-term crisis. The long-term problem was the changing nature of northern abolitionism. By the 1820s, the North's gradual abolition acts had left very few slaves above the Mason-Dixon Line. Yet first-movement abolitionism had failed in its second and perhaps larger goal of eradicating white prejudice and Black degradation, a failure highlighted by the expansion of slavery across the South as well as the hardening of racial prejudice in the North. The colonization movement that started in the 1810s attempted to solve these problems by sending Black Americans away, a quixotic plan that led to the settlement of Liberia but never overcame the many logistical, financial, and moral obstacles that lay in its path.

Many antislavery whites embraced colonization in the 1820s, but free Blacks continued to push—even stronger now that they saw they were not wanted—for the traditional abolitionist goals of ending slavery and eliminating racial prejudice. The free Black abolitionist movement's most emphatic statement came from a Boston used-clothes dealer, David Walker, who published an impassioned *Appeal to the Coloured Citizens of the World* in 1829. Walker was motivated, he wrote, by the desire "to awaken in the breasts of my afflicted, degraded and slumbering brethren, a spirit of inquiry and investigation respecting our miseries and wretchedness in this *Republican Land of Liberty!!!!!!*" He proceeded to outline four main causes of Black "wretchedness," starting with slavery, "the *source* from which most of our miseries proceed." Tying the end of slavery to the achievement of Black rights, he advocated for "men of colour" to work tirelessly for "the *entire emancipation of your enslaved brethren all over the world*" if they hoped to attain "glory and happiness" in this life.[21]

Walker died suddenly, in mysterious circumstances, after making efforts to distribute his pamphlet to southern ports. But the broader Black abolitionist movement survived and inspired a new generation of white allies who similarly rejected colonization and embraced the twin goals of emancipation and equality. William Lloyd Garrison was the key figure in the rise of this "interracial immediatism," as it has been called, which saw slavery as a sin that needed to end. With support from northern Black communities and antislavery whites, Garrison started an abolitionist newspaper, *The Liberator*, in 1831, as a self-conscious successor to Walker's *Appeal*, then helped found the New England Anti-Slavery Society in 1832 and the American Anti-Slavery Society a year later. (He was influenced in part by James Forten, who had been a Black student of Anthony Benezet in Philadelphia and who prized his copies of Benezet's antislavery pamphlets.) Northerners caught up in the Second Great Awakening, a wave of religious revivals sweeping across New England and New York, began to indict southern slaveholders for denying the fundamental equality of all men before God and preventing the religious salvation of their slaves.[22]

The changing nature of abolitionism raised the stakes of any new challenge to southern slavery. In fact, it was widely assumed that abolitionist propaganda was what caused slaves, who were supposedly content, to rise up in violent rebellion. This theory was self-evident to many slaveholders, but it also had a specific source. Back in the 1790s, the British planter Bryan Edwards had provided one of the earliest accounts of the Haitian Revolution in his *Historical Survey of the French Colony of St. Domingo*. The book proved terrifically popular and quickly sold through three editions in the British Isles before going through three American editions as well; Thomas Jefferson, then serving as president, was among the first American edition's subscribers. Edwards said the slave insurrection in St. Domingo was sparked by abolitionist agitation—an interpretation that soon became generalized to the theory that insurrections were always caused by outside abolitionists. To white southerners who lived in fear of slave violence, the theory was borne out by what appeared to be a clear pattern of slave conspiracies following public discussions of slavery—when, for example, the Missouri Crisis was followed within a few years by the Denmark Vesey plot in Charleston.[23]

Another example came in August 1831, less than a year after Garrison started *The Liberator*, when Nat Turner led a slave rebellion that killed about sixty whites near Southampton, Virginia. Fearful for the future, the Virginia legislature debated a plan for gradual emancipation and colonization—the closest that colonization ever came to large-scale implementation. But the eastern and western halves of the state were divided, the governor withheld his support, and the proposal ultimately went down to a narrow defeat as the legislature opted instead for more slave patrols and tighter restrictions on both enslaved and free Blacks.[24]

Not far from Southampton and Richmond, Professor Dew was in Williamsburg following the debate closely; Turner's rebellion and the subsequent legislative session were the specific crisis that prompted him to write about slavery. He was troubled by what he saw as the "false principles and assumptions" underlying the whole discussion. Abolition amounted to a "question of truly momentous character," Dew thought, one that had not been sufficiently studied owing to its magnitude. "It involves the whole frame work of society, contemplates a separation of its elements, or a radical change in their relation, and requires for its adequate investigation the most complete and profound knowledge of the nature and sources of national wealth and political aggrandizement." Dew believed he was just the man to do it.

In his *Review of the Debate*, which was ostensibly about local matters but actually took in the world, Dew explained that slavery had existed in most places across the globe and throughout history. Abraham owned hundreds of slaves, the Egyptian pyramids were built by slaves, and Assyria, Babylon, Carthage, Greece, and Rome all rested on slave labor. In his effort to explain why slavery was so universal, Dew ended up providing the South with a coherent narrative about slavery as an agent of progress: "Slavery is inevitable in the progress of society, from its first and most savage state to the last and most refined. This was no *accident, the mere result of chance*, but was a *necessary and inevitable* consequence of the principles of human nature and the state of property."[25] Examples from ancient history as well as Mexico, Peru, Africa, and the South Seas all attested to the same supposedly fundamental truth: slavery led to greater productivity, better standards of living (especially for women), larger populations, and more flourishing cultures.

As with most books regarded as landmarks, Dew's was not the first to make any of its individual arguments, but it put them all together in a clear synthesis that arrived at exactly the right time. Following on the heels of the failed emancipation proposal in Virginia, it effectively ended all criticism of slavery in the South. At the same time, it became the foundation for a whole new genre of southern pro-slavery studies, which claimed the institution was not a necessary evil but a positive good. For the next three decades, this proof became the central project of southern intellectuals.

The basic idea behind the pro-slavery position went back decades, if not centuries—southerners found similar claims in Aristotle. But it had been largely repressed during the early republic, when Revolutionary commitments to liberty and equality required slavery's defenders to admit its evils and acknowledge its tension with republican values. In contrast, the pro-slavery argument called forth a different kind of defense, one based not just on inertia (slavery is here and there's no good way to end it) but on a more comprehensive investigation of how slavery in general, or at least the enslavement of Blacks in the South, benefited society as a whole.[26]

Economists like Malthus, supported by the harsh realities of labor for lower-class workers in Britain and the North, played a starring role in pro-slavery studies. These dismal scientists provided evidence that free labor's economic efficiency came at a high cost to workers because market forces produced cycles of starvation. In contrast to such heartless cruelty, southerners argued, slavery's alleged economic inefficiency was actually a virtue. Slavery insulated slaves from the destructive laws of supply and demand, and provided them with the kind of comfort and security denied wageworkers. Free labor might be cheaper, in this view, but it was cheaper only because it kept workers suffering at the edge of subsistence. Slavery provided a more humane alternative by regulating population growth and promising subsistence to all members of society.[27]

By the time Cooper was getting into trouble and Dew was writing his *Review*, Bancroft had tired of teaching ten-year-olds at his boarding school in Northampton and decided to devote himself to history and politics. He made the decision public in 1834, when he ran for local office, declared his allegiance to the Jacksonian Democrats, and published the first volume of his *History of the United States*, a project that would occupy the next forty years of his life.[28]

As Bancroft became more politically active, slavery assumed a more prominent place in his social and political thought. In 1831, he reviewed his former professor August Böckh's book on *The Public Economy of Athens*. Free workers in Athens suffered, he saw, because the large number of slaves made labor so cheap. "Mere manual labor could be procured for ten cents a day," a rate comparable to what poor workers received in much of modern Europe. Yet the economics of the Athenian slavery system as presented by Böckh seemed questionable at best. With the average unskilled slave going for twenty dollars, Bancroft reported, "The labor of the slave would . . . do but little more than yield his own support."[29]

In his sense that slavery did not pay and his concern about its effects on free workers, Bancroft was tapping into a line of economic thought that was becoming politically potent in America. The early decades of the nineteenth century saw the rise of new attitudes toward labor, attitudes that had been accelerated by the egalitarianism of the Revolution and that were distinctly at odds with slavery. The kind of gentlemanly leisure made possible by the lowly labor of others, formerly a prerequisite for participation in philosophy and politics going back to Plato and Aristotle, came in for new criticism as it got recast as mere idleness or even exploitation, associated with aristocracy and monarchy. Productive labor, in contrast, was raised up as the proper base of republicanism, elevated in moral worth precisely for its utility. This idea took root more strongly in the North than in the South, where leisure long remained an important justification for slavery. Yet even large slaveholders were starting to be depicted as hard workers. In Parson Weems's famously hagiographic biography of George Washington (it started the cherry-tree story), Weems listed the "glory-giving goddess, *industry . . . rosy-cheeked industry . . . snow-robed Industry*" as one of Washington's primary virtues.

This celebration of work, which started around the time of the Revolution, took full shape by the 1810s and 1820s, partly as a result of important changes in the US economy. Most notably, the dispute with Britain that culminated in the War of 1812 accelerated the development of manufacturing in the United States. Mills and other small factories became a major part of the economy, employing more than one-quarter of the workforce in New England and the Mid-Atlantic. Although factory workers remained a minority until the late nineteenth century, they loomed large in American political thought because they made the traditional equation of independence with property ownership into a problem. As larger workshops and mills rose in the East, the definition of independence shifted to include all men who owned their own labor, which they could hire out to employers for wages. But even then, wage work was still supposed to be a stepping stone toward becoming an independent shop owner or small farmer—the free-labor foundation on which American democracy was supposed to rest.[30]

Bancroft drew the connection between free-labor ideology and antislavery politics in a speech on "Slavery in Rome," which he delivered to the Workingmen of Northampton in 1834 and then published in the *North American Review* ahead of that fall's election. The Roman Republic had once been peopled by proud, independent farmers, Bancroft said, but the spread of slavery turned those farmers into a degraded urban rabble. The result was the death of the Roman Republic and the end of free labor in Italy as wealth became concentrated in the hands of a few. Democracy gave way to aristocracy, which then devolved into monarchy and eventually "Oriental despotism." "The Barbarians did not ruin Italy," he declared. "The Romans themselves ruined it. Slavery had made it a waste and depopulated land, before a Scythian or a Scandinavian had crossed the Alps." Looking west toward the Mississippi River and beyond, Bancroft provided a clear warning of what the expansion of slavery would entail. But he also offered a solution: "Would you abolish slavery? Imitate Gracchus, and pass a law in spirit like his; that none but the free shall till the soil."[31]

As the free-labor ideal gained coherence, it became the source of the most powerful strain of antislavery thought in the United States. Its advocates, including Bancroft, wanted to make access to free land as easy as possible so that Americans could work their own farm and be their own boss. For this vision to be realized, the country needed a vast reserve of open land to the west where workers could settle with their families. Moreover, that open land needed to be restricted to settlement only by free people, not southerners with slaves in tow.

This final stipulation was essential. Some people were starting to see that free land, precisely *because* it provided opportunities to free workers, also generated conditions that fostered slavery. This may seem like a paradox, but Americans who lived in such conditions knew it from experience. Already in the 1750s, Benjamin Franklin observed that Europe was becoming crowded while America still had plenty of land "so cheap as that a labouring Man . . . can in a short Time save Money enough to purchase a Piece of new Land sufficient for a Plantation, whereon he may subsist a Family." These conditions made it difficult to keep free workers; Franklin saw that "hired Men are continually leaving their Master (often in the midst of his Business,) and setting up for themselves."[32] Workers would labor under someone else only as long as necessary, then head west, buy cheap land, and become their own boss.

These conditions were good for poor and middling Americans who could look forward to owning their own land. They were less than ideal for wealthy planters who depended on hired labor to work their property. In such conditions, with wageworkers expensive and liable to leave at any time, owners who wanted a stable labor force larger than their family had few good options. Slavery was one of them.

The basic principle that places with plenty of free land tended to develop slavery (in the absence of laws against it) continued to be rediscovered throughout the nineteenth century, and even into the twentieth. One of the most influential statements of the theory came from the English colonizationist Edward Gibbon Wakefield. Named for the historian Edward Gibbon, who was a distant relation, Wakefield led a criminally caddish youth that included eloping with one young heiress and abducting another. Sent to prison in the late 1820s, he somehow managed to publish a series of newspaper articles called "Letter from Sydney," which purported to be written by a settler in the distant colony of Australia. In this guise he wrote that he had discovered that he needed forced labor if he wanted to undertake any large projects. His fictional settler dreamed of importing "a few thousand Negroes" to New South Wales. Yet Wakefield himself opposed slavery. His realization about the relationship between free land and slavery led him to propose an increase in the price of colonial land, which would restrict the supply of free land and solve the problem of employers not being able to retain workers.[33]

Released from prison in 1830, Wakefield began to promote his plan through the National Colonisation Society, whose supporters included John

Stuart Mill and Jeremy Bentham. His ideas convinced the British Cabinet to end free land grants in New South Wales, but he had trouble persuading the secretary for war and colonies to endorse the colonization plans of his newly formed South Australia Land Company. In 1833, he wrote *England and America*, a comparison of the two countries, to press his arguments further.

Predictably, Wakefield attributed the rise of slavery in America to the "*super*abundance of land in proportion to people." If Americans really wanted to end slavery, he believed, the only practical solution was a land scheme like the one he had proposed for Britain's colonies. The government should raise the price of land, making it harder for laborers to strike out on their own. It should then use the profits from land sales to import poor workers from Europe, which would provide additional labor in America (and help solve Europe's problems of overpopulation and poverty). The goal would be to deliberately create a Malthusian society by increasing the population and decreasing the availability of land until free labor became as cheap and abundant as slave labor. "By means of some plan of this kind," he wrote, "and by no other means, does it seem possible that slavery in America should be peacefully and happily abolished."[34] (This was exactly how George Tucker had predicted that slavery would end in his Missouri speech in 1820, except he envisioned it happening slowly as a result of natural causes.)

When Karl Marx later analyzed Wakefield's work, he claimed that Wakefield had discovered nothing new about colonial settlement. What Wakefield had actually discovered, Marx wrote, was simply "the truth as to the conditions of capitalist production"—that capitalist accumulation for a few depended on the obliteration of opportunity for the many.[35] Whether in the guise of slave plantations or industrial factories, it was inimical to the small landholders, artisans, and shop owners who were the heroes of the free-labor ideal.

Northern advocates of free labor recognized the force of these critiques. They also suffered from Malthusian nightmares about what could happen to capitalist society in a confined space, which is what spurred them to push for the spread of small farms and shops across the continent. If America hoped to preserve its republic, free-labor advocates argued, it needed free land where free men could farm. Otherwise, the country risked becoming like modern Europe, with crowded cities full of impoverished workers who couldn't support a free republic.

BANCROFT EMBRACED FREE LABOR BUT LOST THE ELECTION IN NORTHAMPTON in 1834, in part because people lampooned him as a high-toned intellectual moonlighting as a man of the people. Nevertheless, he stuck with politics, beginning a steady ascent through the ranks of the Democratic Party. Within a few years he landed a cushy, politically powerful position as collector of the Port of Boston, which gave him a good salary as well as plenty of time to keep working on his *History*.[36]

Bancroft's was the first major American history since David Ramsay and also the first, he believed, to be written in a properly skeptical scientific spirit, the spirit of the German seminar, with an emphasis on interrogating sources, correcting errors, and establishing truth. After publication, he even got a nice note from his German mentor, Heeren, congratulating him on his "exact scholarship" and thanking him for being cited in several footnotes: "What higher reward could a teacher wish?"[37]

Bancroft has sometimes been faulted, both in his own time and later, for neglecting slavery as part of the American story. In fact, he discussed the subject more than many American historians of his day while still clearly avoiding divisive debates about it. This may have been a business decision—southerners bought books, too, and Bancroft was in the process of tying his political fortune to a Democratic Party with a strong southern base. It may have also reflected his centrism on the issue, his dislike of what he saw as the extremism of both pro-slavery partisans and immediate abolitionists. He later said the world could be divided into three basic political parties: conservatism, absolute right, and reform.[38] The pro-slavery position was conservative; abolitionists appealed to absolute right; that left him in the corner of reform.

Bancroft thought that abolitionists stirred up trouble. Angelina Grimké, a true abolitionist, once wrote him an angry letter blaming him for providing ammunition to southerners who saw slavery as divinely sanctioned.

Bancroft did not respond. When the National Anti-Slavery Convention invited him to attend in 1839, he declined. Instead, he was a reformer to his core, a believer in the basic goodness of the world as it is as well as its susceptibility to gradual, continuous improvement. This view could shade easily into complacency. He warned his sister Jane not to buy slaves when she moved to Louisiana, largely because he believed that they were a bad investment. She bought some anyway. But when she died, he did not set them free. He quickly sold them to raise money to support Jane's children.[39]

Nevertheless, in the first volume of his *History*, Bancroft did pause to devote roughly half of a chapter to the introduction of slavery in Virginia. He regarded slavery as a threat and a contradiction in a land that was otherwise an "asylum of liberty." Like many Americans at the time, Bancroft did not see slavery as a system that developed naturally in the colonies, but instead one that was imposed from above. "The unjust, wasteful and unhappy system was fastened upon the rising institutions of America, not by the consent of the corporation, nor the desires of the emigrants," he explained. Instead, "it was introduced by the mercantile avarice of a foreign nation" and "subsequently riveted by the policy of England, without regard to the interests or wishes of the colony."[40]

Yet even then, Bancroft noted, the growth of slavery remained quite small for decades, such that as late as the 1670s, the proportion of slaves in Virginia was still less than it would be in many northern states at the time of the Revolution—that is, small enough that emancipation was not out of the question. For the moment, he left the story of American slavery there, pledging that in later volumes he would explore what allowed slavery to grow beyond its small presence in early Virginia—as he put it, "what influence was ultimately extended to counteract the voice of justice, the cry of humanity, and the remonstrances of colonial legislation."[41]

Only in the third volume of his *History*, published at the end of the decade, did Bancroft fulfill his promise. It was there, as he analyzed the place of the early colonies in the larger European colonial system, that he explained why slavery developed despite the countervailing pressures he had identified. The answer, as usual for Americans at the time, was English avarice and commercial ambition; slavery was imposed from afar as an instrument of imperial oppression. The slave trade, Bancroft claimed, was "encouraged by English legislation, fostered by royal favor, and enforced for a century by every successive ministry of England." It was the culmination of the mercantile system by which England exerted control over its colonies: "English ships, fitted out in English cities, under the special favor of the royal family, of the ministry, and of parliament, stole from Africa, in the years from 1700 to 1750, probably a million and a half souls."[42]

At precisely the moment that Bancroft was writing, however, British abolition was complicating the American claim that imperial forces were solely to blame for foisting slavery on the unwitting colonies. In August 1833, Parliament passed the Act of Abolition for the British West Indies. The act ended slavery in Britain's Caribbean possessions, effective August 1, 1834, although slaves were typically required to continue serving as "apprentices" for several more years.[43]

If Britain itself was able to eradicate slavery from the American colonies that it still held, what excuse did the United States have for not doing the same? The newly energized abolitionist movement seized on this issue to spark a handful of specialized inquiries into the history of American slavery. In fact, the first major publication to discuss British emancipation appeared before Parliament's Act of Abolition even received royal assent. It was written by a former Massachusetts schoolteacher named Lydia Maria Child. In the late 1820s, Child had become the leading avatar of a new form of middle-class domesticity. Her homemaking manual, *The Frugal Housewife*, her children's magazine, *Juvenile Miscellany*, and her parenting guide, *The Mother's Book*, made her the most prominent female author in America. In 1828, she married David Lee Child, editor of the *Massachusetts Journal*, and began to edit literary columns there as well.[44]

David had once employed William Lloyd Garrison at the *Massachusetts Journal*, and in 1830 Garrison made it his goal to get Lydia on his side. Meeting Garrison changed her life. She was deeply moved by his passion and by the plight of enslaved people. But she still had significant doubts about what the right response should be. She decided to study the problem. She read Garrison's *Liberator*, which was a treasury of facts and quotations about slavery, and followed up on its references to a wide variety of scholarly and polemical writings, borrowing books from private libraries and her brother's parsonage. She examined slavery from moral, legal, economic, political, and racial angles, and she discussed the different aspects of the issue with friends. After her husband helped Garrison establish the New England Anti-Slavery Society, she attended some meetings there as well, listening silently at a time when women were still not welcome in public debates about politics.

Child's years of research on slavery had two results. The first was that she joined Garrison and her husband as an immediate abolitionist. The second was that she wrote a whole book on the subject, *An Appeal in Favor of That Class of Americans Called Africans*, which is often credited as becoming, upon its publication in August 1833, the first full-scale abolitionist analysis of slavery in American history.

Child's analysis in her *Appeal* rested on a strong historical and comparative foundation. She began with a brief history of the slave trade, dating back to fifteenth-century Portuguese explorers, followed by a description of the trade itself as she traced it from the interior of Africa to the coast and across the Middle Passage to America. From her deep reading on the subject, she then assembled a list of fourteen specific legal aspects of slavery: that slavery is hereditary and perpetual, that slave labor is compulsory and uncompensated, that slaves can't make contracts, that slaves can't be witnesses, and so on. On each count she compared several different slave systems, ancient and modern, to see the precise shape that each system took. Her comparisons led her to conclude, first, that modern slavery was "more odious than the ancient," something she attributed to what she believed was modern slavery's basis in greed, and, second, that within modern slavery the most severe laws of all could be found in the British West Indies and the United States. Moreover, her research revealed that American slave laws were becoming even more severe as southern states passed stricter statutes in the wake of Nat Turner's rebellion.

In contrast to Bryan Edwards's claim that abolitionists caused insurrections, Child sensibly asserted that slave insurrections resulted from nothing other than slavery. "Slavery causes insurrections," she declared, "while emancipation prevents them." If abolition succeeded, after all, slave insurrections would end. She delved into the history of Haiti to show that most bloodshed there occurred either before emancipation or after Napoleon tried to restore slavery, but not in between, when formerly enslaved people enjoyed a peaceful and productive freedom. The process of emancipation in the northern states and in newly independent Spanish American republics such as Mexico provided her with another example, allowing her to predict that British emancipation in the West Indies, which was moving forward just as her book was going to press, would prove peaceful as well.[45]

Child's *Appeal* was the first major abolitionist publication to draw on the example of British emancipation, but it would not be the last. It showed a new generation of Americans that slavery could—and should—be the subject of patient investigation and rational deliberation.

Americans looked to the West Indies, curious about two questions in particular: Would free Blacks kill their former masters? And would they still work? Early newspaper reports provided sensational accounts of violence and suggested that free Black workers were prone to idleness. But the American Anti-Slavery Society doubted these reports. In the summer of 1835, the society asked the prominent New York abolitionist William Jay, son of John, to go to the islands and collect facts for a report. Jay declined; he didn't think it would do any good for a confirmed abolitionist to collect the evidence. He recommended that abolitionists rely on ostensibly objective sources of data such as parliamentary reports and press accounts.

But the American Anti-Slavery Society still wanted boots on the ground. Finally, in the fall of 1836, they got a pair of volunteers, two sickly young men who needed to go south anyway for health reasons. One, Horace Kimball, had been an abolitionist editor in New Hampshire; the other, James Thome, came from a slaveholding family in Kentucky but had converted to abolitionism at Lane Seminary in Ohio. They sailed out near the end of 1836 and spent the next six months touring Antigua, Barbados, and Jamaica, three islands that represented the full spectrum of the emancipation experience: Antigua went for immediate emancipation without any apprenticeship period, while Barbados was regarded as having the best apprenticeship system and Jamaica the worst.

Thome and Kimball went first to Antigua, where they stayed for a few months. The governor told them they wouldn't find anyone who wanted to return to slavery, and their other interviews appeared to bear that out. They spoke to planters who admitted that free labor was less expensive and easier to manage than slavery; they heard from church officials that even their poorest parishioners preferred low wages to none at all. When they stopped one Black man, a former slave, to ask how slaves had celebrated emancipation, "He said they all went to church and chapel." Thome and Kimball saw evidence of tremendous moral and intellectual improvement among the freed slaves, who were showing a remarkable interest in religion, education, and the law. The same was true of Barbados, where they talked with leaders such as the governor and the archdeacon as well as some local "colored" (often mixed-race) planters who had been free before abolition. Even in Jamaica, where the evils of the apprenticeship system were supposedly greatest, Thome and Kimball came to believe that the problems had been greatly exaggerated and were probably the fault of planters scheming to exploit their former slaves.

Thome and Kimball's trip to the Caribbean successfully answered their questions, but it did not fulfill its second function as a health retreat. Kimball died soon after the men sailed home in the summer of 1837, leaving Thome to complete their report, called *Emancipation in the West Indies*, on his own. The American Anti-Slavery Society published it in two versions: a full bound volume and a short pamphlet that could be had for only a quarter. The pamphlet saw much wider circulation. Its main goal was to provide "a simple narrative of facts . . . ," Thome wrote, "*well authenticated facts*, accompanied with the testimony, verbal and documentary, of public men, planters, and other responsible individuals." *Emancipation in the West Indies* bolstered abolitionist arguments in the United States because it was able to provide an eyewitness account, complete with statistics and testimony from local officials, showing that emancipation could be peaceful and profitable. At least one prominent Boston minister considered it "the most important work" that anyone had contributed to the abolitionist cause.[46]

Within a decade, however, a new story was emerging. In the South, profits from slave-grown cotton were surging. Meanwhile, sugar production in the British West Indies declined by about one-third in the decade after emancipation, and the islands were beginning to import indentured laborers from Africa and India. To abolitionists, this return to bound labor appeared as an abandonment of emancipation. To slaveholders, on the other hand, it seemed to provide clear evidence of the failure of free Black labor—and of the superiority of slavery.[47]

AROUND THAT TIME, IN THE EARLY 1840S, BANCROFT TRAVELED SOUTH FROM Massachusetts on a research trip. He toured battle sites and conducted interviews around Philadelphia, then went on to Maryland, where he visited the large Carroll family plantation. Several hundred slaves worked the fields across twelve square miles. Bancroft was impressed by his amiable host and reassured him that the Democratic Party had no intention of interfering with slavery.

Instead, Bancroft focused on territorial expansion, which he saw as the solution to the country's problems. If only there were more free land, he believed (along with many others), then Americans would continue to enjoy an egalitarian, democratic society with plenty of economic opportunity for everyone. The West, Bancroft thought, was where Americans freed themselves "from the bonds of hereditary or established custom" to forge a new society, a process that had been going on since the first English settlements in the 1600s. In 1844, James Polk ran for the Democratic presidential nomination on an explicitly expansionist platform, and Bancroft played power broker at the convention, helping to secure him the nomination. Bancroft then campaigned hard for Polk—to the point of neglecting his own nominal campaign for Massachusetts governor—as he emphasized in his speeches that expansion had nothing to do with slavery.

After Polk won, Bancroft hoped to be repaid with a plum diplomatic assignment in Europe, which would be a boon for his research and also satisfy his self-conception as a refined man of letters. Instead, he was appointed secretary of the navy, a position for which his qualifications were unclear. As secretary, Bancroft strove to make the navy more modern and professional. He tried to abolish the seniority system and introduce competition for promotions, two reforms that aroused significant opposition and failed to go through. He was more successful in the field of higher education, his home turf, where he managed to establish the US Naval Academy—despite lacking congressional approval—by means of creative budgeting and legislative interpretation.

Bancroft's main role in the Cabinet, however, was as an advocate and architect of American expansion. Already in the spring of 1845, he was putting the pieces into place to ensure that the United States would be ready to make war on Mexico as part of a territorial land grab. He strengthened a squadron in the Gulf of Mexico, ordered one commander to the Mexican coast, and told General Zachary Taylor to move to the Texas border; he also instructed an officer in the Pacific to take San Francisco as soon as the fighting started.

War broke out a year later, after a skirmish near the Texas border, and Bancroft backed Polk's goal of using the opportunity to acquire California. The problem was that getting California required also taking the vast stretch of southwestern land connecting California to the rest of the country. That land lay mostly south of the Missouri Compromise line and would potentially be open to slavery. Many northerners, already incensed about the annexation of Texas a year earlier, saw the war as nothing but a southern bid to keep extending slavery through the colonization of free land. They worried that after expanding into Mexican lands in the West, slaveholders would soon push for parts of Central America or the Caribbean. To stop that expansion and preserve free land for free labor, Representative David Wilmot of Pennsylvania introduced a "proviso" to the 1846 war appropriations bill that would have prohibited slavery from any new territory acquired in the war with Mexico. The Wilmot Proviso never made it past the Senate, but it linked the war and the West ineradicably to the question of slavery's expansion.

Perplexed, Bancroft continued to assert that expansion had nothing to do with slavery. In fact, he still believed that expansion would soothe sectional tensions and strengthen the Union by blending North and South together. Firmly behind Polk's policies, he used his suave manners and easy command of European languages to sell the war at the English, French, and Prussian embassies. Then, tired of bureaucratic hassles and wanting to spend more time writing (by that time he had not published a new volume of his *History* in six years), he finally secured himself a diplomatic position as ambassador to England. As with the Missouri Crisis, he was once again an ocean away while the country consumed itself with the question of slavery.[48]

3

LAWS OF NATURE AND NATIONS

The Mexican War ended in 1848 with the US acquisition of much of what is now the Southwest, stretching from Texas to the Pacific Coast. With the California gold rush and the Mormon migration to Utah bringing tens of thousands of settlers to the new territories, Congress could no longer avoid discussing the fate of slavery on the frontier. Some antislavery congressmen wanted to prohibit slavery from all the new territories; in response, southern congressmen threatened secession. The Compromise of 1850 promised to settle the problem, but it only made things worse—particularly the new Fugitive Slave Law, which required federal authorities and even private citizens to help recapture escaped slaves.

A series of standoffs occurred between northern abolitionists and federal marshals, sometimes resulting in casualties. One of the first involved an alleged fugitive named Shadrach, who was arrested in Boston in February 1851. His defense team asked the local US commissioner, George Ticknor Curtis, to postpone the hearing to give them time to prepare. Curtis agreed, but he soon felt fooled when Shadrach's supporters spirited him away to Canada. Two months later, Curtis granted a warrant for the arrest of another alleged fugitive, Thomas Sims, who was taken into custody that night. The case went before Commissioner Curtis—who, having been fooled once, now denied the defense team's request to postpone the hearing. After listening to the arguments, Curtis believed the evidence proved "that the prisoner before me is the identical person described in the record, as having escaped from Georgia, while owing service to James Potter." The next morning, before dawn, armed guards escorted Sims to the wharf. As he walked onto the ship that would take him south, he reportedly paused to ask, "And is this Massachusetts liberty?" It marked the first time a fugitive in New England was legally returned to slavery. When he landed in Savannah, Sims received a public whipping.

Around the same time, a woman named Harriet Beecher Stowe started to have visions of a brutal master ordering two slaves to whip an older slave to death. Stowe turned her visions into the novel *Uncle Tom's Cabin*, which appeared in weekly installments in the antislavery newspaper the *National Era* starting in June 1851. The novel became a sensation. After it was published in two volumes in the spring of 1852, Americans bought more than three hundred thousand copies in its first year in print. The book was wildly popular in the North, but it also sold briskly in the South, where it provoked both angry attacks (Stowe received a human ear in the mail, apparently cut from an attempted runaway) and a rash of pro-slavery novels in response.

Stowe came from a deeply religious New England family, the Beechers, who were steeped in spiritualism and famous for their ministers and reformers. They had moved to Cincinnati in the early 1830s, not long after Stowe turned twenty, and she married a widowed faculty member at Lane Theological Seminary. They stayed in Cincinnati—just across the Ohio River from slave country—and started a family. Her husband also had visions, in his case of forms floating through walls, and the couple believed that they had been visited by her husband's first wife. In 1849, a cholera epidemic killed their eighteen-month-old son. That experience, Stowe said, taught her "what a poor slave mother may feel when her child is torn away from her" and sold to a different owner. Soon after that, Stowe's husband got a job at Bowdoin College, in Maine, and it was from that remove that she wrote *Uncle Tom's Cabin*.[1]

Stowe's novel follows Tom, an elderly slave living on a Kentucky plantation. Kentucky was as close as slavery got, Stowe wrote, to "the oft-fabled poetic legend of a patriarchal institution." Tom is sold south to Louisiana, where he ends up with a kindly owner named St. Clare. After St. Clare dies while trying to break up a fight, Tom is sold again. This time he lands with a nasty transplanted northerner—a stock figure in American writing about slavery—named Simon Legree, who owns a cotton plantation near the Red River. Legree hates Tom for his kindness, piety, and faithfulness, and eventually orders his overseers to whip Tom so hard that he dies from the beating. Tom becomes a Christ figure, enduring his suffering and forgiving those who kill him.

Stowe claimed that her book, though fictional, drew a true portrait of the slave South. "The separate incidents that compose the narrative are, to a very great extent, authentic," she informed her readers. Stowe or her friends and correspondents had seen "characters the counterpart of almost all that are here introduced; and many of the sayings are word for word as heard herself, or reported to her."[2]

Yet as abolitionists had learned, facts on their own could say only so much. In the 1830s, in addition to compiling evidence about emancipation in the British West Indies, the American Anti-Slavery Society also solicited reports about slavery in the South. "Facts and testimony respecting the condition of slaves, in *all* respects, are desired," one notice declared. Correspondents were asked to submit any information they had concerning slave life:

> their food, (kinds, quality, and quantity,) clothing, lodging, dwellings, hours of labor and rest, kinds of labor, with the mode of exaction, supervision, &c.—the number and time of meals each day, treatment when sick, regulations respecting their social intercourse, marriage and domestic ties, the system of torture to which they are subjected, with its various modes; and *in detail*, their *intellectual* and *moral* condition.

The society hoped to use mounds of evidence to prove the evil of slavery beyond any doubt. Accuracy was imperative in order to preserve credibility: "Great care should be observed in the statement of facts."

In 1839, the American Anti-Slavery Society published its most comprehensive collection of facts about slavery, Theodore Weld's *American Slavery as It Is*. Weld worked with his wife, Angelina Grimké, and her sister, Sarah, to compile the book largely from southern newspaper articles and advertisements, taking a page from Anthony Benezet as he turned descriptions written by slaveholders into evidence against slavery. Weld supplied long tables of extracts from "advertisements, which they have published in their own newspapers, describing by the scars on their bodies made by the whip, their own runaway slaves." Nearly twenty pages of excerpts documented different types of cruelty: whipping scars, chains and fetters, gunshot wounds, missing fingers and toes, broken bones, lost front teeth.

Weld also collected evidence of insufficient food, lodging, and medical care. Statements from slaveholders and other southerners revealed that slaves received an average of about a peck (eight quarts) of corn per week. Using *Ainsworth's Latin Dictionary*, an old standard that had been revised and reissued for a century, Weld calculated that ancient Roman slaves received double that amount. He came to similar conclusions about labor (slaves could be forced to work about 1.5 times as long as southern convicts) and clothing ("inadequate, either for comfort or decency").[3]

Stowe knew Weld from his time at Lane Theological Seminary, where he had protested a gag order on campus by organizing a student debate on abolition (his side won) and then dropping out. She relied heavily on *American Slavery as It Is* while writing her novel, later saying that she "slept with it under her pillow at night, till its facts crystallized into Uncle Tom." But it was far from the only source she used. In the 1830s and 1840s, the American Anti-Slavery Society also sought out other new evidence about slavery, including firsthand accounts from former slaves. In 1838, the society printed the *Narrative of James Williams, an American Slave*, the first fugitive slave narrative to be published by an abolitionist organization. Over the next two decades, slave narratives became a key tool of the abolitionist movement. These narratives carried the considerable advantage of authenticity, promising a glimpse into a secret world. They provided a hint, too, that enslaved Black people had their own knowledge of and theories about slavery, which they rarely had a chance to make public. Twenty-five slave narratives were published as books in the 1840s (including Josiah Henson's, which helped inspire Stowe), followed by thirty-three more in the 1850s.

Slave narratives, and compilations like Weld's, were useful to the abolitionist cause only if they were considered both accurate and representative. But southerners were not inclined to trust the accounts because these readers saw slaves as cunning and deceitful by nature. It didn't help that abolitionist editors often shaped the narratives they published, giving them the unmistakable air of antislavery agitation. This could sometimes cause trouble. The American Anti-Slavery Society had to disavow James Williams's narrative after an Alabama editor tried to confirm the details and declared it to be a "*foul fester of falsehood.*" (Williams did exaggerate some stories, and names and locations had been changed.)[4]

After *Uncle Tom's Cabin* was published, southern newspapers immediately set out to refute its claims or come up with counterexamples. Stowe responded a year later with another book, called *A Key to Uncle Tom's Cabin*, in which she documented the real-life incidents and evidence on which her novel was based. The *Key* proceeded almost line by line, "from the first page onward," listing sources, quoting letters, and telling anecdotes to establish the factual ground on which the novel stood.[5]

Stowe hoped readers would take away more than just individual facts and incidents. By that time, descriptions and catalogs of cruelty still mattered to abolitionists, just as evidence of benevolence did to their opponents. But partisans on both sides also saw slavery as an institution that reshaped society in its image, the cornerstone on which all other social relationships rested. Stowe's goal was to show that slavery acted as a system that affected everything it touched. To do this, she turned, like a growing number of abolitionists at the time, to the law. With the work of gradual emancipation essentially complete in the North, antislavery litigation had shifted by the 1840s from securing freedom for people under northern emancipation statutes to helping southern slaves who found themselves in free states, either as fugitives or in the service of their master. These court cases were attractive to antislavery lawyers as a way to help individual slaves, probe the status of slavery in state and national law, and pursue politics by another means at a time when Congress explicitly refused to consider the question of slavery.

After 1850, the Fugitive Slave Law accelerated and consolidated this shift. It revealed that slavery was not just a personal relationship on the plantation but also a state-backed system that necessarily affected, and implicated, every member of society. After the Shadrach and Sims cases, Ralph Waldo Emerson went so far as to call the law "a university to the people," teaching them what slavery was really like.[6]

For abolitionists, the most fundamental law of slavery was that it made a person into property. One of the earliest American analyses of southern slave law, George Stroud's *A Sketch of the Laws Relating to Slavery* (1827), examined the various southern state legal codes to trace the practical effects of applying common-law notions of property to slaves. Because of the strict way he saw the property idea applied throughout the South, Stroud believed that American slavery was among the worst forms of servitude that had ever existed. Slaves in ancient Rome, Greece, and Germany were often allowed to acquire some property of their own, for example, but American slaves legally could not because they were themselves property. Similarly, many countries practiced a form of serfdom in which workers could never be sold away from particular plots of land or have their families broken apart, but in the United States, slaves could be bought and sold at will because they were pieces of property.[7]

Stowe's novel brought this analysis to the masses. But she started to doubt Stroud's accuracy after southern critics pounced on her treatment of slave law, so when she revisited the issue for *A Key to Uncle Tom's Cabin*, she took the time to pick the brains of several "legal gentlemen," whom she thanked for helping her show that "the impressions first derived from Judge Stroud's work were correct." She also turned for corroboration to Jacob Wheeler's *A Practical Treatise on the Law of Slavery*. Published in 1837, Wheeler's *Law of Slavery* was a guidebook for southern lawyers who had to deal with slave law on a daily basis. Wheeler cataloged southern laws and legal holdings on slaves as property (including mortgages of slaves), slave treatment, runaways, kidnapping, suits for freedom, and manumission. He also covered the ways slavery reared its head in a wide variety of other legal fields, from criminal law to wills and estates. The cases Wheeler cited and the legal rulings he explained showed which areas of slave law were in active use.[8]

Because of this, Wheeler's *Law of Slavery* became popular among antislavery writers who wanted to refute the southern claim that slavery was a kinder institution in practice than it appeared in law. Wheeler served, for example, as the primary source for the abolitionist William Goodell's *The American Slave Code in Theory and Practice*, which was published in 1853, the same year as Stowe's *Key*. Like Stowe and Stroud (who reissued his *Sketch of the Laws Relating to Slavery* in 1856), Goodell saw "the foundation principle of American Slavery" as "human chattelhood"—the fact that slaves were classed as chattel, or property, under the nearly absolute power of their masters. He followed the logic of this principle as far as it would take him, attempting to derive the entire system from it just as surely "as any science, in detail, is educed from its fundamental axioms." The chattel principle dictated relationships between master and slave and between slave and government, and it also meant that slave laws would inevitably impinge upon free citizens as well: "The usages of human chattelhood cannot be tolerated in any community without impairing the freedom and invading the rights of *every member* of that community."[9]

This emphasis on "human chattelhood" provided the foundation for abolitionist attacks on slavery throughout the late 1840s and 1850s. Simply piling up evidence of cruelty in compilations or narratives provided an opening for southerners to dismiss those examples as isolated abuses in a broader system characterized by benevolence. But the chattel principle gave abolitionists a way to explain why cruelty in southern slavery was the rule, not the exception. In *Uncle Tom's Cabin*, Tom and all the other slaves were objects that could be sold, like a horse or a piece of furniture, when their masters needed money. The action of Stowe's novel—and of some slave narratives, too—showed how this principle led inexorably to the slave trade, to broken families, to sons weeping as their mothers were sold downriver.

AMONG THE MANY FIERY SOUTHERN DENUNCIATIONS OF *UNCLE TOM'S Cabin*, one came from an English immigrant named George Frederick Holmes. At the time, Holmes was unemployed and living at his wife's family estate in southwest Virginia after several turbulent years in academia.

He considered Stowe's novel "reprehensible," an example of what happened when fiction was "degraded into the domain of falsehood." The problem was not with Stowe's facts, the truth of which Holmes conceded for the sake of argument. The problem was that the interpretations and conclusions she drew from those facts were all wrong:

> The argument of the work is, in plain and precise terms, that any organization of society—any social institution, which can by possibility result in such instances of individual misery, or generate such examples of individual cruelty as are exhibited in this fiction, must be criminal in itself, a violation of all the laws of Nature and of God, and ought to be universally condemned, and consequently immediately abolished.

To Holmes, this was not just nonsense, but patently dangerous, because *all* communities, not just societies with slavery, featured misery and cruelty. There was no "inherent vice in the institution of slavery," Holmes contended, "which does not also appertain to all other institutions whatever." What writers like Stowe were too blind to see, he believed, was that slavery at least rendered those vices less pernicious than they were elsewhere.[10]

When Holmes talked about slavery, he was talking—like his abolitionist foes—about an institution based on a fundamental principle. But for him, the principle on which slavery rested was not the chattel principle of people as property. He thought that was a narrow view bound by time and place, a view that didn't apply to the different forms slavery had taken throughout history. "The more accurate view of slavery," he wrote, was as an institution of "dependence and service."[11] To explain this idea, he had to develop a new, sociological analysis of the role that slavery played in society.

Holmes had come a long way in his journey toward seeing slavery as a social panacea. Born in 1820 in Georgetown, a British colonial outpost on the northeast coast of South America, he soon moved to England with his mother. At seventeen he left home, under uncertain and perhaps dishonorable circumstances, and made his way to Virginia. Brilliant and well educated (he had won a prize scholarship back in England), he found work teaching a huge variety of subjects at a boarding school north of Richmond.

Ambitious and restless, he soon moved again, this time to South Carolina, where he tried to make a living as a lawyer. But he could not concentrate on his cases. He spent his days studying history and languages, and sprinkled his legal files with notes on metaphysics. On the side, he started to write for the *Southern Quarterly Review*.

Somehow this struggling lawyer and scholar caught the eye of Eliza Lavalette Floyd, the daughter of a wealthy and politically prominent family in Virginia. (Her father and her brother both served as governor.) Their marriage in 1845 prompted Holmes to seek out a professorship to provide for his family. Soon he snagged a position at William & Mary—one that had been left vacant by Thomas Dew's untimely death—but like most of the academic jobs Holmes held before the Civil War, it didn't last long. Without Dew's leadership, William & Mary was beset by extreme faculty infighting. When Holmes heard talk of "damned foreigners," he saw the writing on the wall and left—not long before the college board asked the whole faculty to resign so it could start fresh.

In 1848, Holmes accepted the presidency of the new University of Mississippi, founded as part of a broader effort to provide a southern education for southern men. At the opening ceremonies, he decried the southern habit of sending sons to northern colleges "to imbibe . . . delusive views which will infect their minds during their whole life." But the situation in Oxford was enough to send anyone scurrying away: stumps still littered the freshly cut campus, buildings lacked outer doors, there was no library, and at first no one had any textbooks, either. As was common across the country (then as now), students lacked preparation and discipline. Holmes probably did not help matters by stating publicly that he would not make inquisitions or impose harsh punishments, but would simply trust students to do their duty—an early version of the college honor code. Lying and lawlessness took hold; in a single year, more than a quarter of the student body was expelled, suspended, or withdrawn. By the time the trustees saw fit to investigate, Holmes had already left, pulled back to Virginia by a family illness. He was not asked to return.[12]

This was how Holmes found himself unemployed in rural Virginia for much of the 1850s. There, isolated in a mountainous county with relatively few slaves, he churned out an astonishing string of essays that helped redefine how intellectual southerners thought about slavery. His first move, common to many southerners at the time, was to push beyond political economy. According to the conventional wisdom, slavery was an inefficient form of labor that might yield profits early in a country's development but would inevitably die out as the population became denser and the cost of free labor declined. In response, intellectual southerners largely gave up defending slavery on economic grounds. There were exceptions, to be sure, most notably *Cotton Is King*, in which David Christy stepped back from the productivity of slave labor on individual plantations to see how southern slavery fit into the global economy. Slave-grown cotton made the world go around, according to Christy, and as long as it continued in high demand, slavery would remain one of the most powerful and profitable forces on the planet. "This is no exaggerated picture of the present imposing power of slavery," he wrote. "It is literally true."[13]

Still, the most prominent economic analyses of slavery in this period were written by people who worried primarily about its effects on the white working class. In the late 1850s, a spate of books focused on the plight of poor whites in the South. The most influential of these were a series of travelogues that Frederick Law Olmsted, the future designer of Central Park, published in the *New York Times*, and the North Carolinian Hinton Rowan Helper's *The Impending Crisis of the South*, which was published in 1857 and soon took second only to *Uncle Tom's Cabin* in its galvanizing effect on northern readers. Helper printed a lengthy sequence of statistical tables to demonstrate that the free states far outpaced the slave states in population and production, and laid out a plan for his fellow nonslaveholders to take power from the slaveholding oligarchy and legislate slavery out of existence.[14]

In the face of these mounting economic critiques, some southerners claimed that political economy as a field was biased against slavery. Others, including Holmes, lamented that the potentially useful science of economics was so often perverted into a narrow-minded drive for profits. To articulate broader social needs that went beyond the accumulation of cash, he turned to a new science of society. In the 1840s, his wide reading brought him under the influence of the French philosopher Auguste Comte, who is usually credited with coining the word *sociology*. Holmes thought that Comte and his followers were "the most profound social speculators of the day" and had "nearly unveiled the mysteries of the great social problems" facing modern society. But while he believed that they had grasped the problems of a profit-oriented economy, he did not think they had realized the cause or worked out a solution.[15]

Holmes saw a solution right in front of his eyes: slavery. Along with a handful of other southerners in the 1850s, he began to argue for "slavery in the abstract," a sociological theory that made slavery central to society regardless of race, time, place, or any other circumstance. Holmes first explained this idea, which he called "the abstract justice of Slavery," in an 1850 article called "Observations on a Passage in the Politics of Aristotle Relative to Slavery." Over the course of the antebellum period, Aristotle had become a sort of house philosopher for the South; his discussion of "natural slaves" in the *Politics* appealed strongly to those who thought slavery was good for society. "Nature," Holmes quoted from the Greek philosopher, "has clearly designed some men for freedom and others for slavery:—and with respect to the latter, slavery is both just and beneficial."

Following Aristotle's analysis in the *Politics*, Holmes believed that the one constant throughout human history, starting with the very first coupling of man and wife, was the division of societies "into two classes, the dependent and those on whom they depend." Dependent people—wives, children, servants, the poor—relied on others for survival. Moreover, these dependent classes secured their survival by performing service for those on whom they depended—husbands, parents, masters, the rich. To Holmes, slavery was a system for codifying this natural relationship of dependence and servitude to ensure that it would not be abused. The only difference in so-called free societies, he said, was that servitude had been shorn of "those mutual claims on the affection of both parties, which arise from the permanent and acknowledged relation of slavery."[16] Free workers were still bound to their employers by necessity—they were poor and needed to work—but they lacked the legal framework that promised slaves housing, health care, job security, and retirement.

As the 1850s went on, Holmes continued to criticize free society but backed off some of his strongest assertions about slavery in the abstract. He still believed that inequality was a natural part of society, but he admitted that there were several possible systems for dealing with it. "Slavery, serfdom, apprenticeships, and free labour"—each was suited to its own social and historical circumstances. "It is a vain option to select between them in the abstract," he wrote, "inasmuch as their existence is determined by circumstances independent of choice, and is allied with political and social conditions which cannot be arbitrarily disturbed without ruin." A scholar rather than a propagandist at heart, he always stressed the need for more study. "We have only indicated the main topics of inquiry," he admitted at the conclusion of an 1856 essay on "Slavery and Freedom." "Volumes must be written before they are fully elucidated."[17]

By that time, however, the argument for slavery in the abstract had been picked up by other southerners who pushed it further. Like Holmes, these intellectuals preferred Auguste Comte to Adam Smith. They built their idea of society around a web of relationships and institutions rather than on a base of individuals and economic transactions, and at their most ambitious they were groping toward an alternative to the liberal order that had its roots in Hobbes and Locke. Pursued in this way, the study of slavery led to a kind of social analysis that was new in the United States. The first two American books with "sociology" in the title, both published in 1854, articulated visions of society with slavery at their heart.[18]

The first was Henry Hughes's *Treatise on Sociology, Theoretical and Practical.* The distinctive thing about the twenty-five-year-old Hughes was his emphasis on slavery as a relationship that took in not just master and slave but all of society. In fact, he chose not to call it "slavery," which he defined as a private relationship between master and slave that deprived the slave of all rights. In its place, he coined the word *warranteeism* to describe slavery as a *social* matter—a public means of establishing a just, or warranted, order within society. Hughes believed that this was the system practiced in the South. There, the state obliged the "warrantee" (slave) to work for the "warrantor" (master), and in return it obliged the warrantor to provide for the warrantee. By binding together the laborer and the capitalist (words that

Hughes also used) and providing a harmonious blend of power and order, warranteeism formed the proper basis for a just society.[19]

While Hughes was articulating a system of warranteeism that verged on social welfare, the Virginia writer George Fitzhugh was also developing a slave-based critique of free society in *Sociology for the South*, the second American book with "sociology" in the title to appear in 1854. Fitzhugh saw the growing popularity of socialist ideas as evidence that even free society's defenders knew they faced deep and perhaps intractable problems. He wanted these people to recognize that socialism was only the dim shadow of a better solution. "The oldest, the best and most common form of Socialism," according to Fitzhugh, was slavery. "The master furnishes the capital and skill, and the slaves the labor," he wrote, and then they "divide the profits, not according to each one's in-put, but according to each one's wants and necessities."[20] From each according to his ability, and to each according to his needs.

Fitzhugh maintained a friendly correspondence with Holmes, who reviewed *Sociology for the South* soon after it was published. "You, and Hughes, and I, in the last year, it seems to me, have revolutionized public opinion at the South on the subject of slavery," Fitzhugh told Holmes in 1855. Intellectually, Fitzhugh was a derivative and junior partner; he once admitted that Holmes could claim precedence for many of his major ideas. But Fitzhugh was considerably splashier, writing books with provocative titles like *Cannibals All!* while Holmes contributed dense essays to quarterly reviews. Holmes worried that Fitzhugh had a "predisposition to push his doctrines to their extreme consequences, or rather to prefer extreme doctrines to moderate statements."[21]

Indeed, Fitzhugh took the argument for slavery in the abstract all the way to the last stop. "He who justifies mere negro slavery, and condemns other forms of slavery, does not think at all—no, not in the least," he wrote in 1857. This included the enslavement of whites. "White slavery, not black, has been the normal element of civilized society," he declared. He believed that its abolition in Europe had proven disastrous for the working class, perhaps even worse than the more recent results of British emancipation in the West Indies. "We are all in the habit of maintaining that our slaves are far better off than the common laborers of Europe," he pointed out. The logical consequence of this claim, he continued, was that those common laborers should be restored to slavery. Fitzhugh made the most clear-eyed case for where the argument for slavery in the abstract necessarily led: slavery as a "necessitous element of civilized society, without regard to race or color."[22]

VERY FEW PEOPLE WERE WILLING TO FOLLOW FITZHUGH IN ADVOCATING the enslavement of whites. In practice, almost everyone in the South who defended slavery fell back at some point on racial arguments to justify the institution. Even Holmes did so despite his professed belief in "the abstract justice of slavery": "In our own day, the distinct functions of different races in the onward march of human progress promise to be recognized as the principal axiom of historical science."[23]

The result was a rush of research in racial science, with doctors and scientists throughout the South—and beyond—trying to develop racial classifications grounded in detailed scientific data gleaned from experiments and observations. This effort was pursued with ghoulish enthusiasm. "A dead negro, is to me, a perfect treat," one Charleston physician wrote an acquaintance in 1843, "& if you should be so unfortunate as to lose a servant, you could not possibly make me a greater present, than by sending me the body." He probably planned to carve up the corpse, examine the organs, and measure the skull. For this physician and others like him, the goal was to find some scientific basis for the assertion that Black people were inferior humans suited only for slavery. At their most ambitious, these racial scientists also raided the past for evidence that Africans had been enslaved throughout human history, hoping to show that Black slavery was a natural, universal human practice. As one prominent racial scientist, Samuel Cartwright, put it, "The mission of Ethnology is to vindicate the great truths on which the institutions of the South are founded."[24]

Today it is easy to caricature these racial scientists as hopelessly backward and unscientific, but as with eugenicists in a later generation, it is important to remember that they saw their own work as the cutting edge of progressive, modern science. The man who founded the field, Samuel George Morton, was not a crank. He came up through the medical establishment and was trained in comparative anatomy, one of the hottest scientific specialties of the day because it served as a powerful tool (at a time before natural selection and genetics) for classifying the creatures of the animal kingdom. As a student in Philadelphia, he attended a private medical school where he worked with the man who later started one of the first American collections of anatomical specimens. After getting his degree from the University of Pennsylvania, Morton continued his medical studies in Edinburgh and then returned to become a professor of anatomy at Pennsylvania Medical College. He made his name with his study *Synopsis of the Organic Remains of the Cretaceous Group of the United States*, which marked the start of invertebrate paleontology in America when it appeared in 1834.

By that time, he was also collecting human skulls. He had started his collection in 1830, hoping to demonstrate the differences between the five human races that had been classified in the late eighteenth century by the German naturalist Johann Friedrich Blumenbach. It was relatively easy for him to find Caucasian, American (i.e., Indian), and Ethiopian (Black) skulls, but he was frustrated in his attempt to secure Mongolian and Malayan examples. Soon he was using his position as corresponding secretary of the Academy of Natural Sciences to solicit skulls, and within a year he had contacts searching in South Carolina and Arkansas; by 1833, he had received about a hundred.

Morton enlisted soldiers, diplomats, travelers, and doctors across the world in his search. A man of scientific temperament, he took evident pleasure in the simple act of describing each one he received. And he tried to push the science of skulls forward, measuring not just facial angle and length, as others had, but also volume, which he did by filling the empty skulls with liquid mercury or pepper seed and buckshot.

In the late 1830s, Morton's search for skulls put him in contact with the American vice-consul in Cairo, a man named George Gliddon. Enthusiastic about Morton's project, Gliddon soon filled the cupboards and shelves of his Cairo house with ninety-three skulls (much to the distress of his servant). At the time, Egypt was contested terrain in discussions about racial history. Home to one of the world's oldest civilizations and some of its grandest ancient monuments, Egypt also happened to be perched between the "Black" history of sub-Saharan Africa and the "white" history of Greece, Rome, and the Bible. But the ancient Egyptians themselves—were they white or Black?[25]

Morton addressed the Egypt question briefly in his first book on skulls, *Crania Americana*, published in 1839. In a lengthy introductory essay, he speculated not only that Egyptians were Caucasians but also that "the Caucasian and Negro races were as perfectly distinct in that country upwards of three thousand years ago as they are now." Because the accepted time line of human history still adhered pretty closely to biblical chronology, with ancient Egypt coming not long after the Flood, Morton was effectively suggesting that racial differences had existed almost since God created man.[26]

Gliddon echoed Morton's claims after he returned to the United States in 1840. He quickly became famous as the first American lecturer on Egyptology, drawing huge crowds wherever he went. By the end of the decade, an estimated one hundred thousand people had heard him speak. He delivered the prestigious Lowell Lectures in Boston in 1843, telling the audience that ancient evidence showed clear distinctions between white Egyptians and Black Africans as long as four thousand years ago.[27]

Meanwhile, Morton followed up on the idea that ancient evidence could prove the antiquity of the races. He measured more than one hundred skulls that Gliddon sent him and examined a variety of Egyptian sculptures dating back thousands of years. By this time, he was interested not only in race but also in the historical connection between race and slavery. "We have the most unequivocal evidence, historical and monumental, that slavery was among the earliest of the social institutions of Egypt," he determined in *Crania Aegyptiaca*, published in 1844. "Negroes were numerous in Egypt, but their social position in ancient times was the same that it now is, that of servants and slaves." Moreover, he noted, the ancient Blacks depicted on Egyptian monuments looked the same as modern slaves, "precisely as we are accustomed to see them in our daily walks." All this was intended to prove that the various human races were fixed, "as old as the oldest records of our species"—and that slavery was an ancient, maybe even eternal, institution.[28]

Gliddon's lecture tour eventually took him to Washington, DC, where he met with the new secretary of state, John Calhoun, the rabidly pro-slavery politician from South Carolina, who was in the midst of plunging headfirst into a controversy over racial statistics in the census. The 1840 census included data on the number of "insane" people and "idiots" by state, race, and slave status. Soon after the numbers came out, a doctor named Edward Jarvis analyzed them and published an article in the *Boston Medical and Surgical Journal* (forerunner of the *New England Journal of Medicine*) showing not only that Black Americans were more likely than whites to be insane but also that free Blacks were far more likely than enslaved Blacks to be insane. This seemed to prove that slavery saved Black people from the insanity into which they supposedly descended when subject to what Jarvis called "the liabilities and dangers of active self-direction."

Except that it didn't. Jarvis did some more digging and found that the census was riddled with errors. Many northern towns listed an insane colored population that was somehow larger than their *total* colored population. Much to his credit, Jarvis followed up two months later to file a correction. He also started pressing the census to fix the mistake.

These problems did not stop Secretary of State Calhoun, in an April 1844 letter to a British minister, from citing the census as evidence that slavery improved Blacks. This was the moment when Gliddon came to town. Learning of the debate, he recommended that Calhoun read Morton's books (and arranged for Morton to send copies), explaining that they proved beyond any doubt that Africans had been servants or slaves throughout human history.

Calhoun soon faced blowback for relying on the faulty census data, a controversy made worse by the fact that the census was technically under his charge at the Department of State. ("What can be more sad than for a man to serve under John Tyler?" George Bancroft joked. "What: unless it be to found an argument in defence of slavery on fictitious statistics, and address it to a British minister!") Eventually Calhoun was forced to ask the superintendent of the census to investigate the alleged discrepancies, but the superintendent replied that abolitionists were upset only because the data poked holes in their theories.[29]

Jarvis continued to press the issue, now with assistance from the most educated Black American of his era, James McCune Smith. Born enslaved in New York, Smith had been freed by the state's Emancipation Act on July 4, 1827, when he was in his teens. "It was a proud day, never to be forgotten by young lads," he later recalled. While still enslaved, he started to attend New York African Free-School No. 2. Later, as a blacksmith's apprentice, he spent his evenings and Sundays teaching himself Latin and Greek to meet medical school admission requirements. Nevertheless, he was turned away from Columbia's medical school because of his race. Undeterred, he gained entry to the University of Glasgow, and local Black leaders in New York raised the money for him to go. He spent five years in Scotland, where he earned his bachelor's, master's, and MD. Upon his return, at age twenty-five, he was treated as a celebrity, his achievements serving as proof that Black Americans—even Black Americans who were born enslaved—could attain the highest academic credentials if given the chance. Smith went on to pursue a remarkably varied career. He operated a medical practice and pharmacy on West Broadway, served as chief physician of the city's Colored Orphan Hospital, contributed articles to his friend Frederick Douglass's newspapers, and edited several abolitionist papers of his own.

Ever since his return from medical school at Glasgow in the late 1830s, Smith had been speaking out against what he called "the fallacy of phrenology." "Learned men, in their rage for classification and from a reprehensible spirit to bend science to provoke popular prejudices, have brought the human species under the yoke of classification," he lamented. In lectures that he delivered to mixed-race audiences in New York and Philadelphia, he used skulls, statistics, and other anatomical information to show that the supposed science of race had no real substance: measurements like facial angles had no correlation with intelligence. Now he felt compelled to study the census data as well. At first, in early 1844, he drew on Jarvis's reports to write an article about the errors that was published in the *New York Tribune* (and soon reprinted in both *The Liberator* and the *National Anti-Slavery Standard*). Then he continued to study the connection between slavery and health. After two years, he assembled statistics to prove that free Black Americans lived longer and healthier lives than slaves. Jarvis was so impressed that he presented Smith's research before the Boylston Medical Community at Harvard.[30]

But Jarvis's efforts and Smith's research did nothing to derail the new racial science, which continued to gain adherents. Soon after the publication of *Crania Aegyptiaca*, Morton read an article about "mulattoes" in the *American Journal of the Medical Sciences*. The author, Josiah Nott, was a doctor who had attended South Carolina College under Thomas Cooper, received his medical degree from the University of Pennsylvania, and then settled in Mobile. Inspired by data from that infamous 1840 census showing that Africans lived longer than people of mixed race, Nott sought to prove that the reason for the disparity was that "mulattoes" were a degenerate hybrid—not of two distinct races, but of two distinct species.

This theory was known as polygenesis, the idea that each race was created separately and suited to a specific climate and geography. It was something of a fringe view because most Americans still held to what was known as monogenesis, the belief that—following a fairly straightforward interpretation of the Bible—there was a single human creation and that racial diversity developed from environmental causes operating on the descendants of an original pair (namely, Adam and Eve). But in the 1840s, Nott became one of the first scientists to drop the Bible as a guide to human history and follow wherever he thought the evidence led. He often compared himself to Galileo and firmly believed that he was fighting a similar battle to free science from the fetters of religion.

When Morton read Nott's article, he had not yet publicly endorsed the notion of separate creations, but he sent Nott a note that the piece gave him "much pleasure and instruction." Over the next few years, as Morton's health declined before his death in 1851, Nott began to assume leadership of the loose group of doctors and scientists who built on Morton's skull studies. Known as the American School of Ethnology, they articulated increasingly strong views of permanent racial difference as a justification for Black slavery.

At the end of 1848, Nott went to New Orleans to deliver two public lectures on what he called "Niggerology." They provide a good overview of his basic ideas. "We assert that the inspired writings must be abandoned, unless they can be reconciled with the clearly ascertained facts of science," he declared. He believed that the facts showed both that human history extended deeper into the past than standard biblical chronology allowed and that different races were separate species. The goal of racial science should be to find a scientific basis for managing their interactions: "The numberless attempts by the Caucasian race, during several thousand years, to bring the Mongol, Malay, Indian and Negro, under the same religion, laws, manners, customs, etc., have failed, and must continue to fail, unless the science of Ethnography can strike out some new and more practical plan of operation."[31]

Nott's polygenist ideas attracted a variety of supporters. By far the most prominent was Louis Agassiz, a world-renowned professor at Harvard, who went so far as to commission daguerreotypes of several slaves in South Carolina—believed to be the first photographs of American slaves—as anatomical evidence to support the theory. Another adherent was the physician Samuel Cartwright, whose research focused on the "Diseases and Peculiarities of the Negro Race," as the title of one 1851 article put it. Perhaps best known for diagnosing slaves' desire for freedom as a disease (drapetomania), Cartwright had a knack for discovering complex medical reasons why Black people did best under the control of others: "Under the compulsive power of the white man," he explained, "they are made to labor or exercise, which makes the lungs perform the duty of vitalizing the blood more perfectly than is done when they are left free to indulge in idleness."[32]

As the new ethnologists and polygenists made stronger historical and biological claims that Black people were naturally slavish, free Black people responded with their own scholarly accounts of Black history, which tried to distinguish Blackness from slave status. Usually, they aimed to demonstrate Black people's capacity for freedom and citizenship by focusing on the great ancient civilizations of Africa (they claimed Egypt as Black), the heroism of Toussaint L'Ouverture's fight for freedom in Haiti, and the courageous service of Black soldiers in American wars, especially the Revolution. One of these Black historical scholars was William Cooper Nell. Nell had grown up in Boston's Black community, where his father was friendly with David Walker. Nell later worked for William Lloyd Garrison at *The Liberator* and briefly for Frederick Douglass at the *North Star*. He became involved in electoral politics (he ran an unsuccessful campaign for the Massachusetts legislature in 1850), and that plus the desire to prove Black patriotism after the Fugitive Slave Act may have helped spur his interest in the history of Black participation in the Revolutionary War. In 1851, he was part of a group that petitioned the Massachusetts legislature to fund a monument to Crispus Attucks, the formerly enslaved Black man who was one of three Americans to die in the Boston Massacre.

When the legislature rejected the petition, Nell responded by putting together a short pamphlet, *Services of Colored Americans, in the Wars of 1776 and 1812*, published in 1852 with an introduction by the abolitionist leader Wendell Phillips. Three years later, Nell expanded his pamphlet into a full book, *The Colored Patriots of the American Revolution*, with a new introduction by Harriet Beecher Stowe. Going state by state, he provided brief biographical sketches of "colored patriots" who served during the Revolution as well as accounts of abolitionist activity throughout American history, including slave rebels like Nat Turner. For Nell, telling the story of Black service in American wars was a way of claiming for them the potent mantles of manhood, citizenship, and patriotism. He emphasized that first-wave abolitionism was central to the Revolutionary struggle, tying the antislavery cause firmly to the American cause.[33]

Nell's original pamphlet served as a source for his acquaintance Martin Delany, a Black man who had worked with him at Douglass's *North Star* in the late 1840s. Despondent in the wake of the Fugitive Slave Act as well as his own expulsion from Harvard Medical School after white student protests, Delany poured out *The Condition, Elevation, Emigration, and Destiny of the Colored People of the United States* in less than a month in 1852 while also attending to business and lecturing on physiology in New York City. Delany was not as optimistic as Nell about the possibility that Africans would be incorporated into American society. His view of African superiority was balanced, and perhaps even outweighed, by his strong sense of the degradation (a word he used often) that accompanied racial slavery—a degradation that passed down through the generations because of continued white prejudice. He went so far as to call such degradation "almost a physiological function of our system, an actual condition of our nature." According to Delany, even free Blacks in such a system were not really free. He advocated emigration as perhaps the only way to escape.[34]

Meanwhile, Josiah Nott's racial science attracted the support of George Gliddon. In the early 1850s, Gliddon took a break from his successful lectures on Egyptology. He stayed on brand, though, by convincing Senator Jefferson Davis to sponsor a scheme to import camels for use in transportation and mail delivery across the deserts of the American Southwest. Gliddon expected to be tapped for the lucrative position of leading the project. While he was waiting for his appointment, which ultimately went to someone else, he worked with Nott to develop a grand ethnological synthesis called *Types of Mankind*. After Nott's family suffered devastating losses during the Mobile yellow fever epidemic of 1853—seven relatives died, including four of his children—he buried himself in the work and completed it quickly.

Published in the spring of 1854, *Types of Mankind* soon sold out. As usual, the polygenist argument provoked an uproar from religious leaders, particularly Presbyterians. Little was new, but the book brought the main ideas of racial science and polygenesis to a broad audience: the races constituted different "types" of mankind, the types were permanent, and the Black type was made specifically for servitude. Even those unwilling to credit the prospect of multiple creations still read with interest the pair's purportedly scientific proof of Black inferiority. Nott and Gliddon quoted a Latin passage allegedly showing that "the physical characteristics of a 'field,' or agricultural, 'Nigger' were understood at Rome 1800 years ago, as thoroughly as by cotton-planters in the State of Alabama, still flourishing in A.D. 1853."[35]

Black scholars continued to challenge these ethnological conclusions. After discussing the issue with his close friend James McCune Smith, Frederick Douglass decided to deliver a souped-up version of his popular speech "The Races of Man," enhanced with additional research for an academic audience, at a commencement address at Western Reserve College that summer. Douglass worked with a white ethnologist to draw up an extensive ethnological reading list for himself, including Morton's skull studies. The result was a major address called "The Claims of the Negro Ethnologically

Considered," which made an environmentalist case for the fundamental unity of humanity.[36]

Despite criticism from biblical and Black scholars, Nott and Gliddon managed to take an even harder line in their second collaboration, *Indigenous Races of the Earth.* Nott declared he could find no historical evidence showing that one racial type had ever transformed into another type owing to any physical cause. He couldn't even find evidence that any racial type had ever adapted to live comfortably in a new climate. (Blacks supposedly suffered from the cold weather found north of 40 degrees latitude—almost exactly the location of the Mason-Dixon Line.) Meanwhile, he and Gliddon continued to press their earlier assertion that the polygenist view represented true science while monogenists trafficked in speculation and superstition. Free inquiry, the pair claimed, provided irrefutable evidence that the different races of humans were essentially different species; this, in turn, proved scientifically that some form of servitude or slavery was the necessary and proper relationship between the races—everywhere and for all time.[37]

Indigenous Races of the Earth didn't sell as well as *Types of Mankind*, but plenty of people still talked about it when the book was published in 1857. Gliddon, whose life never had a dull moment, left that spring to serve as an agent for the Honduras Inter-Oceanic Railway. Depressed and delirious with tropical fever, he accidentally overdosed on opium and died. Nott survived to keep pushing his scientific view of slavery. "Questions of morals and ethics, pertaining to its consideration," he reportedly said in the spring of 1861, "ought to be referred to the cubic capacity of the human cranium."[38]

Even as sociological and biological ideas swirled through society, the most important questions about slavery in America were always political: What was its status under the Constitution? Where could slaveholders legally take their slave property, and where could abolitionists stop them? This was the point at which competing theories had to cash out.

Whether grounded in sociology or biology, pro-slavery writers said slavery was a universal institution that existed across all times and places, sanctioned by the law of nature and of nations alike. This assertion helped support their claim to a constitutional right to property in slaves, resting on three specific clauses: the three-fifths clause counted "the whole Number of free Persons" and "three fifths of all other Persons" for purposes of representation and direct taxes; the fugitive-slave clause provided for the return of any "Person held to Service or Labour in one State, under the Laws thereof," who escaped into another; and the slave-trade clause denied Congress the power to prohibit "the Migration or Importation of such Persons as any of the States now existing shall think proper to admit" until 1808. Finally, the Fifth Amendment provided extra protection by prohibiting anyone from being "deprived of life, liberty, or property, without due process of law." Slave owners claimed that these clauses, particularly the ones in the main body of the Constitution, were compromises designed to secure southern buy-in to the Union by guaranteeing property rights in slaves.

Yet many abolitionists looked at the Constitution and saw nothing of the sort. It was true that the Constitution protected property rights in general, but abolitionists maintained that slaves were a special sort of property. This had been the import of Lord Mansfield's decision in the *Somerset* case of 1772, the first major victory of the Anglo-American abolitionist movement, which declared that colonial slaves could not be held in England because England had no law of slavery. Similarly, abolitionists argued that freedom was the national default under the Constitution, slavery a local exception. As Theodore Dwight Weld put it in 1838, slavery could only be the creature of "*positive legislative acts*, forcibly setting aside the law of nature, the common law, and the principles of universal justice."[39]

Debates about the status of slave property across state lines went on for decades. In 1857, *Dred Scott v. Sandford* brought the momentous question to the Supreme Court. In the early nineteenth century, Dred Scott had lived as a slave in Missouri. His owner, an army surgeon, took Scott with him to live for several years at posts in Illinois and Wisconsin Territory, where slavery did not exist. Eventually Scott and his master returned to Missouri, where Scott continued to be enslaved. In 1846, however, Scott sued for his freedom, arguing that his residence in places that prohibited slavery rendered him a free man. A decade later, the case finally made its way to the Supreme Court. George Ticknor Curtis—the US commissioner who returned Thomas Sims to Savannah in 1851—helped represent Dred Scott before the court. George's older brother Benjamin sat on the bench.[40]

At first, in chambers, the justices settled on a narrow decision declaring that Dred Scott was still enslaved because he lost his claim to freedom when he returned to Missouri, whose local law considered him a slave. In February 1857, however, the southerners on the court asked Chief Justice Roger Taney to write the opinion—seizing the opportunity, as they saw it, to settle the constitutional status of slavery once and for all. Taney issued his ruling a few weeks later. Regarding Scott, Taney stuck to the idea that his status should be determined by local law in Missouri.

But Taney's decision about Scott himself arrived as the coda to a much longer, more comprehensive discussion of race and slavery in the United States. The first question he addressed was whether Black people were citizens. He said no—a position he had held at least since serving as Andrew Jackson's attorney general in the early 1830s. At the time of the Revolution, he claimed, Africans "had for more than a century before been regarded as beings of an inferior order, and altogether unfit to associate with the white race either in social or political relations, and so far inferior that they had no rights which the white man was bound to respect." No person of African descent had been included in the Declaration of Independence's "all men are created equal" or in the Constitution's "we the people," he declared, and no Black person—slave or free—could be an American citizen. (As several historians had already established, free Black men in many states enjoyed some political rights when the Constitution was ratified, and some Black voters participated in the ratification process.)

Taney's argument that descendants of Africans were excluded from American citizenship meant Scott never had standing to sue for his freedom in the first place. Nevertheless, Taney still took up the substantive question of whether Scott could have become a free man because of his residence in Wisconsin Territory, a free portion of the Louisiana Purchase under the terms of the Missouri Compromise. "The right of property in a slave is distinctly and expressly affirmed in the Constitution," he declared, citing the slave-trade and fugitive-slave clauses. He also trotted out the Fifth Amendment's due process clause to claim that Congress could not deprive a citizen "of his liberty or property merely because he came himself or brought his property into a particular Territory of the United States." According to Taney's view of slave property, then, the Missouri Compromise had been unconstitutional from the start. In fact, so was the more recent innovation of "popular sovereignty" by which the people who settled territories such as Kansas and Nebraska could choose for themselves whether they wanted slavery. Territories had to remain open to slavery, Taney said, and his decision suggested that slaveholders might also be able to take their property into any state they wished.

Needless to say, *Dred Scott* did not settle the slavery question in the United States. Although Taney's was the ruling opinion, the decision was so divisive that every justice issued a separate one of his own. Most concurred with Taney, but there were two dissents, including a biting one from Benjamin Curtis. "Slavery, being contrary to natural right, is created only by municipal law," Curtis wrote. "This is not only plain in itself, and agreed by all writers on the subject, but is inferable from the Constitution and has been explicitly declared by this court." He believed that Taney was interpreting the Constitution according to his own individual will, and he resigned from the Supreme Court later that year.[41]

Taney's decision sparked a number of scholarly responses. George Bancroft, back from his stint as ambassador to England, was busy throughout the 1850s churning out a series of new volumes based on the research he'd done in Europe. In these volumes, the subject of slavery, which he later called "an anomaly in a democratic country," was reduced to a minor subplot in the grander story of the American Revolution, which Bancroft saw in providential terms as springing "from the intelligence that had been slowly ripening in the mind of cultivated humanity." Provoked, however, by Taney's false assertions about Black citizenship at the time of the Revolution, and prompted by a letter in which the abolitionist Theodore Parker passed along information gleaned directly from the Black historian William Cooper Nell, Bancroft included in his 1858 and 1860 volumes a few key passages detailing Black participation in the war: "Nor should history forget to record that . . . the free negroes of the colony had their representatives" at the famous Battle of Bunker Hill.[42]

Taney also had plenty of defenders. The most extended justification of Taney's ruling, as well as the capstone of southern pro-slavery thought, came from a young Georgia lawyer, Thomas Cobb, whose *Inquiry into the Law of Negro Slavery* was published in 1858. Just thirty-five years old, Cobb had been born on a large plantation that had 6,000 acres and 150 slaves at its height. He grew up mostly in Athens, where his father developed what became the wealthy part of town. A bright young man, he entered Franklin College (later the University of Georgia) at age fourteen, finished first in his class, and went into law. He started a legal practice and married a judge's daughter. He also grew wealthy himself, with seventeen slaves, two carriages, and more than two hundred acres of land. He aspired to be a good master and allowed his slaves to read the Bible and go to church. Yet he never lost sight of the fact that slavery was primarily a mode of economic production. He worked his slaves from 5 a.m. to 10 p.m., giving them little time off except for Sunday afternoons and Christmas, and he bought and sold people according to his needs. When an enslaved woman named Susan tried to slap his face, he did not hesitate to sell her and four of her youngest children.

Cobb believed, deep in his soul, that this system was right. In his view, stridency in defense of slavery was unnecessary because the truth of slavery would inevitably win out. He decried "*Calhounism* and *Abolitionism*" in equal measure because he wanted a spirit of comity to prevail. For much of Cobb's career, in fact, comity was his guiding principle in both politics and law. In 1852, the New York Superior Court upheld the seizure of slaves who had been taken by their Virginia owners to New York for a stay of eight days. People in the South were incensed. Cobb drafted a statement about the case for his older brother Howell, then serving as governor of Georgia: "By the comity of nations the personal status of every man is determined by the law of his domicile. A denial of this comity is unheard of among civilized nations, and if deliberately and wantonly persisted in, would be just cause of war."

Cobb started his *Inquiry into the Law of Negro Slavery* around 1850 and worked for eight years. His research brought him to libraries in Philadelphia and New York, and involved peppering a Harvard law professor with queries. He intended his book as a fair-minded attempt to show northerners that slavery was a sound practice. "My confidence," he wrote when he was finished, "is solely in the honesty of every conviction which I have announced as truth."[43]

As with Taney, Cobb's legal reasoning depended on a historical argument about race. His book opened with a "historical sketch" of more than two hundred pages, whose main purpose was to show that Africans had always and everywhere been slaves. "We cannot go back to the origin of negro slavery," he wrote. Israel, Egypt, India, China, Greece, Rome—not only was slavery universal throughout civilized history, but all these places enslaved Black Africans.

Cobb's history laid a clear foundation for his analysis of the law of negro slavery in America: if Black Africans had been slaves throughout world history, nothing in nineteenth-century America could change that. In Cobb's view, the condition of slavery followed the slave wherever he went, no matter the laws on the ground. "The escape of the slave into a non-slaveholding State would not impair the master's rights," he declared.[44] Masters could take their slaves wherever they wanted—in most cases, even into northern free states, according to Cobb—and still own them as slaves.

After the book garnered harsh reviews in the North, Cobb realized that the spirit of comity might not extend as far as he thought. Caught up in sectional politics, he began to embrace southern nationalism, with a focus on education. He drafted a plan for a public school system in Georgia and worked with his father-in-law to start a law school in Athens. He also led an effort to remodel Franklin College into a full university that could compete with northern schools and keep southern students in the South. "As Georgians, should we not be ashamed that our sons are forced to be sent to Northern Colleges in order to receive the highest educational privileges?" he asked in 1858, echoing George Frederick Holmes at Mississippi a decade earlier. "That even *abolitionized Yale* has at this time *forty-five* young men from the South, whose parents prefer to submit to the degradation of placing their sons under the tuition of our worst enemies, rather than deprive them of the best opportunity of becoming educated?"[45]

Meanwhile, Cobb's book caught the attention of a New York lawyer named John Codman Hurd. Hurd was at work on his own very different book on American slave law in the United States. Prompted by Taney's *Dred Scott* decision, he had realized that the domestic law of slavery involved not only local or national statutes but also principles of international law.[46]

The biggest controversies in the slavery debates of the 1850s—including the Fugitive Slave Act and the *Dred Scott* decision—all turned on whether slavery continued across state borders. This was analogous to the question in international law of whether slave status transferred to different jurisdictions. Examining the question historically, Hurd agreed with Cobb that chattel slavery was once an accepted condition in the law of nations, one that was assumed to exist from place to place. But he showed that this largely unspoken law of nations had transformed over the past several centuries. In Hurd's reading of history, slavery had shifted from a universal institution accepted everywhere to an institution peculiar to only a few places, at least in the Western world.

Hurd then applied these lessons from the history of international law to American slavery. He was not the first antislavery lawyer to reach this insight, but he developed it most fully. He claimed that Article IV of the Constitution, which governed relations between the states, acted as a kind of "domestic international law" whose intricacies had never been adequately studied. According to Hurd, the "full faith and credit" and "privileges and immunities" clauses in Article IV functioned to maintain "relations which exist under the dominion of another State. They are therefore international in their *effect*." Legally speaking, he said, different states within the United States stood in the same relation to one another as did different nations in the world at large.

Hurd believed that slave status could carry over between local jurisdictions that practiced slavery—that is, throughout the South—based on comity, but in contrast to Taney and Cobb, Hurd claimed that slave status could not continue into free states and territories unless the local jurisdictions explicitly agreed or Congress enforced a treaty to that effect. In the United States, of course, there was such a treaty: the Constitution's fugitive-slave clause in Article IV, which was enforced by the Fugitive Slave Law of 1850. But the crucial point for Hurd was that slave status could be transferred to nonslaveholding jurisdictions only under the terms of a specific "treaty"—the Fugitive Slave Law—not deeper principles of international or natural law.

Hurd's book was a long, difficult work of legal scholarship, and it took him several years to complete. The first volume, focusing on international law, appeared in 1858, but the second, containing the heart of his analysis of "domestic international law" under the Constitution, was not published until 1862. By that time, the country was in the middle of a civil war. "Whatever its consequences on the law of personal condition may be," Hurd wrote of the war, "it is certain that the opinions and decisions cited in this work are not the least among the causes of the existing civil contest."[47] His book provided the historical background and legal principles that other scholars needed as they confronted new questions about the place of slavery in the laws of war.

AFTER *DRED SCOTT*, THE QUESTION OF CONSTITUTIONAL PROTECTIONS FOR slave property became the paramount issue in American politics. In 1859, Democratic senator Stephen Douglas, who planned to run for president the next year, broke with the southern wing of his party and declared, in a long essay in *Harper's*, that he believed slavery to be the product of local, not national, law. The Democrats soon splintered into sectional parties. Douglas's chief Republican rival, Abraham Lincoln, spent the next few months studying Douglas's essay as well as the *Dred Scott* case for a speech he was scheduled to deliver at Henry Ward Beecher's Brooklyn church. In February, the location was moved across the East River to Cooper Institute, which could accommodate a larger crowd.[48] There Lincoln gave a history lesson about slavery and the Constitution.

Slaveholders, he said, claimed a constitutional right "to take slaves into the federal territories, and to hold them there as property." Did such a right exist? He went step-by-step through the federal government's actions regarding slavery in the territories, starting in the 1780s, demonstrating in his clear, lawyerly accounting that a majority of the Constitution's thirty-nine framers had at some point voted in a way that indicated they believed the federal government could restrict slavery's spread. Moving on to Taney's *Dred Scott* decision, he noted that "it was mainly based upon a mistaken statement of fact" regarding whether the Constitution "distinctly and expressly affirmed" the right of property in slaves. He described the Republican position on slavery as a conservative return to the framers' understanding of it. Slavery was "*an evil not to be extended*," he explained, "*but to be tolerated and protected only because of and so far as its actual presence among us makes that toleration and protection a necessity*." Yet, as Lincoln knew, southerners saw that position as a provocation, a violation of their supposed right to take their human property wherever they wished with the protection of the federal government. The only way to satisfy them, he said, would be for Republicans to "cease to call slavery *wrong*, and join them in calling it *right*."[49] But that was one issue where his party refused to compromise.

Because Lincoln's Republicans took a broad view of their powers under the Constitution to restrict slavery and put it on the course to ultimate extinction, slaveholders saw his election as president on November 6, 1860, as an existential threat. Thomas Cobb learned the news by telegraph the next morning. Three days later, he attended a public meeting in Athens about trying to prevent any slave insurrections that might be inspired by the Republican victory. He also delivered a stirring speech in favor of disunion, which one thunderstruck listener described as "the greatest speech *I ever heard*." Cobb went even further in an address to the state legislature a few days later, in which he declared Lincoln's election unconstitutional because northern states had allowed some free Blacks to vote in defiance of the *Dred Scott* decision.[50]

On December 20, South Carolina became the first state to secede. That night, Cobb marched in a torchlight parade through Athens. Back at his house, he illuminated a large transparency reading "Resistance to Abolition is Obedience to God." By Lincoln's inauguration on March 4, 1861, six other states, including Georgia, had joined South Carolina to form the Confederate States of America.

"A disruption of the Federal Union heretofore only menaced, is now formidably attempted," Lincoln declared in his inaugural address. "One section of our country believes slavery is *right*, and ought to be extended, while the other believes it is *wrong*, and ought not to be extended. This is the only substantial dispute."[51] Yet that dispute, grounded as it was in fundamental disagreements about human nature and society, economics and government, and history and progress, had divided families, severed friendships, and torn the country apart.

Cobb served in the Confederate convention, where he was named to the committee on a permanent constitution. His job was to polish the committee's draft, which he described as "really the old Constitution with the states rights construction incorporated." In what could be read as a tacit admission that their pro-slavery interpretation of the Federal Constitution was not quite correct, the Confederates explicitly wrote slavery into their own document, substituting "slaves" for "persons" in several places and adding clauses protecting "the institution of negro slavery" as well as the right to property in slaves.

Back home in Georgia, Cobb kept up a furious schedule, voting to ratify the Confederate constitution and leading the committee that rewrote the state constitution. That summer, he was elected to the Confederate Congress in Richmond, and he also raised his own legion, gaining a commission as a colonel in the Confederate Army. Neither institution was energetic or efficient enough for his taste, but the army did see considerable success until the Battle of Antietam in September 1862, when the Union Army turned back Robert E. Lee's forces in Maryland. A few months later, at Fredericksburg, Cobb was in a conference with other officers behind the line of battle when a piece of shrapnel sliced open his thigh. Knocked to the ground, he asked for a tourniquet. But the bleeding from his severed artery could not be stopped. Cobb was carried to the field hospital, where he fell into a coma and died, at the age of thirty-nine.[52]

By the time Cobb was buried after a massive funeral in Athens, a new set of thorny legal and moral problems was emerging from the war over slavery. With Union armies marching through the South, slaves were fleeing to federal lines. The loss of these slaves constituted a major blow to the Confederacy, which depended on them for agricultural production and army labor. Some northern officers suggested that the slaves should be returned under the terms of the Fugitive Slave Law; others said they should be kept as "contraband of war" and returned after the fighting ended. By August 1861, the contraband policy had become law. But there was still no consistent practice within the army. The laws of war regarding slaves seemed to permit multiple interpretations. Which interpretation won out would affect not only the outcome of the war but also the future of slavery.[53]

The person who thought most deeply about these questions was a political scientist named Francis Lieber. The confiscation of slave property seemed increasingly "momentous" to Lieber as the war went on. He thought war naturally dissolved the status of slavery, making slaves into *people* deserving protection rather than *property* to be restored to their owners. He sketched his logic for Massachusetts senator Charles Sumner in December 1861. Slavery mixed "the two ideas Man and Thing," Lieber wrote. But war washed away the property aspect of slavery, he believed, leaving only human beings: "The Law of Nature does not acknowledge the difference of skin, and war is carried on by the Law of Nature." That same month, President Lincoln noted in his first annual message to Congress that the slaves confiscated by Union armies were "thus liberated."[54]

At the time, Lieber was a professor of history and political science at Columbia College in New York. He was, in fact, the first professor of political science in the United States, and he embodied the rise of the social sciences in a changing American academic landscape. Born in Berlin in 1798, he had studied at several German universities and received a PhD from Jena before working for a year in Rome with the groundbreaking ancient historian Barthold Niebuhr. Eventually he was forced to flee his native Prussia because his liberal politics resulted in constant run-ins with the police. Landing in the United States in the late 1820s, he rode his energy and intelligence into the most desirable social circles in Boston, New York, and Philadelphia. In 1835, in the wake of the Thomas Cooper debacle over the Old Testament at South Carolina College, he was named the school's new professor of history and political economy. During two decades there, he essentially founded the field of political science in America. Later, at Columbia, he laid the groundwork for one of the key institutions where the modern American research university—based largely on German models—eventually took shape.[55]

Lieber disliked slavery, but during his years in South Carolina, if he wanted a servant or a laborer, his main option was to hire a slave. He even bought some and learned to look at potential purchases with a practiced eye. This distressed him deeply. As time went on, he found life among slaveholders increasingly intolerable, perhaps because of what it forced him to see in himself. (And in his family: his eldest son would die fighting for the Confederacy.) "Such wildness, such wicked shamelessness, such hypocrisy, such ranting, raving imbecility, such godless lying as I am surrounded by, I feel sure has never existed in any period of history, with so little cause," he complained in 1850.[56] This was one major reason that he left the South a few years later.

By then, he was already starting to see that several of the most important issues confronting the country—such as the transportation of slaves into new territories and the status of fugitive slaves—ultimately boiled down to questions of international law that hinged largely on the precise mixture of person and property in the legal definition of a slave. He had begun to study the topic as early as 1849, when the question of California's admission as a free state was first raised. He realized then that if slaves were considered simply as property, like flour or furniture, there would be no good argument against transporting them from state to state or even from country to country. But slavery was also a personal condition, and he thought that the nature of that personal condition was defined differently in nearly every time and place where it existed. Because of those different definitions, Lieber believed, slavery was necessarily "a domestic or municipal institution," with no reach beyond a country's borders.[57] Like Hurd, he thought the only way to bridge the gap between the slave laws of two different countries would be a specific treaty guaranteeing the continuation of slave status across borders.

After Fort Sumter, these ruminations on the legal status of slavery fed into Lieber's analysis of slavery's place in the laws of war. In addition to his letters to Senator Sumner, he delivered lectures on the laws of war at Columbia's law school in the winter of 1861–62. The Lincoln administration got wind of Lieber's work and started to ask him for advice. General-in-Chief Henry Halleck asked him to write legal treatises on war matters, starting with a short essay on guerrilla warfare. Attorney General Edward Bates requested a memorandum on the status of slaves in wartime, and Secretary of War Edwin Stanton wanted one on the "military use of colored persons."[58]

The status of slavery in wartime soon became an unavoidable problem. In early 1862, Congress forbade the return of runaway slaves who made it to Union lines. Around that time, Lieber read John Codman Hurd's second volume on the law of slavery and remarked that the events of the war would soon make a third volume necessary. After the Union victory at Antietam in September, President Lincoln issued the Preliminary Emancipation Proclamation. If the Confederate states continued their rebellion into the new year, the federal government would consider all slaves in rebel territory "then, thenceforward, and forever free." The Union was starting to arm Black soldiers, but the Confederacy declared it would treat them as criminals rather than combatants. Lieber heard reports that the South was starting to enslave Blacks traveling with the Union Army as well as free Black civilians unconnected with the fighting. He considered such enslavement "a relapse into barbarity." He searched his library to find the last time that war captives had been enslaved. "In all probability," he concluded, "this would be the last case in the history of civilized or semi-civilized nations."[59]

By December, around the time Thomas Cobb bled out at the Battle of Fredericksburg, Halleck and Stanton needed to figure out a response. They summoned Lieber to Washington to help compose a set of rules for Union armies in the field. He was still revising it when Lincoln signed the final Emancipation Proclamation on New Year's Day, turning the Union Army into an army of liberation.

Lieber's code, which he completed in January, provided the legal and theoretical framework on which that promise of liberation could hang. About a dozen of the code's 157 articles dealt with slavery, emancipation, or Black soldiers; everyone recognized that they were its most original and important sections. Lieber wrote into the code that slavery "exists according to municipal law or local law only. The law of nature and nations has never acknowledged it." The implication was that even without the proclamation or any other official act, all slaves who reached Union lines should be considered permanently free. Thinking of the reports he had heard of Confederates enslaving Blacks they found traveling with the Union Army, Lieber added,

"The law of nations knows of no distinction of color," specifying that the enslavement of anyone connected with the army, white or Black, should be punished with death.[60]

Lieber's code, known as General Orders No. 100, went into effect in the spring of 1863. Confederate president Jefferson Davis considered it "inhuman," but by late summer, the Confederacy capitulated on one of the main points, distinguishing Black soldiers who had been free (whom it treated as soldiers) from those who had been enslaved (whom it continued to treat as criminals). Meanwhile, good reports flowed north from the front after one Black regiment performed particularly well at Port Hudson. The conduct of the Black regiments, Lieber thought, served as "a distinct sign post on the highway of History."[61] Their success refuted old claims that Blacks constituted an inferior race, perhaps even a separate species, that was unfit for freedom.

Within a few months, Lieber realized that he no longer needed to worry about the survival of slavery in the United States. He declared to Charles Sumner that he couldn't think of "any change of opinion, conviction and feeling . . . equal to the change that has been wrought in the American mind concerning Slavery, within the last one year." Soon he drafted a constitutional amendment for abolition, which he sent to Sumner in the Senate. Sumner thought Lieber was wasting his time. An amendment abolishing slavery was unnecessary, Sumner believed, because the Constitution never used the word *slave*. He thought the passages usually interpreted as referring to slavery didn't *necessarily* refer to slavery, and could remain as written. The clause dealing with the return of fugitives who were "held to Service or Labour," for example, might also apply to apprentices and indentured servants. But Lieber rejected this theory as too convenient by half. "I am convinced there is unfortunately no doubt," he replied. "We know that shoemaker apprentices did not run away in so alarming a degree as to make it necessary to talk of them in the national fundamental Law of America."[62]

By the spring of 1864, Republicans in Congress agreed that an amendment would be the best way to abolish slavery in the United States. The Senate passed one in April. It was not Lieber's version, but it was similar in spirit, its language copied from previous territorial exclusions of slavery dating back nearly eighty years: "Neither slavery nor involuntary servitude, except as a punishment for crime whereof the party shall have been duly convicted, shall exist within the United States, or any place subject to their jurisdiction."

The amendment stalled in the House, where there were still enough Democrats to prevent the necessary two-thirds majority. After Lincoln and the Republicans won a resounding victory in the election that fall, Lincoln convinced the lame-duck House to pass it, with just two votes to spare, in January 1865. Nineteen northern states ratified it within two months—but because Lincoln and the federal government always maintained that states could not really secede, the amendment could not be adopted until three-fourths of all the states, including those in the South, approved it.[63]

Lincoln was assassinated in April, just as the war was ending. "Poor, good Lincoln," Lieber wrote to Sumner when he heard the news. "The South must be literally swept with the sword, all the fiends ought to be driven out or hanged, until the people in the states rise against their own de facto government and offer themselves back to the union, without slavery."[64] By December, enough southern states had ratified the abolition amendment for it to be incorporated into the Constitution.

Four million slaves were now free. Already the meaning of slavery and freedom was being called into question; already southern states were beginning to pass Black Codes to limit the ability of former slaves to work outside the old plantation system. But while these new problems were in the making, there also existed a spirit of celebration—a sense of having achieved a victory not just for the North but also for civilization, for progress, for morality. A year after the war ended, Lieber saw a parade of Black Americans marching down a street in Washington, celebrating their freedom. "It was most touching—I could not help crying," he told his wife. "God bless this land."[65]

Lieber was in Washington as director of the War Department's office for organizing Confederate records. He pored over hundreds of thousands of documents looking for evidence to use in the treason trials of Confederate officials. He also categorized the files for future historians. Soon, he sensed, a tremendous gulf would separate him from the next generation of

Americans. No one alive after emancipation would be able to see slavery as a living institution or a working relationship in the United States. For a while there would still be memories, but then scholars interested in slavery would have to come up with new sources and new methods. They would study slavery not as a practical problem but as a historical puzzle.

Lieber doubted whether anyone would put it all together. "Modern North American slavery," he wrote, "with its hypocrisy and fanaticism in the very teeth of religion and the spirit of the times, with its new-fangled philosophy, moral, mental and economical—will be wholly inconceivable to the next generation."[66]

PART II

RESEARCH

4

STILL FIGHTING IT

EMANCIPATION DID NOT MARK THE END OF DEBATES ABOUT SLAVERY IN America. Even before the Thirteenth Amendment was formally adopted at the end of 1865, there were questions about what actually constituted slavery, what role it played in society, and what it meant to end it. If slavery was primarily a personal relationship between two people, then it could be ended simply by freeing the slaves. In that case, emancipation amounted to a matter of law. But if slavery was a means of regulating the relationship between two fundamentally unequal races, or if slavery was the natural result of certain economic conditions, or if slavery encompassed not just personal servitude but also social and economic discrimination, then the problem became significantly more complex. Must freedpeople also be granted social and economic equality in order to guarantee their freedom? Must the economic conditions that accompanied slavery, such as large landholdings, be abolished? Must entirely new social institutions be devised to deal with the supposedly inevitable racial conflicts that slavery mediated?

Even committed abolitionists had a hard time agreeing on answers. For example, the legendary abolitionist William Lloyd Garrison believed that the Thirteenth Amendment signaled the end of the antislavery cause. In 1865, he shuttered *The Liberator* and called for the American Anti-Slavery Society to dissolve. The society's membership, however, had other ideas and rejected Garrison's motion. Garrison's longtime friend and ally Wendell Phillips took over, continuing to publish the *National Anti-Slavery Standard* and push Congress to support Black equality. Only after the ratification of the Fourteenth Amendment—which secured birthright citizenship, due process, and equal protection—and of the Fifteenth Amendment—which secured Black men the right to vote—did the group finally, in 1870, consider its antislavery mission complete. Even then, the vote to disband was not unanimous.[1]

As for the country as a whole, which included freed slaves as well as former slaveholders, the struggle over these questions would not be short. America's postwar trajectory, from the promise of emancipation to the retreat from Reconstruction and beyond, is often encapsulated in the neat formulation that the South lost the war but won the peace—won, that is, the long-term social, cultural, and political battles (sometimes including real battles with violence) to define the war's meaning and to determine America's postwar racial order. Fifty years after the end of the war, the South was ruled by Jim Crow and lynch law, and the first southern president since the Civil War, Woodrow Wilson, was busy segregating the executive branch and applauding the racist film *The Birth of a Nation*. Instead of statues of fugitive slaves on every town square, as the writer William Dean Howells once suggested, monuments to Confederate soldiers sprouted across the South.[2]

What might be called the southern view of things—racist, pro-slavery, neo-Confederate—may have won out around the turn of the twentieth century, but even that victory was hard-fought, partial, and temporary. There were always plenty of Americans, white as well as Black, who pushed for racial equality. And where that promise seemed most dim and distant, in the South of the 1910s, Black people who had been stripped of their right to vote with ballots decided instead to vote with their feet, relocating in such large numbers that they soon reshaped American politics with the Great Migration.

A similar dynamic occurred in the study of slavery. By the 1910s, the leading American historian of slavery was a southerner who saw slavery as a beneficent institution that served as a school for supposedly childlike Black people. But critics of that view never dropped away, and at times they even dominated the debate. Just as before the war, Americans continued to argue about slavery.

The difference now was that slavery was gone. Over the course of the next two generations, slavery shifted from the realm of firsthand observation and experience to that of memory and, in time, to historical research. Slavery itself stopped being a heated political issue, but it continued to provoke heated debate.

When the Civil War started, few sympathetic histories of Black Americans existed. "History has thrown the colored man out," a former slave named William Wells Brown complained in 1860. "You look in vain to Bancroft and the other historians for justice to the colored people. . . . The colored man is colonized off from the white man, or mentioned in a sort of appendix."[3] Not only were slaves not considered proper historical subjects, but for a long time there were few educated free Blacks who were capable of compiling that history themselves. With slavery gone, however, a new kind of Black history was possible, one that could look back over the entirety of African slavery in the United States and frame it in hindsight as the now-finished first chapter of Black life in America. Brown decided that he should be the first to do it.

Brown liked to suggest that his own life embodied the Black American experience. He had been born in Kentucky to an enslaved woman named Elizabeth; his father was his owner's cousin. Later, after his owner moved to Missouri, Brown fled with his mother to freedom in Illinois. They did not get far. Brown's mother was sold south as punishment, while Brown was whipped and then sold locally, eventually ending up with a steamboat owner. On New Year's Day in 1834, the boat stopped at Cincinnati. As it was unloading, Brown took the opportunity to unload himself as well. He went north and settled in Cleveland, where he worked on a Lake Erie steamboat and started a sideline helping to smuggle fellow fugitives to Canada.

Brown learned to read, moved to Boston, and joined up with Garrison and Phillips at the Massachusetts Anti-Slavery Society, where he became a celebrated writer and speaker. He first achieved fame in 1847, with the publication of his *Narrative of William W. Brown, a Fugitive Slave.* He then went on to write the first African American travelogue (*Three Years in Europe,* 1852, about his period of exile after the Fugitive Slave Act), the first African American novel (*Clotel,* 1853, about the fictional enslaved daughter of Thomas Jefferson), and the first African American play (*The Escape,* 1858, about slaves who flee to Canada).[4]

As the Civil War started, Brown decided to try his hand at history. He was already at work in 1861, when he published biographical sketches of Benjamin Banneker, the famous Black scientist, and Madison Washington, who led a rebellion aboard a coastal slave ship in 1841. Over the next year, he completed about fifty additional biographies for a compilation called *The Black Man: His Antecedents, His Genius, and His Achievements.* Given the paucity of available information about Black history, this was not an easy task. It involved pilfering from previous Black historians as well as reading a huge number of standard historical works and mining what he could from the margins. No less an authority than Frederick Douglass was impressed by Brown's detective work. "It is hard to repress the enquiry whence has this man this knowledge?" Douglass later wrote. "He seems to have read and remembered nearly every thing which has been written or said respecting the ability of the negro."

Brown finished *The Black Man* in early September 1862, setting up one of the best-timed book releases in history. Lincoln issued the Preliminary Emancipation Proclamation later that month. Ads for Brown's book then appeared throughout the fall. The book was published in December, followed shortly by the final Emancipation Proclamation on January 1. Brown's book constituted the most comprehensive survey of African American achievement to that point. Coming at the same moment as the Emancipation Proclamation, it essentially marked the birth of African American history—of Black people being acknowledged as important actors in the

American story. The book sold well, and enthusiastic Black readers quickly spread it as far as they could. Soon after Savannah fell into Union hands, a former slave was distributing copies throughout the city. On nearby Edisto Island, South Carolina, one freedman gave a copy to a friend, inscribing it with the date July 16, 1865.[5]

Many of the biographical sketches in Brown's book told the story of Black men who were born in slavery and rose to great achievements. In just a few short years, Black Americans as a whole were traversing the same ground, going from slaves to soldiers to citizens—a scale of transformation almost unprecedented in world history, one that took them from outside the traditional sphere of historical action to its very center in politics and war. Brown did his part, helping to recruit Black soldiers for the Massachusetts Fifty-Fourth. When the war was over, he wrote a second work of Black history, called *The Negro in the American Rebellion*, in which he recorded and celebrated "the part which the Negro took in suppressing the Slaveholders' Rebellion."[6] For him, as for many other northern abolitionists, emancipation marked the defining event of the war, and formerly enslaved Black soldiers were its heroes.

YET BROWN'S FOCUS ON MAJOR FIGURES WHO CAME UP FROM SLAVERY WAS far from the only way to think about the role of slavery in American life. Another was to study slave culture. Before the Civil War, Black slaves were not seen to contribute anything to American culture as it was usually understood, at least nothing worth recording. White southerners and northern travelers surely would have seen and heard the cultural practices of enslaved Blacks in the South, but such observations usually did not make it into print.

This neglect owed a good deal to slavery and bigotry, but it also reflected a broader lack of attention given to oral "folk" cultures, which tended to be either taken for granted or considered unimportant. Writings on slavery to that point focused more on its political, economic, and social effects, especially its effects on whites. Abolitionists emphasized the physical cruelty and deprivation of slavery, but it would not have helped their cause to celebrate slave culture. White southerners did not become interested in Black music or culture until after the Civil War, when they felt a strong wave of nostalgia for old plantation life. Some "Black" music was known in the North before the war, but it was mostly minstrelsy.[7]

That changed when northern abolitionists, missionaries, soldiers, and teachers had their first sustained encounters with newly freed slaves during the war. Without the blinkers of explicit racial prejudice, these northerners could see Black people as "intensely human," as one of them put it.[8] Still, they often harbored their own prejudices of culture and class. So while they may not have equated Blackness with a permanent condition of barbarism, they did sometimes see Black slaves as temporarily ignorant or backward, in need of a little education and guidance as they made their first steps in freedom. The result was a variety of responses, sometimes sensitive and sympathetic, sometimes condescending or patronizing, often a complex combination. With all its complications, this sudden, mass encounter opened a fresh possibility in the study of slavery: the formal study of slave culture.

The Sea Islands of South Carolina were by far the most important site where this occurred. The navy had secured a beachhead there in November 1861 as part of its larger effort to blockade the Confederacy. The white planters fled the islands. They tried to convince their slaves to come, too, but the slaves—thousands of them—thought better of it and stayed put. These people technically became contraband of war—and soon the subjects of a vast experiment in education and free labor centered on the islands around Port Royal, including Hilton Head and St. Helena.[9] Abolitionist groups in Boston, New York, and Philadelphia raised money and recruited volunteers to serve as teachers, missionaries, and plantation superintendents.

In Philadelphia the city's Port Royal Relief Committee was headed by James Miller McKim, who also helped run the Pennsylvania Anti-Slavery Society. An abolitionist of some distinction, McKim had helped John Brown's wife bring Brown's body north after he was hanged near Harpers Ferry. In early 1862, McKim quickly raised more than five thousand dollars to send to Port Royal. A few months later, the committee decided to dispatch McKim himself to report on conditions there. McKim brought along his eighteen-year-old daughter, Lucy, as his assistant. She, too, was a staunch abolitionist, having briefly attended and then taught at Eagleswood, an experimental school in New Jersey run by the abolitionist couple Theodore Dwight Weld and Angelina Grimké.

James and Lucy McKim arrived at St. Helena late in the spring of 1862. Within a day, Lucy felt she was seeing slavery with fresh eyes. "The pro-slavery folks were right when they said, Go South, Abolitionists, if you want to have your views changed on the subject of slavery," she wrote to her mother. "Mine have been most profoundly." She began to jot down notes about everything she saw.[10]

What captured Lucy's attention most was the music she heard from the freedpeople. She started copying down tunes and lyrics just days after her arrival. A trained musician who had already spent a few years teaching piano, she was better prepared than most people to really hear them. She remained entranced even after her return to Philadelphia in July. She asked the friends she'd made in Port Royal to keep sending her examples, and she began preparing piano arrangements for publication. "Poor Rosy, Poor Gal," the first in her series of "Songs of the Freedmen of Port Royal," came out in October. It was the second published slave-song arrangement in the United States, after a version of "Go Down, Moses," that had been collected at Fort Monroe, Virginia, and published the year before.

Lucy sent a copy of her arrangement to *Dwight's Journal of Music* along with an introductory letter—which, when it was published in November, became the first article in American history to describe the musical style and technique of slave songs. Beyond their purely musical interest, she noted, the songs were also "valuable as an expression of the character and life of the race which is playing such a conspicuous part in our history." She went on to provide a perceptive reading of what the songs revealed: "The wild, sad strains tell, as the sufferers themselves never could, of crushed hopes, keen sorrow, and a dull daily misery which covered them as hopelessly as the fog from the rice-swamps," she wrote. "On the other hand, the words breathe a trusting faith in rest in the future."[11]

Lucy's second arrangement, "Roll, Jordan, Roll," came out in January, just after Emancipation Day. She seems to have had a plan to publish four more, but life intervened; young men to whom she had romantic attachments died in the war, and she then entered into a courtship with Wendell

Phillips Garrison, the son whom William Lloyd Garrison named for his abolitionist ally. Lucy's time was occupied teaching piano and waiting for Wendell to find a steady job so they could get married.[12]

Meanwhile, Thomas Wentworth Higginson had arrived in Port Royal, called there in November 1862 to take command of the First South Carolina Volunteers, a regiment raised from the freedpeople on the Sea Islands. He got the position because he was one of the most fiery abolitionists in America. Before the war, he had become involved in the Underground Railroad and also helped form Boston's Vigilance Committee, which tried to protect fugitive slaves from being recaptured. In 1854, he bought the axes for an ill-fated attempt to free the alleged fugitive Anthony Burns from Boston's Federal Courthouse. In the scrum, he got hit on the chin and acquired a scar that he carried for the rest of his life; a federal marshal was killed, an event that Higginson later recalled with perhaps a hint of pride (and certainly little sadness) as the first casualty of the Civil War. His next act was to take rifles and ammunition to Bleeding Kansas, where he learned about the violent exploits of John Brown. A few years later, when Brown needed help planning and funding his raid on Harpers Ferry, Higginson was one of the so-called Secret Six who provided assistance. After the raid went awry, he was the only one of the six courageous or foolhardy enough to spill his secret; he also raised money for Brown's defense and even planned an armed raid to rescue Brown before Brown learned of the scheme and called it off.[13]

Higginson redirected his energy into a series of deeply researched articles on slave insurrections, including Nat Turner's and Denmark Vesey's, which appeared from 1860 to 1862 in a new magazine called the *Atlantic Monthly*. (William Wells Brown relied on these articles when he was writing *The Black Man*.) Higginson also prepared for war. He didn't volunteer initially because his wife was ill, but by 1862 he could no longer resist, particularly when he got the invitation to serve with Black soldiers in South Carolina, a position he saw as the fulfillment of Brown's legacy. "As many persons have said," he wrote on board the ship taking him south, "the first man who organizes & commands a successful black regiment will perform the most important service in the history of the War."[14]

Higginson thought he knew everything there was to know about slavery from his abolitionist activity before the war. As with the McKims, however, several months in the Sea Islands showed him that he still had plenty to learn from the slaves themselves. At one point his Black corporal, Robert Sutton, took Higginson to the plantation from which he had escaped, and showed him the chains and stocks at the slave jail. In their presence, Higginson felt himself choking, as if he couldn't swallow or get a breath. He realized that Sutton had a "more thorough and far-reaching" understanding of slavery than "any Abolitionist." That sense continued to grow as Higginson talked to his men about their experiences. "It was not the individuals, but the ownership, of which they complained," he later recalled. "That they saw to be a wrong which no special kindnesses could right. On this, as on all points connected with slavery, they understood the matter as clearly as Garrison or Phillips."[15]

At night, Higginson listened to his men as they gathered around their campfires to sing—"these incomprehensible Negro Methodist, meaningless, monotonous, endless chants," he wrote in his journal after about ten days, "with obscure syllables recurring constantly & slight variations interwoven, all accompanied with a regular drumming of the feet & clapping of the hands, like castanets." Soon, though, Higginson learned to love the music, looking forward to it every night, running out of his tent when he heard a new song, writing down all the lyrics he could decipher (sometimes with pencil and notebook hidden in his pocket), and calling on Corporal Sutton to fill in the gaps. He was particularly moved by the "graceful & beautiful" song "I Know Moon-Rise," with its lines "I'll lie in de grave & stretch out my arms / Lay dis body down." "What ages of exhaustion these four words contain," he marveled. "Rivers of tears might be shed over them."[16]

This was not idle talk; Higginson knew artistry when he saw it. In addition to his abolitionist exploits, he was one of the most prominent literary minds in America. He had studied French with Longfellow at Harvard and would later serve as poetry editor of *The Nation* for twenty-five years. Earlier in 1862, not long before he took command in the Sea Islands, a young woman from Amherst named Emily Dickinson had sent him, unsolicited, a few of her poems; recognizing their merit, he wrote back and kept up a correspondence with her for the next two decades. After her death, her family gave her poems to Higginson, who arranged for their first publication—today perhaps his chief claim to fame.[17]

Higginson lasted only a few months in South Carolina. He was wounded in an upriver raid in July 1863 and then contracted malaria. Returning to New England, he began to write about his experiences for the *Atlantic*. One of his articles, which appeared in June 1867, was on "Negro Spirituals." It included the lyrics to three dozen songs. Like McKim, Higginson speculated about the role the songs—and religion more generally—played in slave culture. One thing that had surprised him in the Sea Islands was that while slavery appeared even more brutal than he had imagined, the enslaved people themselves did not seem brutalized by it. He wondered for a while about this paradox and eventually solved it with the songs he had heard. "They were a stimulus to courage and a tie to heaven," he believed. "By these they could sing themselves, as had their fathers before them, out of the contemplation of their own low estate, into the sublime scenery of the Apocalypse." Now that slavery was gone, he wrote, "history cannot afford to lose this portion of its record."[18]

By chance, there had been a historian in the Sea Islands who had also taken an interest in the songs. William Francis Allen arrived in November 1863 after being sent by the New England Freedmen's Aid Society to teach freedpeople on St. Helena. He had studied philology and classics at Harvard and ancient history at Göttingen (where he took classes with George Bancroft's old professor Arnold Heeren). After the war, he would get a job at the University of Wisconsin and become a beloved mentor to the great American historian Frederick Jackson Turner, who always considered Allen the best scholar he'd ever encountered.[19]

Allen's reactions to the slave South echoed those of McKim and Higginson. He was struck above all by the humanity of the people he met. For him, that threw the evil of slavery into even sharper relief. "They seem human beings, neither more nor less," he wrote after a few days in the Sea Islands. "It seems trite and common-place to say so, but I must say that the wickedness of slavery never seemed so clear as when I saw these people (about 240 on this plantation), so entirely human as they appear, and considered how they have been treated, and how little reason there is that they should be selected from all mankind for this awful abuse."

Allen recorded everything he saw and heard: the arrangement of the slave quarters, the location of the slave cemetery, the provisions the slaves had received (a peck of corn each week, some meat and eight yards of cloth twice per year). Trained in philology, he also paid attention to the grammar and vocabulary of the local dialect. "It is really worthwhile as a study in linguistics," he wrote after a few weeks. He kept gathering examples during the rest of his stay, and at the end of the war he wrote an article "to put them on record" before they vanished.[20]

Above all, Allen recorded the songs. He arrived in the Sea Islands late enough that he had already seen some of the earliest articles about them and was primed to appreciate them. He heard slave singing for himself on the Sunday after his arrival, standing outside a packed Praise House in the plantation quarters. All he heard at first was a standard hymn, "Old Hundred," but the style of singing set it apart, with the song "maintained throughout by one voice or another, but curiously varied at every note, so as to form an intricate intertwining of harmonious sounds." He added, "No description I have read conveys any notion of it."[21] He started to copy down all the lyrics and tunes he could.

Allen went back to Massachusetts in the summer of 1864, then returned to South Carolina at the end of the war to serve as assistant superintendent of schools in Charleston. That summer, he started to write dispatches on conditions in the South for a new magazine called *The Nation*, which Lucy McKim's father, James, had just cofounded as a venue for antislavery writers to discuss postwar problems. The McKims probably had a hand in picking the magazine's first literary editor: Wendell Phillips Garrison, Lucy's fiancé. Once he had a steady job, he and Lucy were married on December 6, 1865, the same day the Thirteenth Amendment was ratified.

Lucy had been back in the North since her brief stay in the Sea Islands in 1862, but she remained marked by the experience. Sometime in the first year of her marriage, she seems to have suggested to Wendell the idea of publishing a book-length collection of slave songs. Serious planning was under way by December 1866, and they began to reach out to contributors in early

1867. They knew of Allen from his articles for *The Nation* and quickly got him on board; Allen then brought on his younger cousin Charles Ware, who had collected more than four dozen songs in the Sea Islands during his time there.

The core team for the collection was now in place: Lucy had come up with the idea, Ware was contributing many of the songs, and Allen took over much of the editing in the spring of 1867, when Lucy gave birth to her first child. Allen was teaching in New Jersey at the time, by chance at the same abolitionist academy Lucy had attended a decade before, and he often traveled to New York to work on the book with Lucy and Wendell. He drafted the introduction in May, before he headed west to start at the University of Wisconsin. The editors also got in touch with Higginson, who contributed his own collection of lyrics. The book was ready by late summer, when Lucy, who by that time had a four-month-old infant, spent part of a day with Ware looking over proofs.[22]

Published in November 1867, *Slave Songs of the United States* was the first book on slave music in America as well as the first book on African American culture and perhaps even the first book-length collection of American folk songs of any kind. Among its 136 songs were beloved tunes such as "Michael Row the Boat Ashore" and "The Good Old Way" (also known as "Down to the River to Pray"). In his meticulous introduction, Allen laid out four reasons (besides sheer beauty) why such songs were worth saving and studying. The first was that their content, which illustrated slave customs and religious attitudes, revealed something about slave life, as did their tempo, which provided evidence about the patterns and pace of slave labor. The second reason was that the songs illuminated the ingredients that went into the making of slave culture in the South. In their mixture of African rhythms with Christian symbols, the songs showed that there was clearly some sort of cultural exchange between whites and Blacks under the slave system. This exchange had not operated the same way across the South, however, so the third reason Allen gave for studying the songs was to see variations in slave culture. Different versions of the songs suggested the existence of several regional cultures (seaboard, inland, Gulf Coast) that shared broad characteristics but differed in the details.[23]

The final reason to collect and study the songs was that they were disappearing rapidly under the new conditions of freedom. Already in 1867, Allen said, it was becoming hard to find unaltered slave songs. Some Black Americans regarded emancipation as a new start to their story, with slavery as a shameful prehistory that they did not want to revisit. Much broader forces of cultural change, such as education, urbanization, and modernization, were also at work. Abolitionist teachers across the South were among the culprits in this cultural loss because they sometimes considered the old songs barbarous and often introduced new songs in their classrooms as part of their effort to Christianize and civilize. "Even the 'spirituals' are going out of use on the plantations," Allen lamented, "superseded by the new style of religious music" that conformed to white standards.[24]

At that time, culture was seen as a ladder rather than a buffet. No matter how interesting or affecting, slave culture was still something to be overcome on the path to civilization (typically coded white). From the perspective of the twenty-first century, *Slave Songs* was a landmark book, the only attempt of its kind to preserve the songs with as few modifications as possible. Yet Allen, Ware, and Lucy McKim Garrison's careful work of collection and interpretation was not seen at the time as a contribution to American historical scholarship, or to the study of slavery—or to anything, really. Lucy and Wendell wrote an unsigned review in *The Nation* (one of the perks of being an editor) and arranged for several others, but more popular magazines such as *Harper's* and the *Atlantic* ignored the book. After a reprint in 1871, it languished in obscurity for more than fifty years.[25]

In the meantime, music programs at Black colleges helped keep the slave songs alive, preserving them through practice and performance. Fisk University in Nashville led the way. Starting in 1871, Fisk's Jubilee Singers made a name for themselves and raised money for their school by performing shiny renditions of old spirituals in concert halls and cathedrals across the United States and Europe. Over the next generation, some students and professors at Fisk, Hampton, and Tuskegee continued to collect, sing, and study African American folk music, with instructors gathering songs at religious revivals and camp meetings while students brought local songs from their hometowns.[26]

THE MAINSTREAM OF AMERICAN SLAVERY SCHOLARSHIP TOOK A DIFFERENT path as Reconstruction unfolded. Initially, it consisted of histories of the war itself. The first wave came from journalists just as the war concluded, the second from politicians a few years later. The goal for both groups was to justify their own conduct, and they did so by arguing at length about the war's causes and consequences.

For triumphant northerners, the story was straightforward. They maintained that the war was caused by slavery (or the slave power, or the slave aristocracy) and that its two-pronged meaning was freedom and nationality, as Lincoln established in the Gettysburg Address. The most important early history along these lines came from *New York Tribune* editor Horace Greeley, an antislavery crusader who in August 1862 wrote a famous "Prayer of Twenty Millions" pleading with Lincoln to embrace emancipation. After the major Union victories at Gettysburg and Vicksburg in July 1863, Greeley, finally confident that the war would end in a Union triumph and the abolition of slavery, embarked on a history of its "causes" and "incitements."

During the violent dispute over Kansas in the 1850s, Greeley had written *A History of the Struggle for Slavery Extension or Restriction in the United States*, a comparatively brief account of political debates over the expansion of slavery since the Revolution. He recapitulated much of that material in the opening chapters of his new history, *The American Conflict*, whose first volume appeared in 1864. Except now he had a better sense of where it was heading.

Greeley saw slavery as an anomaly in a republic dedicated to freedom and equality. Like most antislavery Republicans, he thought there had been a rough consensus at the time of the Constitution: slavery would be tolerated where it existed but would not be allowed to spread. That changed with the Missouri Compromise, which Greeley saw as the moment when the country took its first clear step toward civil war. After that, the South kept pressing its advantage to expand slavery. When the North finally stood up behind an antislavery party in 1860, southern slaveholders chose secession rather than compromise or surrender.

Because slavery caused the war, Greeley believed that the war could end only with abolition. His second volume, published in 1866, saw slavery as a central thread in the military history of the war. Early in the war, according to Greeley, many in the administration and the army tried not to disturb slavery. But officials, soldiers, and the public gradually realized that slavery was "the Union's real assailant" and that the war could be won by striking at it directly. Greeley credited Black soldiers with providing clear evidence of that truth. "It is no longer fairly disputable that they played a very important and useful part in the overthrow of the Rebellion," he concluded.[27]

Greeley's counterpart in the South was Edward Pollard. Throughout the war, Pollard, then a writer at the Richmond *Examiner*, issued annual volumes of his *Southern History of the War*, which became widely known. Greeley put Pollard's volumes to good use in his own work; he considered Pollard "utterly untrustworthy as a whole" yet strangely valuable for his complete candor about the Confederacy's goals. "He never dreams of concealing or disavowing the fundamental ideas whereon it is based," Greeley wrote; "it is precisely because it stands and strikes for Slavery that he loves and glories in the Confederate cause."[28]

Pollard's love of slavery stemmed from his education and his experience. He'd grown up on his family's plantations southwest of Charlottesville, where he acquired a paternalistic view of slavery as a reciprocal relationship between master and slave. As a young man, he left this plantation idyll for the wider world, joining the rush for gold in California. He didn't strike it rich, but he did acquire a firm conviction that slaves, protected from the kind of cutthroat competition he encountered out west, were much better off than their free-labor counterparts.

After a sojourn in East Asia, Pollard returned to the East Coast in 1856. When he saw what he called his "first unadulterated negro" back in the United States, he felt an overwhelming sense of comfort and relief: "He looked like *home*." That emphasis on *home* continued in Pollard's 1859 book *The Southern Spy; Or, Curiosities of Negro Slavery in the South*, also published in an enlarged version as *Black Diamonds Gathered in the Darkey Homes of the South*. At a time when the political controversy over slavery was at a fever pitch, Pollard purposefully retreated from politics. He was one of the few white southern writers before the war to describe slave music, folklore, and religion at any length. He also recalled his "sable playmates" and described his deep love for "the faithful slaves of our family," especially one older woman who served as his plantation mammy: "At this moment my eyes are tenderly filled with tears when I look back through the mists of long years upon the image of that dear old slave."[29] This would become the standard tone for nostalgic southern memories of slavery after the war.

Pollard was imprisoned when Richmond was captured in April 1865. After his release, he worked to make sense of the war and its meaning, a task that all southerners had to confront in their own way. Some preferred oblivion: after Appomattox, Edmund Ruffin draped himself in a Confederate flag and shot himself dead. Those who remained had to adjust themselves to a world in which the South no longer represented an alternative world order but was now a dependent province or colony. To negotiate that change, they needed a way to reconcile allegiance to the South with loyalty to a postwar nation in which the Confederacy had been crushed and slavery eliminated.

The solution, as it worked itself out, was for them to minimize slavery as a cause of the rebellion and to anchor the Confederacy in meanings that could gain broader support. At the private level of personal action, the war was redefined around the service and sacrifice of individual soldiers, whose courage was unquestionable and whose cause, now described as defense of home, was unassailable in late nineteenth-century America. Then at the public level of history and politics, the Confederacy's animating idea was shifted from slavery to the twin pillars of white supremacy and constitutional government.[30]

Slavery may have provided the "occasion" for the war, white southerners explained, but it was not the war's true "cause." The real cause ran deeper, either to questions of constitutional interpretation (consolidation versus decentralization) or to a case of conflicting civilizations. Slavery just happened to be the issue that brought these more fundamental problems into politics. In the more cynical version of this argument, slavery was nothing but a tool that northern politicians exploited in pursuit of national consolidation or northern domination (or both). Versions of this interpretation proved terrifically appealing during Reconstruction, when the North experienced mixed success in its attempt to give the federal government greater power and to use that power to reshape the South in its own image. The resistant

South held up the Confederacy as part of the true lineage of American liberty: first, colonial resistance to British domination; then, Confederate resistance to northern domination; now, postwar resistance to Republican domination.

Pollard gave voice to this view. In 1866, he condensed and sharpened his account of the war into *The Lost Cause; A New Southern History of the War of the Confederates*. The phrase *Lost Cause* had been current before the war, when it was used to describe the "Lost Cause" of Scottish independence in the historical romances of Sir Walter Scott. After the war, its meaning migrated to the Confederacy; Pollard's book was the first to put this usage into wide circulation. What, according to Pollard, was the "cause" for which the Confederacy stood? Nothing less, he maintained now, than "the very cause of republican government itself."

Pollard's theory of the war was that North and South constituted separate civilizations, whose differences he traced all the way back to Massachusetts Puritans and Virginia Cavaliers in the seventeenth century. The North was commercial and materialistic, and believed in majority rule; the South was agricultural and moral, and believed in statesmanship and states' rights. Between these two positions, Pollard implied, there was more than enough cause for conflict.

In place of a Constitution that provided systematic support for the Slave Power, as in Greeley's account, Pollard told a story in which the Constitution's prohibition of the slave trade and provisions for commercial regulation enshrined systematic sectional inequalities that protected northern population growth and economic production while leaving the South to shrivel. The South maintained some political power through alliances with northern Democrats as well as "superior and consummate political skill," but the region ultimately knew that it stood no chance against a united North.

This, according to Pollard, was the whole purpose of the slavery controversy: it gained prominence as a way to unite the North and enable that section to gain power over the entire country. "The slavery question was not a moral one in the North, unless, perhaps, with a few thousand persons of disordered conscience," Pollard wrote. "It was significant only of a contest for political power, and afforded nothing more than a convenient ground of dispute between two parties, who represented not two moral theories, but hostile sections and opposite civilizations." Starting with Missouri, every slavery compromise represented not a capitulation to the Slave Power (as it did for Greeley) but another step in the drive to divide the country on the slavery issue so that the North could impose political centralization and its own civilization throughout the land.

One purpose of Pollard's history was to separate the South from slavery so that it might still have some future. He believed that the war had "properly decided" only two issues: "the restoration of the Union and the excision of slavery," issues on which he believed that the South was willing to submit. Now that the war was over, the most pressing question was whether the Republicans' despotic reign of terror would continue or could be stopped, with some remnant of republican government reclaimed. In this "war of ideas," Pollard suggested, the defeated South had a heroic role to play.[31]

The Lost Cause became Pollard's most popular book. He followed it up with a couple of political and military volumes about the Confederacy, then joined one of his brothers in a weekly newspaper venture called *Southern Opinion*. The Pollards could be caustic in their criticism; some choice words about former Virginia governor and Confederate general Henry Wise prompted an attack by Wise's gun-toting nephews. Pollard survived and moved to New York, but a year later, in November 1868, his brother was murdered in Richmond, apparently by a man who did not take kindly to insinuations printed in *Southern Opinion* about his sister's elopement.

During the year between the attacks, Pollard continued to grope for a way to embrace the Civil War's results—the Union and free labor—while remaining a staunch opponent of Republicans and Reconstruction. After the Republican National Convention in May 1868, he quickly wrote a new book called *The Lost Cause Regained*, which was ready in time for the Democratic convention that summer. It was intended as a campaign manifesto that could unite conservatives in both North and South against perceived Republican overreach in matters of racial equality and federal power.[32]

In the interest of making that kind of coalition possible, Pollard continued to redefine the Confederate cause. Now that the war was over and slavery gone, it was possible to see more clearly what was at stake. Slavery had been at most a means to an end. "The true question which the war involved," Pollard declared, "and which it merely liberated for greater breadth of controversy was the supremacy of the white race, and along with it the preservation of the political traditions of the country." These were questions on which the South could still prevail, especially if it had help from northern friends. "If she succeeds . . . ," he continued, "she really triumphs in the true cause of the war, with respect to all its fundamental and vital issues."[33]

Pollard's hoped-for victory did not come, at least not immediately. The Republicans won in November, led by former Union general Ulysses S. Grant and aided at the polls by the votes of Black freedmen. A few months later, after the acquittal of his brother's alleged murderer, Pollard retreated to live with another brother in Lynchburg, Virginia. In pamphlets and articles published mostly in the northern press, he began to argue more strongly for the formation of a cross-sectional conservative party that could serve as a bulwark of liberty against Republican despotism. He thought he saw hope in the form of the Liberal Republicans, a splinter group of largely genteel northerners who despaired for the future of constitutional government in the face of the Grant administration's corruption, expansion of federal power, and pursuit of racial equality.

When the Liberal Republicans convened in the election year of 1872, they nominated for president none other than Horace Greeley. He was named the Democratic candidate as well. Ever since the war, he had been pursuing reconciliation at almost all costs. Already in the first volume of *The American Conflict*, while the war still raged, he was willing to celebrate Confederate soldiers. A few years later, he went much further and helped post bail for Jefferson Davis. Greeley was ready to absolve everyone, even Davis, of blame. In a speech delivered at an African Methodist Episcopal church, he suggested that the country should forget about the Civil War and slavery so that it could move on with life. As a presidential candidate, he campaigned for states' rights and white supremacy in the South, but under the softer names of amnesty and reconciliation.[34]

This was the kind of person that Pollard could get behind. He spent part of 1872 writing a series of pro-Greeley essays. Collected as *A Southern Historian's Appeal for Horace Greeley*, Pollard's articles advanced Greeley as the candidate who could secure the South a solid peace based on "kindness and trust" rather than punishment. Envisioning a conservative paternalism in which whites led and Blacks followed, he endorsed Greeley's support for Black suffrage but not social equality and predicted that Greeley would unite both races across the South, marking the start of a new era. Such a union, Pollard wrote, "would date anew Southern prosperity and Southern power, and realize the vision which has too long floated in our dreams and hesitated in our hopes—a New South."[35]

As in 1868, Pollard's vision did not transcend his dreams. Greeley lost in November, suffering from a fatal lack of enthusiasm among Democratic voters. He died about three weeks later, and Pollard, suffering from kidney disease, died about three weeks after that. Just before his death, however, Pollard completed a short article called "The Anti-Slavery Men of the South," which was published the following year. In some ways, it was the culmination of his postwar work. Throughout the colonial period and the early republic, Pollard explained, slavery had to be maintained because it was "doing its great God-appointed work . . . of making the negro truly fit for freedom." With that education complete, however, the time had come for slavery to end. Perhaps the most cunning part of this argument was the way it co-opted Black success since emancipation as evidence of slavery's virtue. "Emancipation *is* a success," Pollard declared, "and the South may be more ready to acknowledge it when she understands what a tribute this fact implies to the past institution of slavery."

Pollard had finally figured out how to unite pro-slavery thought with emancipation, a union that he believed could foster a broader reconciliation in American life. He predicted this truce would form the basis of national policy going forward, with the South acknowledging Black freedom as long as the North allowed southern whites to manage racial questions as they saw fit, and as they had done successfully (according to Pollard, at least) since slavery times.[36]

Pollard popularized the idea of the "Lost Cause," but he also had plenty of detractors as a result of his open disdain for the inept wartime leadership of Jefferson Davis and other southern politicians. Naturally, these former Confederate leaders wanted to defend themselves—not only from the criticism of fellow southerners such as Pollard but also from the accusation (not unreasonable, given the circumstances) that they were traitors to the republic. So defend themselves they did, often at great length; remarkably, they found publishers willing to print their work. They advanced what soon became the most influential interpretation of the war, draining away even white supremacy to reveal a pure and noble Confederate cause dedicated solely to constitutional liberty. In the process they gave even greater authority to the assertion that slavery was merely a side issue.[37]

Immediately after the war, it was not clear that this would be the case. Confederate vice president Alexander Stephens was imprisoned at Fort Warren, on an island in Boston Harbor. Kept in a cold, damp room, Stephens was miserable. A few months in, he received a visit from Massachusetts senator Henry Wilson. A prominent political abolitionist, Wilson had been at the forefront of congressional antislavery policy during the war. Yet he didn't believe in needless cruelty toward former Confederates. Finding Stephens sick and uncomfortable, Wilson asked President Andrew Johnson to allow him to return home on parole. That request was denied, but Stephens did at least get a better room. He sent Wilson his thanks.

At the start of the war, Stephens had declared slavery the "cornerstone" of the Confederacy. Near its end, he rejected a surrender deal that included emancipation. But faced with defeat, and with plenty of time to think, he began to reconsider Confederate history. "The slavery question had but little influence with the masses," he confided to his journal, adding that he now believed that southern slave owners would have willingly given up slavery to gain independence.

Stephens was paroled in October and returned home to Georgia. These were still the early days of Reconstruction, before congressional Republicans took control of the process, and the Georgia legislature promptly picked Stephens—just a few months earlier the sitting vice president of the Confederacy—to represent the state in the Senate. When Stephens and other former Confederates showed up to Congress, disgusted Republicans refused to seat them and started to design a new Reconstruction policy of their own.

Stephens returned again to Georgia, where he lived in a plantation house he called Liberty Hall. Visited by old friends from the North, he naturally fell into discussions about the war. Out of those discussions grew a long book designed to defend his own record and define the cause he had led.[38]

Stephens wrote his two-volume *Constitutional View of the Late War Between the States* as a dialogue, in the style of classical philosophers such as Plato and Cicero. Stephens himself starred in the Socrates role, explaining at excruciating length (the two volumes ran to about fifteen hundred pages) that the Civil War was nothing but a conflict over the Constitution. He appeared exasperated by the extent to which other writers, mostly northern, focused on slavery as the cause of the war. The real question, he asserted over and over, concerned "the nature of the Government of the United States, and where, under our system, ultimate Sovereign power or Paramount authority properly resides." Like Pollard, Stephens placed the Confederacy on the side of constitutional liberty. Also like Pollard, he believed that the cause was not lost. All that had been lost in the war, he claimed, was "the maintenance of this Principle by arms." But the principle itself remained, and in fact it had become more important than ever in the face of Reconstruction.[39]

Stephens's *Constitutional View* gave him a reputation as a scholar. He was able to expand on his interpretation of the Civil War and bring it to a wider audience in his *Compendium of the History of the United States*, a schoolbook history published in 1872. There he made two moves designed to deny that slavery was ever a source of conflict in American life.

First, Stephens nationalized slavery, drawing on the work of an antislavery northerner, George Moore, whose *Notes on the History of Slavery in Massachusetts* was published in 1866. Moore's book was the first history of slavery to appear after emancipation. Instead of celebrating the state's history of abolitionism, as other writers dating back to Jeremy Belknap had done, Moore dug up a series of primary documents designed to deflate those claims. Slavery came early to Massachusetts, he showed, explaining that the slave trade arrived there in the 1630s and that the colony's 1641 *Body of Liberties* contained, ironically, the very first statute establishing slavery in British North America. In his effort to pop the moralistic bubble of self-satisfied abolitionists, Moore managed, perhaps unintentionally, to make North and

South seem morally equal on the issue of slavery. His book soon became the standard source for anyone looking to show that slavery had been prevalent throughout the North as well as the South, and thus to prove that northern abolitionism was primarily a sectional power play, not a moral movement.[40]

After using Moore to demonstrate a colonial consensus in favor of slavery, Stephens then had the foundation to argue that any later conflicts which *appeared* to be about slavery must have had some other, deeper cause—namely, constitutional principles. This theme carried through the rest of Stephens's book, with dastardly centralizers (the North) pressing the slavery issue to gain power while strict constructionists (the South) mounted a noble defense of the Constitution. The South may have lost the war, but Stephens suggested that the larger struggle against centralization and despotism was not over.[41]

Indeed, he soon joined it himself. By 1873, all the former Confederate states had returned to Congress with full representation. Republicans, anxious to undercut Horace Greeley's support the year before, had adopted the Amnesty Act, allowing ex-Confederates to serve again in government. Georgia quickly named Stephens to a vacant House seat. This time he took office without trouble, making him the highest-ranking Confederate to return to Washington after the war. He soon became a strong opponent of the Civil Rights Bill of 1875, saying it would turn the republic "into a centralized empire" and doing all he could in a failed attempt to prevent its passage.[42]

The most comprehensive response to Stephens's interpretation of the Civil War, which erased slavery from what was supposedly a struggle over sovereignty, came from Henry Wilson, the Massachusetts senator who had once visited Stephens at Fort Warren and helped him secure a more comfortable room. Wilson had been an avid abolitionist since the 1830s. As soon as the Civil War started, he pressed Congress to take action against slavery wherever it had power to do so, especially in areas of federal jurisdiction such as the District of Columbia (he introduced the bill to end slavery there) and the territories. After the war, he continued his aggressive pursuit of Black equality. He helped create the Freedmen's Bureau, introduced the bill to abolish the Black Codes, and was involved in the establishment of Howard University.

But Wilson failed to nab the vice-presidential nomination in 1868 and felt his influence waning as he pressed the Republicans to become a working-class party while they ran in the opposite direction. Worried that he and his generation of antislavery activists would soon be forgotten, he started work on a huge *History of the Rise and Fall of the Slave Power in America*, which eventually weighed in at three volumes and more than two thousand pages. The grandest postwar statement about slavery as the cause of the Civil War, Wilson's *History* made slavery above all a problem of politics. He focused on discussions in the halls of Congress and in the columns of newspapers, working his way methodically through each political crisis over slavery from the Revolution to 1860.

Despite his waning influence in the Republican Party, or conceivably because of it, Wilson was placed on the ticket as Grant's vice president in 1872, the year the first volume of his *History* was published. After Grant defeated Greeley, Wilson, like many vice presidents before and since, found himself with time on his hands. He spent it working feverishly on his *History*, in part because he hoped it would earn him some much-needed money (again, never a good plan). In early 1873, he was writing sixteen hours a day and routinely working long past midnight.

This brutal schedule may have combined with existing ill health to cause a stroke that May. But he was back at work by 1874, when his second volume was published. He immediately threw himself into the third volume, worrying friends who thought the effort would kill him. In the spring of 1875, he also spent six weeks on a tour of the South, ostensibly for relaxation and recovery but actually as the first campaign swing for a planned presidential bid. The effort proved too much: he suffered more strokes that fall, and died soon after.

Throughout his life, Wilson worked hard for equality because he believed that it could be achieved. At the time of his death, he had not quite finished the third and final volume of his *History*, covering the Civil War and Reconstruction. It was completed by his friend Samuel Hunt and published just as the last federal troops were withdrawn from the South after the election of 1876, an event that conventionally marks the end of Reconstruction. "A reaction has taken place," Hunt wrote in the volume's conclusion.

"The old régime is reinstated, and everything, save legal chattelhood, is to be restored." In place of slavery, he believed, the South would simply substitute "caste" as "the 'corner-stone' of Southern civilization."[43]

This was an ironic, depressing note on which to end a book about the rise and fall of the Slave Power, but Hunt was not wrong. As Reconstruction withered, power over civil rights and other racial matters began to revert to state control. It felt to many southerners as if not only their constitutional principles but their whole view of American history had been vindicated. The Lost Cause had been won.[44]

STILL, THERE WERE PLENTY OF AMERICANS WHO CONTINUED TO INSIST that slavery and emancipation were central to the meaning of the Civil War and to the history of America as a whole—who wanted to remember, not to forget. One was a Black man named George Washington Williams—"the greatest historian of the race," according to W. E. B. Du Bois, no slouch himself. As Reconstruction came to a close, Williams showed that it was still possible to see Black history, including slavery, as a defining part of the American story.

Born free in Pennsylvania in 1849, Williams had served as a soldier in the Civil War, lying about his age and his name in order to enlist. After bouncing around for a bit after the war, he enrolled in 1870 at Newton Theological Institute in Massachusetts. He became the leader of Twelfth Baptist, the most important Black church in Boston, and in the summer of 1874 he wrote a history of the church—his first foray into Black history. At the same time, amid reports about the murder of Black southerners by white vigilantes, he helped organize a mass meeting of Black Bostonians to press Congress for action. (William Wells Brown was the main speaker.) After Congress passed a Civil Rights Act the next year, Williams wanted to be closer to the halls of power. He quit the church and moved to the capital to start a new Black journal. "This is a plastic period," he wrote. "The Negro will begin to make history. What manner of history will it be? That is the question."[45]

Williams's journal failed, and he moved to Cincinnati to resume the pulpit. In 1876, he delivered a Fourth of July oration in nearby Avondale; his subject was "The American Negro." The success of his speech convinced him to write a full history of Black Americans, the first of its kind, something that went beyond a brief overview or a collection of biographical sketches.

The idea of a history of the Negro race promised a new history of slavery, as well as a new history of America. Williams had no formal training for it. Yet, as with everything else in his life, he threw himself into the work, performing research at a scale and level of sophistication that was rare at the time. In Cincinnati he used the library of the Historical and Philosophical Society as well as the collection of a local bookseller and publisher who specialized in old and rare American historical works. After he was elected in 1879 as the first Black member of the state legislature, Williams had the state library at his disposal; records indicate that he consulted some 576 volumes as well as scores of newspapers and government documents. Ultimately he claimed to have examined more than twelve thousand books and pamphlets in the course of his work. He even traveled for research, heading east in the summer of 1880 and again for a much longer stay the following year. He corresponded about sources with George Bancroft, the grand old man of American history; Bancroft told Williams that his research on Black history was "of the utmost importance." Williams also spent more than two months doing research in New York, where he got help from George Moore, author of *Notes on the History of Slavery in Massachusetts*, who still worked as a librarian there.[46]

By the end of 1882, Williams had completed his two-volume *History of the Negro Race in America from 1619 to 1880*. (As the title indicates, he was able to correct the old error by which many historians dated the arrival of Africans in Virginia to 1620.) In each colony, Williams discovered a common story. The earliest period featured few slaves and almost no surviving evidence about them; he described the documents as "fragmentary, uncertain, and unsatisfactory, to say the least." Then, as the number of slaves grew, colonies enacted the first laws to define and regulate the institution. Slavery soon received not only legal authority but also judicial recognition and clerical backing. As it expanded throughout the early eighteenth century, it "sent its dark death-roots into the fibre and organism of the political, judicial, social, and religious life of the people." Slavery was "like a cancer," Williams wrote, a malignant growth that spread "until there was not a single colony in North America that could boast of its ability to check the dreadful curse." The spread of slavery set up a situation ripe for hypocrisy during the Revolution, and Williams confronted it head-on. "Slavery flourished during the entire Revolutionary period," he wrote. "The colonists asked freedom for themselves and children, but forged chains for Negroes and their children."

For the period between the Revolution and the Civil War, many postwar histories of the "slavery struggle" focused almost exclusively on political debates. Williams relegated such debates to a secondary role because they had been covered elsewhere—he mentioned Henry Wilson's three mammoth volumes—and, more importantly, because they had little to do with the slaves themselves. "It should not be forgotten," he noted, "that this is a history of the Negro race." When he discussed "anti-slavery agitation," for example, he focused on the efforts of free Blacks in the North and insurrections led by enslaved Blacks in the South. In his section on the Civil War, he examined the role played by runaway slaves and Black soldiers in defining the war's meaning and defeating the South. After emancipation, he used statistics about education and Black churches to illustrate how Black Americans were living in freedom. He concluded his two-volume history with a celebration of what his race had accomplished:

> Under-fed and over-worked; poorly clad and miserably housed; with the family altar cast down, and intelligent men allowed to run over it as swine; and with the fountains of knowledge sealed by law against the thirstings of human souls for knowledge, the Negroes of America, nevertheless, have shown the most wonderful signs of recuperation, and the ability to rise, against every cruel act of man and the very forces of nature, to a manhood and intelligent citizenship that converts the cautious, impartial, and conservative spirit of history into eulogy![47]

Williams made this broader project of racial uplift his life's work. He had boundless energy for such activities and once even went to New Mexico to look at land for a potential Black farming colony; it didn't work out. In the late 1880s, he became interested in Belgian king Leopold II's personal colony in the Congo, where he thought he could recruit free Black Americans to work. This, too, did not work out, to put it mildly: when Williams went to the Congo himself in 1890, he discovered slavery everywhere. He wrote an open letter to Leopold, but then he died of tuberculosis, at the age of forty-one, and his opposition died with him.[48]

Williams's *History* had a different fate. It survived to inform and inspire future generations of Black historians, including Du Bois, Carter Woodson, and John Hope Franklin, and others who stood fast to the emancipationist understanding of the Civil War. Yet despite its influence on future historians and its engagement with postwar debates, it was soon forgotten in the field of slavery studies. For it came at a key turning point when the study of slavery was shifting from interested amateurs to professional scholars as it was incorporated into a new institution—the research university.

5
LOOK AWAY

EARLY POSTWAR HISTORIES OF SLAVERY WERE OFTEN WRITTEN BY THE same people who had been involved in antebellum debates. Politicians like Alexander Stephens and Henry Wilson had been fighting about slavery for most of their adult lives, and after the war they continued to fight about it using many of the same arguments. That situation changed in the 1880s and 1890s, with the coming of age of a new generation that grew up after emancipation and had at most a few early memories of slavery. They were able to approach the subject with somewhat greater distance.

Another reason for the shift in how Americans studied slavery was that the study of American history—including slavery—became incorporated in the early 1880s into a new institution called the research university, where professors and graduate students produced new knowledge in laboratories and seminars. Up to that point, nearly all historians in America had been amateurs, mostly wealthy men with no formal training. As of 1880, the United States had fewer than a dozen professors of history, scattered between Boston and Berkeley. None specialized in American history. For scholars brought up in the classical curriculum and steeped in the supposedly universal significance of ancient Greece and Rome, the history of the United States seemed too shallow for academic study.[1]

At just that moment, however, academic history was coming into its own in America. Young men returned from their studies in Germany with a new sense of history "as a science by itself," as the Harvard professor Ephraim Emerton put it in 1883. The scientific study of history in America was developed earliest and most extensively by Herbert Baxter Adams, a young professor at Johns Hopkins University. Founded in Baltimore in 1876, Johns Hopkins was based on German models and became the first modern research university in America. In the field of history, where Adams presided, Hopkins quickly became dominant, granting fully 40 percent of all history doctorates awarded in America before 1900. By that time, Hopkins men made up two-thirds of the professionally trained historians in the South.[2] Led by Adams, Hopkins defined the academic study of history during these decades, and it also defined the study of slavery.

Adams belonged to a new generation that had little memory of slavery. As a child in Amherst, Massachusetts, during the Civil War, he had watched as volunteer soldiers marched out of town. But he was too young to enlist, too young even to remember much from the debates about slavery, and never saw slavery in the South. He grew up in a free state; the Thirteenth Amendment was adopted before his sixteenth birthday.

After the war, Adams attended boarding school in New Hampshire before returning to Amherst for college. At that time, in the late 1860s, colleges like Amherst remained much as they had in the 1840s and 1850s. The curriculum was capped with a moral philosophy course taught by the college president, which at Amherst meant Julius Seelye. Though largely forgotten today, Seelye struck his students as one of the most dynamic and influential educators of his time. He straddled the edge of a fundamental transformation in American intellectual life, which manifested itself in the shift from moral philosophy to social science as the primary way to study human behavior. Of the men who went on to establish the academic fields of history, political science, economics, and sociology in America over the next few decades, many graduated from Amherst, and they credited Seelye with awakening in them a sense that there was an inherent grandeur in the record of human experience.

Adams was one of them. Up to the moment he stepped into Seelye's classroom, he had seen history as something to read for fun in his free time. Now he heard Seelye describing history as "the grandest study in the world." "That sentence," Adams later recalled, "decided my fate."[3]

To pursue the grand study of history, Adams would need to go to Germany, whose universities were still widely acknowledged as the best in the world. As in George Bancroft's day, Germany drew Americans for the prestige of the professors and the renown of the research seminars—courses that cultivated methods of meticulous, systematic scholarship. Bancroft had experienced an early version of the seminar at Göttingen, at a time when it was still largely restricted to the field of classical philology. By the late nineteenth century, the seminar had become central to the German academic experience for students in a wide range of subjects. "Methods of research. Library work. Laboratory work," Adams wrote of his seminar experience. "Idea of University study. The enlargement of Science. The widening of the sphere of the known." He regarded the professors who led the seminars as "the personification of Science."[4]

Adams got his degree from Heidelberg in 1876 and immediately secured a job at Johns Hopkins University, which was about to open its doors. The school had been planned from the start as a new kind of American educational institution, the only university in the country dedicated to research in the German sense. To carry out this plan, the Hopkins trustees looked to Daniel Coit Gilman, a former professor of geography who since 1872 had been head of the young University of California. Gilman tried to build a German-style university in Berkeley, devoted to specialized research in various departments, but popular resentment of the school and charges of corruption (never substantiated) made the job a headache. When, in late 1874, the Hopkins trustees approached the forty-three-year-old Gilman with an offer to lead their new institution, he jumped. In Baltimore he would have the freedom to build from scratch the school he wanted, establishing many of the forms and conventions that make up the American research university we know today.

Gilman hoped to hire distinguished full professors with long records of original work, but he was more successful in some fields than others. For Greek he lured America's most eminent classicist, Basil Gildersleeve, but for history he found no full professor who fit his standards. Instead, he settled for a string of visiting professors (including William Francis Allen) and an "associate" named Austin Scott. Scott held a Leipzig doctorate and lived in Washington, DC, where he assisted George Bancroft (still at work in his late seventies), but he was willing to commute to Baltimore to teach.[5]

From the start, Johns Hopkins supplemented its professors and associates with a system of fellowships designed to support postdoctoral students at the start of their careers. This was a novel idea in American higher education, certainly on the scale that it existed at Hopkins. Twenty fellows would receive $500 each to do research and some teaching for one year, potentially renewable for up to four. Adams applied for the first fellowship competition in the spring of 1876, as he was finishing his Heidelberg degree, and learned in June that he had secured one of the fellowships.

When Johns Hopkins opened that fall, the new university introduced the German-style research seminar to American higher education in the humanities. The school offered two of them in its first year, but it was the historical seminar, originally directed by Scott, that would ultimately prove most influential. Participants wrote essays based on original research, which were then subjected to criticism by their professor and their peers. During the first year, Scott was still working for Bancroft, so students investigated topics for Bancroft's *History of the Formation of the Constitution*, and Bancroft wrote kind notes encouraging their work.[6]

Adams presented four papers during the first year of Scott's historical seminar and quickly took control. No one could match his energy and enthusiasm. In fact, he was so devoted to his academic work that he once described himself as "wedded to Science," listing his historical publications as "his children by this his first wife." (He never married and had no human children.) By 1878, he had been promoted from fellow to associate and had thrust off all supervision from Scott. Then, in the early 1880s, Scott's contract was not renewed, leaving Adams in full command.[7]

The academic study of American slavery began in Adams's seminar. The crucial moment came in October 1883, when Adams arranged for the

German historian Hermann Eduard von Holst to deliver a series of lectures. For Americans at the time, von Holst was the embodiment of scholarly history, in part because he was the first German scholar to pay serious attention to the United States. At Johns Hopkins, von Holst planned to speak mostly about European history and politics, but he told Adams that he also wanted "to conclude with a specifically American talk."[8] He needed to talk about slavery.

Born to a German family in what's now Estonia, von Holst received a PhD at Heidelberg in 1865. He got a job as a tutor in St. Petersburg, but a liberal pamphlet that he wrote soon earned him exile from Russia. Landing in New York City in 1867, he spent his first hungry winter living in a shared room with three other men, surviving on meager wages from manual labor and tutoring. Soon, his natural ability got him better-paying gigs writing and editing for publications including *The Nation*. He also dove headfirst into American politics, becoming a Republican and battling against Boss Tweed and his Tammany Hall machine. When some wealthy Bremen merchants funded a project designed to explain American democracy to Germans, they picked von Holst to write the articles.

Von Holst started the project, but it quickly became clear to him that if he wanted to understand American democracy, he first had to study American history. The effort took years. His multivolume *Constitutional and Political History of the United States* eventually began to appear in German in 1873 and in English translation three years later, just in time for the country's centennial. By that time, von Holst was back in Germany, where he became a professor at Freiburg. The move away from the United States hurt von Holst's book, he sometimes thought, but his position as a German professor surely enhanced his work's reputation. Regarded as the first truly critical and scientific history of the United States (Bancroft got only up to the Constitution), his book was immediately hailed as a landmark—assigned regularly, cited constantly. It almost single-handedly made American history into a reputable scholarly field.[9]

Like Horace Greeley and Henry Wilson before him, von Holst identified slavery as the central problem of American political history. The final index to the seven-volume English translation of his work would include a staggering thirteen pages of entries for the terms *slaveholders, slave labor, slave representation, slavery, slaves, slave states, slave trade*, and "*slavocracy*," the word he used for the South's political and economic leaders.[10] He was sometimes criticized for having a warped sense of perspective because of his intense focus on slavery, but his analysis displayed an intellectual clarity that cut straight through American squabbles about the causes of their conflicts. "Ever since the end of the civil war," he wrote, "thick books have been written to prove that the slaveholding and free states might have got along with one another till the end of time, if on this side and that, political short-sightedness, fanaticism, and demagogism had not awakened discord and artfully kept it alive." He would have none of it: "The whole history of the Union since 1787 so clearly contradicts this view that it can be attributed only to moral enervation."

Von Holst did not think that the Civil War was the result of a dispute about constitutional principles, nor did he think it was the inevitable result of broader differences between distinct northern and southern civilizations. He thought it was about slavery. The opposition between the sections was not only moral and political, von Holst emphasized, but also, crucially, economic, "a natural result of their different industrial systems." These divergent systems expanded rapidly in the early nineteenth century, but by the 1830s, moral opposition to slavery was growing in the North while the declining "slavocracy" sought, through increasingly extreme positions, to press every advantage before it lost power. Yet the slavocracy's attempts to ensure the perpetual security of slavery only sharpened the struggle until it came down to fine points of principle—and in a contest of principle, von Holst believed, slavery was fated to lose. "This was the curse laid upon the slavocracy," he wrote, relishing the irony, "that every step towards its goal was a step nearer the inevitable doom."[11]

In the late 1870s, between his second and third volumes, von Holst got funding from the Prussian Academy of Sciences to return to the United States to conduct additional research, including a tour of the South. He soon heard from Daniel Coit Gilman, the president of Johns Hopkins, who invited him to give a series of public lectures while he was in the area. Von Holst agreed, but on this first visit he chose to speak on "The German

Empire" so he wouldn't feel like he was lecturing Americans about their own history. Nevertheless, his talks were the most popular Hopkins lecture series to date. He also dropped by the historical seminar one Friday evening to discuss "the idea and modes of conducting a German Seminarium of Historical Science" and to regale the students and professors with an inspiring story about how much time and energy he once put into verifying a single date. Adams, taking the minutes, called the session "the most interesting exercises of the year."[12]

Meanwhile, Gilman, still hoping to hire a distinguished professor of history, thought he had finally found his man. He presented the trustees with a proposal to offer von Holst a $5,000 annual salary. One of the trustees, George Brown, a Baltimore judge and former Confederate who had been jailed at Fort Warren (also home to Alexander Stephens), was hesitant about hiring someone known for his strong opinions on slavery. "I should like to see whether he has modified some of his views on the Slavery Question, which seemed to me to be extreme altho' natural from his point of view," Brown told Gilman. He complained that von Holst seemed to render his judgments without "sufficient allowance for the difficulties of the case, or . . . any reference to the good actually accomplished, but rather as an abstract question of right considered in the light of today." After Brown spent more time with von Holst's work, however, he was mollified by its scholarly rigor and intellectual vigor, and the offer became official. It would have quadrupled von Holst's salary and given him a base in the United States, but he declined. He felt bound to Freiburg and opted to retain his position there, where he had tenure and a pension.[13]

Von Holst returned to the United States again in 1883—this time as a guest of the Northern Pacific Railway, a circumstance that reveals the extent of his celebrity. By that time, he was writing about the early 1850s—the years of the Fugitive Slave Law, *Uncle Tom's Cabin*, and the Kansas-Nebraska Act. He thought it was the single most important period in the development of the "irrepressible conflict," a phrase he did not use lightly. He had come to believe that American politicians in those years were essentially impotent in the face of overwhelming forces beyond their control.

The trouble for von Holst was that he was writing a political history, and there were limits to what he could do to show how forces outside politics constrained political action. This is not to say he didn't try. But to prove the true nature of the "irrepressible conflict," he knew, would take more work—and he knew exactly what kind of work it would require. "It is my firm conviction," he wrote, that "a proof will yet be furnished by the investigation of the history of slavery—I deliberately say slavery and not slavery question—in such a shape as to put it forever beyond the possibility of dispute."[14]

These were the thoughts in von Holst's head when Adams invited him to visit Johns Hopkins in the fall of 1883, and he replied that he wanted "to conclude with a specifically American talk." He clearly had slavery in mind and sensed that the topic would need to be approved first; he told Adams that the precise subject could "be left undecided until I can talk the matter over with the President, Judge Brown"—the trustee who had hesitated about hiring von Holst four years earlier—"and yourself."[15] What he wanted to say must have passed muster, because at the end of his stay, after delivering his scheduled set of lectures on the "Relation of History to Politics," he visited with Adams's graduate students. There, in an informal Friday evening discussion that lasted an hour or two, he "urged upon them the study of Slavery as an historic, economic, and social Institution." He went on to explain exactly what he meant:

> The history of slavery has not yet been written. There has been no attempt to write it. There are, indeed, works which indicate by their titles some bearing upon the subject of slavery, but a scientific treatise upon the same there is not. Accounts of the slavery *question* there are in abundance, but slavery as an historic Institution is yet to be studied. Until the thing itself is known, it is impossible to treat it understandingly in the history of political controversy. Students from the South, trained to a knowledge of scientific methods, should take up the history of slavery—the peculiar institution. Study the slaveholders as such; study their position, occupations, modes of life, their intercourse with the outside world. . . . Such inquiries would show to some extent the character of southern civilization. No individual can complete this

> great task. It will be a work for the coming century. But individuals can contribute a stone to the up-building of this historical structure and by and by it will be finished.[16]

The seminar soon took it up.

At the time of von Holst's visit, in the fall of 1883, Hopkins had recently awarded its first doctorate in history. The seminar was just settling into a new library and meeting space designed specifically for research and collaboration. A new publication series, the Johns Hopkins University Studies, had been launched as a venue for the seminar's work.[17]

And it happened that the following week, the Supreme Court handed down a decision that raised once again the question of the nature of slavery and its relationship to contemporary politics. The decision concerned the Civil Rights Act of 1875, which lame-duck Republicans had passed before a wave of Democrats swept into Congress. The act prohibited discrimination in public accommodations, transportation, entertainment, jury selection, and several other realms of public life. It was far from perfect—a schools provision had been dropped, and the law was rarely enforced because Black litigants had to sue for their rights.[18]

Nevertheless, the Civil Rights Act was at least on the books, if not quite a realized fact. Then, in 1883, it came before the Supreme Court in the *Civil Rights Cases.* The court used the occasion to settle once and for all the question of exactly what the Thirteenth Amendment's promise—that "neither slavery nor involuntary servitude . . . shall exist within the United States"—was meant to prohibit. "Was nothing more intended than to forbid one man from owning another as property?" Justice John Marshall Harlan asked. Harlan reasoned that American slavery had been based on race, so the end of slavery should also mean the end of discrimination based on race. He believed that the Thirteenth Amendment necessarily gave Congress additional powers "to the extent, at least, of protecting the liberated race against discrimination, in respect of legal rights belonging to freemen, where such discrimination is based upon race."

But Harlan stood alone on the bench. The other eight justices, led by Joseph Bradley, agreed with Harlan that the Thirteenth Amendment gave Congress legislative power over "slavery and its incidents." But Bradley concluded that discrimination in accommodations and transportation imposed "no badge of slavery or involuntary servitude." Racial discrimination might violate the Fourteenth Amendment's strictures about equal protection, but it had nothing to do with the abolition of slavery. "The long existence of African slavery in this country gave us very distinct notions of what it was, and what were its necessary incidents," Bradley explained. They could be counted on a few fingers: compulsory service, worse punishments than free people, no freedom of movement, and no right to hold property, make contracts, sue in court, or testify against whites. But that was about it. "It would be running the slavery argument into the ground to make it apply to every act of discrimination which a person may see fit to make as to the guests he will entertain, or as to the people he will take into his coach or cab or car, or admit to his concert or theatre," Bradley declared.[19]

It was in the wake of von Holst's talk and the Supreme Court's invalidation of the Civil Rights Act in October 1883 that Adams's students dove into the historical records and began to produce the first scholarly studies of slavery in America.[20] As the antecedent of the so-called Negro problem in American politics, a question that the Supreme Court's decision had just opened wide, slavery was a topic that would allow Adams's students—scientifically trained scholars at a national research university located close to the capital—to demonstrate the value of their expertise. Slavery was also a local institution whose evolution Adams's students could trace from colonization to emancipation. If each student investigated the history of slavery in a single state, Johns Hopkins would eventually produce the foundation for a comprehensive history of American slavery.

Within a year, two students in the seminar were planning "to make a special study of slavery in some of its institutional phases." To help them get started, Adams arranged for a visit from a DC lawyer named William Birney. The son of an Alabama slaveholding family that later converted to abolitionism, Birney had joined the Union Army during the Civil War and recruited seven regiments of Black troops in Maryland. After the war, he became a collector of southern historical artifacts, and the purpose of his visit to the seminar in 1884 was to discuss "Sources of information for the study of Slavery." Birney pointed Adams's students to old abolitionist compilations such as George Stroud's *Sketch of the Laws Relating to Slavery* and Theodore Weld's *American Slavery as It Is*, which contained laws, travel accounts, and other evidence. He also donated part of his personal collection, shipping Adams an express package of books that marked the start of the Johns Hopkins collections in southern history and slavery.[21]

By the spring of 1885, Adams's students were ready to present "a series of slave & Negro Studies" to the seminar. One of the students interested in slavery soon left to become a lawyer, but the other one—a Harvard graduate named Jeffrey Brackett—stayed at Johns Hopkins and began to bring slavery studies into the emerging American historical profession.[22] In September 1885, he gave the first talk on slavery ever delivered before the American Historical Association, then holding just its second annual meeting.

By the time Brackett spoke to the assembled historians, he had spent about a year researching American slavery. But his was a particular kind of knowledge, different from that of men who had studied—and seen—slavery while it still existed. To study slavery now meant to study the past, to reconstruct something that was once living out of a stack of silent papers.

Brackett used his talk to explain how to pursue this kind of knowledge. The first and most urgent need, he said, was simply a "bibliography of the *institution* of slavery." He believed that the antebellum polemics written by abolitionists and their pro-slavery foes held "little or no value to the student" interested in an accurate account. Brackett urged his fellow historians to ignore those partisan arguments and instead to "enter as much as possible into the life of the old plantation." They could do this, he believed, if they relied on the kinds of sources he saw as impartial, including not only "statute-books" but also "court reports, legislative journals, and newspapers, as well as the testimony of reliable whites and blacks who knew the old régime." The goal was "to know its laws, the interpretations of the courts, and, what is far more important, the historical reasons for the laws, and how far the laws were executed—the real spirit of the people toward the blacks."

Brackett noted that historians of slavery would need to study not only white slaveholders but also Black slaves if they hoped to get a full picture of the institution. For him, this meant examining slaves in America as well as their ancestors in Africa. "If students of the history of our own country must begin with the history of England," he said, "so surely must a study of slavery in America begin with the blacks of Africa." This was not a new idea; it went back at least to Anthony Benezet and had been a standard practice of some antebellum slavery writers as well as African American historians. For Brackett, the reason for focusing on Black slaves and their ancestors was not only historical but also political. Speaking in 1885—midway between the collapse of Reconstruction and the rise of Jim Crow, when the country's racial politics remained uncertain—he hoped a thorough history of slavery would "aid those who are trying to solve the so-called negro problem of to-day" by revealing how a society of whites and Blacks could be peacefully ordered.[23]

Over the next few years, Brackett continued to report on his research at the Hopkins seminar. In 1889, he finished his study *The Negro in Maryland*. It was the first dissertation ever written about American slavery—the first book-length study of slavery based on research in primary sources and supported by the authority of the new research university. It was written primarily to advance knowledge (and to fulfill an academic requirement), not to make a political argument. Its evidence and conclusions might suggest certain policies or political ideas, but that was not the main point. "The object of this study is simply to trace, as clearly as possible, the growth of African slavery, as an institution, in Maryland," Brackett wrote.[24]

As with many dissertations, Brackett's fell far short of the ambitious plan he had laid out a few years before. Instead of tracing slavery back to the Old World, he skipped quickly over ancient slavery and medieval serfdom as essentially irrelevant to the development of modern slavery in the New World, which he considered a separate institution. And he often did little more than transcribe the relevant statutes from the Maryland archives. He consulted some court cases to try to determine "the rigor or mildness" with which slave laws were enforced, but confronted by a lack of sources about how punishments were meted out in the private court of the plantation, he ultimately fell back on old slaveholder claims. "There is every reason to believe that the great majority of slaves in Maryland were properly and kindly treated," he concluded, having considered almost no evidence from the point of view of the slaves. He acknowledged that there must have been a few bad masters just as surely as there were a few bad parents (he went on to a career in social work), but he believed that this "brutal side of human nature" could be seen in any society. He saw little reason to condemn slavery as especially cruel.[25]

Brackett confessed to Adams that he did not "feel at all satisfied" with his work.[26] But he did think it made at least one major contribution: it demonstrated that slavery could be studied separately from the slavery question. Those who lived through the Civil War had spent the previous quarter-century arguing over past politics, but no one had bothered to investigate the subject that those past political debates were supposedly about. Brackett and the rest of the Johns Hopkins seminar in historical and political science hoped to change that, and to reframe the subject of slavery so that it could be analyzed scientifically by people trying to solve the problem of postwar race relations. They wanted to make it possible to look at the subject impartially, without the old passion, so that the country could finally move forward.

ADAMS HOPED THAT HIS STUDENTS WOULD EVENTUALLY DEVELOP "A COMplete study of the negro in the various Southern states." By the time Brackett published his dissertation, in 1889, several younger seminar members were already taking up the subject.[27] Bernard Steiner was studying slavery in Connecticut, Edward Ingle was looking at Washington, DC, and John McPherson was working on a history of Liberia, which had been settled by freed slaves.

Meanwhile, the university was expanding its library collections to make it easier for Adams's students to study slavery. In January 1891, the library acquired five more boxes of "books and pamphlets on slavery" from William Birney, giving Johns Hopkins what was then believed to be the most complete collection of materials on American slavery in existence. Later that year, the university also acquired the collection of J. Thomas Scharf, a Baltimore lawyer and state government official who had spent the decades since the Civil War gathering thousands of manuscripts, letters, public documents, and pamphlets related to secession and the Confederacy. The Birney and Scharf collections represented "the first serious attempt on a large scale to insure the preservation of the history and literature of the South as written by her own people," President Gilman declared.[28]

By 1896, students at Hopkins had used those southern history collections to produce sixty-one studies of southern history, economics, and politics. These were not necessarily great works of scholarship. They were not really meant to be; they were exercises to develop certain skills. Still, they were published and read, and they cannot entirely be excused as the work of students who were still figuring out how to be historians. In general, the Hopkins slavery studies were narrow and shallow, and they relied too heavily on the sources that were easiest to access, such as statute books, despite Adams's warning that law "may be very misleading; it may represent the plans, the designs, the hopes, the desires of legislators, but not realized facts."[29] The result was a series of studies that largely recapitulated legislative records.

Yet this was not only an accident of source material. As professionally trained social scientists like Adams and his seminar students began to take over the production of scholarship, they made a show of avoiding any strong partisan stance. They depoliticized slavery by saying that disinterested scholars could present a more truthful view of slavery than partisans who pressed a side and by focusing on institutional evolution instead of political debate. "The non-partisan, objective study of slavery is what has been done so well by Johns Hopkins," Adams declared. He saw a vast gulf between the Hopkins-style study of slavery as an institution and what he deemed "controversial papers on the Civil War" that dwelt on political debates and moral guilt—a description that could have included von Holst.[30] As Adams's students pioneered the academic study of slavery in the 1880s and 1890s, they celebrated the reunited nation, drained the slavery question of any moral or political element, and excused slavery as a social and economic expedient that had little to do with the Civil War.

Indeed, at the same time as they saw their work as a contribution to national policy, the Hopkins scholars also sought to make the study of slavery a local issue that lay outside the realm of politics. This process was happening beyond the academy as well. At the time the Hopkins studies took shape, the idea that slavery and race were national political issues was giving way to the notion that the Negro problem was peculiar to the South. Many white Americans in the North as well as the South had turned against older dreams of equality and universal suffrage as the United States struggled with the question of how to incorporate new classes of foreign immigrants, freed slaves, and industrial workers into the republic. As a new generation searched for methods of social control, a growing nostalgia for the plantation and the Old South took hold across America. In addition to providing a model for race relations, crumbling plantations seemed to offer an ennobling alternative to the enervation caused by modern materialism and machinery.

The moonlight-and-magnolia stories that characterized what became known as the "plantation school" of southern literature showcased chivalrous gentlemen, beautiful ladies, and loyal bondsmen. They evoked a sentimental version of the South that appealed strongly to the nationwide desire for political, racial, and economic harmony after decades of vitriol and violence. Literary magazines such as *Scribner's* and *Century* published southern romances by the bushel, and by the 1890s, the Boston-based *Atlantic*, a bastion of New England sensibility, was also running nostalgic stories about southern plantations. The Virginia writer Thomas Nelson Page proved especially popular; even an old abolitionist like Thomas Wentworth Higginson, who had funded John Brown and fought to end slavery, was known to weep over Page's plantation romances. Page, who had grown up on a plantation just before the war, perfectly expressed the politics of plantation nostalgia when he worried about what would happen to society "as the older generation which knew the ties between master and servant passes away."[31]

Alongside this conservative paternalism, which envisioned a place for free Blacks (and immigrants and industrial workers) in American politics under the guiding hand of educated elites, some white Americans went so far as to argue that free Blacks would not be able to survive without the structure and support provided by slavery. This was paternalism turned on its head. Cut off from the daily contact with civilized whites that slavery had facilitated, the Harvard professor Nathaniel Shaler predicted, free Blacks would inevitably "revert to their ancestral conditions" of savagery. After the 1890 census, which seemed to show a decline in the rate of Black population growth and the concentration of that shrinking population deeper in the South, some began to believe that a race war wouldn't be necessary: released from the protection of slavery into the fierce Darwinian struggle for survival, Blacks in America were supposedly going extinct.[32]

Needless to say, this dream (or nightmare) of racial purity did not come to pass. But with the North no longer invested in Reconstruction and Black Americans seemingly stuck in a state of half-civilization in the South, the "Negro problem" was removed from national politics and returned to the South—where some 90 percent of Black Americans lived—to be solved. This was confirmed in 1890, when Congress failed to pass a bill intended to protect Black voters in federal elections. It turned out to be the last gasp of the Republican Party's commitment to equal rights. At precisely the same time, southern states began to take political and civil rights away from Black citizens, starting the system of racial segregation that we know as Jim Crow. Over the next ten to fifteen years, southern states effectively eliminated Black participation in electoral politics.[33]

By that time, many whites in both sections were reaching a tacit agreement that the Civil War's legacy was national reunion and white supremacy rather than emancipation and racial equality. Hopkins students turned out not to have a problem with that. They often assumed without question that Blacks did not deserve to be the social equals of whites, and that allowed them to affect a tough-minded realism when drawing lessons from the American experience with slavery. Edward Ingle, for example, called for "the calm, impersonal, scientific sifting of the evidence on both sides of the slave question" as well as "the honest, unprejudiced, and equally scientific consideration of facts about the condition—social, moral, political, and religious—of the negroes of to-day." He added: "Truths may be revealed which may be distasteful, but they must be told if the best interests of this country are to be subserved." Perhaps unsurprisingly, the "truth" he discovered was that there had been a "favorable side" to slavery in the way it gave Blacks a "practical education."[34]

The supposedly objective Johns Hopkins model wasn't the only way for scholars to study slavery. One of Harvard's top history professors was Albert Bushnell Hart, who had studied with von Holst in Freiburg just before von Holst urged students at Johns Hopkins to examine slavery. In 1887, Hart encouraged one of his female students at the Harvard annex, Marion Gleason McDougall, to take up the subject of fugitive slaves. After four years of work, McDougall published her study in 1891. Much of the book looked like an institutional history straight out of Hopkins, with chapters tracing colonial regulations, constitutional clauses, state and congressional acts, and court cases. In addition, McDougall asked a different kind of question, one that may not have occurred to the men in Baltimore, because she also wanted to understand the experience of running away. "Perhaps a better point of view than that of the outside observer will be gained by placing ourselves in the position of the slave," she suggested, "and examining his motives for flight, the difficulties which he encountered at home, the manner in which he overcame them, and, finally, the various paths open to him, and the agencies which befriended him and forwarded him on his way."[35] This was an attempt at a history of the slave as a human being, motivated by the same love of freedom and family, the same fear of punishment and separation, as anyone might feel.

But historians trained in Germany and at Johns Hopkins believed that real scholarship focused on institutions, not individuals. Institutional history strove to be impersonal and objective. It traced changing laws, not individual choices, and excused the rise of slavery as the inescapable product of larger social pressures, such as the need to civilize Africans or the need for New World colonies to be profitable. Yet few social pressures are truly absolute, and even those that are, such as the need to eat or to reproduce, can usually be attained in more than one way. How they are attained is ultimately a matter of individual choice and responsibility.[36] Institutional historians like those at Johns Hopkins, on the other hand, looked at the chance events of the past and saw in them the latent order dictated by the unfolding logic of institutional germs. They excused southern whites for the sins of slavery, instead blaming impersonal forces for which no one was at fault.

YET HISTORIES OF SLAVERY AS A NATIONAL MORAL AND POLITICAL PROBLEM never disappeared, not even at the end of the nineteenth century. In fact, the single most influential account of southern slavery in these years fell into that category. It came from an amateur northern historian named James Ford Rhodes, who doubled down on antebellum debates and rankled southerners by recapitulating the antislavery analysis of the 1850s.

Rhodes was one of a handful of gentleman amateurs who lingered on, able to support themselves with independent incomes, as the field of history became increasingly professional with the rise of graduate schools at places like Johns Hopkins. Born in Cleveland, he had attended college for a few years in the 1860s before being called away to help manage his father's iron and steel firm. This he obediently did for nearly two decades, until he had an epiphany. "One evening in 1877," he later recalled, "while reading [Richard] Hildreth's History of the United States, I laid down my book and said to myself why should I not write a History of the United States."

Rhodes continued to work at his father's firm until he amassed enough money for himself and his family to continue to live comfortably. Then, in 1885, he quit his job and started to write his *History of the United States from the Compromise of 1850*. Making use of trained research assistants and a professional editor, Rhodes compiled notes and drew up an outline. He finished drafts of the first two volumes (of an eventual eight) by the end of 1891. "I rejoice to say that I never worked as hard in the pursuit of gain, as I have worked on this book the last 3 1/2 years," he told a friend.[37]

The first two volumes of Rhodes's *History* covered the sectional crisis from 1850 to Lincoln's election in 1860. Rhodes built himself up as a modern Thucydides, and his account of the run-up to the Civil War immediately established his reputation as one of America's most influential historians. Northerners and Europeans praised his work almost unanimously. "You are fair and dispassionate to a degree which makes Von Holst's volumes appear more than ever like the argument of an intense partisan," one Boston-based writer told him.[38] Southerners interpreted things differently. What outsiders perceived as fairness, they saw as bias and sensationalism, especially on the subject of slavery.

For the most part, Rhodes provided a standard political history. But in the first volume, wedged between the presidencies of Millard Fillmore and Franklin Pierce, he also included an eighty-page chapter on slavery. "It is my wish to describe the institution as it may have appeared before the war to a fair-minded man," he began, only to concede that "nevertheless, this chapter can only be a commentary on the sententious expression of Clay: 'Slavery is a curse to the master and a wrong to the slave.'" The rest of the chapter leaned heavily on Frederick Law Olmsted's accounts of his travels through the South in the 1850s. Rhodes himself had been south only a few times, but he believed that Olmsted was a trustworthy guide. "His aim was to see things as they were and describe them truthfully," Rhodes explained. "He has admirably succeeded, and his books are invaluable to one making a study of this subject."[39] He cited Olmsted two or three times per page, using Olmsted's observations as evidence for nearly every point he made.

Today Olmsted is remembered primarily as a landscape architect who transformed the look and feel of American cities with his designs for Central Park and an astonishing number of other urban green spaces that we now take for granted. But before the Civil War, he was a gentleman farmer and a well-known journalist. In the early 1850s, Henry Raymond, who had recently founded the *New-York Daily Times*, asked him to become a "Special Correspondent" in the South, writing periodic dispatches about conditions in the countryside. Raymond, like Olmsted, was a moderate when it came to slavery, and both men hoped to influence the inflamed debate by providing accurate information and objective observations. In his newspaper articles about the South, where he spent thirteen months over the next two years, Olmsted distilled to its essence the free-labor ideology that would soon give rise to the Republican Party. "I shall be able to show conclusively, I think, that free labor is cheaper than slave," he told a friend twelve days into his journey.[40] He turned his articles into three popular books published between 1856 and 1860, plus an abridged version of the whole in 1861.

Rhodes reproduced most of Olmsted's main arguments, establishing a framework of analysis that would be followed for years. He started with basic living conditions—food, clothing, housing, working hours, and so on—and showed that standards for slaves were far inferior to those for northern workers. He then examined slave treatment, things like punishment and slave breeding, both of which he said were essential to making the plantation economy profitable. He allowed that slave auctions were played up for sentimental value in abolitionist propaganda, but he had little doubt that an "extensive traffic in slaves" existed across the South. He said masters kept their slaves "in a state of dismal ignorance and moral darkness," one unfortunate aspect of which was the loose morals of slave women—a subject whose effects on southern society exercised him for several pages.[41]

Rhodes went on to reflect at great length on slavery's baleful effects on southern whites, plantation owners as well as the poor, who lived in a social and political system that made a virtue of cruelty and elevated a few at the expense of the rest. Southern slaves and poor whites suffered so that the planters might achieve something great. This was a goal that Rhodes, a former Gilded Age captain of industry, did not reject out of hand. "They displayed good breeding, refined manners, and dignified deportment . . . ," he wrote of the large planters, with more than a hint of admiration. "When we compare the cream of society in both sections, the palm must be awarded to the slave-holding community." But that cream consisted of only a few thousand men in a society of several million. As for the rest, immigration statistics alone made it clear that the North was the more attractive and prosperous society. Rhodes, like Olmsted, found antebellum southern culture mostly stale, especially compared to "the opportunities for culture in the ancient world given the existence of slavery." He lamented that southern intellectuals "waste[d]" their "varied ability in a doomed cause," and he indicted southern politicians such as Calhoun and Davis for defending "an unrighteous cause."[42]

Rhodes believed Olmsted to be an objective reporter, but southerners were especially keen to criticize Rhodes for what they perceived as bias. In a review published in June 1893, John William Burgess, a political scientist at Columbia University, acknowledged that Rhodes's *History* was the best work so far on the run-up to the Civil War. But Burgess believed that the historical work of scholarship, if carried out properly, should also perform the political work of reconciliation. "Almost thirty years have now passed since the great civil war in the United States . . . ," he wrote. "It would seem, therefore, as if the time had at last come for something like an impartial narration of the events, and an unprejudiced presentation of the ideas, which prepared the way for that demonstration of fratricidal fury." A few years later, in his own history of the antebellum period, Burgess would name the establishment of "national cordiality" as his explicit goal. He thought Rhodes's work failed at this central task. "Mr. Rhodes had a great opportunity for mediating a more complete reconciliation," he lamented, "and he has not made full use of it."[43]

Burgess had deep personal reasons for seeking a reconciliation between North and South. He had been born, in 1844, to a slaveholding family in the small town of Cornersville, Tennessee. But his family, like many in the Upper South, remained loyal to the federal government even after secession. During the first year of the war, when he was seventeen, he saw some of these fellow Union loyalists "hanging by the neck from the limb of a tree" for their views. He later fled to Union lines, took an oath of allegiance, and enlisted in the US Army. But his experiences during the war shook him to the core. He emerged a wreck, physically and psychologically, and his family lost all its property, including its property in slaves. He decided he would dedicate his life to figuring out "how to solve the problems of man on earth and construct his institutions by means of the still, small voice of human reason instead of through the roar of cannon and the rattle of musketry."[44] He hoped to keep his country from devolving again into civil war.

By the 1890s, Burgess had built a successful political science program around himself at Columbia—one successful enough, in fact, to overtake Johns Hopkins as the most important center for social scientific research in America. He taught that the main story of US history was the development of national sovereignty, something he saw as the peculiar province of the "Aryan race." In this view, the issues of slavery and emancipation receded into the background, or worse. Slavery entered Burgess's interpretation of US history only insofar as it forced crucial questions about national sovereignty to the fore, while sectionalism (an attempt to destroy US sovereignty) and Reconstruction (an attempt "to pollute it with non-Aryan elements") both constituted equal "sins against American civilization."[45]

Burgess had seen slavery "face to face," as he put it, and to him Rhodes's history of slavery read like the work of an abolitionist who was still fighting the same old battles. "The time has gone by when it was necessary to exaggerate the evils of slavery in order to nurse the passions of men for its overthrow," Burgess wrote. "The time has arrived for the cooler impartial study of the nature of this temporary relation between the highly civilized white race and the deeply barbarous negro race—for the discernment of the great problem of history which was solved through this relation."[46] He was calling for reconciliation based on an acknowledgment by southerners that they had been wrong to secede and a recognition by northerners that slavery had played a necessary role in US race relations. For him, as for many other men of his time and station, slavery was starting to be remembered above all as a beneficent form of social control.

A few months after Burgess's review, an anonymous critic piled on in an article that ran in the *Atlantic*, deriding Rhodes's volumes as "a superior sort of anti-slavery pamphlet" in which the main features of American history were "thrown hopelessly, almost grotesquely, out of proportion." The unnamed author was Woodrow Wilson, the future president, who was then a young political scientist at Princeton. Originally from Virginia, Wilson had studied at Johns Hopkins in the early 1880s. As it happened, he was there at the same time that Hermann von Holst visited the seminar to encourage the study of slavery. At a seminar meeting a few months later, during a lively debate about von Holst's history, Wilson energetically led the opposition. Wilson hated von Holst's heavy Germanic style and northern sympathies so much that he once threw a volume across the room and broke the book's back. Now he added Rhodes to the list of authors who failed to deal fairly with slavery and the South. (For Wilson, a fair accounting of slavery was that it "had done more for the negro in two hundred and fifty years than African freedom had done since the building of the pyramids.") Most important, Wilson claimed that Rhodes's focus on slavery caused him to miss "the real life of the times." There was "a deeper guiding principle" to

American life in those years, Wilson wrote, "an infinitely profounder complexity" than the debate over slavery, although he did not go into the details in his brief review.[47]

Rhodes feared that these criticisms represented a troubling mood. He worried that they were pushing the "new idea" that slavery was just a subplot in the dramatic clash between North and South, not the main story. "I think we should insist that without slavery, without Cuffee, there would have been no war," he told a fellow historian soon after he saw Wilson's review. "It is not the historians who make slavery too prominent—it is the events themselves and the spirit of the time."[48]

Rhodes was wrong that this was a "new idea." It had been around for decades; Burgess and Wilson were adding little to what men like Alexander Stephens and Edward Pollard said twenty years earlier. Still, Rhodes was right to be concerned: Americans in the 1890s were much more amenable to reconciliation than they had been two or three decades before. And this goal did require a new interpretation of the role that slavery played in American history.

As Rhodes received blows from Burgess and Wilson in the summer of 1893, a grand Historical Congress was getting under way in Chicago. It was being held in the midst of that year's World's Fair, which was celebrating four centuries of progress since Columbus arrived in the New World. (The fair's organizers were a year late.) A former Johns Hopkins student and good friend of Wilson named Frederick Jackson Turner was invited to give a paper, which he called "The Significance of the Frontier in American History." The title made Turner's point: what was significant in American history was not slavery but the western frontier, where settlers turned wilderness into civilization. This, it turned out, was the "deeper guiding principle," the "infinitely profounder complexity," that Wilson was describing. It amounted to a striking new framing of slavery's place in the American past.

Born in Portage, Wisconsin, a former fur-trading town about forty miles north of Madison, Turner had grown up in a world that seemed completely divorced from the struggle over slavery then consuming the states farther south and east. As a boy, he heard French names all around him, relics of the fur trade. There were still Indians near Portage who would come into town to sell furs; wandering in the woods, he sometimes stumbled upon their camps.[49] These experiences made up his everyday life, and it was only when he moved away that he began to see in them some larger significance.

First, Turner stayed close to home to attend the University of Wisconsin. There he came under the wing of the ancient historian William Francis Allen, who had taught in the Sea Islands during the Civil War and later edited *Slave Songs of the United States*. "From Allen I learned what historical scholarship meant," Turner later recalled. What it meant, Turner learned, was that history encompassed not just political events or institutional evolution but also social and economic forces. He adopted Allen's practice of not discriminating between disciplinary methods in his efforts to reconstruct society as a whole—an approach that caused some later scholars to view him as sociological in his thinking.[50]

After receiving his bachelor's degree, Turner taught alongside Allen for three years before heading to Johns Hopkins for his PhD. It was only then, when he moved to Baltimore in the fall of 1888, that he turned toward the frontier as the organizing principle of American history. In the seminar with Adams, he suddenly saw with great clarity (and some exaggeration) the difference between his own experience in the West and the way American history was taught in the East. Less than a month after he arrived, he reported home to Allen that the Hopkins history program completely lacked "any proper conception of the Great West. Not a man here that I know of is either studying, or hardly aware of the country beyond the Alleghanies—except two."[51]

Turner's experience in Baltimore improved in the spring, when Woodrow Wilson came to deliver a course of lectures on "Administration." Turner loved the course, and he also loved spending time with Wilson. They were staying at the same boardinghouse, and they often talked there over cider and doughnuts. Wilson was from the South, Turner from the West, and they bonded over their shared sense that their sections got no respect in American historical writing—as well as their shared ambition to change that. "I got new ideas of the South and its dynamic side in my talks—sometimes my arguments—with Mr Wilson . . . ," Turner recalled thirty years later, when Wilson was in his second term. "I was bringing to him words from lands he didn't know, as he was giving me a new conception of the South, as well as a new outlook upon politics in general."[52]

After Turner returned to Wisconsin, he and Wilson kept up an occasional correspondence about the ideas they'd discussed in Baltimore as they began to apply them in their own work—Wilson in *Division and Reunion*, a relatively brief history of the United States since the inauguration of Andrew Jackson, which he finished in the summer of 1892, and Turner in a few sharp essays and reviews. In the fall of 1892, Turner criticized von Holst "because in his attention to slavery he has lost sight of the fundamental, dominating fact in United States history, the expansion of the United States from the Alleghenies to the Pacific." With his new understanding of the significance of the South and the West, as well as his belief in the primacy of social and economic forces, Turner had become frustrated with what he saw as the inflated importance that historians like von Holst assigned to the slavery struggle. "The struggle over slavery is a most important incident in our history," Turner wrote, "but it will be seen, as the meaning of events unfolds, that the real lines of American development, the forces dominating our character, are to be studied in the history of westward expansion."[53]

By the next year, when he received an invitation to speak at the Historical Congress at the Chicago World's Fair, Turner was ready to expand on this idea. On the evening of July 12, he declared that American democracy was above all the product of frontier individualism. The frontier of settlement, he explained, had been the "meeting point between savagery and civilization" as Americans moved across the continent, the place where the wilderness stripped off settlers' "garments of civilization" and thrust them back into primitive conditions. Gradually settlers transformed the wilderness, building up trading posts and plowing up farms and laying out towns; by that time, the frontier had passed, had moved farther west, only to begin the same process over again. "This perennial rebirth," Turner said, "this fluidity of American life, this expansion westward with its new opportunities, its continuous touch with the simplicity of primitive society, furnish the forces dominating American character."[54]

Turner's frontier talk is remembered as the most influential address ever delivered by an American historian. Yet in the moment, at the end of a long day, his audience reacted with complete indifference. The assembled historians headed straight back to their rooms without discussing Turner's talk at all. Even Turner's own father, who visited the fair and had his son show him around the White City, didn't say a word about the speech when he reported home.

Nevertheless, Turner's frontier thesis caught on after its publication by the State Historical Society of Wisconsin at the end of the year. Like most works seen as landmarks, it said little that was new, but it brought several existing concepts together into an elegant synthesis that arrived at exactly the right time. "I think you have struck some first class ideas," Theodore Roosevelt, then a successful western historian, told Turner a few months after his talk, "and have put into definite shape a good deal of thought which has been floating around rather loosely."[55]

Turner's talk consolidated a larger shift whose fulcrum lay somewhere around 1890. With the rise of urbanization and industrialization, scholars were becoming interested in new questions of social and economic organization. The old scholarly emphasis on law and politics, as at Johns Hopkins, went along with a society convinced of its ability to imagine a new world and then to make it real—to abolish slavery through legislation, to remake the South and West through Reconstruction. But it was becoming apparent that there were still real limits to the power of law to reshape the world.

One clear example for many Americans was the experience of Reconstruction, in which liberal universalist dreams ran up against the hard reality of either prejudice or inferiority, depending on one's perspective. Another was the growing unrest among farmers and industrial workers, which reached a fever pitch with the formation of the People's Party in 1892, a financial panic in 1893, and a nationwide Pullman railroad workers' strike in 1894. Social and economic factors were playing a more prominent explanatory role for historians and other social scientists.

This new conception of the proper objects and ends of historical study held out, in theory, the prospect of a new analysis of life and labor under the slave system. Yet slavery remained conspicuously absent from Turner's account. His West was the Old Northwest where he grew up, not the Old Southwest of Mississippi plantations and New Orleans auction blocks. Traders, ranchers, miners, and farmers all made their appearance in his American pageant across the continent, but never slaves. Turner knew slaves had been there, doing much of the work of making the swamps and forests of the South fit for settlement. But he did not highlight their presence.

In Turner's telling, the parallel march of free and slave across the West wasn't a political struggle for the future of the United States. Instead, it was a cooperative process—indeed, *the* cooperative process—by which the American nation was formed. "On the tide of the Father of Waters," Turner said, "North and South met and mingled into a nation."[56] This was exactly the kind of history that reconciliation-minded scholars like John William Burgess and Woodrow Wilson wanted to see.

For Turner, at least at that time, the slavery struggle amounted to an "interlude," a parenthesis, an aberration, a deviation from the main lines of American development. Turner's own goal was simply to reduce the emphasis on slavery, not write it out of existence, but as other historians followed him in turning away from the politics of slavery, the subject continued to be downplayed and depoliticized until it nearly disappeared.

Perhaps the best example of this was the historian Charles Beard, who, two decades later, wrote a famous and influential book examining the Constitutional Convention from an economic perspective. Beard mentioned slavery occasionally but had a hard time finding a place for it within his controlling scheme of capitalists versus agrarians—a dichotomy that couldn't accommodate slaveholders. A few years later, as coauthor of a large *History of the American People*, Beard warned against "the impression that the people of this country, between 1820 and 1860, lived either by presidential administrations or by the slavery controversy alone."[57]

At the same time, even as scholars began to concentrate on economic questions and the working class, they focused primarily on the development of the urban, industrial workers who characterized their own world. Slave labor was seen as a historical reversion to the economic necessities of primitive societies, not as an aspect of modern industrial development. As the socialist A. M. Simons explained, "Chattel slavery in America was an historical atavism, and not a stage in social evolution." The progressive economist John R. Commons, who worked alongside Turner for a few years at Wisconsin, published a multivolume *History of Labour in the United States* that ignored slave labor completely.[58]

Other forces were also working against the study of slavery in the United States. Turner's frontier thesis was part of a shift in the structure of social scientific knowledge. In the generation since elective courses were first introduced at Harvard, in 1869, electives and specialization had transformed the American university. The elective system allowed students to choose their own courses, and scholarly specialization gave them new courses to choose from. Not only were students no longer confined to the classical curriculum, but the requirement to take the classics began to drop out altogether. Professors organized themselves into academic departments—new bureaucratic structures on the university landscape—which resulted in divisions and distinctions that were often arbitrary. Individual scholars began to know their particular corner of the world in greater detail than ever before, but they also grew more likely to see that corner of the world as an island unto itself. US history began to stand on its own, both more independent and more isolated than before.[59]

Turner's frontier thesis, with its emphasis on a break between Europe and America, contributed in a small but meaningful way to this larger transformation. As a result, wide-ranging subjects like slavery, once seen as a river running continuously through history and overflowing the boundaries of any one particular discipline, were dammed up and diverted into many smaller and more easily managed channels. Just as the nation was defining the "Negro problem" as a southern problem for southern states to handle on their own terms, so the historical profession was starting to see slavery as a southern problem for southern historians to interpret as they saw fit, while others focused on the real issues that supposedly shaped national life.

6

DIXIE LAND

THE MAN WHO ULTIMATELY DID THE MOST TO MAKE AMERICAN SLAVery a subject of southern social and economic history was Frederick Jackson Turner's student and colleague Ulrich Bonnell Phillips. During his career, Phillips became the first professional historian of American slavery, writing books and articles in the early decades of the twentieth century that redefined the way the subject was studied. Despite, or perhaps because of, their frank statements about Black inferiority and the beneficence of slavery, they stood as the standard histories until the 1950s. Even today, their influence lingers.

Phillips first met Turner in the summer of 1898, when Phillips was a twenty-year-old student working on a master's degree in history at the University of Georgia. Upon learning that Turner was offering a course of lectures at the University of Chicago, he rushed off to listen. It was probably his first trip outside the South, and it proved to be a life-changing experience.

Phillips had been born in 1877 in Troup County, Georgia, in a region that W. E. B. Du Bois once called "the centre of the Negro problem,—the centre of those nine million men who are America's dark heritage from slavery and the slave-trade." His parents originally named him Ulysses, but at some point he decided that his given name was too closely associated with Ulysses S. Grant and had it changed. Before the Civil War, the Phillips family had owned some two dozen slaves along with fifteen hundred acres of land. After the war, with slavery over, the family had trouble making ends meet. Phillips's father worked odd jobs, and his mother had to earn money as a seamstress.

In the fall of 1893, the gangly, fifteen-year-old Phillips arrived at the University of Georgia and soon came under the influence of a professor named John McPherson. Educated at Hopkins, where he wrote a dissertation on the African colonization movement, McPherson was now busily making Georgia's History Department into a replica of what he had experienced in Baltimore, complete with spacious history rooms, research alcoves, and a departmental library.

Phillips walked into those rooms during his second year and absorbed a passion for history. He was soon allowed to teach the freshmen and to serve as assistant librarian, helping to collect and catalogue historical documents. He pored over so many faded manuscripts and newspapers that he had to spend a semester recovering from eyestrain—a semester he spent on a cotton plantation. This devotion to research in original sources stuck with him all his life.[1]

It may have been McPherson who first alerted Phillips to Turner's summer course of lectures at Chicago in 1898: McPherson and Turner had attended Hopkins together a decade earlier. Little evidence from the initial encounter between Phillips and Turner survives, but the men must have made an immediate impression on each other. The following year, they corresponded about Phillips's master's thesis, "State Rights in Georgia." Turner encouraged Phillips to focus on "social origins and economic characteristics" rather than pure politics. Phillips diligently mapped elections county by county to figure out the social and economic fault lines across the state.

Turner and Phillips also discussed where Phillips should go for his PhD. A generation earlier, a person in his position would have sailed for Germany without hesitation. But by the late 1890s, the prestige of US universities had begun to eclipse those in Germany. Johns Hopkins had entered a period of decline, but John William Burgess at Columbia had built up the best department in the country, one that would go on to produce more history doctorates than any other school over the next three decades. Moreover, one of Burgess's younger associates, William Dunning, had just made a name for himself with his *Essays on the Civil War and Reconstruction*. Phillips chose Columbia and headed to New York to work with Dunning.[2]

Today, Dunning has become synonymous with historical racism for his negative portrayal of Reconstruction, and perhaps even more for the way his students—the so-called Dunning School—demonized northerners and Blacks while lionizing white southerners. In his own lifetime, however, Dunning was known as a pragmatist and a joker who cultivated a healthy skepticism of all historical accounts. Older historians like von Holst and Burgess may have felt the need, as Dunning once wrote, to be "tendenziös (I think that's it) for affect on the rising generation; so that the citizens of the U.S. should not go to cutting one another's throats again too soon." But more than a generation since the Civil War, he believed that those considerations no longer applied. "We kids are living in the time of calm reflection," as he cheerfully put it, "when 'What's the use?' sums up the creed of all true philosophical historical students."[3]

This attitude was not just a pose. Later on, Dunning would become president of the American Historical Association. In his presidential address, called "Truth in History," he provided the philosophical justification for his easygoing attitude of acceptance. Characteristically, he cared most about the jokes—"All the jokes caught on," he told his wife after his talk—but he also made an important point about his pragmatic approach to history. He believed that it was not the historian's job to congratulate himself for showing people in the past to have been mistaken, or to celebrate the supposed moral superiority of the present. Instead, the historian's task was simply to uncover how people had lived and what beliefs had motivated their actions. "Whether these ideas were true or were false, according to the standards of any other period, has nothing to do with the matter," Dunning declared. "That they were the ideas which underlay the activities of the men of this time, is all that concerns the work of the historian."[4] In other words, the historian should not care whether past practices and beliefs—the enslavement of human beings, say, or the theory of Black inferiority—were right or wrong. That was beside the point.

Dunning was generally regarded as the most intelligent man in any room—but he often wished to escape the room. He had been expelled from the first college he attended, Dartmouth, for participating in freshman pranks, but then graduated from Columbia with nearly perfect marks in every subject. "In my inmost heart," he wrote in his journal during graduate school, "I think I should like to retire from this quest of learning, take a refined & congenial girl, & settle down in life." It would help, he added, if the girl had "a little—only a little—money."

Dunning buckled down, finished his degree, and then remained at Columbia for the rest of his life, receiving his PhD in 1885 and an academic appointment in 1886, after a year's sojourn in Germany. By the 1890s, he had become an established scholar. He was starting work on what he considered his magnum opus, a massive, three-volume *History of Political Theories* that took him twenty years and covered everything from Plato to the present. "I have been so exclusively devoted to Kant lately," he once wrote, "that I don't even feel sure there ever was a Civil War or Reconstruction."[5]

Yet it was Dunning's *Essays on the Civil War and Reconstruction* that defined his career and his reputation. One of the first scholarly attempts to delve into the constitutional and political history of the Civil War and its aftermath, the book described Reconstruction as misguided and claimed that it ended in disaster. Dunning believed that it was "reckless" to give political power to Black southerners, but his essays were not devoted entirely to denouncing the Negro-loving North. He also showed genuine admiration for the complex political and administrative work of Reconstruction, calling it "one of the most remarkable achievements in the history of government."[6]

On the whole, however, the keynote of Dunning's collection was that Reconstruction failed because it attempted to legislate equality between races that he saw as unequal. A few years later, he wrote a new essay, "The Undoing of Reconstruction," which appeared in the *Atlantic* in 1901 and was included as the final chapter in future editions of his *Essays*. In the brief time since Dunning had completed the first version of his *Essays*, in 1897, the United States had fought the Spanish-American War and acquired new overseas territories in the Philippines, Puerto Rico, and Guam. It had quickly become apparent that governing these territories would not be easy, especially in the Philippines, where warfare continued for years as the United States attempted to subdue an independence movement. This suggested to Dunning an instructive parallel with the South.

In the Philippines and other overseas territories, he thought, the United States was encountering the same problem the South had faced throughout its history: "the coexistence in one society of two races so distinct in characteristics as to render coalescence impossible." In the South, he explained, slavery had provided a solution to that problem, but slavery was not its source—a distinction that was forgotten, he believed, during "the abolitionist fever." With slavery gone, he went on, "its place must be taken by some set of conditions which, if more humane and beneficent in accidents, must in essence express the same fact of racial inequality." This was what white southerners had accomplished in rolling back Reconstruction and implementing white supremacy. In the wake of the country's resort to similar solutions abroad, Dunning believed that the North would now be more willing to endorse them at home as well.[7]

Dunning's work helped turn the Faculty of Political Science at Columbia into a center for scholarship sympathetic to the South. Droves of white southerners, including Phillips, came to study with him. According to Dunning's pragmatic view of history, these southerners could write as if from Charleston while northerners wrote as if from Boston, and capital-T Truth (if such a thing existed) would work its way out somewhere in the middle. Was this an abdication of moral responsibility? Absolutely. The work of Dunning and his students, which demonstrated the supposedly deplorable effects of allowing Black Americans to wield political power, would be used to prop up Jim Crow for years to come. But it's important to remember that Dunning and his students largely reflected the common sense of the South and to some extent the nation in the decades after Reconstruction ended; they did not create it. As Dunning joked to a friend in 1901, "The only way in which a man can attract any attention now" in writing about Reconstruction would be to "take the ground that the whole business was ethically, socially, and politically right."[8]

Ultimately Dunning didn't believe that slavery or race or sectionalism mattered enough to distract him from his three-volume history of political philosophy (which he saw as his true life's work) or from the really pleasurable things in life: fishing and golfing at his summer house ("Dreamland") on the shore of Lake Sunapee in New Hampshire. While others argued about American history, he would be catching bass and practicing his drive, and puzzling out Plato while sailing slowly and peacefully around the lake.

Dunning's pragmatic approach to history may have been the most influential idea that he passed on to Phillips, perhaps along with his sense of style. Phillips mostly took courses on social history, sociology, and economics at Columbia. The dissertation he produced, *Georgia and State Rights*, was simply a revised and expanded version of his master's thesis. But it won him a prize from the American Historical Association and set him up for a successful career. Graduating in 1902, he sought a job at Wisconsin, where Turner headed the History Department, and with Turner's help, he secured the position.[9] There he would start to rewrite the history of slavery.

By the end of Phillips's first year at Wisconsin, he had already attracted a crowd of enthusiastic students who had never heard southern history taken seriously as a subject in its own right. "The history of the United States has been written by Boston and largely written wrong," he told an official at the Georgia Historical Society. "It must be written anew before it reaches its final form of truth, and for that work the south must do its part in preparation."[10] He was ready to make southern history his life's work.

Part of that work involved fostering and funding the professional study of history and other social sciences in the South. This had mixed results. As of 1902, only two universities in the entire South employed more than one man to teach history. Many of the rest continued to assign historical subjects to some poor professor whose portfolio also included a laundry list of other courses. This was one reason why Phillips had ended up at Wisconsin.[11]

The slow growth of professional history in the South had several causes. Partly as a legacy of slavery, the region had a dearth of colleges and universities compared to the North, and the funding for those that existed was meager at best. Just as important, the South proved inhospitable to all but the most timid of scholars in these years before the rise of a strong culture of academic freedom. The historian William Dodd, who received his PhD at Leipzig before joining the faculty at Randolph-Macon College in Virginia, lamented in 1902 that public opinion and publishers in the South enforced a strict party line. According to Dodd, scholars who taught history in the South were required to "subscribe unreservedly to two trite oaths: (1) that the South was altogether right in seceding from the Union in 1861; and (2) that the war was not waged about the negro." Historians were expected to justify southern beliefs, not question them. "Under such conditions, no healthy criticism can exist," Dodd noted. "The results of investigation are fixed for an author before his work begins." The aftermath of Dodd's article unfortunately proved his point: he became embroiled in a dispute with the Grand Camp of Confederate Veterans, who tried to get him fired. Randolph-Macon supported him, but a few years later he left for Chicago.[12]

As Dodd's experience revealed, heritage groups had amassed great power in the South. These groups, including the United Confederate Veterans and the United Daughters of the Confederacy, had blossomed in the late 1880s and early 1890s as white southerners paired the restoration of "home rule" with a renewed celebration of the Confederacy. The UDC, which soon became the largest women's group in the South, paid particularly close attention to history and even had a position called historian-general. One prong of this campaign involved public monuments; thanks to UDC fundraising efforts, roughly half of all Confederate monuments in the South were built in the decade from 1903 to 1912. A second prong involved preservation and education. This contributed to the rise of state archives and other collections of artifacts, such as the Confederate Museum in Richmond, which opened in 1896. But this activity was always in the service of what the UDC called the "true" history of the South, which depicted harmonious race relations on idealized plantations that served as schools for Black slaves. American slavery ranked highly, a UDC historian-general wrote, among "the greatest missionary and educational endeavors that the world has ever known."

The UDC had considerable success in southern primary and secondary schools, where the group monitored textbook selections, sponsored essay contests, and promoted birthday celebrations for Jefferson Davis and Robert E. Lee. By the 1920s, most southern states had adopted pro-Confederacy textbooks as a result of the UDC's campaigns. The group attempted to influence higher education as well by funding professorships, scholarships, and essay contests. But colleges proved less conducive to the UDC's indoctrination efforts. Many scholars at the time held views on slavery and race that lined up well with the UDC's, which was one reason the UDC supported the professionalization of history. These scholars, however, insisted that they should control their own field—an assertion that sometimes brought them into conflict with heritage groups because scientific scholars tended by temperament and training to tolerate a fairly wide range of views. When such conflicts occurred, as in Dodd's case, Confederate veterans, sons, and daughters could combine to bring considerable public pressure to bear, often causing the offending scholar to move north.[13]

Phillips avoided such controversies, partly because he ignored what he called the "propagandist efforts by patriotic societies" such as the UDC, partly because his views lined up well with theirs, and partly because he did not find the academic situation in the South attractive enough to spend much time teaching there. He didn't need to. As sectional resentment receded and history departments grew, it became standard practice for southern topics to be covered by southern men—even at northern schools. Phillips was able to spend most of his career at Wisconsin, Michigan, and Yale, with just a single three-year stint at Tulane, in New Orleans.[14]

It was during the summers that Phillips went south to perform the other preparatory work that he saw as necessary for rewriting American history from a southern perspective: finding, collecting, and preserving southern historical records. Interest in the collection and preservation of American historical records spread across all regions at the turn of the twentieth century as a growing number of students wrote dissertations on the United States. This movement felt especially urgent in the South, where historical documents remained largely scattered in private hands or rotting in county courthouses. In Georgia, for example, the most important state records documenting the antebellum period and the Civil War were stored in a small room with no attendant, where they sat in packages that might or might not be labeled, arranged in an order that might or might not be purposeful. "The documents might almost as well be in a promiscuous heap upon the floor," Phillips lamented.[15] Aside from Johns Hopkins, no other southern university had taken any serious steps toward the preservation of southern historical documents. But as young, professionally trained scholars like Phillips confronted the lack of sources in their field, they began to push for the collection and preservation of old southern documents before they all disappeared.

Phillips was already on the prowl. One of the things that distinguished him throughout his career was his zest for finding new sources, and new types of sources, about slavery and southern history. He dove enthusiastically into old manuscripts, which he saw as a necessary tonic for the traditions and myths that had grown up around the history of the South. In the spring of 1903, his first year at Wisconsin, he submitted a grant proposal to the Carnegie Institution of Washington, a new research-funding agency. He sketched a plan for "a systematic productive study of the historical development of the South in the American Union" and asked for $1,000 per year to pay for traveling around the South and copying documents (which at that time had to be done painstakingly by hand). "I feel that I am getting a much better grasp of the subject in its unity and entirety than has yet been shown by any one writer," he wrote in his proposal, before thinking better of the boast (he was, after all, just a year out of graduate school) and crossing it out.[16]

Phillips failed to get full funding for the project. Thanks to Turner's influence, however, he continued to seek out evidence that other historians had neglected. He collected postcards showing southern scenes: slave quarters near Milledgeville, Georgia; Negroes carrying freight; trainloads of cotton; the sugar house on a Louisiana plantation. He asked law firms in rural Georgia towns to dig into the county clerk's records and send him old quotes of slave sale prices. He devised a filing system to keep all of this straight as he gathered more and more material over the course of his career. One folder was stuffed with notes and outlines about "Negro Slavery," but there were also folders on everything having to do with plantations—"Plantation Economics" and "Plantation Labor" and "Plantation Management" and "Plantation Life," plus a "Plantations Described" folder full of details culled from old notices of plantations for sale or for rent—as well as nearly a dozen folders dealing with the various subdivisions within the subject of slavery: the African slave trade, prices, hiring, runaways, insurrection, and so forth. Documents and manuscripts eventually filled every nook and cranny of his office, which he usually kept open at all hours for students to use as a kind of extra-special collections library.[17]

Plantation records and slave prices struck Phillips as particularly valuable. They contained what he saw as objective and indisputable evidence regarding the daily operations, productivity, and profitability of plantations. The problem was that they were maddeningly time-consuming to find. "The documents containing record of slave prices, I have found, are usually either probate returns or bills of sale," he explained. "They occur sometimes in local archives and sometimes in state archives, and the only thing that I can do in general is to search until I find them." Phillips believed that these unconscious records carried more truth than any published account. "As soon as this material shall have been brought to light," he predicted, "it is safe to prophesy that the travelers' accounts, fallacious as they usually are, will be duly relegated to a place of very minor importance."[18]

As he dug for sources across the South, Phillips also sought to address the Negro problem by drawing on the social and economic history of plantation slavery. As he put the question, "How can improvement be made in industrial conditions, known to be unsatisfactory, and how is civilization to be promoted among the mass of Southern negroes who are beyond question in need of further and higher development?"

To correct the problems that came with progress, Phillips pushed conservative reforms designed to preserve cherished aspects of an older way of life. Just like his mentor, Turner, and many other progressives (both scholarly and not), he sought to cut the transformations of the Civil War and Reconstruction cleanly out of US history. With those incidents out of the way, southern history could return to its main line of development in the form of the plantation—a model of social and economic organization that would now be free from what Phillips came to see as slave labor's inefficiency.[19]

When Phillips wrote about recent southern history, he implied that antebellum plantations dissolved after the Civil War into small farms worked by free Black families, which he portrayed as dismally inefficient and unproductive. He later cited census reports showing that the production of cotton and corn in Deep South states such as Alabama and Mississippi decreased by 40 percent per capita between 1860 and 1900. According to Phillips, this decline in productivity proved that Blacks worked more efficiently as plantation laborers than as peasant farmers. "Average negroes under compulsion are nearly twice as productive as when left to the control of their own impulses," he concluded.[20]

What Phillips did not say was that the South actually replaced slavery with sharecropping, vagrancy acts, and a convict-lease system, all designed to yoke supposedly free Black workers to white landlords. Many workers remained free to move around and sell their labor to the highest bidder, but some became stuck in endless cycles of debt that restricted their options. At the bottom end of the spectrum, where coercion entered the equation, workers were compelled to toil in debt bondage. This was particularly true in the rural South, where, as W. E. B. Du Bois wrote at that same moment, "the spirit of the Thirteenth Amendment is sadly broken." This was what Phillips's hoped-for plantation revival looked like in practice.[21]

Phillips spent the summer of 1904 in the South, where he was teaching for a term at the University of Georgia. While there, he used a stipend from the Carnegie Institution to visit county archives in search of records of the slave trade and slaveholding finance. "I am busily delving into great stores of material that never met the eye of the student before," he rejoiced. But he worried over how to divide plantation history into discrete pieces for publication, and he struggled "to find some central theme, some key to the situation," that would help tie together his evidence. Over the summer, he put together a preliminary article on "The Economic Cost of Slaveholding in the Cotton Belt."[22]

Soon Phillips accumulated enough data to deepen his analysis of the plantation, which he developed in a groundbreaking series of articles over the next few years. Digging deeper into that analysis helps draw out the differences Phillips saw between slave labor and plantation organization, and highlights some of the contradictions in his view of slavery that he was never fully able to resolve. Slavery's fundamental economic characteristic, he believed, was that it transformed laborers into commodities. In other words, masters owned their workers as property and could buy and sell them in the market. This fact not only distinguished slavery from serfdom and other forms of bound labor; it also made the slave trade a defining feature of southern slavery. "The American slave-labor régime was developed under a money economy," Phillips explained, "to enable European settlers and capitalists to exploit American resources with the aid of African labor. Any fixing of laborers to the soil as in serfdom, would have hindered the purpose in America." The property aspect of slavery allowed masters to deploy labor in response to market conditions without worrying about the sorts of messy entanglements that might prevent a free family from moving. If a master wanted to migrate, he simply took his slaves with him. If the demand for labor in developing parts of the South caused the price of slaves to rise, masters in older areas could sell their slaves for a nice profit.[23]

Yet Phillips believed that the slave trade also had important limitations that threatened the long-term viability of the entire slave-labor system. This was why he spent part of his career unearthing and analyzing relatively obscure economic data on slave prices. To test whether slave prices made economic sense, he compared them with cotton prices in Georgia from 1800 to 1860. Because slaves in Georgia primarily produced cotton, the relationship between the prices of the two commodities should have remained fairly stable over the years, other things being equal. Phillips found that in 1800 a prime field hand cost $450 and a pound of ginned cotton could fetch thirty cents, meaning the slave was worth fifteen hundred pounds of cotton. But instead of remaining stable, Phillips noticed, the cotton-price of a prime field hand rose sharply over the decades. By 1818, it had more than doubled to thirty-five hundred pounds; by 1837, it had hit ten thousand. In the late 1850s, the cotton-price of a prime field hand topped out at fifteen thousand pounds: prime field hands sold for more than $1,500, but the price of cotton had sunk to just eleven cents a pound.

What could explain the huge antebellum increase in the cotton-price of slaves? Not any fundamental changes in the cotton or the slaves. Phillips believed (incorrectly, it would turn out) that the slave of 1860 still did about the same work as the slave of 1800 and that "a pound of cotton in 1860 was not essentially different," he dryly noted, "from a pound of cotton in 1800." Not all other things remained equal in the intervening years; the early nineteenth century saw important developments in transportation and marketing that affected the way slaves and cotton were bought and sold. But Phillips maintained that those changes alone could not account for the tenfold increase in the cotton-price of slaves. Strikingly, he believed that the basic problem lay at the heart of slavery, in the way that it turned labor into capital.

As Phillips explained it, slavery involved the permanent purchase of labor as a capital investment. Instead of paying weekly wages to hired hands, planters laid out huge sums up front to buy their slaves. Worse still, at least from an economic perspective, they couldn't lay off those slaves when a task was completed or demand slackened. An extensive system of slave hiring sprang up throughout the South to satisfy the demand for cheap and flexible short-term labor, but this was just a symptom of the deeper problem. "When capital and labor were combined . . . ," Phillips wrote, "there was an irresistible tendency to overvalue and overcapitalize slave labor." Planters constantly bid against one another when they bought slaves. Slave prices spiraled upward, but planters were willing to pay the high prices because they saw slaves as a capital investment that would keep going up in value, much as people bid up house prices in hot real-estate markets.

In theory all these expensive slaves could be liquidated for cash if necessary, but in practice that proved impossible, according to Phillips, because the economy of the antebellum South suffered from a fatal lack of diversification. Planters all bid against one another to buy slaves, driving the price up. They all used their slaves to grow cotton. Then they all tried to sell the cotton, and their competition drove the price down. As slave prices went up and cotton prices went down, it became increasingly difficult for planters to turn a profit. On top of all that, Phillips noted, planters were stuck using a rigid system of capitalized labor in an industry—agriculture—that had inherently uncertain returns. If there was a bad harvest, planters couldn't simply fire their slaves. They had to sell. But because the southern economy wasn't diversified, other planters were inevitably in the same dire position. Whenever one was hurting and needed to sell a slave, it was likely that others were hurting, too, and couldn't afford to buy. As Phillips put it, "Any crisis threatened complete bankruptcy."[24]

Phillips's economic analysis led him to resurrect the free-labor critique of slavery. Like countless antislavery commentators, he thought that the South's precarious slave-and-cotton economy hindered the region's economic development for decades before the Civil War. He believed that southerners recognized this and would have discarded slavery on their own, without northern interference. Masters knew they could earn larger profits by allowing their slaves more freedom to direct their own labor or by giving them some share of what they produced. Such reforms would make slaves more efficient workers, as economists like Adam Smith had long argued.

But Phillips never blamed southern planters for holding on to slavery as long as they did, because for him slavery was more than a mere system of labor, ruled by calculations of profit and loss. Slavery also operated as a system of social control:

> With the negroes once on hand in large numbers, . . . the enormous contrast between them and the whites in intelligence, standards and institutions—in a word, in race character—brought up a social problem which over-shadowed all economic issues. Slavery, originating as a system of labor control, was maintained as still more valuable in safe-guarding the standards, institutions and social well-being of the few whites against possible demoralization and overthrow by the numerous blacks. . . . Plantations and slavery made up a system of tutelage and police combined, providing education in civilized industry and life and at the same time preventing successful outbreaks of negro revolt against white control.

Originating as a means of controlling a lower class to make a profit, Phillips believed, slavery was retained as a means of controlling a lower race to secure a civilization. "In the divergence of economic interests and social needs," Phillips wrote, "it became increasingly clear that the social needs were paramount." With slavery gone, the New South had become a place where it was easier to turn a profit but harder to maintain order. "The slave labor problem has disappeared," he wrote, "but the negro problem remains."[25]

Even later in his career, as he shifted his emphasis to the social side of slavery, Phillips continued to discuss the domestic slave trade in narrowly economic terms: labor mobility, price, capital investment. Yet he always kept the crass commercialism of the slave trade separate from the sanctuary of the plantation, just as antebellum southerners had in their own heads. The slave trade may have been a cutthroat market in which slaves were bought and sold like commodities, but somehow the plantation was a school or a settlement house that operated at a loss for the beneficent purpose of educating and civilizing Black workers. There was a potential contradiction here between the central economic role of the slave trade and its seemingly negligible influence on the social life of the plantation, as well as between the booming trade in slaves and the supposed unprofitability of slavery. Phillips tended not to dwell on these problems, but that didn't make them go away.

As the years passed and the articles piled up, Phillips's position at Wisconsin gradually deteriorated. His situation had seemed promising when he first started, fresh out of graduate school, but after five years he was still an instructor without tenure. For a while, Turner was able to deflect outside offers with soothing words and more money, but Phillips's stock was rising, and he knew it. He was too ambitious a man to stay in an undesirable position for long. In 1908, Tulane dangled before him a plum professorship in history and political economy. He could return to New Orleans, where he had spent part of his childhood at the Tulane Preparatory School. He would have easy access to nearby plantations and their moldy manuscripts. He bit.[26]

Before Phillips left Wisconsin for good, he finished a book called *A History of Transportation in the Eastern Cotton Belt to 1860*. Over the strong objections of his publisher, he insisted on dedicating the book "To the dominant class of the South"—who, he wrote, "in the piping ante-bellum time schooled multitudes white and black to the acceptance of higher standards . . . and who in the troublous upheaval and readjustment which followed wrought more sanely and more wisely than the world yet knows."[27]

PHILLIPS DOMINATED THE STUDY OF SLAVERY IN THE EARLY TWENTIETH century, but his interpretation was not the only one available. The implications of his ideas come into sharpest focus when set in contrast to their alternatives—particularly the alternative offered by W. E. B. Du Bois, the one Black scholar who had anything approaching the same stature as Phillips.

As the first Black American to earn a PhD in history, Du Bois represented something new in the United States—a scientifically trained scholar who was not a white man. Before him, there had been educated Black Americans who studied slavery in a scholarly way, but they tended to be ministers or journalists like George Washington Williams. But in the decades since Williams published his *History of the Negro Race in America*, in 1882, the professionalization of history and the social sciences had transformed the US intellectual landscape. Du Bois became the first Black person in America—and basically the only one before World War I—who was able to engage with the new breed of professional scholars from a position of relative equality.

William Edward Burghardt Du Bois was born in 1868 to a free Black family in the North and grew up in Great Barrington, Massachusetts, where he attended integrated schools. At his high school graduation in 1884, he gave an oration on the abolitionist Wendell Phillips. After staying at home for a year to care for his ailing mother, he started college at Fisk University in Nashville. More than a decade earlier, the school's Jubilee Singers had become famous by performing spirituals and other songs across the United States and Europe. The money they earned had built Jubilee Hall and raised the school's profile, turning it into a solid liberal arts college that attracted wealthy Black students from across the South (and, in Du Bois's case, beyond). Du Bois took courses in ancient and modern languages, theology, moral philosophy, history, and natural science. He also received an education outside the classroom. He spent two summers teaching in a rural county just east of town, where he later recalled that he "touched the very shadow of slavery." In Nashville itself, the racial situation was such that students often armed themselves when leaving campus.[28]

Du Bois graduated in 1888 and headed to Harvard. At the time, Harvard was technically open to all men, but cost, concerns about racial prejudice, and the inadequacies (real and perceived) of Black education made it difficult for Black students to attend. Du Bois's Fisk degree counted for only two years in Cambridge, for example, so he had to enroll as an undergraduate (making him one of only two Black students in the college). He concentrated in philosophy, studying with William James, but he also developed a good relationship with the historian Albert Bushnell Hart, who had received his PhD under Hermann von Holst in Germany and encouraged students in his undergraduate seminars to study slavery. The "son and grandson of abolitionists," as he put it, Hart would go on to write *Slavery and Abolition* (1906), essentially a one-volume version of James Ford Rhodes's antislavery account. Hart's course on "The Constitutional and Political History of the United States" focused more on social context than formal structure, and it included one lecture on the conditions of slavery in the South. Du Bois got an A+.[29]

After he got his second bachelor's degree, Du Bois was determined to go on to graduate school. Like white scholars at the time, he was interested in applying social science to the Negro problem, in his case by promoting "the social and economic rise of the Negro people." He received a fellowship from Harvard and embarked on a study of "The Suppression of the African Slave Trade in America." Du Bois's work impressed Hart, who arranged for his student to present at the annual meeting of the American Historical Association—the first Black person ever to do so. In his talk on "The Enforcement of the Slave Trade Laws," Du Bois claimed that the North looked away as thousands of Africans were imported illegally after the formal ban on the trade in 1808. "Here was an audience of white men listening to a black man," the New York *Independent* reported—"listening, moreover, to a careful, cool, philosophical history of the laws which have not prevented the enslavement of his race." It marked an important moment.[30]

Du Bois's next ambition was to earn a German doctorate. He was able to secure a fellowship from the John F. Slater Fund for the Education of Negroes and sailed for Europe in 1892. After spending the summer learning German, singing Wagner, and drinking beer, he enrolled at the University of Berlin, where he worked with the economist Gustav von Schmoller. A practitioner of historical economics, Schmoller believed that economic studies had to be grounded in empirical research, including not just statistical data but history and culture. He suggested that Du Bois do a comparative study of the living standards of German peasants and rural Black southerners. At some point the comparative element dropped out, and Du Bois ended up with a dissertation on "The Large and Small-Scale System of Agriculture in the Southern United States."[31]

Du Bois finished his thesis in December 1893. He needed another semester in residence before he could take his doctoral exams, so he applied for an extension of his Slater Fund fellowship. The trustees denied his request, however, because they did not really believe it was a good idea for Black people to be educated in Europe. They told him to come home to America if he wanted to get a PhD, and they redirected the fund's remaining money to teacher training and school construction.

Forced to return to the United States, Du Bois took a job teaching classics at Wilberforce University in Ohio, the oldest Black college in the country, and revised his Harvard master's thesis on the slave trade to qualify for a doctorate. Hart approved it in 1895 and arranged for Du Bois's dissertation, "The Suppression of the African Slave-Trade to the United States of America, 1638–1870," to be published the following year as the first volume of the Harvard Historical Studies, making it the first book-length work of scientific scholarship by a Black American.[32]

Throughout the book, Du Bois punctured self-congratulatory accounts of abolitionism as a moral movement. He claimed that fear and self-interest were what really drove people's actions, which was why laws to end the slave trade were so long ignored. In his concluding remarks, he could not hide a certain disgust with his fellow Americans: "We have the somewhat inchoate idea that we are not destined to be harassed with great social questions, and that even if we are, and fail to answer them, the fault is with the question and not with us."[33]

This tendency offended Du Bois morally and politically, but also professionally. He had studied philosophy, history, and economics, but he was really a sociologist, the kind of scholar who saw society as a whole. At the time, sociology as a field of empirical research (as opposed to abstract theorizing) was just coming into being as social scientists began to direct their attention to the problems that attended industrialization, urbanization, and immigration. Sociology proved especially attractive to Black scholars like Du Bois, who saw in it a way to study Black social problems and to counter racial theories about innate Black inferiority.

In 1896, Du Bois was hired by the University of Pennsylvania to conduct a sociological study of Philadelphia's Black residents. (He was an untenured assistant and was not allowed to teach; predominantly white colleges would not begin to hire tenured Black faculty until after World War II.) A year later, he spent the summer in Farmville, Virginia, studying a rural Black community for the Bureau of Labor Statistics. Du Bois's Philadelphia and Farmville projects became the first major studies of urban and rural Black communities in the United States, respectively, and also among the first empirical sociological studies of any kind in America, after Jane Addams's work at Hull House.[34]

In both places, but especially the rural southern community around Farmville, Du Bois saw firsthand the ongoing effects of slavery on Black life. This suggested one way to explain racial disparities without resorting to nature: Black people might be poor or have supposedly loose morals, for example, but the reason was the history of slavery, not the biology of race. It also suggested to Du Bois a plan for future work. "One cannot study the Negro in freedom and come to general conclusions about his destiny without knowing his history in slavery," he explained to the American Academy of Political and Social Science a few months after he was in Farmville. Yet he regarded existing studies of slavery as wholly inadequate to the task. He launched into a stinging rebuke:

> The slaves are generally treated as one inert changeless mass, and most studies of slavery apparently have no conception of a social evolution and development among them. The slave code of a state is given, the progress of anti-slavery sentiment, the economic results of the system and the general influence of man on master are studied, but of the slave himself, of his group life and social institutions, of remaining traces of his African tribal life, of his amusements, his conversion to Christianity, his acquiring of the English tongue—in fine, of his whole reaction against his environment, of all this we hear little or nothing, and would apparently be expected to believe that the Negro arose from the dead in 1863.

Du Bois hoped to convince some white university in the North (where the money and the scholars were) to form an alliance with some Black college in the South (where the Black people were) to conduct large-scale sociological research in Black communities.[35] He found no takers. Instead, he ended up trying to do all the work himself.

By that time, Du Bois had moved to Atlanta University, one of the top Black colleges in America. He was hired specifically to build a sociology department there and to continue the school's annual studies and conferences on Negro problems, which had begun in 1896. He later said that his time in Atlanta was when his "real life work was done." He quickly made Atlanta a hub for research about Black life, laying out an ambitious plan for the Atlanta University Studies: ten research topics would be repeated every decade for a century to create a body of long-term data on Black businesses, churches, health, and family. Each year, teams of Atlanta University students, other Black college alumni, social scientists, and community leaders would dive into research and fieldwork on the assigned topic, followed by a conference in May and the publication of a report assembled by Du Bois. Because no one else was doing research on urban Black life on such a large scale, Du Bois was able to attract a slew of talented collaborators, including the early Black sociologists Monroe Work, George Haynes, and R. R. Wright Jr. Just as important, he got leading white politicians and scholars to attend his annual conferences: Georgia governor Allen Candler, Harvard president Charles William Eliot, social workers Florence Kelley and Jane Addams, and anthropologist Franz Boas.[36]

Du Bois believed that racial problems were based in history rather than nature, so his Atlanta University Studies typically included historical sections tracing their topics back to slavery days and even to Africa. These chapters constituted some of the only studies of slave society and slave culture being conducted at the time.

Two major ideas distinguished Du Bois's analysis of slavery in these years. The first was his emphasis on historical dynamism—the dynamism of slaves, whom he recognized as people with their own ambitions and intentions, and of the slave system, which he saw as evolving over time. Along with other economically minded scholars of his day, he identified the rise of large-scale cotton cultivation in the early nineteenth century as the main turning point in the history of American slavery. This fed into the second striking feature of Du Bois's writings on slavery, which was that his analysis was not as relentlessly negative as one might expect. To be sure, he was never in favor of slavery. But the Victorian-minded scholar in him believed that the smaller-scale slavery that prevailed before the cotton revolution had fostered certain improvements in Black life—for example, in the form of increased religiosity and the rise of monogamous families. "One can easily imagine in this development how slavery might have worked itself out for the good of black and white," he wrote in his report on the Negro family.[37]

In 1903, Du Bois published a collection of essays, simultaneously lyrical and empirical, called *The Souls of Black Folk*. The book began with his famous observation that "the problem of the Twentieth Century is the problem of the color line" and went on to sketch a social history of Black America, looking at economics, education, religion, and relations with whites. "How does it feel to be a problem?" he asked, before answering that it yielded what he called a "double-consciousness," a "sense of always looking at one's self through the eyes of others, of measuring one's soul by the tape of a world that looks on in amused contempt and pity." His former adviser, Albert Bushnell Hart, called *Souls* "the only literature published by a Harvard graduate in forty years." It sold ten thousand copies within half a decade, a huge number for a complex and controversial book about race by a Black author.[38]

Two of Du Bois's essays dealt specifically with slavery. The first, "Of the Faith of the Fathers," focused on religion, the same topic as that year's Atlanta University Study. As in his report, he emphasized that Black religion could be traced back to Africa and that it had served under slavery as a source of both submission and compromise, on the one hand, and radicalism and revolt, on the other. In other words, Black religion was integral to understanding the American past. "The study of Negro religion is not only a vital part of the history of the Negro in America," he wrote, "but no uninteresting part of American history."[39]

Du Bois identified "the Music of Negro religion" as "the one true expression of a people's sorrow, despair, and hope," and it was that music which formed the subject of his second essay on slavery. Throughout the book, at the head of each essay, he made a point of pairing a few lines of European poetry with a few bars from a Negro spiritual, placing the two cultural forms on an equal level. The single exception to this pattern was the essay on slave songs, the last one in the book, where the European poetry was replaced by lines from the spiritual "I Know Moon-Rise," the same song Thomas Wentworth Higginson had praised so highly some forty years earlier. (Du Bois seems to have known of Higginson's article and Lucy McKim Garrison's arrangements, but not the book *Slave Songs of the United States*.)[40]

Du Bois sketched an account of the slave songs' historical evolution—one that doubled as an account of American culture itself. In the beginning, he wrote, was primitive African music, the kind sung by his great-great-grandmother, who'd been seized by a Dutch trader some two hundred years before: "Do ba-na co-ba ge-ne me, ge-ne me! / Ben d'nu-li, nu-li, nu-li, nu-li, ben d'le." Du Bois no longer knew what the lines meant, but they had been passed down through his family all the same. The next stage of development was one he called "Afro-American," with songs "of undoubted Negro origin" and "peculiarly characteristic of the slave." Among these he listed "Nobody Knows the Trouble I've Seen" and "Swing Low, Sweet Chariot." The third step started to show the influence of white American culture. The result remained "distinctively Negro," Du Bois noted, as in the songs "Bright Sparkles" and "I Hope My Mother Will Be There," but "the elements are both Negro and Caucasian." Finally, he identified a fourth step of cultural evolution in the rise of white American songs that were influenced by Black melodies, as in "Swanee River" and "Old Black Joe."

"What are these songs, and what do they mean?" Du Bois asked. Against the popular plantation myth of the time, which deployed slave songs as evidence of happiness and contentment, he declared (just as Higginson, Allen, Ware, and Lucy McKim Garrison had decades earlier) that they were in fact "sorrow songs." "They are the music of an unhappy people, of the children of disappointment," he wrote; "they tell of death and suffering and unvoiced longing toward a truer world." At the same time, he saw in them a breath of hope, "a faith in the ultimate justice of things . . . that sometime, somewhere, men will judge men by their souls and not by their skins." Yet with

Black political rights being rolled back and a regime of racial segregation rising all around him, he could not help but wonder, "Is such a hope justified? Do the Sorrow Songs ring true?"[41]

Soon Du Bois was chafing at the constraints he faced as a Black scholar in the South. Scientific scholarship was beginning to seem impotent in the face of racial discrimination and violence, which were pushing him to political activism. A Black man named Sam Hose was lynched and burned outside Atlanta in April 1899, his charred knuckles displayed in a shop window; a month later, Du Bois's two-year-old son, Burghardt, died of diphtheria, which Du Bois blamed in part on his struggle to find a Black doctor; in 1906, a violent white mob, some ten thousand strong, rampaged through the city until "the sidewalks ran red with the blood of dead and dying negroes," as the *Atlanta Constitution* reported.

The same racial environment that produced these problems was also making it nearly impossible for Du Bois to fund his work. One reason for his funding woes was that he had made a public break with Booker T. Washington, the principal of Tuskegee Institute in Alabama, who was the most influential Black man in America. Washington had been born into slavery and believed that the institution served as a civilizing force for Black Americans, a force that needed to continue through the kind of industrial education in manual labor that he championed. This view clashed with Du Bois's desire for Black Americans to gain greater access to higher education and to push for political rights, but it dovetailed nicely with that of many whites at the time, allowing Washington to gain a degree of power. In the world of social science and social work, in particular, white scholars and funding organizations frequently turned to him for advice and approval. With Washington standing in that gatekeeping role, it proved increasingly difficult for Du Bois and his employer, Atlanta University, to attract much-needed money.[42]

In 1906, Du Bois sent the Carnegie Institution an ambitious research proposal requesting at least two thousand dollars per year to fund a series of historical studies of Africa, the Atlantic slave trade, and American slavery, as well as comparative studies of slavery across the Western Hemisphere. He did not get the funding. Instead, it went to one of Ulrich Phillips's friends, Alfred Holt Stone, an amateur scholar who presided over hundreds of Black tenants on his Mississippi plantation. Phillips sometimes visited Stone's property, called "Dunleith," to observe the workings of a modern cotton plantation, and the two men also shared an interest in collecting documentary source material about the economics of slavery.[43]

But Stone concentrated mostly on the contemporary race problem. He believed that feelings of racial animosity were "natural" and "instinctive," as was common at the time, but he thought they could be managed as long as a clear racial hierarchy was maintained. As he told the American Sociological Society in 1907, "The absence of *ante-bellum* racial friction was due to the general acceptance by the negro of the status assigned him by the white race." Stone foresaw the potential for greater friction ahead as the generation of people educated to that kind of "acceptance" under slavery died away. "Why they selected him and neglected an established center like Atlanta University, I cannot imagine," a rueful Du Bois later wrote. He had to subcontract with Stone to get enough funding to carry out his annual Atlanta University Study.[44]

Eventually Du Bois tired of struggling in the South. In the summer of 1909, he participated in the National Negro Conference in New York, which led to the establishment of the National Association for the Advancement of Colored People. A year later, he resigned from Atlanta University to join the NAACP as its director of publicity and research.

Before he left the academic world behind, Du Bois appeared on a panel on southern history at the American Historical Association's annual meeting in New York. His topic was "Some Actual Benefits of Reconstruction"—a nearly heretical idea at a time when William Dunning and his students were describing the era as somewhere between a mistake and a living hell. Black suffrage, usually derided by whites as a disaster, became for Du Bois a signal achievement, marking both the end of slavery (because it gave Black people political power) and the renewal of the South.

With Dunning and Phillips sitting nearby, Du Bois patiently outlined how Reconstruction-era governments based on Black voters gave their states democratic constitutions, free public school systems, and new social legislation, all of which laid the foundation for southern prosperity ever since. "Practically the whole new growth of the South has been accomplished under laws which black men helped to frame thirty years ago," Du Bois concluded. "I know of no greater compliment to negro suffrage."

Dunning sat through Du Bois's talk and praised it afterward, pragmatist that he was. But when Phillips was asked to "speak extemporaneously" in response, he reminded the audience that "post bellum conditions have proceeded directly and problems have been inherited from the ante bellum régime. The people involved have not differed in any way from the general run of people of similar stocks and similar circumstances throughout the world"—seemingly an endorsement of plantation hierarchy rather than multiracial democracy. Indeed, Du Bois later found out that his talk had "greatly exercised" Phillips—as well it should have, because it undermined the assumption of inequality that lay behind his valorization of the plantation as a system of paternalistic racial control.[45] This would not be their last disagreement.

IN THE YEARS AFTER HIS CONFRONTATION WITH DU BOIS, PHILLIPS continued to develop his ideas about slavery and the plantation. After moving to Tulane in 1908, Phillips hadn't stayed there for long. In 1911, he married Lucie Mayo-Smith, the daughter of the economist Richmond Mayo-Smith, who had been a strong force at Columbia during Phillips's years there. Lucie loathed the South. The same year he married her, he took a job at the University of Michigan, which she probably saw as an acceptable stepping stone to Columbia or Yale. She expected Phillips to make a name for himself, so he finally resolved "to leave off the production of isolated essays and stick to some larger project." He began to outline "A History of American Negro Slavery."[46]

At Michigan, Phillips was at best an indifferent teacher: he had no interest in lesson plans, gave little guidance, and probably put away too much gin at lunch for his afternoon classes to be entirely lucid. Still, his teaching provided space for him to think about the plantation: "The plantation system, with its dependence on staple crops, unfree labor, free trade, and local autonomy, is taken as a key to the development and policy of the South," one course description read. For some students, these ideas came as a revelation and could lead to a conversion experience; one graduate student who came from an old abolitionist family switched to southern history after taking a course with Phillips.[47]

Phillips labored for years on his big slavery book, and ultimately he had to return to the South to finish it. In the fall of 1917, he secured a sabbatical and drove to Atlanta, taking his family, his notes, and his draft. The United States had entered World War I earlier that year, so he decided to visit Camp Gordon, a new army base just northeast of the city. The camp housed more Black recruits than any other army camp in the country, nearly nine thousand by the end of 1917. Phillips volunteered almost on the spot to help the Young Men's Christian Association in its educational efforts there, which reached Black soldiers as well as whites. He began by teaching English and French, quickly rose to the position of education director, and eventually spent much of each day rushing around the camp doing a little bit of everything. "This camp work," he told a Michigan colleague, "is the most inspiring thing I have ever experienced." He was enjoying himself and felt as fit as he had in years. His wife tired of the South, however, and returned with the children to Michigan. Phillips, his notes, and his draft stayed in Georgia.[48]

Living in Georgia again reminded Phillips of the basic harmony he felt in southern life, which he attributed to the beneficent influence of plantation organization. He described his experiences at a meeting of the Georgia Historical Association in April 1918. "At Camp Gordon it is a pleasure to be with the negroes," he said, speaking without notes, "for they are, for the most part, plantation negroes, and it is easy to manage them." He saw thousands of them being managed peacefully by relatively few white officers, with none of the riots or mutinies that white Atlantans had feared when the camp was first established. "The spirit of the plantation was that of neighborliness," Phillips explained, "and that again is a thing to be cherished."[49]

When Phillips finished *American Negro Slavery* that year, it ended up being as much a study of the plantation as a history of slavery. He traced the development of the plantation system from the West Indies to Virginia, the Carolinas, and the Deep South. Not all plantations received his approval.

He saw the sugar plantations of the West Indies, for example, as capitalist to the core. They became speculative ventures for absentee investors who managed them with an eye on the bottom line. This led to abuses that Phillips deplored. "The laborers were considered more as work-units than as men, women and children," he wrote. "Kindliness and comfort, cruelty and hardship, were rated at balance-sheet value; births and deaths were reckoned in profit and loss, and the expense of rearing children was balanced against the cost of new Africans."

What distinguished the plantations that developed on the North American mainland, according to Phillips, was the way they fostered mutual respect and affection. He recognized that caring for slaves could amount to nothing more than cold calculation: slaves constituted a huge capital investment, and it paid to keep them fit for work. But he always maintained that the southern slave plantation operated on fundamentally different principles from the modern industrial factory, which he thought sacrificed workers on the altar of efficiency.

According to Phillips, the patriarchal plantation was able to save slaves from the hell of alienated industrial labor because it was more like a loving home than a ruthless factory. As a home, the plantation served important social as well as private and commercial purposes. In fact, Phillips thought, it performed exactly the same social role as Jane Addams's Hull House, which taught poor immigrants how to live in a modern industrial city. "Each white family served very much the function of a modern social settlement," Phillips wrote, "setting patterns of orderly, well bred conduct which the negroes were encouraged to emulate." In training and educating a supposedly backward race to take its place in American society, the plantation was just as progressive as the settlement house—if not more so. Phillips regretted that the laws of slavery resulted in a "lack of any regular provision for the discharge of pupils upon the completion of their training," yet he still concluded that the slave plantation "did at least as much as any system possible in the period could have done toward adapting the bulk of them to life in a civilized community."

Earlier in his career, Phillips had shown that slave plantations became less profitable over time, until finally many planters drowned in debt. He continued to believe that operating a slave plantation in the middle of the nineteenth century made little business sense, and this belief bolstered his growing emphasis on the fundamentally philanthropic nature of the plantation. "Plantation slavery had in strictly business aspects at least as many drawbacks as it had attractions," he wrote.

But the strictly business aspects of slavery were not, ultimately, the point. Slavery's supposed limitations from a capitalist point of view became, for Phillips, a kind of moral virtue. No one expected a school or a settlement house to turn a profit. Similarly, plantation slavery served a role in southern society that outweighed any simple calculation of profits and losses. "In the large it was less a business than a life," he wrote; "it made fewer fortunes than it made men." Phillips knew that slavery had many shortcomings, yet he could not help but admire the society it supported:

> There were injustice, oppression, brutality and heartburning in the régime,—but where in the struggling world are these absent? There were also gentleness, kind-hearted friendship and mutual loyalty to a degree hard for him to believe who regards the system with a theorist's eye and a partisan squint. For him on the other hand who has known the considerate and cordial, courteous and charming men and women, white and black, which that picturesque life in its best phases produced, it is impossible to agree that its basis and its operation were wholly evil, the law and the prophets to the contrary notwithstanding.[50]

American Negro Slavery quickly became the standard history of slavery in the United States. A generation later, it was still assigned regularly in graduate schools across the country.[51]

Still, there were dissenting voices—Du Bois above all. He savaged the book at length in the *American Political Science Review*. "Mr. Phillips' work is not a history of American slavery," he began. Instead, Phillips had written "an economic study of American slaveholders"—a book that amounted to "a defense of American slavery—a defense of an institution which was at best a mistake and at worst a crime." A true "history of slavery," Du Bois declared, would necessarily start from the premise that Black people constituted "a living mass of humanity with all the usual human reactions." It would have to "deal largely with slaves and their point of view."[52]

But such a project would take time. Whatever his faults, Phillips was able to write his history of slavery because he had first spent decades uncovering new sources about slaveholders. Anyone wanting to write Du Bois's history of slavery would need to do the same for slaves.

PART III

REVISION

7

NEW FOUNDATIONS

After Phillips published *American Negro Slavery*, the established avenues of scholarly publication about slavery languished. Yet behind the scenes, a new foundation for the study of slavery was being laid. During the two decades between the first and second world wars, books and articles ceased to be central to the work of studying slavery, but a new energy infused the collection, preservation, and publication of sources, spurred in part by new ideas about race and culture that made it possible to tell the history of slavery from the perspective of the enslaved.

During those interwar years, scholars were saddled with too much teaching and not enough time for research and writing. Progressive Era efforts to expand access to public high school had been so successful that there was now a crush of college students, whose numbers expanded more than fivefold between the wars. Doctoral programs and faculty numbers grew as well, but there was still a lot more teaching to go around. At the same time, faculty salaries failed to keep up with the cost of living. Many professors took on even more teaching in the summers to earn extra money, leaving them with little time for research and writing.[1] Funding problems became more pressing during the Great Depression, and they played an even larger role in the lives of Black scholars, who were still segregated at relatively poor Black institutions.

In addition, once Phillips published his comprehensive synthesis of the subject, no one who agreed with him about slavery was going to do it again anytime soon. Phillips's work fit neatly into the racial consensus that prevailed in US politics in these years. In 1912, for the first time since the Civil War, the Republican Party platform dropped any mention of Black civil and political rights, with President William Howard Taft saying he was fine with Black Americans coming "under the guardianship of the South." Taft lost his reelection bid to Woodrow Wilson, the historian and political scientist who once spent a semester in Baltimore at the same boardinghouse as Frederick Jackson Turner, and who in the early 1900s presided over Princeton at a time when it was the only Ivy League school to refuse to admit Black students. With his victory, Wilson became the first southern president since Reconstruction. He soon oversaw the segregation of the executive branch.[2] For roughly the next quarter-century, until the late 1930s, Jim Crow was generally accepted by the North and rarely questioned in the white South.

During these decades, it was common for American historians to see slavery as a side issue that had little influence on the country's development. In *The Rise of American Civilization* (1927), the most influential general history of the United States of the era, Charles and Mary Beard relegated slavery to a minor role. To the Beards, "slavery was but one element, and if the number of abolitionists is any evidence, a minor element" among the forces that brought on the war. The Civil War was indeed a revolution, they maintained, but the fundamental change wasn't from slavery to freedom. The North was driven by a capitalist desire to exploit the South, not an abolitionist desire to end slavery, and the war primarily signaled a shift from agriculture to industry, which the Beards saw as a much more important transformation in US history. Over the next decade, this interpretation proved tremendously attractive to historians during the Great Depression, when they had a fresh round of reasons to be skeptical of capitalism, and particularly in the South, where some saw the New Deal as another northern invasion.[3]

In the meantime, the collection of sources and evidence about slavery provided a way to study the subject without raising too many contentious questions. This reflected broader trends in the development of the social science disciplines. Social scientific data attained new authority during World War I, when the social sciences became yoked more tightly than ever before to government and business. The ideal of serving society through empirical data continued after the war, when funding came from a new group of philanthropic foundations whose mission was to improve social and economic policy by basing it on neutral, objective facts. To the extent that money was available for the study of American slavery in these years, then, it was for the compilation of sources and evidence.

These collections, in the fields of Black history as well as southern history, formed part of a larger process of cultural modernization in the United States. New forms of transportation, communication, and entertainment (the automobile, the radio, the movies) were breaking down old regional barriers and creating a mass national culture. This process carried in its wake the impulse to preserve aspects of the ethnic and regional cultures that were being erased. Indeed, one way of defining modernism is simply as romantic antimodernism—that is, the discovery and valorization of other groups and cultures as alternatives, with difference not necessarily coded as negative. Only a modern scholar would feel the impulse to collect and preserve evidence about premodern cultures, including the cultures of the Old South and of Black slaves.

The preservation of sources about slavery and the South had been in progress for at least a decade or two before World War I. Indeed, it was a central part of the work that Phillips had been doing since the start of the twentieth century. But it was vastly accelerated during and after the war.

One of the key ingredients in the making of a mass national culture was the movies, and the first modern movie in America was *The Birth of a Nation*. When it came out, in 1915, the film introduced much of the syntax of modern cinema, with fast-paced cuts between different shots. It also marked the moment when moviegoing became a mass experience. More

Americans saw *The Birth of a Nation* than would see any other film for the next fifty years.

What they saw was a historical epic that depicted the Ku Klux Klan saving the United States from the twin terrors of Black political rule and Black sexual violence. The film implied that emancipation was a mistake and celebrated the Klan's violent response to Reconstruction as marking the birth of a reunited nation grounded in white supremacy. The film had intertitles to explain the action—this was the era of silent movies—and it drew them from the work of Woodrow Wilson, then in his first term as president. A screening was arranged for Wilson at the White House, making *The Birth of a Nation* the first movie shown there. "It is like writing history with lightning," the president famously remarked (according to the filmmakers), "and my only regret is that it is all so terribly true."

But not everyone was so impressed. Some Union veterans' organizations opposed what they called the film's "false history," and the NAACP launched a nationwide protest. The group scored a few small victories, including bans in Pasadena and Wilmington, but as with many such campaigns, it succeeded primarily in drawing even more attention to the film. The filmmakers seized the opportunity to offer the NAACP's president a $10,000 prize if he could find any factual mistakes—a fool's errand for a subjective work of fiction—then skillfully deployed Wilson's comment about "writing history with lightning" to claim the historical high ground.[4]

A different mode of resistance developed in Chicago, where an Exposition of Negro Progress celebrating the fiftieth anniversary of emancipation was being held that summer. A Black historian named Carter Woodson was there, hawking books on Black history and photos of famous figures such as Frederick Douglass. At night, in his room at the Wabash Avenue YMCA, he dreamed of starting an organization for the preservation and publication of historical material about Black Americans. His goal was to make "the world see the Negro as a participant rather than as a lay figure in history," as he later put it.

Woodson had recently become the second Black American to earn a doctorate in history, after Du Bois. But unlike Du Bois—and probably unlike any other American ever awarded a history PhD—his parents had been enslaved. His father, James Henry Woodson, worked as a plantation carpenter who was hired out, allowing him to develop some independence, and his mother was a former field slave named Anne Eliza Riddle, whose mother and two brothers were sold to pay their owner's debts.

After the war, Woodson's parents worked as sharecroppers, then managed to buy their own land east of Richmond. That was where Woodson was born, in 1875. He worked on the farm with his six siblings and attended a one-room school for a few months each year. As a teenager, he followed two older brothers to West Virginia to work in the coal mines. There he became friendly with an old Civil War veteran who had a library of books on Black history, including George Washington Williams's *History of the Negro Troops in the War of the Rebellion*. Woodson devoured them all and decided he would devote his life to the subject. He returned to high school at age twenty, then proceeded on a path through Berea College for his bachelor's degree, Chicago for his master's, and finally Harvard for his PhD. It was not an easy journey. Woodson had to earn his way through school and was often teaching while taking classes. At Harvard, some of his professors seemed intent on blocking his progress—including, oddly, Albert Bushnell Hart, who had previously worked with Du Bois. But he eventually received his degree in 1912, at the age of thirty-six.[5]

By the summer of 1915, Woodson had published his first book, *The Education of the Negro Prior to 1861*. He mined sources such as slave narratives and fugitive-slave advertisements to find fragmentary evidence of education under slavery. That July, the book received a glowing review from a sociologist named Robert Park. According to Park, Woodson's book was the first real attempt to show "the negro himself as he was" before emancipation.[6]

Park was based at the University of Chicago, where he taught a course called "The Negro in America"—perhaps the first such course at a white university in the United States when Park started it in 1913. He told his students that he wanted to "get beyond and behind the faces of people we study." He collected notecards full of references to sources that might help him figure out "what the negro was thinking during the 18th century." In other words, he took slaves seriously as human beings, not just as property or as the object of laws and political debates. He recognized that they possessed complex ideas and emotions, and he was interested in discovering how they understood their own lives.[7]

In the summer of 1915, around the time he reviewed Woodson's book, Park decided to organize a conference on Black folklore. His goal was to undermine the negative portrayal of Black Americans in *The Birth of a Nation*. The collection and dissemination of Black folklore could demonstrate Black humanity to whites, he believed, while also instilling a sense of shared culture among Black Americans. Park invited Woodson to his conference, but Woodson passed, explaining that he was not a folklorist.

Yet Woodson recognized that he and Park were thinking along similar lines. He soon got Park on board with his plan for a Black history organization, and in early September, at the Wabash Avenue YMCA, he formally established the Association for the Study of Negro Life and History. Woodson and his organization did not create the field of Black history, which could trace a lineage back through Du Bois to George Washington Williams and William Wells Brown (and even as far back as Anthony Benezet). But he did lay the foundation for Black history as a legitimate and even influential academic field—a field that inevitably fostered new ways of seeing American slavery.[8]

Back in Washington, DC, where he worked as a high school teacher, Woodson quickly started the *Journal of Negro History*, which he would edit for the rest of his life. Starting with the first issue in January 1916, every single edition of the *Journal of Negro History* that appeared under Woodson's watch—which lasted about thirty-five years—included some kind of content on slavery. More often than articles about slavery, Woodson published collections of primary documents that would allow other scholars to approach the subject from a new angle. The first of these, a collection of eighteenth-century writings on slavery by Black men, was printed in the journal's inaugural issue under the title "What the Negro Was Thinking During the Eighteenth Century" (the same heading that also appeared in Park's notes for his "Negro in America" course). Woodson's second issue carried a collection on "Eighteenth Century Slaves as Advertised by Their Masters." Later that year, he followed up with another collection, this time of "Travelers' Impressions of Slavery in America from 1750 to 1800."

Over the next fifteen years, Woodson printed some two thousand pages of primary sources in his journal. They marked the start of a new study of slavery in the United States, providing a window into slave life other than the one offered by slaveholders.[9]

To promote his new association and journal, Woodson sent copies of the first issue to prominent scholars around the country, hoping to gain subscriptions and support. He got that and more from John Franklin Jameson. When Jameson learned about Woodson's new organization, he promptly subscribed to the journal, added his own "small personal contribution," and offered to meet with Woodson at his convenience. "I am warmly interested in the work which you are doing," he added.[10]

Jameson's support had the potential to be extremely valuable; he was the most influential behind-the-scenes figure in the whole historical profession. In 1916, he was managing editor of the *American Historical Review* and director of the Department of Historical Research at the Carnegie Institution, an independent research organization with an endowment of $10 million (more than $300 million today). In those roles and others over the course of his career, he had a hand in an astonishing number of major projects, from the *Dictionary of American Biography* to the National Archives.

Crucially, Jameson had also been interested in slavery almost as long as he could remember. At age seven, he joined his family on a trip to the West Indies and kept a journal of what he saw as he visited sugar plantations with his father. He went on to graduate as valedictorian from Amherst, where he was influenced, like everyone else, by Julius Seelye, but in his case also by John William Burgess, who had spent a few years at Amherst before settling at Columbia. Jameson then moved to Baltimore to begin graduate work at Johns Hopkins. He received his PhD in 1882, making him the first person to get a doctorate in history at Hopkins, and stayed on for several years as an instructor. He was there for Hermann von Holst's visit in October 1883, and then he watched Jeffrey Brackett present the first fruits of his slavery research to the seminar some eighteen months later. He felt inspired. "It was excellent in spirit and execution," Jameson wrote in his diary; "mighty good thing to work up the real history of slavery, and I wish I could take a hand in it."

Eventually Jameson began to chafe under Herbert Baxter Adams, whose ideas of history he found alternately boring and absurd, and whose personality he considered small and petty. In 1888, he moved to Brown, where he would be free from Adams's quirks—and where he began to develop a broader conception of history, one based on people rather than politicians. Yet there always remained a tension beneath the surface of his work, as if the evidence were pointing him one way and he had to make a conscious effort to keep it in check. Politically conservative and somewhat patrician, he never entirely overcame his disdain for the masses, describing the Populists as "a vast horde of unintelligent farmers" and the Jacksonians as "a vast mass of ignorant voters" whose political ideas were "crude and half understood." To his credit, Jameson seems to have recognized this about himself, and rather than publish work that would strain his soul, he devoted most of his career to collecting evidence that would make it possible for others to draw their own conclusions.

And just as he was conflicted about social history, so he was also torn about the significance of slavery. Like Turner and other scholars at the time, he saw American history as essentially continuous if you just sliced out the "foreign body" of slavery. But in contrast to many of his contemporaries, he could never convince himself to write slavery off as a sideline. He may have described it as merely "an episode" in American history, but he always added that it was "an episode of gigantic dimensions."[11]

In 1901, Jameson moved to the University of Chicago, where he acted immediately to incorporate slavery and other social history topics into the curriculum. In his very first year, he arranged to give a graduate lecture course on "The History of American Slavery" in the spring quarter of 1902, one that focused on "the social and economic history" of the subject. This was probably the first course on slavery at an American university. But Jameson taught the course only once more before he resigned from Chicago to take over the Carnegie Institution of Washington's Department of Historical Research, where he could focus on the work he always loved best: publishing historical documents and funding the scholars who might use them.[12]

A decade later, when Woodson sent him the first issue of the *Journal of Negro History*, Jameson was moving his Department of Historical Research into the field of Black history—although almost no one else knew it yet. Up to that point, the Department of Historical Research had specialized in producing archival guides and documentary collections, which were extremely valuable to historians at a time long before online searches and digital reproductions. These kinds of publications provided a foundation for other scholars to build on—and Jameson believed that Black history needed a similar foundation if it hoped to become a body of knowledge instead of an airing of opinions. "A hundred years from now inquiring minds will be eagerly seeking for knowledge of American slavery . . . ," he had declared soon after he first taught his slavery course at Chicago. "Now is the golden time to collect the data, before it is too late."[13]

But he worried that no one else would take on the work. Surveying the field, he saw that surprisingly little had changed since von Holst's visit to Johns Hopkins some three decades earlier—"that while the history of the agitation for the abolition of slavery has been very abundantly recounted," as he later recalled thinking, "comparatively little has been done toward the history of slavery as an actual economic and social institution in America." For scholars to tackle that subject, he knew, they would need "a much larger body of documents made easily accessible." Yet as things stood at that time, it seemed clear to him that no southern university or historical society would take on the work, and neither would the national government. "Therefore," he concluded, "there was a distinct call upon an endowed department like this to fill in this gap in the documentation of United States history."

By the fall of 1915, he had decided to act. He focused first on the slave trade, assigning the project to an assistant named Elizabeth Donnan, who had a degree from Cornell and had been working under him for several years at the *American Historical Review*. Her task was to collect published and unpublished documents that illustrated the operation of the African slave trade to America from its fifteenth-century origins to its nineteenth-century end.[14]

Donnan was just getting started when Jameson began to exchange letters with Woodson in the spring of 1916. Jameson soon mentioned the project to Woodson, along with his plans for an extensive program of future collections focused on slavery, setting up a negotiation during which he and Woodson would divide the world of Black history between them to avoid duplicating their efforts. Because Jameson had a stable budget, he thought his department should focus on big projects that required sustained work over a long period of time. He placed "the case of the laws respecting the negro and slavery" in this category because it would take years "to present all laws or portions of laws relating to the negro and to slavery." Woodson, on the other hand, would be better equipped to handle short-term projects at the local level, such as locating and transcribing documents held in private hands or county courthouses. Jameson considered these local sources essential for illustrating the everyday facts of slavery. "I remember well how much advantage—in the way of local color and vivid and solid reality—my old friend Jeffrey Brackett, when writing his book on The Negro in Maryland, derived from the records of the county courts," he wrote.[15]

This division guided their work over the next two decades, with Woodson focusing on local records and free Blacks while Jameson directed large-scale documentary publications. The first of Jameson's big slavery projects was already under way, with Donnan traveling up and down the East Coast in search of slave-trade material. Soon, Jameson also started a second slavery project, this one consisting of extracts from American law reports. One goal for this collection was to document the development of slave law over time, but Jameson had broader ambitions. Extracts from cases involving slaves would be able to "give us glimpses, and in the mass a pretty large view, of slavery in its actual operation," he explained, in much the same way "as the following of murder cases in our newspapers lifts the roof off from many houses and shows us how some people live." In the spring of 1918, Jameson assigned the project to an older woman named Helen Catterall, the widow of one of his former students at the University of Chicago, who had just finished law school at Boston University.

Meanwhile, Jameson was following the publication of Ulrich Phillips's *American Negro Slavery* with keen interest. He was especially struck by dissenting views of the book from Black scholars and relayed Du Bois's pointed criticisms to Catterall as an example of why her project was necessary. "He declares, to put it briefly, that Phillips whitewashes the whole institution of slavery," Jameson reported, adding, "I rather think he does." Yet given the state of knowledge about American slavery at the time, Jameson believed that there was no way to say for sure. "We shall continue to have merely one man's opinion against another's on what slavery was really like until we bring out a body of evidence that is unimpeachable as representative of the sum total," he told her. This was what his documentary projects were intended to do.[16]

As Jameson anticipated, both Donnan's slave-trade documents and Catterall's judicial reports took many years of work. He liked for them to work slowly; he wanted them to do the work so well that no one would ever have to do it again. Catterall's progress was unexpectedly delayed when she suffered a nervous breakdown and checked into a sanatorium in Wisconsin. (She claimed it had nothing to do with her work.) Meanwhile, Donnan's progress stalled after she began to teach at Mt. Holyoke and then Wellesley in the early 1920s. At times, it proved all too easy for Donnan and Jameson to deploy the metaphor of the long slave voyage for her project. "I suppose that you have put the niggers down in the hold, have battened down the hatches, and are sailing within two points of the wind," Jameson wrote in the middle of one academic year. "You were altogether correct about the present location of the negro cargo," she replied. "They have been stowed away in the hatches so long that I fear to investigate lest I find most of them smothered."[17]

But these comments, however unfortunate, belie the tremendous time and effort that Jameson, Donnan, and Catterall put into their projects, time and effort that they never would have spent if they did not believe that their slavery collections made an essential contribution to American history. Jameson thought the work was so significant that he encouraged Donnan and Catterall to give talks about their topics at American Historical Association meetings—talks that he then published in the *American Historical Review*. As the years of work stretched on, he shepherded things along: smoothing the way with librarians, arranging for copies, and measuring piles of manuscript as they grew.

Even as Jameson pursued his own slavery projects with Donnan and Catterall, he continued to support Woodson's work in Black history. The main problem Woodson faced was financial. Even with his tremendous energy and determination, his organization would fail if it had no money. Woodson himself gave $1,000 to his association in its first two years (at a time when his annual salary as a high school teacher was only $2,000), and he borrowed $400 against his insurance policy to print the journal's first issues.[18] This was not sustainable.

Things improved somewhat when Woodson joined the Howard faculty in 1919. He had an immediate effect, quickly expanding the History Department's offerings from four courses to twenty-two, convincing the trustees to approve Black history instruction, and establishing a master's program in the history and culture of the Negro. But Woodson rarely worked well with others. He clashed mightily with the school's white president, who fired him after only one year.[19]

By this time, however, the landscape of funding for the social sciences in America, and particularly for research about the Negro, was rapidly changing. The reason, in brief, was World War I. The war forced the US government and business interests to act on an unprecedentedly large scale to mobilize troops and production for a conflict halfway around the world. Progressive Era technocrats and efficiency experts believed that the best way to do so was with detailed data. Beginning even before the United States entered the war, there was a national industrial inventory to gather information about the country's production capacity. Social scientists also enlisted directly in the war effort. The American Psychological Association convinced the War Department to use intelligence tests to classify recruits, which had the by-product of generating loads of data that psychologists could analyze later. Among historians, Jameson worked with Frederick Jackson Turner to organize the National Board for Historical Service, which soon left their control to become a subsidiary of George Creel's infamous Committee on Public Information.

These wartime experiences proved that social scientific data could help government and business manage complex problems. And at just that moment, the "Negro problem" suddenly reemerged on the national political scene for the first time since it was handed back to the South around 1890. The war had spurred a massive rearrangement of the US population. With European immigration effectively halted by the hostilities but industrial demand on the rise, Black southerners whose rights had been curtailed seized the opportunity to move north. By 1920, more than three hundred thousand Black southerners had moved to northern cities, a stream that flowed more or less consistently for the next five decades.

This Great Migration, as it became known, had numerous far-reaching effects on American politics, society, and culture. One of the most immediate was to generate racial tension in northern cities that had never seen such large concentrations of Black residents. Lynchings increased in the late 1910s, as did race riots, which peaked in the summer of 1919, when white soldiers were coming back to work and Black soldiers who had experienced precious freedoms in France were frustrated to return to familiar constraints at home.

Woodson found himself in the middle of one such riot that summer in Washington. Returning home one night in July, he accidentally walked into a white mob that was making its way along the street. He hid in a store entrance while it passed. When he stepped back onto the street, he saw that the mob had caught some unlucky Black man, whom they seized and shot. A week later, an even larger riot engulfed Chicago, which had received an influx of some sixty thousand Black migrants during the war. Racial violence raged for nearly a fortnight; thirty-eight people died and hundreds were injured as stores and houses burned.[20]

In the wake of the Chicago riot, Robert Park was appointed chairman of a Joint Emergency Committee that the NAACP and several other Black-welfare organizations established to assist Black residents who had been arrested. Soon the governor set up a separate Chicago Commission on Race Relations to investigate the riot's causes. Park was involved with it, too, and Woodson was brought in to evaluate some of the data. One of Park's most promising Black sociology students, Charles Johnson, wrote much of the final report, which became the first major study of US race relations after the war. It was not the last. Eager for any information that might help them manage race relations peacefully, establishment leaders demanded better data about Black Americans. Money started to flow toward social scientists who were willing to conduct empirical studies of Black life.[21]

Because the federal government gave almost no support to social science research at American universities at that time, the funding came from a handful of private foundations that had been established over the previous two decades, primarily by the Carnegie and Rockefeller families. These new foundations had enough money to reshape US higher education. In 1909, a single Rockefeller organization, the General Education Board, had funding equivalent to one-fifth of all American college and university endowments at the time, and the Carnegie Corporation (separate from the Carnegie Institution, where Jameson worked) spent more money on education in 1913 than did the entire federal government.[22]

In the spring of 1920, as Woodson was on his way out at Howard, his small association was surviving on an annual income of only $6,000. If he was going to keep it alive, he needed access to the new world of foundation funding. Jameson helped him get it, turning on a spigot of money that transformed Woodson's fortunes. First, Jameson got Woodson to submit an application for Carnegie Corporation funding; then he personally recommended Woodson's application to the Carnegie president, who was a friend of his. The corporation's trustees remained wary of giving a large grant to a relatively new organization directed by a Black man, but that difficulty dissolved when Jameson agreed to supervise Woodson's work. This arrangement satisfied the corporation's trustees while preserving Woodson's independence, for Jameson was perfectly willing to leave Woodson alone. The corporation pledged $5,000 per year for five years starting in 1921, nearly doubling Woodson's budget on the spot. He paid off the association's debts and was able to give up teaching to devote himself full-time to the association and the journal. A year later, he successfully parlayed the Carnegie gift into a separate $25,000 grant from the Laura Spelman Rockefeller Memorial.[23]

Woodson's large grants laid the foundation for his work throughout the 1920s. Among other things, they enabled Woodson to spend some of his time collecting manuscripts and other sources about slavery directly from Black Americans. In 1921, he began to survey surviving former slaves and the relatives of former slaves. He gathered information about their food, housing, clothing, and working conditions. In 1925, he also began to collect letters written by Blacks before the Civil War. By the time he held the first Negro History Week celebration, in 1926, he had a large store of sources about slavery and Black history, most of it thanks to his own efforts and to voluntary donations of documents. He displayed these collections at Negro History Week exhibits, hoping they would inspire even more contributions.[24]

Throughout these years, Woodson also had the support of a new constellation of anthropologists, artists, and intellectuals, mostly concentrated in New York, who shared his interest in Black history. In the early 1920s, he began to work with the Columbia University anthropologist Franz Boas, who joined the executive council of Woodson's association in 1922.

Originally from Germany, Boas was a Jewish scholar who had come to believe that racial differences had environmental rather than genetic causes, and that the primary sources of racial inequality were prejudice and discrimination. Like Woodson, Boas was trying, as he put it, to "devise some means of bringing home to the negroes the great achievements of their race." And for him, as for Robert Park, this largely took the form of collecting Black folklore. He saw the study of folklore as a way to demonstrate racial equality because he believed that a sympathetic understanding of a people's folklore could go a long way toward explaining their thought and behavior as the result of culture and society rather than genetics.

Boas had begun this project as early as the 1880s, when he helped found the American Folk-Lore Society and the *Journal of American Folk-Lore*. From its start, the journal was supposed to devote fully one-quarter of its space to Black folklore. The trouble was that most anthropologists and scholarly collectors lived in the North, while the overwhelming majority of Black Americans still lived in the South. Boas and his colleague William Wells Newell, the journal's first editor, had some success with amateur collectors based at southern Black colleges. But these efforts sputtered after a few years, in part because Boas was simultaneously pushing for the professionalization of the field, a cause that cut against the work of amateurs. By the early 1910s, he had begun to use the *Journal of American Folk-Lore* as an outlet for his own students' publications, which usually focused on

American Indians (the subject of much of his own research). Boas urged the collection of Black folklore at American Folk-Lore Society meetings, but he didn't follow through.[25]

That changed with the war and the Great Migration. Among other things, the migration solved the problem of the distance between northern anthropologists and southern Blacks. Now, all Boas and his students had to do was walk down the hill from Morningside Heights to Harlem. At the same time, Boas was censured by the American Anthropological Association in 1919 for his critical views of Woodrow Wilson and the war. After that, he decided to redirect his energy toward publishing Black folklore and training Black graduate students. With the help of a wealthy white anthropologist named Elsie Clews Parsons, Boas made a renewed push in those areas. Starting in 1917, fourteen single-topic "Negro Numbers" of the *Journal of American Folk-Lore* appeared over the next twenty years, many of them underwritten by Parsons. Parsons also convinced Boas to relax his methodological strictures so that they could rely on amateur collectors again, and she developed a lecture on the preservation of Black folklore that she began to deliver to Black groups in Harlem and Black schools across the South.[26]

In the early 1920s, Woodson and Boas briefly sponsored a joint award for the study of Black folklore, but Woodson ended up rejecting most of the candidates as falling beneath his lofty standards. A few years later, in a similar spirit of trying to foster talented Black students, Boas and Parsons sent Woodson a promising Black Barnard College graduate named Zora Neale Hurston. Boas arranged for her to get funding from Woodson to collect Black folklore and interview former slaves in Florida and Alabama. In Mobile she sought out an old man named Cudjo Lewis, who had been born in Africa and was at that point the last known survivor of the last known slave ship to reach the United States. Woodson published Hurston's essay about Cudjo in the *Journal of Negro History*.[27]

The collection of Black folklore was central to the rise of the New Negro movement of the 1920s, also known as the Harlem Renaissance, whose goal was to cultivate race consciousness in pursuit of equality and integration. As artists, writers, and intellectuals created a new Black identity, folklore stood at its center, serving as a symbol and source of cultural pride. Alain Locke's influential *New Negro* anthology of 1925, often considered the defining statement of the movement, included an entire section on folklore as well as a separate essay specifically on the spirituals. The bibliophile and collector Arthur Schomburg's contribution, called "The Negro Digs Up His Past," made the recovery of Black history and culture central to the Black future. "The Negro has been a man without a history because he has been considered a man without a worthy culture," Schomburg wrote. New collections of Black historical sources promised to provide "materials not only for the first true writing of Negro history, but for the rewriting of many important paragraphs of our common American history." A year later, the Carnegie Corporation gave $10,000 to the New York Public Library to buy Schomburg's extensive book collection—the roots of today's Schomburg Center for Research in Black Culture in Harlem.[28]

MEANWHILE, AT THE CARNEGIE INSTITUTION, JAMESON SPENT MUCH OF the 1920s supervising Elizabeth Donnan's collection of slave-trade documents and Helen Catterall's work on judicial reports. It's worth reflecting on the fact that Jameson chose two women to direct these projects. Aside from Lydia Maria Child, Harriet Beecher Stowe, and Lucy McKim Garrison, Donnan and Catterall are the first two women to play a significant role in this history—and the only two women for some time to come. Women's absence before this point is easy to explain: they had little chance to participate in scholarly work. As was also the case with Black colleges, the first major wave of women's colleges didn't open until the third quarter of the nineteenth century. Even then, they weren't as rigorous or research oriented as most men's schools. Nevertheless, some women did absorb the German research ideal that dominated the American academic world. Initially, however, it proved difficult for them to get into American graduate schools. Instead of pursuing postgraduate education, academically inclined women usually had to turn to elementary or secondary teaching.

Facing this lack of opportunities, female college graduates organized in the 1880s to push for greater access to postgraduate education. They were remarkably successful. At the start of the 1890s, women were still largely shut out of graduate school; by the end of the decade, only a few universities prevented female graduate students from enrolling, and a total of 228 women had received doctorates from US institutions (and some had gone to Europe). This is not to say that it suddenly became easy for women to get the same education as men. But it was now possible, at least, for white women from relatively comfortable backgrounds. These women avidly pursued the opportunity. By 1920, women made up 45 percent of all college faculty and students.

The moment when Jameson hired Donnan and Catterall, then, was almost the first moment in American history when lots of university-educated women were floating around the academic world. Still, these women continued to face worse options for academic advancement and less encouragement to pursue independent research than their male colleagues. They remained concentrated at women's colleges or in marginal positions, not on the permanent faculty of research universities, in large part because many men (and some women) continued to believe that even well-credentialed women were less capable of high-level intellectual activity. Jameson's use of Donnan and Catterall to compile documentary collections was in line with this general view. Jameson believed strongly in the enduring value of documentary collections, but they were still less prestigious scholarly productions than writing one's own articles and books, and therefore were suitable for women's work. It may also have been cheaper for Jameson to hire women because he based their pay in part on the salaries at women's colleges.[29]

Yet even this small window of opportunity for women in the scholarly world would soon close. The 1920s turned out to be a high-water mark for women in higher education; after Donnan and Catterall, no woman would make a major contribution to the study of slavery for many years. Over the next three decades, women's percentage of the total college student population declined, while their representation on college faculties stalled. There were several reasons for these trends, including discrimination in hiring practices and the lingering belief that women's education should be directed toward domestic concerns. As American universities and doctoral programs expanded in the 1920s, women's colleges lost prestige, and men's enrollment in higher education outpaced women's. Then, during the straitened circumstances of the 1930s and early 1940s, women were more likely to forgo college, and universities facing tight budgets became even less likely to hire them as professors. Finally, after World War II, women's numbers in higher education were dwarfed by the sudden influx of soldiers going to school on the GI Bill. The number of female students began to tick up again in the 1950s, but representation on faculties lagged. It was not until the 1970s that women regained the same presence in American higher education that they had attained, briefly, some fifty years before.[30]

It's possible that Jameson chose Donnan and Catterall to conduct the slavery collections because, on some conscious or subconscious level, he thought that women would be seen as less threatening than men when researching and writing about a controversial subject such as slavery. But in at least one instance, even Donnan's ladylike demeanor and her project's "colorless" quality (as Jameson put it) were not enough to secure her access to a private archive. This was the case with the Brown family of Rhode Island, best known as the benefactors of Brown University, who were at that time still extremely sensitive about the fact that some of their ancestors had been involved in the slave trade. Jameson and Donnan tried for years to gain access to the Brown family papers, but they faced repeated rejections and delays. "It is unfortunate that Miss Donnan's interest should be in the slave trade," the head of the John Carter Brown Library eventually wrote, adding, "Under the present circumstances it is better that the situation should not be discussed."[31]

Jameson probably would have kept pushing for Donnan to gain access to the Brown papers, but soon he faced bigger problems of his own. For the better part of a decade, he had been butting heads with his boss at the Carnegie Institution, a paleontologist named John Merriam, who believed that Jameson's documentary projects were not scientific enough to merit funding. In 1927, Merriam played his trump card, informing Jameson that he would not be allowed to work after he hit the mandatory retirement age in two years—and that funding for Jameson's Department of Historical Research would then be redirected to fieldwork in Mayan archaeology. Jameson was distressed, but less for himself than for the slavery projects, whose future was now up in the air. After several months of internal negotiations, he managed to secure funding for the slavery publications going forward. With that done, he promptly jumped ship a year early, joining the Library of Congress as chief of manuscripts.[32]

Despite their differences, Merriam honored his pledge to maintain funding for Jameson's slavery projects. It helped that both Catterall and Donnan were close to the finish line. During a productive sabbatical year in the late 1920s, Donnan arranged her material into three volumes, later spilling over to four, which appeared in rapid succession from 1930 to 1935. Putting it all together, she realized now, if she had not before, that the mass of evidence she'd managed to assemble proved that the slave trade played a central role in making the modern world. It was the "big business" of the seventeenth and eighteenth centuries, she saw, a global trade that spurred new corporate practices, caused world wars, exploited the resources of a whole hemisphere, and provided the foundation for English industrial growth. "It accomplished the largest human migration the world has ever seen," she concluded, "and it has left a set of social problems as yet unsolved."[33]

Meanwhile, Catterall had published the first volume of her *Judicial Cases Concerning American Slavery and the Negro* in 1926. No less an authority than Ulrich Phillips was impressed. "The introductions are excellent, and the editing beyond reproach," he wrote.[34] A second volume followed three years later, a third volume another three years after that.

Even though Jameson was no longer associated with the Carnegie Institution, he remained deeply invested in the slavery projects he had started. When Catterall passed away in the fall of 1933, leaving two volumes of her *Judicial Cases* series unfinished, he jumped into the breach. First, he solicited recommendations for an editor to complete her work; then he found someone new when the original replacement turned out to be a dud—and worked alongside him throughout late 1934 and early 1935 to make sure that the final volumes maintained Catterall's high standards.[35]

At almost the same moment as Jameson was completing the manuscripts for Catterall's volumes, Donnan published the final installment of her *Documents Illustrative of the Slave Trade*. When Jameson got his copy, he seems to have been overcome by emotion. One major part of his life's work was reaching its end. "Surely there never was a finer piece of work done in the making of any book of documents for American history . . . ," he told Donnan. "I am proud to have had a hand in starting the series."[36] His pride was merited. His Carnegie projects helped remake the study of slavery in the United States, allowing scholars to see the workings of slavery and the slave trade in incredibly fine-grained detail.

By this time, southern history was coming into its own as an academic field—the Southern Historical Association was established in 1934—and Jameson, now in charge of manuscripts at the Library of Congress, faced significant competition for the collections he was hoping to acquire. "The old plantations are no longer the happy hunting grounds for the Division of Manuscripts," he reported after one collecting trip, "for Hamilton and Boyd and other energetic persons, scouring South Carolina in their own cars have gathered most of what is to be salvaged at all."[37]

He was referring to J. G. de Roulhac Hamilton and William Boyd, two former students of William Dunning at Columbia who had then taken jobs down the road from each other at the University of North Carolina and Trinity College. Both schools had been transformed in the 1920s by massive infusions of money, in Trinity's case from the Duke family of tobacco barons and philanthropists, who paid generously for the school to remake itself as Duke University, and in Carolina's from the new social science foundations, which invested in the school as a laboratory for the study of the American South. The centerpieces of these growing universities were their libraries, in particular their collections of southern historical documents, which took shape in rivalry with each other.

As was often the case in the competition between the schools, the most significant developments occurred in Chapel Hill. Hamilton started teaching there in 1906 and soon began to drive around North Carolina collecting old manuscripts, which he'd been dismayed to find scattered in private hands while he was researching his dissertation on Reconstruction in the state. He flipped through local phone books in search of historically significant surnames and stopped at any old plantation house that looked as if it might have a trunk of papers collecting dust. He wanted everything, even documents and letters that donors thought worthless, because, as he later wrote, "the run-of-the-mine stuff is more important and interesting."[38]

The pace of Hamilton's collecting increased significantly in the 1920s, when he started to receive money from the university's Institute for Research in Social Science. Run by the sociologist Howard Odum, who had his own long-standing interest in Black folklore, the institute owed its existence to a large grant from the Laura Spelman Rockefeller Memorial. With funding from Odum's institute, Hamilton dreamed of building what he called a "national southern collection" in Chapel Hill and began to extend his trips beyond the state's borders. Driving around the South in his Ford, Roulhac Hamilton gathered so many documents that he earned the nickname "Ransack" from detractors who didn't like to see all the region's historical records flowing to North Carolina.

When the university opened a grand new library in 1929—the first fireproof library on campus—Hamilton finally had a suitable place to house his prized collection. That same year, a donation of $25,000 from the philanthropic Kenan family secured stable funding. Hamilton became the founding director of the Southern Historical Collection when it was established as an official part of the university library in January 1930, and he devoted the rest of his life to it. Soon southerners stopped complaining that Hamilton was "ransacking" their states and started celebrating his achievement.[39]

Hamilton's Southern Historical Collection later became central to the study of slavery in the United States. Hamilton anticipated this and welcomed it because it would vindicate his acquisition of everyday records that few other collectors considered important. "If ever there is written a definitive history of African slavery in America," he believed, "it will be largely based upon southern material of this sort in which its realities appear."[40]

At the time, though, Hamilton's Southern Historical Collection, like many other growing archival collections in the South, could be hard for Black scholars to access. Across the region, a patchwork of Jim Crow laws, paired with inconsistent interpretation and enforcement, made it nearly impossible for Black scholars to predict exactly what would happen when they arrived to do research. Some libraries required a formal referral; many placed Black patrons at separate tables or in separate rooms. In nearly all cases, white librarians had latitude to make life either a little easier or a lot harder for any Black researchers who showed up at their desks. In Chapel Hill, where Jim Crow laws formally prevented Black scholars from sitting in the same reading room as whites, Hamilton was known to give some Black historians access to the stacks, where they could do their work safely out of sight. (Even so, Black women had to walk across campus to find the nearest restroom that was open to them.) In other cases, Black scholars could gain furtive access to valuable sources through the good graces of a Black janitor, who would smuggle material out in the evening and place it back on the shelves in the morning without anyone being the wiser.[41]

The Library of Congress, in contrast, was open to all without discrimination. This was one thing that made it an attractive institution to Carter Woodson and also allowed it to be the site of yet another fruitful collaboration between Woodson and Jameson during Jameson's tenure at the library in the 1930s. As chief of the Division of Manuscripts and chair of American history, Jameson accelerated the library's transition from the research branch of Congress into a national cultural treasury. Notably, he focused his efforts in part on collecting the papers of abolitionists and plantation owners. He was particularly interested in acquiring "records of old plantations as would serve to illustrate the economic history of the ante-bellum South," he told one contact. His acquisitions not only helped make the Library of Congress a leading center for the study of slavery and abolition but also established that those subjects merited an important presence in the nation's cultural memory.[42]

Jameson was eager to acquire documents from Black Americans, and Woodson was eager to supply them—provided, as always, that he could find some funding for the project. Building on his collection efforts from earlier in the 1920s, when he began to interview ex-slaves and gather documents from Black families, Woodson now dreamed of getting a large foundation grant that would allow him to hire field-workers to canvass the South for sources. In 1928, he drew up a proposal for "An Exploratory Effort to Collect Manuscript Materials Among Negroes." The Social Science Research

Council approved the project in 1929, awarding Woodson a one-year grant of $4,000. He collected more than 2,500 documents, a haul that he promptly deposited with Jameson at the Library of Congress.[43]

When Woodson turned to the Rockefeller Foundation for additional funding, the foundation awarded him $10,000 for one year. (Ulrich Phillips and Roulhac Hamilton both recommended giving him the money.) Characteristically, Woodson then submitted an even more ambitious proposal directly to John D. Rockefeller Jr., requesting $50,000 to fund a three-year collection project. In his proposal he explained that the goals of the collection were "to make possible the study of the social and economic conditions of the Negro from authentic documents which unconsciously disclose the whole truth in contradistinction to most literature of the sort now available" and "to improve interracial relations by acquainting the public with the inner life of a people long seen but hitherto given little attention and, therefore, misunderstood and despised."[44]

As usual, Jameson wrote a strong letter of support, noting that Woodson had already deposited a valuable trove of documents at the Library of Congress, including "a bill of sale of a slave of Thomas Jefferson." If Woodson had the means to continue his work on a larger scale, Jameson added, he could "make here a very rich collection such as I do not know of as existing elsewhere." But the Rockefeller Foundation awarded Woodson less than half the money he asked for. It also required a matching contribution, which Woodson generated by laundering his own salary into anonymous donations.[45]

This was the last major white foundation grant that Woodson would receive. His own ornery insistence on independence was partly to blame. The number of Black college students had increased by a magnitude of ten over the previous decade—another result of the Great Migration—and foundations responded by shifting their priorities from funding independent organizations like Woodson's association to pouring money into Black institutions of higher education. Not wanting to duplicate efforts or fritter away funds, the foundations warned Woodson that he needed to affiliate his association with a Black college if he hoped to keep receiving money. But Woodson refused, preferring to maintain his autonomy.[46]

Then, with the onset of the Depression, the big foundations reduced their budgets and became leery of large commitments. Now that their pockets were not quite as deep, they wanted to ensure that their limited resources went to projects that would have practical applications. They ceased their practice of providing fluid, open-ended research funds to universities and other organizations, and shifted to funding specific projects aimed at identifying concrete solutions to contemporary problems.[47]

Woodson's Black history work didn't fall into that category. By 1935, he was struggling. He hadn't had any major infusions of grant money in several years, leaving him to rely for the first time on small donations from Black Americans. "We are living on the nickels and dimes received from those Negroes who are not yet in the bread line," he told Jameson. But it wasn't enough. "We must have other help," he went on, laying out his reasons for submitting yet another proposal to the Rockefeller Foundation to fund "our former project of collecting manuscripts for the Library of Congress." Jameson quickly sent his usual letter of support, this time noting that with the recent completion of the Carnegie Institution's slavery projects, "Dr. Woodson's Association" now stood alone as "the chief means of promoting that line of study."[48] But no funds were forthcoming.

Undaunted by his failure to secure new grants, Woodson continued to collect Black history sources throughout the 1930s. His pace slowed considerably without any dedicated funding, but by 1941, he had deposited a total of some five thousand documents at the Library of Congress.[49]

YET WOODSON'S DONATION WAS NOT THE MOST IMPORTANT SET OF SOURCES about slavery to become available at the Library of Congress that year. Instead, that distinction belonged to the Slave Narrative Collection—more than two thousand interviews spanning some ten thousand pages—which represented the culmination of this era of collection and preservation.

Jameson, who had been overseeing the library's accumulation of sources about slavery, did not live to see it. He had hoped to make it to the age of ninety before enjoying cigars and gin for the rest of his life, but he did not quite reach that promised land. In March 1937, at the age of eighty-seven, he was hit by an automobile outside the library. He appeared to make a full recovery, but then he got pneumonia and died. Woodson wrote an admiring obituary calling him "one of the greatest promoters of the study of the Negro."[50]

Woodson had started to interview some surviving ex-slaves in the early 1920s, but it is a striking fact about the study of slavery from emancipation to World War I that former slaves were rarely consulted as sources. At the time, historians also ignored antebellum slave narratives or dismissed them as abolitionist propaganda. Instead, they relied largely on the writings and reminiscences of the master class while lamenting that "the lives of the American slaves are without annals," as Ulrich Phillips told his students. As late as 1930, more than a hundred thousand people who had been enslaved were still living, but almost no one had put their experiences on record.[51]

It was only in the late 1920s that efforts to collect testimony from ex-slaves expanded beyond Woodson's interviews. These new collecting projects grew out of the developments of the previous decade: the Black scholarly reaction against the plantation ideal, the renaissance of Black culture after World War I, recent anthropological and sociological interest in studying Black culture, the growth of Black colleges, and the rise of foundation funding for empirical studies of Black life. Then, during the Depression, the collection of ex-slave interviews increased exponentially thanks to a new and unprecedentedly large source of money and manpower: Franklin D. Roosevelt's New Deal.

Systematic interviews with former slaves started at Fisk University. In 1927, Fisk got a five-year, $200,000 grant from the Laura Spelman Rockefeller Memorial to hire new faculty and increase its research activity in the social sciences, with the idea that the school would focus its work on race relations. The memorial's leaders then ensured that Charles Johnson, the student of Robert Park who had worked on the Chicago Commission on Race Relations after the 1919 riot, would be hired away from the National Urban League to lead the program. Johnson used his large stream of funding to establish a Social Science Institute, probably based on Park's Local Community Research Committee at Chicago (also funded with memorial money), and began to study the Black community around Fisk's Nashville campus.

These were the first sociological studies of the Black South since Du Bois's Atlanta University Studies a generation before.

Johnson and his students relied heavily on personal interviews for their work. They soon realized that they were talking to lots of older Black people who retained memories of slavery. Recognizing the value of these firsthand accounts, Johnson's team expanded their interviews to cover rural Tennessee, Kentucky, and Alabama. The interviews were stored in the Social Sciences Department at Fisk, where at least one professor began to use them in his work.[52]

At the same moment in the late 1920s, another Black scholar, John Cade, also began to lead his students in interviewing formerly enslaved Black Americans in the area around Southern University in Louisiana. Thirty-six students conducted a total of eighty-two interviews, and Cade summarized the answers in an article aptly titled "Out of the Mouths of Ex-Slaves," which appeared in Woodson's *Journal of Negro History*. The interviews included enough detail about punishments and family life to undermine any simplistic view of slavery as benign. "In no phase of slavery do we find it more cruel and heartless than in family relationships," Cade wrote, before presenting stories of broken families, forced marriages, and rape. Cade and his students then conducted hundreds more interviews after he moved to Prairie View, near Houston, in the mid-1930s.[53]

By that time, the collection of ex-slave testimony had also become a federal project. One of Charles Johnson's students at Fisk, Lawrence Reddick, had gone on to become a Negro history professor at Kentucky State Industrial College. In 1934, Reddick approached the director of one of the big New Deal relief agencies, the Federal Emergency Relief Administration (FERA), with a proposal "to study the needs and collect the testimony of ex-slaves." Johnson and Woodson both supported the proposal, which resulted in the first government-sponsored attempt to interview former slaves. Reddick supervised more than 250 interviews and presented a paper on the use of slave testimony at the Association for the Study of Negro Life and History's annual meeting in 1936.[54]

FERA was intended as a temporary agency and was gone by then. But some of its work was being continued by a new agency, the Works Progress

Administration, that was established as the Depression dragged on. Among the WPA's many activities was the Federal Writers' Project, whose purpose was to provide work for unemployed authors—including the likes of Richard Wright, Ralph Ellison, and Zora Neale Hurston. Eventually the Writers' Project grew to nearly 6,700 employees spread across all 48 states, and its main product was a nationwide series of state guidebooks, some of which became classics.

In the course of producing those guidebooks, Writers' Project employees conducted a lot of local research, including the collection of folklore and oral history. In the South this meant they encountered a lot of former slaves. The Georgia office started to purposefully collect autobiographies from ex-slaves in 1936, and the Florida office—which employed Zora Neale Hurston—was doing the same. Some of the Florida interviews were sent to national headquarters early the next year. They landed on the desk of the WPA's folklore consultant, John Lomax, who immediately recognized their value.[55]

Lomax was a white folklorist who remains best known for his collections of cowboy songs, including "Home on the Range" and "Git Along, Little Dogies." But his interest in Black folk music ran just as deep. He had recently been traveling to southern prison farms and penitentiaries with one of his sons to record songs from elderly Black inmates, which they then deposited in the Library of Congress's new Archive of American Folk Song. (It was on one of these trips that they discovered Huddie Ledbetter, better known as Leadbelly, at a prison farm in Louisiana.) Lomax was just a few months into his role with the WPA when he saw the ex-slave interviews that some Writers' Project workers were starting to conduct. Based on his long experience as a folklorist and collector, he drew up a list of "detailed and homely questions" designed to "get the Negro interested in talking about the days of slavery": *Where and when were you born? Describe your home and the "quarters." What work did you do in slavery days? Tell about your master, mistress, their children, the house they lived in. How many acres on the plantation? How many slaves on it? Was there a jail for slaves? Did you ever see any slaves sold or auctioned off? Now that slavery is ended what do you think of it?* The list went out to Writers' Project workers, and by the summer of 1937, the collection of slave narratives had become a systematic project across the southern and border states.[56]

Over the next year or so, before the WPA redirected its resources elsewhere, the Writers' Project collected more than two thousand ex-slave narratives. This amounted to roughly one-third of all American slave narratives in existence. A by-product of the process was that the Writers' Project practically invented the field of oral history in the United States.

In 1939, the WPA shifted from federal to state control, and most state Writers' Project offices sent their ex-slave interviews to the Library of Congress. A library folklorist named Benjamin Botkin spent two years supervising the organization of the material into seventeen volumes of typescript in the Rare Books Division, where they became known as the Slave Narrative Collection. Botkin then condensed those seventeen volumes into a single three-hundred-page book intended to bring the narratives to a broader audience. He called the resulting anthology "a folk history of slavery."[57]

From a scholarly point of view, Botkin knew that the WPA's ex-slave interviews suffered from severe limitations: the amateur interviewers, mostly whites, often betrayed their own prejudices, while their Black informants sometimes exaggerated, dissembled, or simply misremembered. Still, Botkin claimed, even as "a mixture of fact and fiction" or "a kind of legendary history," the narratives had significant value. He found that they revealed the slave "as an individual rather than a type, a person rather than a symbol, with normal sensibilities and intelligence, portrayed as only the Negro can portray his own kind." To him, the narratives demonstrated with visceral reality that enslaved people always retained a will of their own in the face of their owners' attempts at control: "It is this stubborn and rebellious will—tragic, heroic, defeated, or triumphant—that, more than all else, haunts us, as it haunted the master."

Botkin was clearly moved by the narratives, which seem to have taught him about not only slavery but also humanity. As he reflected, "From the memories and the lips of former slaves have come the answers which only they can give to questions which Americans still ask: What does it mean to be a slave? What does it mean to be free? And, even more, how does it *feel*?"

Yet few other scholars at the time saw what he did. His anthology of excerpts, *Lay My Burden Down*, proved to be a popular success upon its release in 1945, going through eight printings over the next twenty-five years. But historians still avoided the narratives, which were hard to use (there was just that typescript at the Library of Congress) and widely viewed as unreliable. It was only a generation later, in the wake of the civil rights movement, that scholars would begin to cite the interviews more extensively in their work.[58]

8

THE PROBLEM OF SLAVERY

DURING THE GREAT DEPRESSION AND WORLD WAR II, SOME OF THE fundamental assumptions behind American slavery scholarship changed. The most important of these shifts, one that was absolutely foundational to all future writing about American slavery, was the decline of scientific racism—the belief that Black people were innately inferior to whites. Implicitly or explicitly, this idea had long grounded much American slavery scholarship, which often took it for granted that Black people had certain natural racial characteristics that suited them—at least temporarily, if not permanently—for enslavement.

By the end of the interwar years, this belief dropped away for many educated Americans. The shift came slowly and then all at once, the result of a confluence of intellectual, political, and economic changes. Sharp immigration restrictions implemented in the early 1920s relieved American anxieties about foreign bloodlines, while the rise of cultural modernism and a surging economy reduced the sense that different races and ethnicities were engaged in a zero-sum struggle for survival. Then, when the Depression hit, it left no groups unscathed. Failure was so widespread that it became untenable to argue that it was the result of racial causes. Yet only toward the end of the 1930s, when the Nazis stepped up anti-Jewish legislation and violence as they prepared to expand across Europe, did various learned organizations publicly declare that there was "no scientific basis for discrimination against any people on the ground of racial inferiority," as one statement read. This marked the symbolic end of scientific racism as an acceptable belief among educated Americans.[1]

The idea that racial differences were at root cultural rather than biological had several important corollaries when it came to the study of slavery. First, historians could no longer rely on the explanatory power of supposedly innate racial characteristics. Instead, they would need to investigate the cultural inheritance of the different groups that entered into their stories. Second, the kinds of negative social traits that once would have been blamed on the Negro's supposed animality or sexuality or laziness could now be laid at the feet of slavery itself. This meant that slavery had to be examined almost sociologically, in terms of the roles and relationships the system created, and the ways it enabled certain human impulses while suppressing others.

None of this was news to Black scholars and some older white scholars, who had been approaching the subject in this way for decades. But it was only during World War II and after that new political, social, and intellectual pressures opened the way to a full-scale reinterpretation of slavery. What some of these pressures were, and how they worked, can be seen most clearly in the Carnegie Corporation's Negro Problem Study, which got started in the late 1930s and ended up having a huge influence on American ideas about slavery and race in the postwar period.

The Carnegie Corporation was one of the wave of new foundations supporting social science research in the early twentieth century. From its start in 1911, it funded Black education in the South, and in the early 1920s, it gave money to Carter Woodson for his Black history work. Outside the United States, it also sponsored two large-scale studies of race relations in Africa. In the early 1930s, one of the corporation's trustees, Newton Baker, began to wonder whether it should do similar work in America. The son of a Confederate officer, Baker lived in Cleveland, where he saw that the Great Migration was making the "Negro problem" into a national problem. Amid the ongoing economic distress of the Depression, he was concerned about the potential for racial unrest in northern cities such as New York, where there was a riot in Harlem not long before the Carnegie trustees assembled in the city in the fall of 1935.[2]

After Baker raised his concerns with other trustees at that meeting, the corporation's head, Frederick Keppel, began to plan for a US race-relations study along the lines of the ones the Carnegie Corporation had already funded in Africa, with one project director supervising a large team of researchers. After considering some American options for the project director, Keppel ultimately decided to pick a European scholar to ensure that the project would be seen as unimpeachably objective. He landed on a Swedish sociologist named Gunnar Myrdal.

Myrdal arrived in the United States in the fall of 1938. He had been there once before, in the early 1930s, for a Rockefeller-funded study of politics and economic theory, an experience that instilled in him a deep admiration for American democracy. But he had no background in race relations. This was more or less what the Carnegie trustees wanted, but it meant that Myrdal had to rely heavily on his team of American researchers and informants. Working out of the forty-sixth floor of the Chrysler Building in midtown Manhattan, he used his lavish budget of several hundred thousand dollars to assemble an all-star team of more than fifty researchers. One of them was Melville Herskovits, a Jewish anthropologist who had studied with Franz Boas at Columbia. Another was E. Franklin Frazier, a Black sociologist who had studied with Robert Park at Chicago. Both men had been investigating the historical background of Black America for about a decade, but they had come to strikingly different conclusions. Frazier became friendly with Myrdal and influenced the study, while Herskovits ended up in a fight and did not.[3]

Frazier's scholarly specialty was the Black family, which he'd begun to study in the late 1920s at Chicago. Because the family was a primary social institution for forming individual roles and personalities as well as passing down customs and traditions, Frazier saw it as the best unit for studying "the assimilation of the Negro and his adjustment to modern civilization" in America. In his assessment of Black assimilation and adjustment, Frazier was particularly influenced by the ideas of his mentor, Robert Park. In an early article called "The Conflict and Fusion of Cultures," Park wrote that "the Negro, when he landed in the United States, left behind him almost everything but his dark complexion and his tropical temperament." No other immigrants to America, Park went on, "have been so utterly cut off and estranged from their ancestral land, traditions and people."[4] Frazier agreed with Park's claim that Black Americans had lost most of their African past. This emphasis on cultural loss meant that he placed a large interpretive weight on the experience of slavery in the forging of Black society and culture.

Frazier finished his book *The Negro Family in the United States* in 1939, just as the Myrdal study was getting under way. For his information about the Negro family in slavery, he drew in part on the ex-slave interviews conducted by Charles Johnson and his students at Fisk, where Frazier taught for a few years in the early 1930s. He did not see it as impossible for strong slave families to take shape, particularly in situations where patriarchal slavery prevailed and masters showed some regard for their slaves' moral development, religious instruction, and marital bonds. Yet he placed greater weight on all the social and economic forces that worked to make slave family life fragile: the loss of traditional norms regarding sex, marriage, and family; the imbalance of male and female populations that made permanent pairing difficult; the practice of forced mating for slave breeding; the prostitution and rape of enslaved women; the economic imperative for women to return to the fields soon after giving birth; and the looming threat of sale and separation.

Frazier's analysis of the slave family amounted to an attack on Ulrich Phillips and the broader phenomenon of plantation nostalgia. In contrast to Phillips, who saw slavery as an economic drain but a social benefit, Frazier believed that slavery on large plantations was an economic boon that proved socially destructive. On large cotton plantations, according to Frazier, slavery became "a purely industrial institution" where slaves "were treated more like cattle." Even the most stable slave families remained "always insecure," he wrote. "No matter how far the moralization of the slave went, his group life, including his most intimate relations in his family, could not resist the fundamental economic forces inherent in the slave system."[5]

Myrdal thought Frazier's book on the Black family was excellent, agreeing that Black culture retained few African influences. But Melville Herskovits strongly disagreed. Herskovits thought Frazier was wrong to assume "that all African patterns have been completely forgotten," as he glossed Frazier's book, "and that only the tradition of slavery remains as background." He believed that this error about the Black past had huge social and psychological ramifications, ramifications that continued to constrain the Black present and future by fostering discrimination among whites and demoralization among Blacks.[6]

As part of Myrdal's team, Herskovits wrote a lengthy research memo summarizing the African influence on Black American culture. But Myrdal disagreed with Herskovits about the extent of that influence, and about the proper scope of the Carnegie study, and he grew tired of what he saw as Herskovits's irrational obsession. "Mel Herskovits is rather crazy at present," Myrdal complained to another researcher. "He sees everything in the light of African inheritance." Frazier, for his part, would push for downplaying Herskovits's claims in Myrdal's final report, and Herskovits's memo itself was cut entirely—but it did not end up at the bottom of a drawer. When Germany invaded Denmark and Norway in the spring of 1940, Myrdal hurriedly returned to Sweden, and his project was placed on hold. In the meantime the Carnegie Corporation decided to publish some of his team's research reports as separate books. Herskovits made sure that his was one of them. It was published in 1941 as *The Myth of the Negro Past*.[7]

According to Herskovits, the "myth" was that the Negro had no past—that Black Americans derived from the childlike dregs of savage African societies, and that whatever culture they may have brought with them was replaced by Euro-American models that they imitated under slavery. He believed that this historical void was what licensed the idea of Black inferiority and allowed slavery to be portrayed as a school for civilization. A proper appreciation of the true Negro past, he believed, would improve both Black self-esteem and white attitudes toward Black Americans. His whole book amounted to a lengthy and at times heated account showing complex, highly developed African cultures as well as people who resisted enslavement and who, despite the destructiveness of the Middle Passage and the plantation, nevertheless retained important African influences in their social structure and cultural life.[8]

Herskovits's ideas about African cultural survivals gained few supporters over the next twenty-five years. Frazier and some other scholars attacked him—not only because they believed that he exaggerated the evidence for African survivals but also because they worried that his emphasis on a distinctive Black culture would strengthen the case for segregation. Frazier thought it was naive to believe, as Herskovits seemed to, that proving Black people had a separate "cultural past" would somehow elevate their status in American life. In fact, Frazier suspected something closer to the opposite would be the case: "Is he not saying that even more fundamental barriers exist between blacks and whites than are generally recognized?"[9]

Meanwhile, Myrdal was able to return to the United States in 1941. He spent a year digesting his team's research memos and cobbling together his final report, which stretched to more than a thousand pages. Myrdal had been hired to write a study of the "Negro problem," but he found that Black Americans were not the problem at all. "Little, if anything, [can] be scientifically explained in terms of the peculiarities of the Negroes themselves," he wrote. "As a matter of fact, in their basic human traits the Negroes are inherently not much different from other people." Instead, Myrdal believed that the "problem" resided in the minds of white Americans, who faced a troubling tension between two sets of commitments. On the one hand, he said, all white Americans harbored some level of anti-Black prejudice. On the other hand, they all believed in what Myrdal called the "American creed": ideals such as freedom, justice, equality, dignity, and opportunity. White Americans might exclude Blacks from society and see them at times as a menace, according to Myrdal, but they simultaneously felt guilty about those actions because they also knew, on some level, that they were violating their deeper commitment to equality and opportunity. Thus the title of his study: *An American Dilemma*.

Because Myrdal was interested in the dilemma that racial prejudice posed in the minds of white Americans, he saw slavery's most important legacy as the idea of Black inferiority itself. It was the need to defend slavery as it expanded across the cotton belt in the wake of the Revolution,

Myrdal believed, that gave rise to a racial doctrine whose main purpose was to shield slavery from the incompatible principles of the American Creed. "*The need for race prejudice is, from this point of view,*" he explained, "*a need for defense on the part of the Americans against their own national Creed, against their own most cherished ideals.*" It was this powerful "heritage of slavery," according to Myrdal, that was the heart of the American dilemma.[10]

Myrdal was writing as the United States entered World War II. In rhetoric and reality, the war amounted to a defense of democracy, and particularly multiracial democracy, against authoritarianism and racial oppression. Myrdal believed in American democracy, and he saw his book as part of the US war effort. Slavery had become associated with foreign dictators, whose regimes were seen as a kind of political enslavement. The United States, in contrast, defined itself as the leader of the free world, displaying its ideals of liberty and equality around the globe.

But the war also dragged American racial discrimination into the global spotlight. Myrdal called such discrimination "America's greatest and most conspicuous scandal," and he saw it as the biggest obstacle to American leadership in the postwar world. Even as American soldiers fought for freedom, their regiments remained segregated—to the extent of having Jim Crow blood banks. At home, racial conflicts erupted in Detroit and Harlem in the summer of 1943, the largest episode of racial violence in more than twenty years. "For its international prestige, power, and future security," Myrdal wrote, the United States "needs to demonstrate to the world that American Negroes can be satisfactorily integrated into its democracy."

Myrdal was confident that this would be the case. He outlined all the improvements he saw as a result of the Great Migration and the New Deal. In the North, where a growing number of Black Americans lived, they had voting rights and equality before the law. In the South a rising group of racial liberals stressed the "equal" part of "separate but equal," or even questioned the Jim Crow system as a whole. New Deal programs brought new public services to Black people while sending liberal-minded federal officials across the country, where matters previously defined as local, including race relations, fell increasingly within their purview. The same federal courts that started to uphold the constitutionality of New Deal policies also proved less willing to allow the South to restrict Black civil and political rights. For the first time in more than forty years, Black Americans began to see the federal government as an ally that might not only define the rights of citizenship but also defend them.

World War II served as a crucial test of Black integration into American democracy. With the war framed explicitly as a fight between freedom and slavery, the circumstances could hardly have been more favorable. Before the United States even entered the war, A. Philip Randolph's March on Washington movement pressured President Roosevelt into issuing an executive order barring discrimination by defense contractors. An exuberant Randolph went so far as to call the order a "Second Emancipation Proclamation." It wasn't quite that, but it did mark the first direct presidential intervention on behalf of Black civil rights since Reconstruction—no small thing. Then, when the fighting began, the "Double V" campaign for victory over fascism both at home and abroad made the stakes even more urgent.

For the war to have meaning, Myrdal believed, America and its allies had to stand for the freedom and equality of all peoples. Glancing forward to a postwar world in which the United States would be competing with communist Russia for the allegiance of people of color across the globe, he suggested that nothing less than the future of democracy hung in the balance: "The development of the American Negro problem during the years to come is, therefore, fateful not only for America itself but for all mankind."[11]

Published in two volumes in 1944, *An American Dilemma* proved massively influential. It went through four printings in its first year, and its ideas underpinned nearly every project on race relations in the postwar period. Along with the experiences of the Depression and the war, Myrdal's work helped stamp segregation as un-American and antidemocratic, a failure to live up to the country's true ideals. Soon, President Truman created the President's Committee on Civil Rights. In 1947, its final report, *To Secure These Rights*, officially declared, for the first time since Reconstruction, that the federal government had the responsibility to secure the civil rights of its citizens.[12]

As the federal government began to put its weight behind desegregation, it also started to acknowledge the negative side of slavery—in part so that it could point to the progress that had been made, and was still being made, in race relations. In fact, it turned out that one paradoxical effect of wartime rhetoric about American freedom and democracy, including Myrdal's emphasis on the American Creed, was to highlight even more starkly the seeming anomaly of American slavery. Recently seen as benign, now it began to appear that slavery in the United States must have been horrible, perhaps even uniquely so, if its effect had been to exclude Black Americans so lastingly from full democratic citizenship.

In this view, slavery and segregation began to be seen once again, for the first time in about a generation, as major problems in American political and intellectual life. They no longer reflected a supposedly natural racial order. Instead, as aberrations from American ideals of democracy and equality, they required new explanations. And they also acquired new explanatory power of their own: with the decline of heredity as an explanation of racial difference, what other causes could account for the inferior social status of Black Americans? History, especially the history of slavery, held the key.

BY THAT TIME, IN THE MIDDLE OF THE 1940S, A SUBSTANTIALLY NEW INTERpretation of American slavery was starting to emerge out of the scholarship of the previous few decades. And not just a new interpretation of slavery, but a new interpretation of Black history as a whole. But there wasn't yet a book that put it all together. Meanwhile, starting in the 1930s and accelerating during World War II, Black activists and parents were pushing for new textbooks that didn't reproduce racial stereotypes.[13]

Roger Shugg, an editor at Alfred A. Knopf's College Department, recognized the opportunity. In 1944, he commissioned a manuscript from the Black historian Charles Wesley, who had received his PhD from Harvard two decades earlier and had worked for a while with Carter Woodson. But when Wesley submitted his manuscript, Shugg was disappointed. He didn't know quite what to do, so he consulted with Woodson and with Arthur Schlesinger Sr., a history professor at Harvard. Schlesinger pointed Shugg to a Black student of his who had recently finished his PhD and was then teaching at a Black college in North Carolina: John Hope Franklin.

Originally from Oklahoma, Franklin had followed roughly in Du Bois's footsteps by first attending Fisk and then going on to Harvard—where, thanks to recent investments and improvements at Fisk, Franklin became the first graduate of a historically Black college not to have to repeat parts of the undergraduate program. He worked his way through school, doing odd jobs like dishwashing and typing, and even took a year off to teach before he was able to secure some fellowships. He then taught again at Black colleges in Raleigh and Durham while he was writing his dissertation on free Blacks in North Carolina, which he completed in 1941.

Franklin represented something new in the world of Black historians: not an amateur like George Washington Williams, not an "advocate" like Du Bois and Woodson, but a consummate professional, working fully within the structures and standards of the scholarly game. He made African American history into an implicit argument for integration by showing that it had always been embedded in the broader story of American history. And he embodied that in his own life and career, too, becoming friendly with white historians, publishing in mainstream journals, and attending—sometimes integrating—the conferences of the major historical organizations. He would go on to become the first Black chair of a department at a historically white college, an event that made the front page of the *New York Times*.

It was at the end of World War II, while Franklin was teaching in Durham, that Shugg came calling about the Black history book. Initially, the idea was for Franklin to join the project as coauthor, but Charles Wesley wanted no part of that and promptly withdrew. So Shugg offered Franklin, then just thirty years old, a chance to write the book on his own, saying that it would satisfy "an urgent and widespread need."[14] Franklin agreed and got to work.

Knopf hoped to have the book available by the fall of 1947, just eighteen months away, so Franklin had to write extremely fast. He had already been teaching some Negro history courses, which may have helped him organize the material quickly. Even so, the library at North Carolina College for Negroes contained only two prior examples of what he was trying to do: a book by Carter Woodson called *The Negro in Our History* and the two volumes of George Washington Williams's *History of the Negro*, a work that Franklin hadn't even known existed.

Nevertheless, he wrote with astonishing speed. Within months, he was able to send Shugg the first five chapters of his book and an outline of the rest. Then, using the first half of his advance—only $250—he moved to Washington for the fall to do research at the Library of Congress. By December, he had drafted ten more chapters and outlined the entire book. By January, another ten chapters were on paper, and the rest were finished within just a few more months. The production of the book, by this time titled *From Slavery to Freedom*, was so compressed that Franklin was reviewing proofs of his opening chapters while he was still writing his final pages. But the whole thing miraculously came together in time to be published on the eighty-fifth anniversary of the Preliminary Emancipation Proclamation in September 1947.

Somehow Franklin had managed to write nearly a quarter-million words in little more than a year. And not only did he write them, but he did it so well that the book received strong reviews for its balanced take—this at a time when whites often assumed that Black scholars could not maintain the requisite neutrality on racial topics. The book sold a few thousand copies and soon entered the curriculum at several dozen historically Black institutions across the South. More important, *From Slavery to Freedom* helped give the field of Black history a new legitimacy just as liberal white scholars were starting to pay more attention to the subject.[15]

Because of the conditions of its composition, Franklin's Black history survey necessarily relied on existing scholarship. This proved particularly problematic in the sections on slavery. Many of the slavery studies that Franklin consulted struck him as "inadequate and inconclusive," to the point that he was "quite hesitant to use them to any great extent." But drawing on some old Johns Hopkins studies, Donnan's slave-trade documents ("monumental"), Du Bois's scholarship, and even Ulrich Phillips, Franklin was able to piece something together. His book showed the slave trade—first transatlantic, then domestic—as the big business of its day, and it portrayed life in "That Peculiar Institution," as he titled his chapter on antebellum slavery, as unpleasant for everyone involved, whites as well as Blacks. It was a brutal system focused on economic gains, Franklin maintained, one that "bred indecency" rather than civility. "Few of the four million slaves in 1860 led anything except the most barren existence in which their only moments of pleasure were in the singing of a plaintive melody, the strumming of a banjo, the telling of a tale, or the playing of a game," he concluded. Yet he also emphasized that enslaved Blacks never lost their desire for freedom, and he left no doubt that slavery was the root cause of the Civil War.

This was a solid short survey of American slavery. Still, Franklin could not help but feel unhappy with it because he knew there was still more work to be done. "I believe that any satisfactory generalizations on the subject will have to wait until many more careful studies of the subject have been made," he lamented.[16] But he would not be the one to do it.

The study of slavery in the civil rights era was rife with ironies. One of them was that even as scientific racism became intellectually indefensible, as American society and the American academy became more open to Black participation, and as white scholars became more interested in Black history, the number of Black scholars in the field declined precipitously. Woodson died in 1950, Du Bois in 1963, and by that time, the early Black scholars they had inspired and supported in the 1910s and 1920s were nearing the end of their careers. Some of the most important organizations that funded Black graduate education in the interwar period, such as the Rosenwald Fund and the General Education Board, shut down soon after the war. The benefits of the GI Bill went largely to white men, and the overall proportions of both Blacks and women in higher education fell. The Harvard History Department—which had educated Du Bois, Woodson, and John Hope Franklin—graduated no Black doctorates between 1941 and 1956.[17]

When this generation of Black scholars did go to graduate school, they tended to have limited financial support (because of the Depression) and to be older (because of the war), and they graduated into a world where their employment prospects were limited to poorly funded Black institutions with heavy teaching loads. Scholars with doctorates were in high demand at these schools and were quickly given full professorships or sucked into administrative duties. In no case was there much incentive or support for research. It was not until 1956, when Franklin was hired at Brooklyn College, that a Black historian received a full-time appointment at a historically white school.

Meanwhile, the same sense of racial progress that pulled some white scholars into the field of Black history paradoxically pushed Black scholars away: they no longer felt the same moral and political obligation to put Black history to work. Throughout much of the 1930s and 1940s, Black scholars completed more than 80 percent of all dissertations on Black subjects at US universities. By the 1950s, however, with integration the order of the day among liberal scholars, Black students often took the opportunity to study other subjects.

Sometimes this was a political choice, a matter of proving that Black scholars could study anything they wanted, and sometimes it was pragmatic, for avoiding Black history meant also avoiding potentially segregated libraries and archives in the South. Another consideration was the job market—which, for Black scholars who were just starting to have serious opportunities beyond historically Black colleges and universities, dictated choosing dissertation topics that would sell in any climate. When one Black student, Nathan Huggins, went through the history program at Harvard toward the end of the 1950s, he chose to study Boston charitable organizations—despite his strong interest in Black history—because he didn't want to be pigeonholed and also because he believed that the charity topic would make him a better candidate for jobs across the country. (He got one in southern California.) Huggins and others received encouragement in this ambition from white scholars who wanted to support their Black students in branching out—or who, in some cases, continued to voice concern that Black people could not be properly objective on topics related to race.[18]

Thus, just at the moment when doctrines of scientific racism were collapsing, when the experience of the Depression was encouraging greater egalitarianism, when World War II was making slavery and segregation seem like problems instead of solutions—at the moment, in other words, when new space was opening for the study of American slavery, white scholars were the ones to do it.

The democratization of American higher education began at least a generation before the GI Bill of 1944. By the interwar period, the Progressive Era expansion of public secondary schools was yielding a larger pool of college applicants and growing college enrollments. The raw number of college students quintupled between the wars, and the percentage of the college-age population that was enrolled more than tripled. It's worth noting that as larger numbers of students finished high school and went to college in these years, their textbooks and much of the latest scholarship were still teaching them to see slavery as a beneficent institution that was ultimately a side issue in American history.

Much of the increase in the student population came from white men, but in percentage terms Black college enrollment gains actually led the pack—largely as a result of the Great Migration, which gave Black migrants and their children access to better educational opportunities in the North and West. Still, the proportion of college-age Black Americans who were enrolled continued to lag significantly behind, and most of those who were in school attended all-Black institutions in the South, which became so overcrowded that they had to turn people away.

The doctorate was also becoming democratized. Instead of having most history PhDs come from a handful of schools—Johns Hopkins, Columbia, Chicago, Harvard, and a few others—there were now many more strong departments graduating good scholars, most notably at a rising group of state universities in the Midwest, West, and even the South. And at the elite schools, the graduate-student demographics were changing as the sons and grandsons of Jewish immigrants, who had their own experiences with discrimination, started to get in the door.

The annual number of history PhDs more than doubled in the second half of the 1920s, then grew by another quarter through the 1930s. These annual increases compounded year over year, such that the number of history doctorates awarded in the fifteen years from 1926 to 1940 was more than double that of the previous five decades combined. Meanwhile, despite the financial crunch of the Depression, faculty positions continued to increase as schools tried to keep up with growing enrollments. The result was an exceptionally rapid generational change in history departments across the country as freshly minted graduates gained employment in large numbers.

The effects of a generational shift are often exaggerated or even invented, but in this case they were real and significant. This cohort of young professors came of age during the Depression and saw its effects every day. They had a strong egalitarian streak and were not inclined to attribute failure to any inherent ethnic or racial traits. They eagerly adopted the environmentalist views of race that were becoming more prevalent among educated Americans over the course of the 1930s.[19]

Having come of age when the capitalist system was experiencing its most spectacular collapse in history, this younger generation was sympathetic to alternatives. They joined the Communist Party or at least attended Communist meetings—at a time when Communists were the primary political group in America committed to complete racial equality. While older professors sometimes ignored current events, even in economics courses, the younger generation gathered in informal study groups to read Marx and, later, to discuss the Spanish Civil War. These proved to be central, formative experiences in their lives. The Radical Left later fragmented when the Nazi-Soviet nonaggression pact became public in 1939, then largely evaporated amid the tense witch hunts of the early Cold War. But the legacy of 1930s radicalism remained—if not in public policy, then certainly in the lives and ideas of the people who took part.[20]

Several members of this cohort proved particularly significant for the study of slavery in America. Comer Vann Woodward, who went by Vann, was among the oldest of this group, and his early work helped set the stage for the others because he did more than anyone else to put the study of southern history on a new course. Born to a former slaveholding family in Vanndale, Arkansas, he graduated from Emory in 1930, at the start of the Depression, and then got a fellowship to study at Columbia. In New York he fell in with a mixed-race crew of Communists and radicals. "No one could escape it entirely in the 1930's," he later recalled of Communist influences. "It was all about, even in the South in those days." He didn't join the Communist Party, but he visited the Soviet Union in 1932 and came away committed to working for greater equality in America. Back home in Atlanta, where he was teaching, he briefly became involved in the defense of Angelo Herndon, a Black Communist Party organizer who was charged under an old insurrection statute intended to prevent slave uprisings.[21]

It was with this background that Woodward turned to history. He wanted to write a biography of the southern populist politician Tom Watson, and because Watson's papers were held in the Southern Historical Collection at Chapel Hill, Woodward enrolled in graduate school there. In his classes he found the previous generation of southern historians invariably stale and obsessed with vindicating their ancestors' virtue, and he bristled at the pro-segregation stance of older professors such as de Roulhac Hamilton. In despair, he spent his time pacing Franklin Street and hanging out with the radicals who congregated at Ab's Intimate Bookshop.[22]

It may have been at Ab's that Woodward picked up a copy of Margaret Mitchell's sensationally popular Civil War novel *Gone with the Wind* almost as soon as it came out in the summer of 1936. A journalist in Atlanta, Mitchell based the book on stories about the old days that she'd heard from friends and relatives. Chock-full of plantation nostalgia and bitter Reconstruction memories, it was a novel in which the southern white women make houses into homes while the southern white men raise good cotton, ride well, shoot straight, and dance lightly. The most memorable of the "darkies" is Mammy, "shining black, pure African, devoted to her last drop of blood to the O'Haras," and often described primarily in terms of her ponderous breasts. When the book's white heroine, Scarlett O'Hara, encounters other Black people who have become free after the war, she thinks of them as "black apes" and "monkeys" who have been set up by devilish Yankees "to terrorize Southerners." Ultimately a Democratic governor ends Negro rule and redeems the state for "her own people," and the novel concludes with Scarlett yearning for Mammy's "broad bosom" and "gnarled black hand" as her "last link with the old days."[23]

Woodward didn't make it that far in his own reading. He quit after about a hundred pages, dismissing the novel as a tawdry story "about how a tart little bitch gets all the men in North Georgia in a rut." Nevertheless, it became the best-selling book in the country for two years in a row, and then the movie made the story popular all over again. Something about its depiction of the southern struggle for survival during the Civil War appealed to Americans in the depths of the Great Depression. The story also reflected, in simplified and exaggerated form, the common sense of the country regarding slavery, the Civil War, and Reconstruction—particularly in the South, where many whites saw slavery as a happy time, the Civil War as a senseless slaughter, and Reconstruction as a tyrannical intervention in southern life that was thankfully undone by Redeemers who reinstated white rule and laid the foundations for the southern regime which persisted to that day.[24]

It was precisely this kind of writing about the South that Woodward was reading in his history courses and finding wrongheaded, making him fear that he had ended up in a field with no future. But instead of giving up, he found a way forward. Woodward may have been training to become a historian, but in his heart he saw himself as part of the Southern Literary Renaissance—William Faulkner, Thomas Wolfe, and Robert Penn Warren, writers who were beginning to trouble the dogmas of southern history. In his Tom Watson biography, which he completed in 1937, Woodward played up Watson's outreach to Black voters in the late nineteenth century to make a point about the neglected possibilities of interracial politics. Later, in *The Origins of the New South* (1951), he sharply criticized the so-called Redeemers at a time when their reaction against Reconstruction was being celebrated as a way to shore up white-supremacist policies and resist federal interference.

With those books, Woodward opened up southern history to a fresh blast of analysis and critique. At the same time, he knocked an important prop out from under the regime of segregation by redefining its founders from Redeemer heroes to corrupt capitalists.[25] This was one significant step toward a new history of American slavery.

WHAT WOODWARD STARTED WOULD NEXT BE TAKEN UP BY TWO YOUNGER historians who approached the problem of slavery together during World War II. Richard Hofstadter and Kenneth Stampp first met in the fall of 1942, when they were both hired as young professors at the University of Maryland. On the day they met, Stampp recalled, they walked to a drugstore near campus "and sort of looked at each other suspiciously": Stampp was a German from the heartland, and Hofstadter was a half-Jewish New Yorker with a Jewish wife. Meeting in the midst of World War II, they didn't know what to make of each other.[26]

But it turned out that their backgrounds were remarkably similar. Stampp was a few years older. Born in 1912 in Milwaukee, he grew up in a community of German Social Democrats. Milwaukee had a Socialist mayor throughout Stampp's youth, his local congressman was the only Socialist in the House of Representatives, and his family subscribed to a Socialist newspaper. Starting as a Social Democrat, Stampp turned even more radical at college during the Depression. He went to Young Peoples' Communist Party meetings and had friends who plotted revolution. Stampp never joined the Communist Party—he tended toward pacifism and could not endorse violence—but he later described himself as a "fellow traveler" in those years.[27]

Stampp's story must have reminded Hofstadter at least a little of himself. Four years younger than Stampp, he came from a lower-middle-class German neighborhood in Buffalo. He also fell in with left-leaning groups during the Depression, in his case at the University of Buffalo. By temperament he was not much of an activist, but his girlfriend and later wife, Felice Swados, certainly was, going so far as to call for a dictatorship to end American capitalism. After they moved to New York City later in the 1930s, they attended Young Communist League meetings together, and they also briefly joined the Columbia graduate school unit of the Communist Party—Hofstadter until the Moscow trials in early 1939, Swados until the Hitler-Stalin pact a few months later.[28]

At Maryland, Hofstadter and Stampp became fast friends. They lunched in each other's offices as they wondered about the future of capitalism and fascism in America. Theirs were the sorts of conversations in which FDR was criticized for being too far to the right, the New Deal for supporting the capitalist structure. Soon Stampp and Hofstadter were so close that their families found apartments in the same complex in Hyattsville, a suburb between College Park and Washington, DC.

Stampp and Hofstadter enjoyed each other's company, but they disliked a lot of things about Maryland. The school and the whole society were segregated, the university president was a despot, and the year-round wartime teaching schedule was relentless. They were determined to publish their way out. In Stampp's case, that meant going down to Washington every Tuesday, Thursday, and Saturday to do research at the Library of Congress and the National Archives. On one of his early trips to the city, he took a detour to visit Carter Woodson, who at that time was still running the Association for the Study of Negro Life and History and the *Journal of Negro History*. Stampp told Woodson about his master's thesis on the antislavery movement in the South and pitched a couple of spin-off articles, which Woodson was happy to take for the next two issues of the journal.[29]

Back at Maryland, Stampp and Hofstadter's conversations eventually led into the history of slavery. Not long before the Hofstadters arrived in Maryland, Hofstadter's wife, Felice, who wrote medical and science columns for *Time*, published an academic article questioning the common assumption that masters had an interest in keeping their slaves healthy. From her reading of antebellum medical journals, she saw striking evidence of diseases such as tetanus, pneumonia, rheumatism, and dysentery among slaves. "The popular conception of the slaves as a sleek, robust, hearty group, enjoying a high degree of welfare on the old plantations, is false," she concluded. Slave sickness was not only "a major economic problem" in terms of lost days and doctors' bills; it was also, more importantly, "a grave human problem, one which casts a heavy shadow on the conventional picture of idyllic plantation life."[30]

This was the basic tenor of Hofstadter and Stampp's conversations about slavery scholarship. Having absorbed modern ideas about race and Depression-era epiphanies about equality, the young men felt they could see straight through the tattered premises and prejudicial assumptions of the "plantation legend." In the spring of 1944, they both put their ideas on paper.

Stampp's article came first. Called "Our Historians and Slavery," it appeared in an early issue of Dwight Macdonald's short-lived publication *politics*. The heart of the essay was a review of a recent book called *American Negro Slave Revolts*, which was representative of a new development in slavery scholarship during the second half of the Depression. The book's author was Herbert Aptheker, a young historian who had begun to research slave revolts in graduate school at Columbia in the late 1930s, at the same time as he was joining the Communist Party and engaging in efforts to combat peonage. As a Communist, Aptheker was primarily interested in uncovering a revolutionary working class, but studying slave revolts also served for him as a way to challenge the prevailing interpretation of slavery as a beneficent institution. Where Ulrich Phillips maintained that American Negroes "were more or less contentedly slaves," Aptheker claimed to have found evidence of some 250 revolts in the two centuries before the Civil War. He finished his dissertation in 1942 and published it the following year, its title a conscious echo and refutation of Phillips's *American Negro Slavery*.[31]

Aptheker's work was part of a surge of interest in slave revolts in the late 1930s and early 1940s, which took shape in direct response to rising labor activism during the Depression. Two students at Northwestern, Raymond and Alice Bauer, produced the most perceptive of the slave-revolt studies by examining everyday activities such as malingering, breaking tools, and slowing down. These actions had long been attributed to the Negro's supposedly slothful, careless, and deceitful nature, but with the decline of scientific racism, they needed a new interpretation. The Bauers saw them as a form of "day to day resistance" that allowed enslaved people to live in outward compliance with the overpowering slave system while still mounting some measure of protest and "indirect retaliation." In this view, the Bauers concluded, the Negro slave "was not a cheerful, efficient worker, as has been assumed. Rather, he was frequently rebellious, and almost always sullen, as any person faced with a disagreeable situation from which he cannot escape will normally be."[32]

In his review, Stampp praised Aptheker and the new wave of slave-revolt studies for challenging one of the central props of the pro-slavery argument: the notion that slavery effectively solved all labor problems and class struggles through the harmonious relationship of master and slave. "The very foundation of this allegation is destroyed," he wrote. Perhaps the Old South was less a land of easy laughter and love than a dreadful place of "perpetual terror."[33]

Hofstadter's article on slavery scholarship appeared a month later in the *Journal of Negro History*. While Stampp attacked the previous generation of slavery scholarship somewhat obliquely, through a review of a new and (he thought) better book, Hofstadter took direct aim at Phillips and the "plantation legend." He began with a narrow critique of Phillips's reliance on data from the largest plantations in the Old South, which he showed were not representative of American slavery as a whole. But this technical point didn't really get to the heart of the problem. In the final pages of his essay, Hofstadter mounted a broader assault on Phillips's romantic view of the Old South, describing Phillips's work as "a latter-day phase of the pro-slavery argument." He ended with a plea for some young scholar, some scholar from his own generation and with his own sensibilities, to write a new history of slavery:

> Let the study of the Old South be undertaken by other scholars who have absorbed the viewpoint of modern cultural anthropology, who have a feeling for social psychology (a matter of particular importance in the study of a regime in which status was so vital), who will concentrate upon the neglected rural elements that formed the great majority of the Southern population, who will not rule out the testimony of more critical observers, and who will realize that any history of slavery must be written in large part from the standpoint of the slave—and then the possibilities of the Old South and the slave system as a field of research and historical experience will loom larger than ever.[34]

Not yet thirty years old, Hofstadter was still building his reputation as a historian (and fishing for a job somewhere other than Maryland), and he sent copies of the article to established scholars across the country. Remarkably, he received at least nine responses. All agreed that his takedown of Phillips was long overdue. "It was about time that something be done to deflate Phillips's special approach to the Southern plantation," Arthur Schlesinger Sr. replied.[35]

On the question of how to start a new history of American slavery, however, the responses were considerably more mixed, revealing latent tensions that would eventually surface as the study of slavery moved to the center of US historical scholarship over the next few decades. "Why 'must' the history of slavery be written 'in large part from the standpoint of the slave'?" one historian asked. "Is there a danger, in pointing out the limits of Phillips' view on the negroes, in going too far in the other direction?"[36]

If there was, Hofstadter would not be the one to find out. Although he showed some interest in race and slavery early in his career, any future in the field got short-circuited by circumstances largely beyond his control. As his article on Phillips went out into the world, he learned that his beloved wife had cancer. The Hofstadters moved back to Buffalo to be near family, and he cared for Felice as she declined over the next year, finding relief only by throwing himself into a new project—a book of essays about major American political figures—that he could write using the inadequate resources of the Buffalo Public Library. Felice succumbed in the summer of 1945, around the time that Hofstadter got a book contract with Knopf and a new job at Columbia. He moved back to New York and soon published his book of essays, *The American Political Tradition*, which became one of the most popular history books of the postwar era and made him perhaps the most influential academic historian of the age. He never developed his critique of older slavery scholarship into something more.[37]

Around the time Hofstadter left Maryland for Columbia, Stampp received his own offer from the University of California. At the time, Berkeley was so far removed from the rest of American intellectual life that Stampp didn't know quite where it was. (He guessed southern California.) Upon his arrival, however, he discovered with relief that California was not purgatory but paradise. He would always remember his first glimpse of the Bay and the Golden Gate Bridge, and he mostly stayed within sight of them for the rest of his life.

By the spring of 1948, Stampp was finishing up his second book, a study of the coming of the Civil War, and was casting about for a new topic. He had digested Myrdal's *American Dilemma* by then, and it helped give him a more solid foundation for his belief in the fundamental equality of whites and Blacks. In his courses, however, he continued to assign Phillips's books on slavery and the Old South, as nearly every American history professor in the country did, because there weren't any better options available. To some extent, Stampp turned this to his advantage, making it into what we call a teachable moment. His undergraduate lectures on the Old South amounted to a lengthy argument against Phillips, and he peppered his graduate seminar with the suggestion that somebody needed to write a new history of slavery.

Then, one day, a student finally called him on it: "Well, why don't you write it?" Surprisingly, the notion of writing a book about slavery had never occurred to Stampp. There were two reasons for this odd blind spot. The first was that slavery was still regarded as a topic for southerners, and Stampp thought any substantial revision of Phillips's interpretation of slavery would need to come from another southerner in order to avoid being tarred as the work of a northern abolitionist. The second reason was that Stampp saw himself as a political historian, but he considered slavery to be a "strictly nonpolitical" subject. This may seem like a strange stance from someone who had recently described slavery as "the most explosive issue dividing the nation and the focal point among many sectional irritants," but it reflected the profound influence of the previous generations of historians who had successfully separated slavery from politics in US historical writing.[38]

Stampp eventually got over those mental hurdles and began to read everything he could find about slavery in the Berkeley library. By 1950, he was ready to make a statement about the subject. At the American Historical Association's annual meeting in Chicago, he announced the start of a new era: "No historian of the institution can be taken seriously any longer unless he begins with the knowledge that there is no valid evidence that the Negro race is innately inferior to the white, and that there is growing evidence that both races have approximately the same potentialities." In his view it was impossible any longer to maintain that slavery was a school for the civilization of Black slaves or that Black slaves were a virtual necessity in the South because they worked better than whites in the subtropical climate. This kind of "loose and glib generalizing" on questions of race and slavery needed to be swept away, he said, ideally through a fresh round of research that viewed the sources at least in part from the perspective of the slaves. Stampp's slavery talk appeared in the *American Historical Review* in April 1952. Hofstadter predicted that it would have "pretty profound repercussions."[39]

At the same time, Stampp won a Guggenheim Fellowship, allowing him to spend the next academic year making his way to as many southern archives as he could. In the fall, he and his family returned to Hyattsville, the DC suburb where they'd lived in their Maryland days. Stampp spent most of his time going through newspapers and manuscripts at the Library of Congress and the National Archives. He lunched with a group of historians at the Supreme Court cafeteria, one of the only spots near the Library of Congress that wasn't segregated. This was important on principle and because the group included John Hope Franklin, who was then teaching at Howard. Among liberal historians, Franklin was becoming a hero. He had conspired with Vann Woodward to integrate the Southern Historical Association meeting in 1949, and most recently he had become the first Black scholar to speak at the annual meeting of the Mississippi Valley Historical Association (now the Organization of American Historians).

When he'd written the slavery sections of *From Slavery to Freedom* a few years earlier, Franklin lamented the lack of "careful studies of the subject." Now Stampp was doing the kind of careful study that Franklin desired. Stampp read Franklin's slavery chapters, and he discussed the subject with Franklin at some length. Franklin's chapters appear to have provided an important model, in both tone and interpretation, for what Stampp was trying to accomplish on a larger scale and in much greater depth.

After spending the fall in Washington, the Stampps moved south to Carrboro, North Carolina, then still a mill town adjacent to Chapel Hill. Stampp spent long days at the Southern Historical Collection, where he pored over the plantation manuscripts that Roulhac Hamilton had assembled a few decades earlier. He made some side trips, too, and when he explained his project, he inevitably received lectures on slavery from heads of local archives or historical societies. A few people called him a "damn Yankee," but no one obstructed his work, and some librarians even brought obscure material to his attention.

Many of Stampp's sources were the same ones Phillips and other early historians of slavery used. But Stampp added a few new elements. Mindful of

Hofstadter's criticism of Phillips for focusing on large plantations, he sought out records from smaller slaveholders wherever he could find them. More important, however, was his perspective. He read books about the psychology of race and of role-playing, and he tried to think through questions such as when and how enslaved children would have learned that they were slaves, and to what extent slaves' interactions with their masters reflected conscious role-playing or unconscious adaptation. He was trying, as best he could, to imagine what it was like to be enslaved.[40]

As Stampp worked on his history of slavery, American society was changing. In the spring of 1953, during Stampp's semester in North Carolina, the Supreme Court heard several cases about school segregation, which were later grouped together as *Brown v. Board of Education*. Instead of issuing a decision immediately, the court scheduled them for a rehearing, asking the lawyers to provide additional evidence about the Civil Rights Act of 1866 and the Fourteenth Amendment. At the NAACP Legal Defense Fund, Thurgood Marshall's team of lawyers drafted a group of historians, including John Hope Franklin and Vann Woodward, to help.[41]

As Franklin and Woodward researched Reconstruction for the *Brown* case, they also huddled to brainstorm topics for a prominent series of lectures that Woodward, who was then teaching at Johns Hopkins, had been invited to deliver at the University of Virginia the following year. Nothing came together until after the Supreme Court's decision declaring segregation unconstitutional in public schools was issued in May 1954. In its wake, Woodward decided to take aim at the notion that segregation was the only peaceful means of regulating race relations. Far from a natural or immutable system dating to time immemorial, he believed, Jim Crow was instead a historical creation that had been implemented scarcely two generations before. With this framework in place, he wrote quickly all summer, finishing his lectures by early September. He sent a copy to Franklin, then stopped by Franklin's house in Washington a few weeks later to discuss the draft on his way to speak at Charlottesville.[42]

The lectures were a great success, drawing large and enthusiastic crowds. Oxford University Press rushed them into print the following spring as *The Strange Career of Jim Crow*, going almost straight from speaking notes to bound volumes. The book soon became a central document of the budding civil rights movement. In the field of history, it proved just as influential, making race relations a legitimate subject for white scholars by placing segregation at the center of a national drama that was still unfolding.[43]

It was against this tumultuous background that Stampp returned to Berkeley and set down to finally write the book on slavery that he had been researching for some five years. At first he found the task nearly impossible, in part because he was keenly aware of the book's potential significance at that precise moment. He wrote the first chapter, and then he wrote it again and again, almost giving up in despair before landing on something that sounded right, a calm, detached tone that couldn't be confused for an abolitionist tract. He sent it to Hofstadter to see what he thought.[44]

Hofstadter wrote a long, nitpicky response—"not because it isn't good," he noted, "but because it's got to be perfect." He acknowledged that he knew "next to nothing substantively" about slavery, so he homed in even more than usual on matters of style. He objected to the term "anxiety," for example, as "too laden with technical psychiatrical overtones," and instead suggested "trouble," which struck him as "truer to the life of the slave." He went on in this vein for pages but also acknowledged his deep admiration for what Stampp was doing. "I am much moved by the more personal and emotional passages," he wrote, adding, "You will put UB Phillips in limbo."[45]

Stampp worked his way into a rhythm and churned out chapters over the course of 1954. Hofstadter's stylistic criticisms gradually subsided, but something else kept bugging him. Finally, he brought it up. "The one thing the [manuscript] has lacked except in a few spots has been an emotional or dialectical surge to add the extra iota of interest . . . ," he told Stampp. "Before you reach the end let more passion and argument appear, since this was and is a controversial institution."[46]

This was a reversal of roles—usually, Hofstadter was the detached observer, Stampp the fiery radical—but in this case Stampp's radicalism was yoked to a deep sense of responsibility. He knew he needed to write a book that could not be rejected on what he regarded as spurious grounds. So he resisted his friend's advice—and Hofstadter quickly relented, perhaps realizing that his vision for the book was somewhat different from Stampp's. "My criticism was made largely from the standpoint of reaching the maximum audience than from the criterion of the substantive intellectual quality of what you were doing," he wrote in apology.[47]

Stampp spent the spring of 1955 at Harvard, where he was visiting for the semester. There he finished the book that now bore the title *The Peculiar Institution*, which he sent to Knopf later that summer. In the book's preface, he left little doubt about its purpose. "With the historian it is an article of faith that knowledge of the past is a key to understanding the present . . . ," he wrote. "I firmly believe that one must know what slavery meant to the Negro and how he reacted to it before one can comprehend his more recent tribulations."

But Stampp also believed that the equation could be reversed: "Knowledge of the present," he explained, "is clearly a key to [the historian's] understanding of the past." For Stampp, this present knowledge consisted above all in new insights from the natural and social sciences regarding "the basic irrelevance of race." "I have assumed that the slaves were merely ordinary human beings, that innately Negroes *are*, after all, only white men with black skins, nothing more, nothing less," he continued. "This gives quite a new and different meaning to the bondage of black men; it gives their story a relevance to men of all races which it never seemed to have before."[48]

The rest of Stampp's book amounted to a thoughtful and thorough application of that principle. He used all the research he accumulated during his year in the South, but he was also able to draw on all the scholars who had approached the subject with similar assumptions over the previous two or three decades. He focused primarily on the final thirty years before the Civil War, a period when he believed that the institution was so "rigid and static" that it could be analyzed "institutionally with only slight regard for chronology." At the same time, even though he was examining the period whose political controversies about slavery provoked the Civil War, he persisted in the tradition of treating slavery itself as separate from politics.

Essentially, if not explicitly, Stampp responded to Phillips point by point. Where Phillips saw slavery as an economic failure that was maintained for its social benefits, Stampp claimed that slavery was a social failure whose only justification was economic profit. Where Phillips saw slave life as basically fulfilling, Stampp described dreary conditions and lack of opportunity. Where Phillips saw slaves as docile and pliable, Stampp showed them to be "a troublesome property." Where Phillips saw slavery as a school for civilization, Stampp believed that it destroyed African culture but provided no substitute, leaving slaves in what he called "cultural chaos" or a "cultural void." Where Phillips saw slavery as a solution to the problem of race, Stampp considered slavery itself as the problem—in fact, "America's most profound and vexatious social problem" before the Civil War. Finally, where Phillips concluded that "modifications might easily be lamented, and projects of revolution regarded with a shudder," Stampp reminded his readers that at emancipation, "the Negro, in literal truth, lost nothing but his chains."[49]

The Peculiar Institution was the product of Depression-era radicalism, but it arrived in a different moment. Published in October 1956, it came two years after the Supreme Court's decision to desegregate schools, one year after Emmett Till's open-casket funeral and the start of the Montgomery bus boycott, and just a few months before the successful conclusion of that boycott with a Supreme Court decision declaring segregated buses unconstitutional.

Stampp received some negative reviews in the South and from southerners, who accused him, as he'd feared, of abolitionist bias, and of what they saw as his ahistorical emphasis on slavery as a monstrous evil. But he got the one southern review that really counted, a glowing one from Vann Woodward in the pages of the *New York Herald Tribune*. Stampp's book was "an important undertaking, carried out with intelligence, insight, and imagination," Woodward wrote. "It firmly rips off a lot of flattering unctions we have laid to our souls and a lot of blindfolds we have used to shut out realities." Stampp prized the review because of his respect for Woodward—and because he knew Woodward remained a critic of capitalism who harbored at least a little grudging admiration for the supposedly aristocratic planters of antebellum days.[50]

Hofstadter was delighted about his friend's success. "I think you are going to have a great deal of impact on the thinking on this subject," he predicted. He was right. A generation of Black and white scholars, including

Hofstadter, had worked to undermine Ulrich Phillips's interpretation of slavery, and now Stampp's book stood as the culmination of that effort. Arriving when it did, *The Peculiar Institution* made it impossible for American academics to talk about slavery the same way ever again—or to ignore it. More than forty years later, the book was still selling about five thousand copies per year, and some scholars continued to regard it as the single greatest history of American slavery ever written.[51]

9

CULTURE AND CONSCIOUSNESS

One of the few substantive notes Hofstadter gave Stampp about his drafts of *The Peculiar Institution* came in the second half of 1954. "One of the things I have been struck with—whether this has significance for you I don't know—is the similarity between the parent-child relation between masters & slaves and the deliberate infantilization of the slaves," Hofstadter wrote. He went on to explain: "They wanted to keep the Negroes childlike & then of course complained, when they succeeded, that the slaves were irresponsible."

There was a reason Hofstadter was thinking along these lines about the potential of the slave system to damage its subjects. He didn't mention it to Stampp, but he had a pair of graduate students who were at work on an essay about slave psychology—and who, that very summer, were camping out in Hofstadter's office to write it.[1] Their names were Stanley Elkins and Eric McKitrick, and their essay, which was published a few years later in a book called *Slavery*, would become one of the most influential and infamous studies of the subject in American history.

In a way, Elkins and McKitrick were what might have happened if Hofstadter had been split neatly in two. Elkins was the Jewish, East Coast half, his grandfather having immigrated in the early 1900s to Brooklyn, while McKitrick was the Protestant, Great Lakes half, his family hailing from the miscellaneous Midwest. Both were born in the 1920s and had their educations interrupted by service in World War II before completing college on the GI Bill. In 1949, Elkins started graduate school at Columbia and chose Hofstadter as his adviser. It was there, in Hofstadter's seminar, that he met McKitrick.

Hofstadter thought that Elkins and McKitrick were two of the best students he ever had. He considered McKitrick, in particular, to be a genius, once confiding that he had "the uncomfortable suspicion that he has taught me more than I have taught him."[2] Elkins and McKitrick became a team in 1952, when they started teaching to earn some money while they were working on their dissertations. Pressed for time, they decided to develop their lectures together. Elkins was the ideas man, dreaming up analogies and developing paradigms, while McKitrick did a lot of the writing and usually polished the final draft. This collaborative process worked so well that they never stopped. They began to refer to themselves as "the Organization" or "the Corporation," and they became convinced, not without reason, that they were going to remake the study of US history.

Vann Woodward would later say that the Corporation's specific strength lay in the "fresh and original conceptualization of problems," something they were able to do by bringing together an array of ideas from across the social sciences.[3] They drew heavily on Hofstadter, of course, but also the literary critic Lionel Trilling, the sociologists Robert Merton and David Riesman, and the growing field of psychology. As a result, their work encapsulated the intellectual culture of the 1950s, addressing both the practical problem of how society functioned and the more metaphysical one of what gave humans a common core.

It may have been Merton who had the most decisive influence. From his work the Corporation learned the method of functional analysis, which they thought promised "as big a step away from older methodology as the step from Newton to Einstein in the natural sciences." The big step, as they saw it, was from simply describing a thing to seeing how it worked—what its functions were—in the context of society as a whole. Elkins and McKitrick were bewitched by this way of thinking, which marked a major change from the morally inflected class struggle that characterized intellectual life in the prewar years.[4]

For the lecture course they developed together in 1952–53, Elkins and McKitrick drew on all these influences to sketch what they called "a general and unified theory of American history & culture." Their goal was to make each lecture revolve around some central problem, illuminating it with a "bright idea" that would give it life and interest. One of these problems was slavery. "What is the nature of this institution," they wondered. Its nature, they came to believe, was to leave deep and perhaps lasting effects on the people who were subject to it—to produce a distinctive personality, in fact, that made slaves different from other people.[5] This "bright idea" about slavery would break the field wide open, changing what it meant to think about slavery's effects on the enslaved and launching debates that lasted for years—and in some ways have never really ended.

The slavery lecture was "Stan's special baby," McKitrick acknowledged, "since both the original idea and the structure of the argument are pretty much his." Elkins began with a few nuggets of observation. In his army years, he had noticed that many white southerners viewed Black people as lazy and stupid. He saw the same thing historically in Thomas Jefferson's *Notes on the State of Virginia* and in the writings of Jefferson's contemporaries. Given that this stereotype was so widespread, Elkins wondered, might it reflect something real? If so, it wouldn't be innate racial difference; Elkins accepted that there weren't any significant biological differences between peoples. And it wouldn't be cultural background because Elkins also knew that enslaved Africans came from advanced societies. What, then, could explain the stereotype of lazy, childish slaves?

It was at this point that Elkins recalled a mimeographed essay that he'd first read in college and that he'd encountered again more recently in a sociology course at Columbia. The essay, called "Individual and Mass Behavior in Extreme Situations," was by the psychologist Bruno Bettelheim, and it dealt with how German concentration camps affected the character of the internees. Bettelheim drew on his own experience as an early internee at Dachau and Buchenwald before they became true death camps. Their population at that time came from a broad cross-section of the German population, not just Jews, and their mortality rate, while high, was still around 20 percent, allowing a large number of people to survive and form a new life there. In that new life, Bettelheim was surprised to see, many adults displayed a childish personality—presumably because they were placed, like children, in positions of utter dependence.

"That's it," Elkins thought. The basic mechanism that Bettelheim described—the shock of imprisonment, the necessity of forming a new society and personality, the effects of doing so from a position of powerlessness—all this seemed similar enough to enslavement that the effect—a childish personality—might also have been the same.

But this raised a second question because Elkins and McKitrick believed that the stereotype of the stupid, loyal, lazy slave developed mainly in the United States, not in other New World slave societies. Why the difference? To find out, they compared slavery in the "paternalistic, Catholic society" of Latin America with slavery "as developed in the liberal, Protestant, democratic, capitalist society" of British America. The key difference in Latin America, they believed, was the existence of three institutions—the crown, the church, and the planters—whose competing interests opened important pockets of space in the slave system. The United States, on the other hand, lacked any traditional institutions, allowing capitalism to develop unimpeded. On the plantation, this meant slaves were defined as property within a "closed" system in which all lines of authority began and ended with the master.

First, Elkins and McKitrick analyzed this closed system of slavery from the perspective of the slaves: "What 'other' would seem more 'significant' than his master: the man who holds the key to everything." Then they came at it from the side of the masters: "If you were setting up an ideal slave system for capitalist staple production, what would you specify as the ideal character for your slaves." This was how the Corporation explained "the sociological development of a stereotype . . . stupid—loyal—gay—irresponsible: Sambo."[6]

At the end of the year, Elkins and McKitrick sent a copy of their full course of lectures to several of their intellectual heroes. They got glowing responses. The few pages on slavery were particularly provocative. "Your treatment of slavery delights me," David Riesman replied—yet it was a delight bordering on horror. "Middle Passage an early concentration camp—nothing left but color," he wrote. "Jesus, here again you see it, about three lines down! Almost gives me the shivers." When Elkins got that response, and another from Trilling, he grinned for a week straight. "We really are as good as we said we were," he exulted. Soon the Corporation signed a contract with Knopf to expand the lectures into a thick book. They threw out their old dissertation topics and got to work.[7]

The first "problem" the Corporation developed in full was a functional analysis of the frontier, which they finished in early 1954. They sent a copy to Trilling, who was floored. "This is, I think, the first historical account—chronicle apart—of American life that has ever fully engaged my imagination," he replied.[8] Next they turned to slavery. After working through the summer in Hofstadter's office and then into the fall, they eventually completed three linked essays by January 1955.

As usual, Elkins and McKitrick sent the essays to their intellectual heroes, fishing for praise from the likes of Trilling. But this time they also sent the essays to an additional idol, Vann Woodward. In his response, Woodward foreshadowed nearly everything that would later be said about the Corporation's slavery work, both good and bad. He led with the positive, which was very positive indeed: "I feel strongly that here you have provided at last a way out of the blind alleys down which the Herskovits and Apthekers and Cravens and Schlesingers and Randalls have led us—which are not awfully different from those where the Garrisons and Calhouns left us long ago—and through which we have all been wandering so long."

He saw pitfalls, too, particularly in the personality essay with the concentration-camp analogy. Woodward allowed that the analogy "opened up a ghastly treasure of insight," but he worried that its sheer explosiveness might undermine the larger meaning of their work: "For here you have done more than anyone probably to rescue this dispute from the clutches of the abstract moralists and put it into a concrete psychological framework. And yet you go tossing about moral dynamite with what seems reckless abandon." Southerners were sure to take offense, particularly at the implied comparison of Thomas Jefferson to an SS guard. "This just won't quite do," Woodward told them. "Can't you suggest that the analogy is not complete. That the moral depravity, the bestial sadism, the planned and plotted diabolism, the genocide ovens were not standard equipment of the Southern plantation." He suggested that they take a closer look at slave testimony and other sources which might demonstrate that American slavery, for all its faults, was not a completely "closed" system: "Were there not perhaps more opportunities for the development of moral personality and individuality under slavery than you suggest?"[9]

Woodward's response to the "Slavery and Personality" essay—along with that of Hofstadter, who was "deeply offended"—convinced Elkins and McKitrick that they'd somehow gone wrong. But not too wrong—they had too much self-confidence for that. They still believed that their basic line of reasoning was correct; they just needed to work on their presentation. "We were so intent on isolating the mechanisms themselves . . . ," McKitrick replied to Woodward, "that we overlooked the inevitable—that our parallels would be taken both as psychological and as moral parallels."[10]

And there the Corporation's production stalled. Just as they were finishing their slavery essays and while they were still graduate students at Columbia, they both took three-year positions at the University of Chicago. Their writing had to be set aside as they rushed to develop a new set of courses. Then their grand plans went sideways. It proved impossible to develop essays that would be short enough to include in their book yet of sufficient depth to satisfy a dissertation requirement. Eventually they tore up their Knopf contract and returned their advance. In the meantime, they selected two of their original problems—slavery for Elkins, Reconstruction for McKitrick—to serve as dissertations that would allow them to graduate and get permanent jobs.[11]

This was when a more serious obstacle presented itself. In the fall of 1957, when Elkins presented part of the Corporation's slavery work to a faculty seminar at Chicago, his talk set off alarms with several professors, most notably Daniel Boorstin. It turned out that Boorstin and the Corporation had fundamentally different conceptions of history. Boorstin thought history should be told as a dramatic story devoted to "the rich particularity of experience" and showed no patience with Elkins and McKitrick's style of social scientific theorizing. With Boorstin "wield[ing] the fine thin blade," according to McKitrick, the department charged them with "a prioristic" reasoning, insufficient original research, and uneven writing quality. What it all amounted to was a complaint that their work was too sociological in nature, not historical.

The consequence was that their contracts went unrenewed—an action that carried the implication that they were no good, leaving them in a tough position for getting new jobs. McKitrick wrote long, distraught letters trying to explain what had happened and to figure it out for himself. "Dick," he asked Hofstadter, "what I still can't really understand is, why, when people are adversely struck by what we do, is the response so damned visceral?"[12]

As a result of their difficulties, Elkins and McKitrick rushed to finish their dissertations in the spring of 1958. Yet the same problems that Woodward and Hofstadter originally saw in the slavery essays remained there roughly three years later. Hofstadter's moral revulsion to the concentration-camp analogy had mellowed, but he still thought it absurd to call a chapter "Slavery and Personality" and then discuss the Nazi camps at such length that "all other aspects of the slave situation" dropped out. "No one could help but wonder why all the literature of slave myths, slave songs, slave folklore, the observations of visitors on the slave system are neglected," he told Elkins, pressing for the analogy to be condensed. Woodward agreed. "I am not saying do not do this," he warned. "I am saying, make what concessions you can and prepare for the consequences."[13]

The Corporation missed the spring deadline for McKitrick's dissertation on Reconstruction, which didn't go to the typist until the fall, but Elkins managed to defend his dissertation at Columbia in May. Even then, Hofstadter and Woodward continued to stress the need for "extra precaution before publication." But Elkins was impatient because he was still trying to land a permanent position somewhere. He submitted the dissertation almost immediately to the University of Chicago Press—where it landed on the desk of Roger Shugg, who had moved on from Knopf a few years after commissioning John Hope Franklin's *From Slavery to Freedom*. Shugg reached out to Woodward for his opinion. "It will be attacked from both sides,"

Woodward told him. "But of one thing I feel confident and that is that it will not be ignored."[14]

Woodward's endorsement held sway. The Corporation spent the spring of 1959 getting the book—now called *Slavery: A Problem in American Institutional and Intellectual Life*—ready for publication. After the criticism they'd received over the previous couple of years, their self-confidence was turning to self-consciousness. Their editor picked up on this tone and suggested that instead of cluttering up the main text with caveats and counterarguments, they should add an appendix summarizing and responding to the main lines of critique they'd heard. They went through it all: the use of law as evidence, the comparative method, the concentration-camp analogy, the reality of the Sambo stereotype, the use of "cross-disciplinary 'gimmicks,'" the book's "implications about 'human nature.'" Perhaps heeding Hofstadter's and Woodward's warnings, they also made sure to declare that the book "does not pretend to be a history" and described it as "more properly a 'proposal' . . . that certain kinds of questions be asked in future studies of the subject."[15]

With all that done, McKitrick finally received his first copy of the finished book in November. Holding the hardcovers in his hands revived his former pride. "Well—all I can say is that the thing is sweet, sweet . . . ," he told Elkins. "It is so obviously & serenely Triple-A that nobody else in that league who really matters will fail to recognize it."[16]

The book received a few cutting reviews, but in general it stirred little immediate response compared with the storms it generated before publication. Meanwhile, after feeling for a year or two as if their futures were in peril, both Elkins and McKitrick secured good jobs. McKitrick landed at Columbia, thanks largely to the efforts of Hofstadter and Woodward, while Elkins got a spot at Smith College, just a few hours' drive north in Massachusetts. Elkins and his family moved into a rambling old house with plenty of rooms for the McKitrick clan to stay when they came up for weekends and summers. The Corporation would be able to continue their work. They soon turned to the next problem they wanted to tackle: politics in the early republic.

But they couldn't leave slavery behind just yet. "The state of discourse on this subject is no longer the same, never can be quite the same again,"

McKitrick told Elkins in 1961, noting that their book had "made one whale of a difference." The Corporation had defined the basic problem—the inner life, the consciousness, of the enslaved—that would dominate the study of slavery over the next two decades. Elkins agreed. "You are perfectly right about Slavery," he replied. "We've started an argument that will continue for a long, long time. No one will write on the subject for a good many years without coming to terms, in one fashion or another, with those essays."[17] He was more right than he knew.

IN 1963, THE CIVIL RIGHTS STRUGGLE BECAME A MASS MOVEMENT THAT NO one in America could avoid or ignore. That spring, Martin Luther King Jr. led a wave of demonstrations in Birmingham, where local police countered them with high-pressure hoses and attack dogs. Footage of the violence aired across the country. The months that followed saw the most sustained wave of protests for equal rights in US history to that point. In June, President John Kennedy announced his support for a new civil rights bill; in August, King delivered his famous "I Have a Dream" speech from the steps of the Lincoln Memorial to a crowd of a quarter-million people.[18]

At just this moment, the publisher Grosset and Dunlap put out a paperback edition of Elkins and McKitrick's *Slavery*. Soon it was selling more than ten thousand copies per year. The book fit the times. It provided the perfect historical foundation for this phase of the civil rights movement, which drew on a model of Black psychological damage to push for desegregation. Slavery had stripped Black people of their African culture, the argument implicitly went, so now, with no cultural baggage to hold them back, the only things preventing their full assimilation into American society were prejudice and discrimination. The head of the NAACP Legal Defense Fund cited *Slavery* in a Supreme Court brief, and Hannah Arendt was recommending it as the best book for understanding the Negro situation. With interest in the historical background of racial problems rising, sales soared to twenty-five thousand per year throughout the mid-1960s.[19]

Yet even as the civil rights movement spurred interest in *Slavery*, it also resulted in an extraordinary backlash against the idea that slavery shattered Black Americans. Nowhere was this shift more apparent than among Black Americans themselves, who began to assert—partly out of fear, partly out of faith—that there was, in fact, a distinctive Black culture worth preserving and even celebrating, that as new civil rights legislation broke down the formal barriers of segregation which had kept Black Americans apart, they could not and would not be assimilated as undifferentiated Americans.

This new attitude grew out of multiple streams. The most direct was the movement itself, which proved (if it needed proving) that Black Americans had not been broken by slavery and segregation—and, moreover, that they had significant resources in their own culture and communities to mount and sustain a long-term political struggle. A secondary stream was the process of African decolonization, which, starting with Ghanaian independence in 1957, provided dozens of examples of Black African political power and leadership on the world stage. Africa took on a new valence among Black Americans, who now gained greater pride in their African past and found there a bank of alternative traditions. "We must recapture our heritage and our identity if we are ever to liberate ourselves from the bonds of white supremacy," Malcolm X declared.[20]

At this point, however, Black-authored history was more likely to be found in magazines available to the masses than in articles aimed at scholars. *Ebony* was the most popular Black consumer magazine of the postwar period, and starting around 1954, it began to carry regular articles on Black history. Many of them were written by Lerone Bennett Jr., a journalist who joined the magazine's staff that year and who consistently pushed for more historical features in its pages. By 1961, he had the freedom and support to start a "Negro History" series, beginning with an article on "The African Past" that drew on Carter Woodson and Melville Herskovits, cited recent archaeologists and anthropologists, and included a scholarly bibliography. More followed over the next few months: one on the transatlantic slave trade, another on antebellum slavery. Bennett discarded the conciliatory tone that *Ebony* writers had previously used when discussing slavery in favor of visceral descriptions of violence. He deployed Elkins and the concentration-camp comparison to great effect, yet he also showed that not all or perhaps even many slaves fit the Sambo stereotype; one of his articles covered slave revolts.

Reaching an audience of roughly six hundred thousand, Bennett's articles were a revelation to Black people who had little access to scholarly books. Bennett quickly compiled them into a book of his own and published it on the one-hundredth anniversary of the Preliminary Emancipation Proclamation in the fall of 1962. Called *Before the Mayflower*—because the first Africans were brought to Virginia one year before the Pilgrims landed in Massachusetts—the book was unabashedly popular in style, making contemporary comparisons whenever possible. There was a "Cotton Curtain" that echoed the Iron Curtain, and the plantation appeared as a totalitarian institution. Yet Bennett drew on more than a year of scholarly research to stress the centrality of Black people to US history. He predicted that his readers would be "astonished by the richness of the Negro's heritage."[21]

The goals of this push for more inclusive history were the same as the goals of previous generations of racial-justice advocates going back to the eighteenth century: to reduce white prejudice and promote Black uplift by demonstrating Black people's capacity for freedom. Culture would be used to foster consciousness. Malcolm X was gaining prominence for articulating this point as early as 1962. After the violent scenes that came out of Birmingham in 1963, many young Black activists, including those associated with the Student Nonviolent Coordinating Committee (SNCC), began to move in Malcolm's direction—a shift that accelerated over the next year as SNCC leaders took a trip to Africa and set up freedom schools in Mississippi.[22]

One of the key influences in the rise of these new views of Black history and culture was the French Caribbean psychiatrist and scholar Frantz Fanon. In his books *Black Skin, White Masks* (1952) and *The Wretched of the Earth* (1961), Fanon asserted that cultural integrity and psychological strength were essential to the anticolonial freedom struggle. His works helped convince Black activists in America that they were an internal colony of the United States, with a white majority imposing a colonial culture on them, and that their own freedom struggle required the formation of a collective Black identity grounded in Black history and culture. After *The Wretched of the Earth* was published in the United States in 1965, it went on to sell 750,000 copies in the next five years. "Every brother on a rooftop can quote Fanon," said one radical editor.[23]

Among American intellectuals, the most influential statements of this new concept of Black culture came from Ralph Ellison, whose novel *Invisible Man* had won the National Book Award a decade earlier. Black life was hard, he allowed, but it was not an unmitigated horror. It had "a fullness, even a richness" to it that flowed from the creativity and culture of Black people themselves. Ellison developed this point over the course of several essays in the early 1960s, which gained even greater power when they were published together in *Shadow and Act* in 1964. A few years later, he did an interview for *Harper's* in which he took direct aim at what he called "the Stanley M. Elkins 'Sambo' argument." Ellison continued: "Any people who could endure all of that brutalization and keep together, who could undergo such dismemberment and resuscitate itself, and endure until it could take the initiative in achieving its own freedom is obviously more than the sum of its brutalization."[24]

It was during the Freedom Summer of 1964 that Black culture began to take center stage in the civil rights movement. The most prominent goal of Freedom Summer was voter registration, but its larger purpose was to educate poor Black Mississippians for political action, a mission that was carried out through community centers and freedom schools. In addition to reading and writing and arithmetic, the most important subject at these schools was history. In a curriculum designed in part by the radical white historians Howard Zinn and Staughton Lynd, students learned for the first time about Black historical figures beyond Booker T. Washington. Teachers drew on Black authors such as Du Bois, Woodson, and John Hope Franklin to demonstrate both the bad side of slavery and the ability of Black Americans to develop a vital culture in the face of deprivation. The goal was to show that the civil rights movement fell into a long tradition of Black and white resistance to racism and inequality, and also to instill a sense of pride in the Black community and its past. By learning about the Black past, the thinking went, Black Americans would gain greater consciousness of their Black identity while also experiencing a sense of psychological liberation from the norms of white society. As they recognized that they had been brainwashed into feeling shame about their past, they would reorient themselves toward a search for an authentic Black identity based in Black culture and history.[25]

The new appreciation and even celebration of Black culture became dominant among Black activists in 1965. One especially catalyzing event in this intellectual transformation came when Daniel Patrick Moynihan, then an assistant secretary of labor in the Johnson administration, issued a report called "The Negro Family: The Case for National Action," which was intended as a blueprint for what the administration saw as the next phase of the civil rights movement. Despite the significant gains the movement had made over the previous decade, Black Americans continued to face discrimination when they tried to find jobs and housing. Income and employment figures had stalled, and many Black workers were stuck in unskilled jobs.

Moynihan's case for national action to support the Negro family was based on the damage that Black Americans suffered in the past. For information about slavery, he turned to Elkins. At some point he'd received a copy of *Slavery* from a colleague, and he reached out to Elkins personally for advice. He also relied heavily on Franklin Frazier's study of the Black family, which provided detailed evidence of its fragility—first under slavery, and later as a result of the destabilizing forces of emancipation and the Great Migration.[26]

Moynihan finished the confidential report in March. He led with a compelling picture of the family problems that needed to be addressed. He identified "the roots of the problem" in slavery, drawing on Elkins to declare that "American slavery was profoundly different from, and in its lasting effects on individuals and their children, indescribably worse than, any recorded servitude, ancient or modern." Perhaps most important, Moynihan wrote, "It was by destroying the Negro family under slavery that white America broke the will of the Negro people." This historical summary occupied perhaps two or three pages in a fifty-page report that spent much more time on urbanization, unemployment, and poverty as the immediate causes of Black family problems. The report ended by calling for new federal programs designed to strengthen "the stability and resources of the Negro American family" to help Black people escape the "tangle of pathology" in which they were enmeshed.

Circulated within the administration in the spring of 1965, the report made enough of an impact that President Johnson used it as the basis for a speech he was scheduled to deliver at Howard University's graduation ceremony in June. At Johnson's request, Moynihan wrote most of the speech and used it to make the case for the policy changes he'd recently recommended in his report. "Much of the Negro community is buried under a blanket of history and circumstance," Johnson declared in the speech, describing "the devastating heritage of long years of slavery; and a century of oppression, hatred and injustice." These problems, he continued, were not the fault of Black Americans but were largely the responsibility of whites. He advocated policies to strengthen the Black family as part of a broader effort to end the cycle of Black deprivation. "This is the next and more profound stage of the battle for civil rights," he declared. "We seek not just freedom but opportunity—not just legal equity but human ability—not just equality as a right and a theory but equality as a fact and as a result."[27]

Johnson considered it the greatest civil rights speech he ever gave, and it received a lot of support from Black leaders. Ralph Ellison sent a glowing letter to the White House, and Martin Luther King Jr. declared that "never before has a president articulated the depths and dimensions [of the problems] more eloquently and profoundly."

Yet the administration's goal of implementing a broad new policy program on behalf of Black Americans failed spectacularly. The Watts riot in August changed everything. Five days of destruction in Los Angeles left thirty-four people dead and about a thousand injured before National Guard troops quelled the worst episode of urban violence in US history. Johnson was furious and felt betrayed by the Black rioters, and many white liberals were shocked and scared. Almost overnight, white liberal attitudes toward poor Black city dwellers went from a paternalistic concern for victims to an alarmist terror of predators.

At the same time, the administration was becoming distracted by Vietnam. In July, Johnson announced the escalation of a war that would soon overwhelm all other issues in US politics and undermine support for his presidency. Over the next few years, the earnest early 1960s desire to end the hypocrisy of American democracy curdled, in the cauldron of Vietnam and its accompanying credibility gap, into a cynical sense that American democracy was hypocritical at its core, its stated ideals nothing but tattered rags to cover up naked assertions of power. The combined influence of Watts and Vietnam ended the Great Society by forcing liberals to recalibrate the scale of transformation that they thought they could achieve.

By the time of the Watts riot, Moynihan had left the administration to run for New York City Council. But news outlets latched on to his report, which had recently been made public, as the government's semiofficial explanation of urban unrest. A flood of commentary followed, much of it accusing Moynihan of "a new form of subtle racism" for implying that Black people needed to do a better job of adapting to middle-class white culture. In fact, one of the controversy's lasting results was the phrase "blaming the victim," which the psychologist William Ryan coined during the debate.[28]

Many of the attacks on Moynihan were misplaced, based on nothing more substantial than secondhand summaries of the report. Nevertheless, the criticism stuck, and the White House quietly let the whole issue fade away. But if the Moynihan affair accomplished nothing in terms of public policy, it did consolidate a broader shift in discussions of the Black past. Among people sympathetic to the civil rights movement, "damage" had long been the keyword for understanding the effects of slavery and segregation on Black Americans, as in Elkins and McKitrick's concentration-camp analogy. But over the next decade, sympathy for civil rights would lead to a strikingly different interpretation of slavery. The "damage" argument that was now personified by Moynihan (and by Elkins, who was often lumped in with him) became a convenient target as activists, and scholars, sought to show that instead of being destroyed by the experience of slavery, enslaved Blacks had managed to forge a community and a culture that resisted slavery and ultimately laid the foundations for the civil rights movement.

THE CIVIL RIGHTS MOVEMENT BROUGHT A WAVE OF AMERICAN SCHOLARS to the study of slavery as they tried to understand the roots of Black discontent and the origins of America's racial situation. The most significant of them was a young historian named Eugene Genovese. For about a decade in the late 1960s and early 1970s, Genovese stood near the center of almost every important development and debate in the field. In part, this was because he liked to court controversy and would stick his nose in any fight. It was also because he was fiercely intelligent and his ideas were often worth fighting about. Yet Genovese always occupied a paradoxical position in the profession. Elkins once described his work as "idiosyncratic and sui generis; to a considerable extent it begins and ends with himself," and another scholar later wrote that "no important modern historian has influenced more, and persuaded fewer."[29]

Genovese might have enjoyed this paradox; he had a Marxist's love of contradictions and dialectics. Indeed, he came to the study of slavery from his commitment to communism. The son of Sicilian immigrants in Brooklyn, he absorbed from his dockworker father a class-conscious pride in being a worker. He became a Communist as a teenager, around the end of World War II, and remained convinced for more than four decades of "the moral as well as material superiority of socialism over capitalism." At Brooklyn College, however, he went against the Communist Party line in some internecine squabble and found himself excommunicated. This was hard on him, but it had the effect of freeing him from a future within the party. Instead, like many other students at the time, driven by the desire to understand the complicated postwar world they had inherited, he decided to become a historian.[30]

Genovese was smart and could be very funny, but he admired Stalin unironically and conducted his own affairs in a similarly dictatorial style. He was in many ways a jerk, the kind of person ostentatiously committed to economic equality who also makes racist jokes and brags about his weakness for college coeds. He collected grudges by the dozen, his friendships were fragile, and his departmental relationships often deteriorated. During the 1960s, he cycled through four colleges and multiple marriages.

Yet Genovese was at this point in his career omnivorous when it came to scholarly influences, open to discussion and debate with anyone who crossed his path. He sincerely believed that every effort to tell the truth about the human condition would ultimately advance the socialist cause. As a result, he kept up a feverish publishing schedule, a pace driven by his own opinionated brilliance as well as his conviction that scholarship really could change the world.

Genovese got his PhD from Columbia in 1959, around the same time as Elkins and McKitrick. He seems never to have crossed paths with them, however, because he started graduate school not long before they left to teach at Chicago. By that time, Genovese had become interested in studying the Old South because he believed that slaveholders represented the only alternative to bourgeois capitalism that the United States had ever seen.[31]

Soon after he received his doctorate, Genovese picked up a copy of Elkins and McKitrick's *Slavery*, which was published the same year. He found almost every part of it fascinating, he soon wrote in a review, especially its "ingenious analysis of the social psychology of the slave." He also thought that almost all of it was wrong. For Elkins and McKitrick, American slavery was the product of a society that was liberal and capitalist to its core, while Genovese's interpretation was nearly the opposite. "That which made the Southern planters unusual and opened the way to absolute power over the slave was not the capitalist element," he claimed, "but the political quasi-independence of the planters, who were fundamentally opposed to bourgeois values and society."[32]

Genovese sent a copy of his review to Elkins. Then, over the next few years, he elaborated on what he meant. Profits were not the same as capital accumulation, he said, nor could a balance sheet reveal anything about its own social and political significance. Slaveholders may have been acquisitive, but the things they wanted to acquire were status, which rested on land and slaves, and honor, which they pursued through politics and the military. Cash could help achieve these goals, Genovese allowed, but it was not an end in itself, nor did it shape social relations. Slaveholders equated slavery with civilization, and no amount of potential profit could convince them to give that up. Ultimately, however, this placed the South in a dilemma. By the 1840s and 1850s, slaveholders were steadily losing ground to the capitalist North, which was gaining the power to determine the country's economic direction and destroy the South's distinctive civilization. Secession made sense in these circumstances, according to Genovese, because political independence was the only way for slaveholders to try to sustain their "special civilization built on the relationship of master to slave."[33]

This was the case Genovese made in his first book, *The Political Economy of Slavery*. Published in the fall of 1965, it had an enormous influence across the field of American history. For one thing, it demonstrated that Marxists could do sophisticated analysis, not pure economic determinism or party-line orthodoxy. At the same time, the book placed slavery at the heart of American history and pushed it to the center of the conversation, especially among young scholars.

Around the time *Political Economy* appeared, Genovese became embroiled in controversy. He was now on the faculty at Rutgers, and at a teach-in there he declared, "I do not fear or reject the impending Vietcong victory in Vietnam. I welcome it." He received death threats and became a convenient talking point in that year's New Jersey gubernatorial election, with the Democratic candidate supporting academic freedom and his Republican opponent calling for Genovese's removal. Former vice president Richard Nixon swooped in and gave speeches attacking Genovese across the state.[34]

Genovese didn't end up getting fired for his Vietnam statements, but he knew he had no future at Rutgers. He soon went into semi-exile at Sir George Williams University in Montreal, which was close enough to New York that he could return regularly to look after his elderly parents, complete his psychoanalysis, and keep his subscription to the Metropolitan Opera.[35]

By this time, Genovese was at work on a new project about slavery. He had read deeply in the works of the German philosopher Hegel, one of Marx's major influences (and one of George Bancroft's professors in Berlin), and he was particularly taken by a passage in Hegel's *Phenomenology of Spirit* on the dialectic of lordship and bondage. The dialectic goes like this: a lord commands his bondsman as an instrument of his own will, but he is paradoxically dependent on his bondsman to acknowledge his own identity as master. Meanwhile, a bondsman must do his master's bidding, but it is through that very labor that he gradually acquires a sense of his own power and independence. For Genovese, this provided the philosophical and psychological foundations for his own understanding of the master-slave relationship. And it meant that in order to understand the masters—still and always his primary interest—he would also need to know something about the slaves.[36]

Another influence came from the new field of working-class social history. The main model came from Britain, where Marxist scholarship was accepted somewhat earlier and more fully than in the United States. In *The Making of the English Working Class*, the British historian E. P. Thompson expanded traditional labor history to take in all the other aspects of life through which early nineteenth-century English workers forged their own sense of identity. Thompson showed that culture could be a site of resistance and a source of power, particularly for marginalized groups that had little access to the usual levers.

Thompson's book became widely available to US historians in 1964, and it had an immediate influence, particularly on younger scholars whose sensibilities were being forged by the civil rights movement and, soon, the antiwar movement as well. Many of these younger scholars turned away from political and intellectual history, which focused on elites, and toward social history, which promised to uncover the experiences of the masses. "History from the bottom up" became the slogan of the day. The proportion of dissertations done in the field of social history quadrupled from 1958 to 1978, and a new *Journal of Social History* was founded in 1967 (with Genovese on its editorial board).[37]

As Genovese embarked on his new slavery project, he also continued to wrestle with Elkins and McKitrick, whose analysis of slave psychology he saw as necessary but not sufficient. Genovese delivered his main critique at the Association for the Study of Negro Life and History meeting in October 1966 and published it in *Civil War History* a year later, in an issue that contained two other critiques of Elkins—by that time, criticism of Elkins was becoming a cottage industry. The problem, according to Genovese, was that Elkins showed little sense of the dialectical quality of human life—the way that it naturally generated its own contradictions and negations. Slavery could make people into Sambos, Genovese believed, but it could also make them into Nat Turners. In fact, he planned to call his slavery book *Sambo and Nat Turner*. Elkins had explained one but not the other.[38]

Neither, at the time, could Genovese, who kept trying to think through the complex problem of accommodation and resistance. He knew that slaves were not docile Sambos and that they did plenty to protest and resist enslavement, but he also saw little to celebrate in activities such as arson, stealing, and breaking tools. For Genovese, these acts of day-to-day resistance played straight into masters' negative image of slaves and amounted to little more than "individual and essentially nihilistic thrashing about." It was not that the slaves were incapable or incompetent, Genovese said in a talk at the Socialist Scholars Conference in 1966, but simply that their situation was ill-suited to successful resistance: they were a minority in a region with strong cohesion among the white ruling class, which had the support of a powerful state behind it. The result, according to Genovese, was that slavery and its aftermath "emasculated" Black Americans for generations. The problem was "not docility or infantilization," he specified, "but innocence of organized effort and political consciousness." This was why he supported Black nationalism to a limited extent: Black leadership on a local or even regional scale, he suggested, "offers the only politically realistic hope of transcending the slave heritage." (But not Black Power beyond the Black community; in private, Genovese described himself as "a great advocate of Black Power—provided it stays on the other side of 125th Street.")[39]

From this rather negative view of "the slave heritage," with its explicit dichotomy between docile, childlike Sambos and violent, rebellious Nat Turners, Genovese began over the next few years to see the significance of culture as a way to bridge the divide—both between these two aspects of slave psychology and between slaves and masters. A crucial moment in this shift came in the fall of 1967, when Genovese attended the meeting of the Association for the Study of Negro Life and History in Greensboro, North Carolina. There he saw two young Black scholars, Vincent Harding and Sterling Stuckey, speak about slave culture and slave religion. Stuckey, who was then in graduate school at Northwestern, had the larger influence. Responding directly to Elkins and McKitrick, who claimed in passing that the fantasy lives of slaves were "limited to catfish and watermelons," Stuckey used slave songs and folktales to demonstrate that "slaves were able to fashion a life style and set of values—an ethos—which prevented them from being imprisoned altogether by the definitions which the larger society sought to impose." Stuckey saw folklore as essential to understanding both "the institutional aspects of American slavery" and "the larger dimensions of slave personality and style." Over the course of some intense discussions, Stuckey convinced Genovese that he had to include a cultural dimension in his project on slave life. And Stuckey convinced plenty of other people, too; his talk was published the following summer and soon became a touchstone.[40]

Genovese came to believe that historians needed to embrace the questions Elkins asked about slave psychology but jettison his answers, returning to the archives to see what the evidence revealed. Like Stampp and Phillips before him, Genovese traveled across the South looking at plantation journals, letters, and court records. By the time he was done, he would have five and a half double-column pages listing all the manuscripts he had used: sources in Chapel Hill and Durham and Charlottesville, Nashville and Jackson and New Orleans.[41]

But now there was also other material. One of the old chestnuts of slavery studies in America was the ritual lamentation of the lack of sources for studying slave life. That had begun to change in the early twentieth century, when scholars such as Carter Woodson and J. Franklin Jameson started to collect and publish sources about slavery. But it was only in the 1960s that those sources, and others like them, began to be widely used. This had something to do with race, as prejudices continued to drop away. But it also grew out of the valorization of working-class and marginalized peoples; the rise of anthropology, psychology, and other social sciences; and the so-called new sensibility of the 1960s, in which critics began to approach all different kinds of culture, high and low and otherwise, with a similar intellectual interest. Historians began to use folklore (as in Stuckey's talk), long-neglected slave autobiographies, and the WPA's slave narratives from the 1930s, which became much easier to access when they were published in a new sixteen-volume collection.

Despite their disagreements, Genovese and Elkins were on friendly, joking terms. In 1967, Genovese asked Elkins to write some recommendations for fellowships that would allow him to finish the research for his book "demolishing this Elkins guy on the nigger question," specifying that Elkins should "tell them how badly we need someone to clean up the mess that that racist running dog of world fascism, S. M. Elkins, caused in this field." Elkins cheerfully complied, and Genovese was able to take a year off from teaching in 1968–69. He thought he had only six more months of research before he could begin writing, but as he worked, he found that the book's scope continued to expand. "It grows and grows and grows," he reported to Elkins at the end of the year. "And I wonder, and wonder, and wonder."[42]

By that time, Black history was taking on a new national significance. Vice President Hubert Humphrey lamented "the psychological backlash of the Negro history gap," while a bill to create a national commission "to study all aspects of the problem of preserving, collecting, and ultimately integrating evidence of the Negro past into the mainstream of American history" attracted support from scholars such as Vann Woodward. New York's Schomburg Library, home of its Black history collections, was now packed with young scholars.[43]

This change, which was starting to be felt in the study of slavery, also reshaped college campuses and the curriculum. In the early 1960s, the number of Black students on historically white campuses had begun creeping upward—into the high single or low double digits. Then Black enrollments increased exponentially in the wake of the Civil Rights Act, which prohibited racial discrimination, and the Higher Education Act of 1965, which vastly expanded access to college among lower-income students through new federal grants and loans. In a single year, the number of Black students attending historically white colleges rose by some 70 percent.[44]

At Northwestern, for example, there were twenty-six Black students in 1965—and twenty of them were athletes. A year later, the school admitted fifty-four Black freshmen. The university regarded them as "culturally deprived" and saw its goal as educating them for inclusion in elite white society; Black students were not supposed to room together. Attitudes and policies like that, coupled with ongoing discrimination (Greek groups didn't admit Black students; Black men weren't supposed to date white women), led to discontent among the growing Black student population. Feeling isolated and unwelcome, Black students on campuses across the country banded together to press for local change, shifting their focus from the federal or state level to the quad and the curriculum. At Northwestern, they formed two new organizations in 1967 to build unity and raise consciousness through activities that included discussions of Frantz Fanon.

Black students initially asked for new Black history courses and programs in the mid-1960s, but universities typically resisted their requests. Then the assassination of Martin Luther King Jr. in April 1968 sparked a wave of demonstrations that swept the country. Black college students turned to more confrontational tactics, protesting on almost two hundred campuses over the next year. And they began to make more radical demands that followed directly from the philosophy of Black Power: separate student groups and dorms and dining halls, places where they could cultivate or maintain a Black identity and not be subject to white surveillance; separate courses, told from a Black perspective, that placed Black people at their center and would be free from white depictions that they saw as stereotypical or demeaning; and separate Black studies programs or departments, under at least partial student control, that would serve as a source of personal self-definition and group empowerment. And they wanted these things—new programs, new departments, new faculty—to happen immediately.

At Northwestern, Black students demanded to be allowed Black roommates and to have new Black studies courses taught by Black professors who would be selected by the students themselves. The university brushed them off. Then a sit-in at the university's business office—which handled the school's finances and admissions—brought the administration to the table within two days. The school agreed to increase its recruitment of Black students, secure dedicated space for Black student activities, and expand "studies of black history and black culture in the University." The administration refused to give students power over faculty hiring, but it did consult with them before inviting Lerone Bennett of *Ebony* magazine to join the faculty that fall. Bennett's courses on Black history, which used his own books as well as those of Du Bois and Herbert Aptheker, proved very popular.[45]

So many Black studies programs, departments, and centers were started at the same time in the late 1960s and early 1970s that it proved impossible to staff them all. Students often demanded Black faculty to teach Black studies, but there were essentially no Black professors to be found. Fewer than 3 percent of all doctorates in history were held by Black Americans (the figure was less than 1 percent for doctorates in all fields), and many of those were older men who had earned their degrees in the 1930s and early 1940s. When one historian asked Woodward, who by that time was at Yale, for the "names of any young Negroes specializing in Afro-American history," Woodward admitted that the supply fell far short of the demand. "In despair," he joked, "I have finally resorted to the device of applying burnt cork to achieve the proper shade of historian." He was trying to do his part by training two Black graduate students, but they—and their whole cohort of Black students who entered graduate school in the mid-1960s—were still at least a year away from being ready to start teaching. One result was that many early Black history courses were taught by whoever was available, often white historians who had relatively little expertise in the field. Black students experienced this, not unreasonably, as an insult because it implied that Black history didn't require any special knowledge or training.[46]

New Black history courses disturbed some older integrationists such as Stampp and Franklin, who thought it better not to segregate subjects by race. These separate courses also raised the question of what story they would tell about America: a halting struggle to fulfill the ideals of freedom and equality or a relentless litany of white oppression in which the only heroes were Black rebels? In the first camp stood most mainstream white historians as well as Franklin and Benjamin Quarles, the two fathers of postwar Black history, along with some younger Black historians such as Woodward's student John Blassingame. In the second camp stood some radical whites and many younger Black scholars, most notably Sterling Stuckey and Vincent Harding but also Lerone Bennett. That second camp was where, for a significant moment in the late 1960s, much of the energy seemed to be.

The scholars who were influenced most heavily by Black Power dropped chronology in favor of continuity, with American history as a static story of white power and Black powerlessness. In 1968, Bennett published an article in *Ebony* that described Abraham Lincoln as a "white supremacist." For Harding, meanwhile, Black history demonstrated that the American dream was really an illusion or even a nightmare, and that the country's conception of freedom meant little more than the freedom to enslave. He became a poet of darkly prophetic statements. "Black History," he said, "is our journey into the void where our fathers believed America to be." No wonder then that he, and others like him, rejected integration in favor of transformation or separation. As Harding himself asked, "Who wants to integrate with cancer?"[47]

Demands for separate departments and programs, which involved larger questions of faculty and curriculum, provoked even greater conflict than Black history courses. To the extent that the programs were meant to make up for the fact that white scholars had long neglected the Black experience, such demands were welcomed or at least tolerated. But to the extent that they rested on more radical claims, such as that white pretensions to objectivity were nothing but a cover for ethnocentrism, they were treated as foundational threats. Richard Hofstadter worried that the frenzy of interest in Black studies and Black scholars would "end either with segregated substandard departments or divisions in many institutions, or, still worse, a headlong assault on university standards in the name of racial politics."[48]

Genovese had nothing but disdain for historians who he thought allowed their politics to pollute their scholarship—a path that he believed always ended up serving power. He was old enough, and had experienced enough marginalization as a result of his Marxist views, to trust in the importance of objectivity as an ideal. "Historians who do not respect historical truth, who sneer at objectivity and fear disorienting the masses . . . ," he warned, "can end only by serving the ruling class they think they are opposing or, at best, some new and exploitative elite." Thus, he led the resistance to a proposed American Historical Association resolution against the Vietnam War—despite his own opposition to the war—because he believed that a scholarly organization such as the AHA had no business taking a stand. Similarly, he was open to Black studies programs and courses in theory but deeply critical of efforts to police offerings along lines of racial identity or political affinity, calling them "ideologically fascist."[49]

Such controversies may have scared some white scholars into abandoning or avoiding Black history, but they never dominated the field. For the most part, university administrations rejected demands for exclusive Black control of Black studies, and even at the height of the for-us-by-us moment, in 1969, it was still possible for white historians to give talks about slavery that were applauded by Black nationalists. The controversy then flamed out as colleges hired more Black faculty, which satisfied the most pressing concerns, and as the Black radicals who were not jailed or killed at the end of the 1960s got mired in internecine squabbles in the 1970s.[50]

By the time the relatively brief boom in Black studies passed its peak, most historically white schools had courses in Black history, which became for several years one of the most popular fields in the discipline. When John Hope Franklin's publisher finally issued a paperback edition of *From Slavery to Freedom* in the fall of 1969, the book sold fifty thousand copies in six months. Dissertations on Black topics exploded, and professional meetings overflowed with sessions on Black history. The *Journal of Southern History*, once a bastion of old-school white southerners, became increasingly hard to distinguish from the *Journal of Negro History*.[51]

Yet even with Black history being incorporated into the college curriculum, there remained the question of what the substance of that history would be, particularly when it came to slavery. "To this day," Genovese lamented in the spring of 1970, "despite a library full of books on slavery, we do not have more than a few fragmentary studies of slave life, of the activity of the quarters, of slave religion . . . , or on slave folklore."[52]

A prolific scholar himself, Genovese had little patience for people who made programmatic pronouncements about what history should look like but weren't willing to put in the work of researching and writing it themselves. "If you say that black folk life can be unearthed and made relevant, then do it," he admonished Vincent Harding; "if white historians—for whatever reasons—have been blind to whole areas of black sensibility, culture, and tradition, then show us." But when Harding published his piece on slave religion, Genovese was deeply disappointed. It looked as if Harding had little research to back up his claims. "What the hell are these guys up to?" Genovese wondered. "Harding's thesis is sound, but that is all he has—a thesis. No analysis of key problems, no data, no nothing."[53]

By that time, however, there were starting to be scholars who had done enough research about slave life to say something substantial. One of the first major examples of the new slave-culture studies came at the end of 1969, when a white historian named Lawrence Levine gave a talk on "Black Songs and Black Consciousness: An Exploration in Neglected Sources" at the AHA's annual meeting. Originally a political historian who studied with Hofstadter at Columbia, Levine had started a new project in the mid-1960s that was supposed to be a deep history of the civil rights movement. After getting interested in grassroots ideas and going further and further back in time, he ended up, a few years later, as a cultural historian writing about slave songs and tales. Those essays, which were first published in the early 1970s, eventually became the heart of his book *Black Culture and Black Consciousness* (1977).[54]

Another important early example was John Blassingame, who became the first scholar in this era to publish a full book about slave life. A young Black historian who had graduated from a historically Black college in Georgia, Blassingame got his master's degree at Howard and then enrolled in the PhD program at Yale, where he studied with Woodward. As one of a small handful of Black historians in the PhD pipeline and as a moderate on questions of Black Power, Blassingame benefited from the Black studies boom. In 1970, Yale hired him while he was still working on his dissertation, a study of Black life in New Orleans during Reconstruction.

Blassingame later recalled having first encountered Elkins and McKitrick's *Slavery* in 1964 and said that his dissatisfaction with its conclusions caused him to embark on a five-year program of reading the autobiographies of ex-slaves to see what they had to say about their experiences. At the same time, he responded to the Moynihan Report by seeking data on Black family formation as part of his broader dissertation on Black New Orleans. Given the prevailing assumptions about Black family instability, Blassingame was astounded to find little difference in the statistical data between white and Black families. "Your data on the stability of the Negro family is of revolutionary significance," Woodward told him.

Soon Blassingame started to spend his nights reviewing literary sources for additional evidence about the slave family. In 1969, he gave a talk about life in the slave quarters, and then, over the next two years, he quickly compiled a book on the subject. He conceived it as a direct response to, or rather elaboration of, Elkins and McKitrick's *Slavery*. "I have accepted the book the way that Elkins hoped it would be received," he explained, "as a 'proposal,' or series of hypotheses to be tested." The main difference was that he would test them using Black sources instead of white ones, and see whether the Sambo stereotype held up to scrutiny.[55]

In doing so, Blassingame overturned nearly every single element of Elkins and McKitrick's argument. On the plantation, he showed, there were limits to how hard an owner or overseer could push his slaves, and also limits to white surveillance and supervision, which could never extend to all times and places. Far from a closed system, the resulting "variegated pattern of plantation life" meant that slaves had sources of meaning other than the master and roles other than that of the abject dependent. In fact, they composed a coherent community in which they were related to one another in a variety of different roles, and through which they passed down and produced a slave culture that both provided them with a collective identity and imbued their lives with meaning. "As long as the plantation black had cultural norms and ideals, ways of verbalizing aggression, and roles in his life largely free from his master's control," Blassingame concluded, "he could preserve some personal autonomy, and resist infantilization, total identification with planters, and internalization of unflattering stereotypes calling for abject servility."[56]

Blassingame published *The Slave Community* in 1972. "It is a stereotype-buster of a book," Woodward congratulated him. Nevertheless, Woodward harbored doubts about it, fearing it had been rushed. But he knew Blassingame to be a solid historian and a decent man. He thought it was important for Yale to grant tenure to a Black historian, and he decided to push Blassingame's case. As part of the process, he solicited opinions of *The Slave Community* from Genovese, Stampp, and some other slavery scholars. Genovese begged off because he was too busy trying to finish his own long-awaited study of slave life. Meanwhile, Stampp had a hard time getting a copy of

Blassingame's book. Woodward might have been worried about what he would say and did nothing to help him; instead, he worked to get Blassingame's tenure quickly approved.[57]

Stampp finally got a copy of *The Slave Community* a few weeks later. "I do not think the book is very good," he told Woodward, describing it as a somewhat sloppy "synthesis of recent scholarship." Stampp's letter would have blocked Blassingame's promotion, Woodward admitted, but luckily it had arrived too late. "I still think our decision was justified," he reassured Blassingame. Woodward then made the questionable decision to share Stampp's letter with Blassingame, shorn of any identifying marks. Blassingame was baffled by the criticisms, especially the one about the book as a derivative synthesis. He could think of nothing else, no other "general study of slavery," he fumed, "which has a chapter on the family, culture, or the African background treated in the same fashion as in The Slave Community." Still, the response did not surprise him. "My own feeling," he told Woodward, "is that age, ideology, and the intimacy of involvement in the slavery issue will determine many reactions to The Slave Community."[58]

Yet Stampp was not the only one who thought the book seemed outdated upon publication. The reason was that everyone else had come to similar conclusions in the late 1960s, and in the early 1970s they began saying the same thing all at once: there were plenty of sources that allowed scholars to study slave life from the perspective of the slaves. These sources showed that the experience of enslavement did not strip slaves of their culture, nor did it turn them into helpless children. Instead, slaves created their own culture, partly African and partly American, which was passed down through the fairly stable families that served as the foundation for cohesive slave communities. Slave culture and community took shape largely or partly outside the influence of white masters and overseers, and constituted a key buffer to oppression and dehumanization.

Even with ritual caveats about the cruelty of slavery, the story that emerged from this new wave of studies showed life for Blacks under slavery in a strikingly positive light. To some extent, what was happening was a straightforward attempt to recover the experiences of Black people under slavery and to celebrate their survival as an act of resilience and resistance. At the same time, new data about the transatlantic slave trade indicated that slaves in the United States experienced unprecedented demographic growth compared to other slave communities in the New World—suggesting that their situation could not have been as uniquely horrible as Elkins and McKitrick claimed.[59]

But new scholarly interest in slave culture and the slave community also coincided with a broader change in US politics and society after the middle of the 1960s, as disillusionment with what was seen as a corrupt political system and a diseased society led many people who had recently believed in the possibility of radical social transformation to spend their time instead pursuing personal authenticity and setting up their own alternative communities.[60] Rather than seeing slavery as a problematic exception to the American liberal tradition, scholars now viewed slave society as a preindustrial community with an authentic culture that had resisted the impositions of the Man.

Elkins and McKitrick mostly observed these changes in the interpretation of slavery with detached bemusement, coolly cashing royalty checks while they watched a character called "Elkins" be set up as a straw man. But they also believed that the new wave of studies understated the damaging effects of slavery, with potentially worrisome effects. "Stanley has a theory that anyone writing about slave culture these days is under fearful psychological pressure to put the best possible face on it, and to make every reasonable effort to tell the black community what it most wants to hear," McKitrick told one of those writers about slave culture, Lawrence Levine, in 1972. "Of course he freely admits that he has a certain vested interest in putting the worst face on it, having to play his role as the bête blanc of Smith College. But it does in a way give him a certain detachment, in the face of what seems to be a general drift, to appreciate some of the consequences of this pressure." McKitrick went on to outline those consequences:

> The actual institution of slavery itself is appearing in more and more benign colors—much more room for expression, maneuver, and so forth, than we thought—in short, it's edging back closer and closer to Ulrich Phillips every day. Something peculiar is happening here, and with it, something important

> may be slipping away. Now my question is, can we not explore slave culture sympathetically and at the same time reserve in our theoretical framework some principle for keeping account of the damaging, disintegrative, destructive effects of slavery itself? Are we forgetting that slavery was a poisonous and corrosive system which corrupted everything and everyone it touched? We shouldn't; we can't afford to; after all, we're still paying for it.[61]

Eugene Genovese's life settled down somewhat after he started dating Elizabeth Fox, a Harvard graduate student in European history, in the spring of 1968. The day after they met, he took her to a symposium on slavery that Elkins was hosting at Smith College. They married a year later and spent part of their honeymoon (a small part, one hopes) reviewing the proofs of a short book about slaveholder ideology that Genovese had just completed. One major difference between Genovese's work and the other slave-culture studies from this period was the sympathy he always extended to the masters. "The trouble with the old white historiography was not that it presented the view from the great house but that that was all it did," he explained. "To write a history of slavery without sympathetic attention to the master class—which need hardly imply approval—would be to repeat all the old mistakes in another, if more politically acceptable, form."[62]

In 1969, the year he got married, Genovese also moved to a new position at the University of Rochester. At first the university's administration balked at the hire, but when the History Department's leaders responded by resigning their roles, the administration not only reconsidered its decision but also made Genovese the department chair. He joined an already impressive collection of slavery scholars. One of them, Herbert Gutman, had started as a historian of the working class. In the wake of the Moynihan Report, he had decided to investigate the structure of the free Black family in upstate New York and was surprised to find stable two-parent households instead of Moynihan's "tangle of pathology." By the end of the 1960s, Gutman was expanding his research to include southern locations as well, and he kept seeing similar patterns everywhere he looked. Soon, he had enough data from New York and Mississippi to feel confident that his findings "cast severe doubt on . . . most sociological writing on the subject, and on much recent black history."[63]

Another couple of colleagues, Robert Fogel and Stanley Engerman, were investigating the economics of slavery. They were among a new wave of quantitative economic historians, known as cliometricians, who used the power of computers to apply large-scale data analysis to the study of history. From its start in the late 1950s, the field of cliometrics had cut its teeth on the subject of slavery, a relevant topic with lots of available data (in the form of plantation accounts and agricultural statistics) that had never been analyzed in any systematic way. What Fogel and Engerman were finding was that southern slave plantations remained productive and profitable throughout the antebellum period, confirming the claims of Stampp and some earlier cliometricians. But not only that—in contrast to at least two centuries of economic orthodoxy, Fogel and Engerman were also finding that slave labor was in some cases more efficient than free labor. To study the issue, they were starting to get large grants from the National Science Foundation, eventually totaling some $360,000 (nearly $3 million today).[64]

In his first couple of years at Rochester, Genovese regularly lunched with Gutman, Fogel, and Engerman, with all of them genially sharing data and discussing ideas. But this happy family of slavery scholars didn't last long. As chair of the History Department, Genovese immediately tried to make it, almost by sheer force of personality, into the greatest collection of scholars in the country. But he had trouble attracting anyone to upstate New York, and within two years his efforts had not only foundered but also earned him new enemies along the way. Anonymous letters requesting his resignation were circulated, some ending up as far away as Woodward's mailbox at Yale.

Gutman, who had helped bring Genovese to Rochester, felt saddened by the fractious atmosphere, which he laid at Genovese's feet. "I have learned," he wrote, "to my great disappointment, that one must work for or against him and not <u>with</u> him." Gutman soon left for City College. But neither he nor Genovese left behind their resentments, which festered into a legendary grudge match. Over the next few years, as Genovese, Gutman, and Fogel and Engerman each finished their big books, the reviews they gave one another often had the character of barroom brawls.[65]

Fogel and Engerman finished their book first. They'd worked at breakneck pace, believing that their study was so significant, and had such startling conclusions, that it would completely remake the field. Fogel started to send drafts to Woodward and other scholars in the second half of 1971. Woodward was fascinated by Fogel and Engerman's data and arguments regarding the profitability and efficiency of slavery, but he was dogged by doubts about nearly all the details. He implored Fogel to slow down, to be more respectful of prior historians, and—most important—to include full documentation for all his claims.[66] Fogel and Engerman slowed down a little, but Fogel, who was a relentless self-promoter, didn't back down from making bold claims that exaggerated the novelty of their work.

Fogel and Engerman published their book, called *Time on the Cross*, in the spring of 1974. It marked an ironic culmination of the wave of slave culture and community studies that were undermining the old view of slavery as damaging to Black Americans. According to Fogel and Engerman, slaves were efficient workers who enjoyed nutritious food, decent housing, good health care, and strong family life. Fogel and Engerman used something called the "geometric index of total factor productivity"—a ratio of output to average inputs—to show that southern slave plantations were roughly 40 percent more efficient than northern free farms. And it turned out (again, according to Fogel and Engerman) that slaves got back about 90 percent of the income they produced thanks to the investments owners made in the care of their slaves. Slave owners were profit-seeking capitalists, in this view, but conveniently the interests of masters often coincided with the interests of their slaves. Owners promoted population growth by encouraging stable families, not by breeding or abuse. They encouraged productivity with carrots like promotions to managerial roles rather than with sticks (or whips). Few slaves were sold south; few slave marriages were broken by sale. This was the slave plantation reimagined as a post–World War II corporation, complete with insurance benefits and a pension plan.

But that was not all. Fogel and Engerman had the gumption to present their conclusions as a courageous defense of Black Americans against the long tradition of abolitionists and, later, historians who cast aspersions on the Black work ethic under slavery. In Fogel and Engerman's telling, everyone was racist except for them; they alone had uncovered the true "record of black achievement under adversity"; they alone recognized that Black slaves were productive and efficient workers, a finding that they presented as dangerous and slightly illicit because it showed that morality and material progress were not always aligned. The tone of the book itself was similar, promising to show readers things that were surprising and maybe even a little naughty; one critic went so far as to liken it to "a modern sex manual" in that regard.[67]

The publicity for *Time on the Cross* outpaced anything on record for a work of academic history. The authors gave plenty of interviews and even went on the *Today* show, and the book was covered in major newspapers, magazines, and literary journals. In the fall, Genovese and Engerman organized a conference at Rochester to discuss the book. Nearly one hundred scholars attended; Stampp, Elkins, and Woodward were all there.

By that time, however, the inevitable backlash had begun. The strongest attack, and the longest, came from Fogel and Engerman's former colleague Herbert Gutman. He had read drafts of *Time on the Cross* in the summer of 1973 and declared much of the book "dead wrong. So wrong it's unbelievable." His main objection was what he saw as the book's model of slave socialization, which assumed that slaves adopted the culture and social structure of their owners without making any contributions of their own.[68] When the book came out with no new caveats or clarifications, he set out to demolish it, taking time out from his own work on the Black family to write the equivalent of a short book in response. He called it "The World Two Cliometricians Made: A Review-Essay of F+E=T/C"—a title that managed to be a dig at both Fogel and Engerman ("F+E=T/C" mocks their formula-heavy approach) and Genovese ("The World Two Cliometricians Made" echoes the titles of two of his books).

Fogel and Engerman often built broad claims on slender shreds of evidence, and it turned out that Gutman had a special genius for turning those slender shreds into kindling for a fire. The most famous example concerned the Barrow Plantation in Louisiana, where Fogel and Engerman used entries from the slaveholder Bennet Barrow's plantation diary to determine that there were "an average of 0.7 whippings per hand per year." Gutman had the good sense to step back from this calculation (whose accuracy he also questioned) and recalibrate it from a different perspective: that of the people who might have received or seen one of those whippings. Based on the number of whippings and the number of slaves, Gutman estimated that each slave on the Barrow Plantation would have witnessed more than one whipping per week. That sounded rather different from 0.7 whippings per hand per year—it sounded, in fact, like an effective and even terrifying form of social control. Gutman's review piled on for about 180 pages in that vein, showing the ways in which Fogel and Engerman's data, assumptions, and interpretations were all flawed.[69]

Time on the Cross quickly generated at least two other full works of criticism. Within a few years, the book's trajectory resembled that of a mining boomtown: a meteoric rise followed by an equally spectacular fall. Its final effect was to reinforce the cultural turn in slavery studies. Fogel and Engerman's blustery dismissal of nearly all previous scholars of slavery had done nothing to endear them (particularly Fogel) to more traditional historians, who then proved eager to ignore *Time on the Cross* when its various problems were pointed out. And they ignored not just *Time on the Cross* but almost the entire economic side of slavery, which became for many years an arcane subspecialty within economic history. The mainstream study of slavery became even more tightly restricted to the realms of slave society and culture. It would take more than thirty years for American historians to get seriously interested in the economics of slavery again.[70]

MEANWHILE, FREED FROM THE HEADACHES OF THE ROCHESTER HISTORY Department by an idyllic fellowship at the Center for Advanced Study in the Behavioral Sciences in the hills above Palo Alto, Genovese was able to complete his own big slavery book. He wrote at a torrential pace in the fall of 1972, with more pages making their way to the typist all the time. His sense that masters shaped the lives of slaves, just as slaves also shaped the lives of masters, informed his growing conviction that the central theme of

Black history was "the unique and dual nature of the black experience in the United States"—something that was distinct but also inseparable from the rest of America. "I expect it to be slammed," he told Woodward that fall. "The integrationists will hate it as too pro-nationalist; the nationalists will hate it because I (a honkey) wrote it before they did. . . . And the radicals will hate it because there is no revolutionary tradition to be found in it." He dropped his original title (*Sambo and Nat Turner*) in favor of *Roll, Jordan, Roll,* which he thought did a better job of capturing the role that religion had come to play in it.[71]

By January 1973, Genovese was starting to send packets of his growing manuscript to friends. He laced his letters with characteristically profane jokes. "Could I lean on you good souls to read my [manuscript] on the Nigger Question?" he asked Elkins and another colleague. "The fucking thing is already 800 pages long, with about 400 more to come," he warned. He went on, in a jab aimed specifically at Elkins: "It is a good thing that the buggers were infantilized. Imagine what a job I would have sorting them out if they had resisted infantilization and become complicated adults!"[72]

In the spring, Genovese sent Woodward the first six hundred pages, which arrived just in time for Woodward to pack them for his usual spring-break trip to the Caribbean. He took the draft out to the beach at Guadeloupe and read it while sipping a steady stream of rum punches as the sun shone through palm leaves and bougainvillea blooms. At first he was surprised to find that a manuscript claiming to describe "the world the slaves made" started with several hundred pages about the masters. "But I see very shortly," he wrote in his notes, "that I complained too soon." Deep into his fourth rum punch, with the sun sinking slowly toward the horizon and the surf sloshing softly on the beach, he found himself almost overcome by emotion—"into the rum punch splashes one salt tear"—as he arrived at a section about slaves asserting the right to have their service repaid with kindness. "Maybe, Gene, you are the only one who could get by with this," Woodward wrote. "Who else would dare? One more rum punch and I will be prepared for whatever comeuppance you will deal out to ole Massa. After all, he in de cole, cole ground."[73]

Woodward's opinion of Genovese's manuscript continued to rise as he kept reading and thinking about it, even when sober. Soon he told Genovese that *Roll, Jordan, Roll* might become the first really good book ever written about slavery.[74]

Genovese's full draft stretched to more than 1,300 pages. He then spent months slashing out large chunks, and the shorter but still substantial final version was published in the fall of 1974. Given Genovese's intellectual style, it's almost certain that he saw the book as the dialectical synthesis that united Ulrich Phillips (thesis) and Kenneth Stampp (antithesis). "Cruel, unjust, exploitative, oppressive," Genovese began, "slavery bound two peoples together in bitter antagonism while creating an organic relationship so complex and ambivalent that neither could express the simplest human feelings without reference to the other." Over the course of hundreds of pages, he packed in details about everything from work rhythms to family roles to dinner recipes (he was particularly proud of his recipe for parboiled and roasted opossum), showing always how white and Black southerners shaped one another's lives.[75]

Genovese characterized the master-slave relationship as "paternalist," a term whose Hegelian complexity he sought to unpack in a brief introduction. He defined *paternalism* as a system in which masters provided for and protected their dependents, whose labor they received in return. Central to Genovese's story of the Old South was his sense that slaves and masters developed different interpretations of the paternalist ethos. For masters, this ideology justified their appropriation of slave labor as a proper return for the protection and direction they provided. For slaves, on the other hand, it provided an implicit recognition of their humanity through its insistence on the mutual obligations of master and man.

Genovese despised bourgeois liberalism—after the collapse of the Soviet Union, he would convert from Communism to Catholicism—so he ignored or simply couldn't see all the appeals to liberal rights in the writings of former slaves like Frederick Douglass. Instead, he sought the source of slave resistance in the coiled spring of the master-slave dialectic. Slaves bought into the paternalistic ethos of their masters, Genovese claimed, but in buying in they also gained the ability to shape the social order through their own interpretations of their rights and obligations. Slaves saw kindness as their due, an interpretation that turned paternalism into self-protection and dependence into interdependence. "The slaves' acceptance of paternalism . . . ," Genovese wrote, "signaled acceptance of an imposed white domination within which they drew their own lines, asserted rights, and preserved their self-respect." Similarly knotty paradoxes characterized the whole book, in which lines of logic typically unfolded, looped around, and got tangled in complexity and ambiguity.

Masters tried to convince themselves that they had their slaves' happiness at heart, according to Genovese, but that happiness was possible only through the creation of an autonomous cultural and spiritual life—an autonomous cultural and spiritual life whose very existence undercut the rationale for slavery and exposed the illusion that slaves were simply extensions of their masters' wills. The heart of Genovese's book, then, became an analysis of that cultural and spiritual life, represented most powerfully by religion. Slave religion embodied all the contradictions Genovese saw in slave culture: it encouraged collective consciousness while simultaneously asserting individual equality; it forged a proto-nationalist spirit while at the same time offering a universalist vision of forgiveness and reconciliation; it taught love and solidarity while preventing the emergence of a political consciousness.

Roll, Jordan, Roll was rich enough that it could be read in multiple ways. It was about the roots of Black nationalism; it was also about the relationship between labor and ownership in corporate America. But it was ultimately a book about why slaves didn't unite to resist their oppression, not a book that celebrated the creation of alternative cultures and communities as ends in themselves. The slave community enabled resistance to slaveholder ideology—but only within the system of slavery. Slave culture became a precious possession—so precious that slaves preferred not to lose it through rash acts of rebellion. In that regard, the book served as another ironic capstone to the culture and community studies of the 1970s. As Genovese concluded, "The slaves' success in forging a world of their own within a wider world shaped primarily by their oppressors sapped their will to revolt, not so much because they succumbed to the baubles of amelioration as because they themselves were creating conditions worth living in as slaves while simultaneously facing overwhelming power that discouraged frontal attack."[76]

Even though it arrived amid a flood of new books about slavery, *Roll, Jordan, Roll* sold strongly in its own right. The Yale Co-op sold out of its first copies within minutes and struggled to keep up with demand. The Book of the Month Club was stunned at the number of people requesting copies. Even Gutman had to admit that Genovese had written "a powerful work." As he told Woodward, "It makes Fogel and Engerman look like overseers . . . not 'masters.'" Many readers were baffled by Genovese's interpretive superstructure of hegemony, paternalism, and Black nationalism, but no one interested in slavery could ignore the book. "Only once before, with Ulrich B. Phillips, has the work of a single scholar seemed so central to the study of [American slavery]," one young historian wrote, predicting that Genovese's work would remain "influential for decades to come." He was right: *Roll, Jordan, Roll* became one of the most widely read US history books over the next two decades, and in the early 2000s one writer declared it the single most enduring work of historical scholarship published since World War II.[77] Nearly every scholar studying American slavery during the rest of the twentieth century would respond to it in some way.

PART IV

INTEGRATION

10
THE BIG PICTURE

THE CIVIL RIGHTS MOVEMENT QUICKLY DELIVERED ON ITS PROMISES of legal equality and enfranchisement. The racial income gap steadily declined throughout the 1960s and early 1970s, giving rise to a new Black middle class. Black mayors were elected in major cities such as Cleveland, Detroit, and Atlanta, and a Black woman became the University of Alabama's homecoming queen. By the middle of the 1970s, the percentage of Black high school graduates heading to college already matched that of whites, as did the incomes of young Black couples with college degrees. The success of the Black middle class and the repression of Black radicals meant that the Black liberation movement largely gave up on radical visions of transformation and was content to seek incremental change within the system.

Many whites saw these changes and assumed that the civil rights struggle was over—something they could confirm by placing it safely into the past, where it could be viewed in retrospect as a success that ultimately vindicated American values and left a legacy of color-blind individualism. In 1976, fifty years after Carter Woodson held the first Negro History Week, President

Gerald Ford officially recognized all of February as Black History Month, a move that he tied to both the success of civil rights and the nation's impending Bicentennial. "In celebrating Black History Month," Ford declared, "we can take satisfaction from this recent progress in the realization of the ideals envisioned by our Founding Fathers."[1]

Nothing symbolized this assimilation of Black history into the American story more than the *Roots* phenomenon. Published at the same moment as the Bicentennial, Alex Haley's story followed a single Black family from Africa through enslavement to freedom. Haley had first made his name working with Malcolm X on his as-told-to *Autobiography* in the early 1960s. Then, talking to relatives at a reunion in Kansas, Haley began to hear stories that traced his family history all the way back, he discovered, to "the original African who was taken into slavery." Starting with that ancestor in Africa, he realized, he would be able to tell an epic that encompassed all of American history. His goal was to integrate slavery into the shared story of America, showing "how the Negro is part and parcel of the American saga."[2]

After identifying The Gambia as his ancestral home, Haley traveled there twice in the spring of 1967. With a good eye for publicity, the recently independent Gambian government organized a "Haley Committee" to help him find, or forge, a family connection. They eventually hit on something that would work in the village of Juffure. There Haley learned about an eighteenth-century villager, Kunta Kinte, who ventured out for firewood one day and never returned. Kunta's family suspected that he was captured and sold into slavery. Hearing this, Haley was overcome with emotion: he believed that he had found the missing link between his family's stories in America and the oral traditions of this West African village. It was the holy grail of Black history.

However unlikely it was that Haley actually discovered his ancestor, the details were close enough to make the story plausible and compelling. Kunta Kinte would soon become the most famous African in American history, a stand-in for every Black family's missing link.

As Haley worked on his book over the next several years, he tested out his story and generated advance publicity by delivering lectures around the country. Coming in the midst of the Black studies boom, Haley's talks about his search for Black ancestors proved enormously popular. Hundreds of thousands of people heard him speak. When he saw how his story moved them, he became convinced that his book would sell at least a million copies. He sold the hardcover and paperback rights, and soon the film rights, too.

Roots was listed as a nonfiction book, but even Haley himself described it as "faction," a mix of fact and fiction, a novelization based on the details he knew. The saga begins with an idealized West African village, the kind of place where one could hear women pounding couscous and preparing breakfast. But everything changes when a young Kunta Kinte is taken captive one morning while out to chop wood. Kunta survives the harrowing Middle Passage, which Haley described in visceral detail, and is sold into slavery in America. After multiple attempts at escape, he gradually learns to accept his new life—even though doing so kills "something precious and irretrievable" inside him. He gets married and has a daughter, Kizzy.

Drawing on the WPA interviews with former slaves, Haley included scenes where enslaved people cared for their families, passed down oral traditions, and played together in their own spaces. Yet his depiction of the Kintes as a family like any other made it even more distressing to see slavery tear them apart. When Kizzy is a teenager, she is suddenly sold away as punishment for assisting an older boy's escape. Distraught, Kunta goes to his cabin, grabs the gourd where he's been collecting pebbles to mark the time since his enslavement, and flings the thing to the ground, scattering pebbles in all directions. This quietly devastating moment is our last glimpse of him. The story shifts abruptly to Kizzy, who is raped almost immediately by her new master, and follows her descendants through several hundred more pages into freedom.[3]

When *Roots* was published, in the fall of 1976, it sat at the top of the nonfiction bestseller list for five months and soon sold 1.5 million copies in hardcover—proving Haley's instincts right. But even those numbers were dwarfed by the audience for the eight-part miniseries that aired on ABC at the end of January. The network worried that the miniseries, which had a mostly Black cast, might not catch on with white audiences, so executives decided to show the episodes on eight consecutive days to ensure only one week of dismal ratings if no one watched. The schedule may have started as a hedge against low viewership, but it quickly became a driver of intense interest and anticipation as more and more people saw each night's new installment. It was as close as the 1970s got to the binge-watching experience of the streaming era. By the end of the week, more than 100 million people tuned in for the final episode—more than half of all households with a television in the United States—surpassing *Gone with the Wind* to make it the most-watched television program in US history. Over the full week, some 85 percent of the country saw at least part of the series.

The book received special citations from the Pulitzer Prize Board and the National Book Foundation, while the miniseries garnered dozens of Emmy nominations and nine wins—even as Haley soon faced charges of plagiarism, one of which he settled out of court. Some historians faulted Haley for what they saw as his romanticism regarding the slave community, even though it echoed many of the scholarly studies that were appearing at the same time. Stanley Elkins concluded that *Roots* played the same role for Black Americans that *Exodus* did for his own Jewish family: "good soap opera but bad history," full of "cardboard characters" designed to satisfy "the deep need of the black community for ancestors."[4]

Yet rarely in American history had so many people engaged with the subject of slavery. Never before had they done so from the perspective of the enslaved. One historian has gone so far as to call *Roots* the first national memorial to slavery, while LeVar Burton, who played Kunta Kinte, probably spoke for many viewers when he described the experience of filming the series as an education. "We got schooled through *Roots*," he said, "of the human cost of that equation."[5]

But if *Roots* schooled Americans in the human cost of slavery, it also assimilated the Black experience as a classic immigrant story of individual opportunity and upward mobility. True, the migration was forced, and the mobility was from slavery to freedom, but the outline was essentially similar to that of other immigrant sagas, such as *The Godfather*, which also proved astoundingly popular in the 1970s as white ethnics shared in the search for identity by exploring their own roots. The overall story of US history remained largely the same, with any changes occurring in the margins—sometimes literally, as in the case of textbook sidebars to cover the new cast of multicultural characters. The goal of integration was displaced by individual opportunity; difference became a promise rather than a problem.[6]

In the decades immediately following World War II, American history was often framed in direct contrast to the foes that the United States was fighting. America was not fascist or communist or totalitarian; it was a land of freedom, capitalism, and democracy. But with the seismic shocks of the 1960s and early 1970s—the civil rights movement, the women's movement, Vietnam, Watergate—Americans faced new questions about their history and identity. At the broadest level, faith in the country and its future was faltering.[7]

It was at precisely this moment, in the second half of the 1970s, that slavery was becoming central to the scholarly understanding of American history. And it was against this background that scholars had to determine how slavery, which for much of the early twentieth century was considered a subfield of southern history, would be reintegrated into the national story. They also had to figure out how that integration might affect the larger story the country told about itself.

Yet the study of slavery itself changed, too. The so-called golden age of slavery studies in the 1970s gave way to a gap that stretched all the way to the late 1990s, the next moment when a comparable burst of excitement and interest could be seen. Of course, the subject didn't disappear in these years. Slavery still mattered, and the number of new publications about it continued to grow. But the rate of increase slowed considerably.

And more important than the sheer volume of studies, slavery stopped being the most significant subject in the field of American historical scholarship. During the civil rights movement, antebellum slavery had served as a useful analogue because it demonstrated that a vast historical iniquity could suddenly be ended. Just as slavery was eradicated with emancipation, so racial discrimination would die with civil rights legislation. But now, as some forms of inequality lingered more than a decade after the Civil Rights and Voting Rights Acts, it appeared that the solution would not be that simple. At the same time, as the US political and economic system came in for deeper critiques in the wake of Vietnam and Watergate, it became harder for scholars to lay all the problems of Black people at the feet of slavery and segregation.

The intellectual energy that had gone into the study of slavery over the previous two decades began to bleed into Reconstruction as scholars compared the fate of the civil rights movement with the failure of America's earlier effort to enact a more racially egalitarian democracy. Some historians believed that this shift opened up greater space for a more objective and disinterested study of slavery. At the very least, it relieved the subject of some of its contemporary social and political burden.[8] Slavery may have become central to American history—but it had also been relegated firmly to the past.

Among those who continued to study slavery, the nature of their scholarship shifted. For at least a generation, the shape of American slavery scholarship had been short but thick, with a large number of scholars focused on what slavery was like for a few decades in a few states at the very tail end of its history in North America. Now that shape became broader but thinner as scholars branched out from the antebellum period to see what slavery was like in other times and places. A string of studies demonstrated not only that slavery was a diverse and dynamic institution but also that it had existed from New England to Texas (and beyond) over the course of more than two centuries. These studies reminded scholars that slavery was nearly everywhere you looked in early America.

Several historians advocated studying slavery across time and space in the 1970s, but the one who became perhaps most influential was none other than Eugene Genovese's nemesis, Herbert Gutman. Ever since the late 1960s, when he first started to investigate Black family structures in the wake of the Moynihan Report, Gutman had been slowly assembling a book on *The Black Family in Slavery and Freedom*. He completed a draft in the early 1970s, but then he spent years overcooking it, adding and revising until he wound up with endless repetition, sixty-eight pages of appendices, and giant footnotes fighting with Genovese. His book was finally published in 1976.

Gutman believed that slaves developed a world that was largely their own, one that was not shaped in any kind of dialectic with whites (as Genovese would have it). There existed "distinctive slave feelings, beliefs, and especially institutions," he claimed, and the slave family was the central institution that bound together the slave community. His analysis of slave naming practices, for example, showed that the choice of names typically lay with slaves, who used them to reinforce kinship bonds by naming children for fathers or grandparents. "Enslavement was harsh and constricted the enslaved," he concluded. "But it did not destroy their capacity to adapt and sustain the vital familial and kin associations and beliefs that served as the underpinning of a developing Afro-American culture."[9]

Aside from his emphasis on the adaptive character of slave culture, Gutman's most important insight was to see slave culture as something that developed over time—and time was a dimension that he believed several generations of slavery scholars had neglected. "Nearly the entire literature on slavery," he once complained to Vann Woodward, "stretching from Phillips to Stampp, to Elkins and even to my former colleague Genovese," failed to deal "adequately with the ways in which slaves accumulated a culture (historical experience over time)." According to Gutman, it was in the middle of the eighteenth century, a period of heavy direct importation from Africa, that a new Afro-American culture developed and slave communities took on "a distinctive character." And he examined not just how slave culture developed over time but also how it "*moved in space*," as he put it, as a result of the domestic slave trade, which carried cultural practices across the Old Southwest.[10]

After completing his *Black Family* book, Gutman spent the 1975–76 academic year at Princeton's Davis Center for Historical Studies. He shared a house and often had lunch with another Davis Center fellow, Ira Berlin, who'd recently published a book on free Blacks in the South before the Civil War.[11]

Berlin began to follow up on Gutman's suggestion that historians should pay more attention to slavery's evolution. He had a rough version of his research ready by the end of the year he spent with Gutman, and in 1980 it was published in the *American Historical Review*. He identified three separate patterns of African American life in the colonial period—one in the North, one in the Chesapeake, and one in the Carolinas—and showed how differences in immigration patterns, demographics, and local economies influenced the experience of slavery and the shape of Black society in each region. Berlin's basic point was that American slavery was a diverse system that was difficult to generalize, and that the different forms that slavery took had important effects on Black society and culture. "Thus no matter how complete recent studies of black life appear," he concluded, "they are limited to the extent that they provide a static and singular vision of a dynamic and complex society."[12]

This set the agenda for the next generation of slavery scholars. Berlin himself spent two decades charting the evolution of slavery across mainland North America, which he laid out in the late 1990s in a book called *Many Thousands Gone*. He divided slavery's development into three periods, or "generations"—Charter, Plantation, and Revolutionary—and in each generation he outlined how slavery changed across four regions—the North, the Chesapeake, the Carolinas, and the Lower Mississippi. This highly schematic outline simplified and streamlined a story of tremendous diversity and variability, somewhat undermining Berlin's earlier message about the dangers of generalization, but it proved perfect for college courses. *Many Thousands Gone* and Berlin's subsequent book, *Generations of Captivity*, which condensed the colonial material and carried the story through another two generations to emancipation, became standard assignments in classrooms across the country.

Studying slavery across the depth and breadth of American history was not the only way that scholars expanded slavery scholarship in these years. Studies combining the Caribbean with the colonial South began to proliferate as scholars situated slavery into a larger framework focused on the Atlantic slave system as a whole. Some cast an even wider net, going back to the medieval Mediterranean or ancient Athens to trace the origins of slavery, define its essence, and tease out its relationship to apparently antithetical phenomena such as freedom, democracy, and capitalism. The person who did the most to broaden the story of slavery in this way—to provide a "Big Picture" perspective, as he would later put it—was the historian David Brion

Davis. From his position at Yale, Davis virtually defined the study of slavery in the late twentieth century—and he was adamant about seeing slavery as central to understanding not just America but also the entire human experience.

For Davis, slavery was above all a problem in philosophy and morality. As a young man, he'd left home three days after his high school graduation in 1945 to report for duty at Camp Gordon—by coincidence, the same place Ulrich Phillips served during World War I. When Hiroshima and Nagasaki ended the war in August, his assignment suddenly shifted to police work in postwar Germany. Struck by the contrast between the Germans, who were supposedly Aryan supremacists yet welcomed Americans regardless of race, and the Americans, who supposedly fought for freedom and democracy yet maintained a segregated army, Davis soon decided to become a historian. He explained his reasoning to his parents in a long letter just before he returned to America: "When we think back into our childhood," he wrote, "it doesn't do much good to merely hit the high spots and remember what we want to remember. To know why we act the way we do, we have to remember everything. . . . Perhaps such teaching could make us understand ourselves."[13]

Back in the United States, Davis studied philosophy at Dartmouth on the GI Bill and then moved on to the graduate program in American civilization at Harvard. During his final year in Cambridge, he happened to live near Kenneth Stampp while Stampp was there finishing up *The Peculiar Institution*. They often got together to talk. It was during these discussions that Davis realized just how little he had learned about slavery. As is often the case in such retrospective realizations (then as now), part of the problem had been Davis's own lack of interest or understanding; he doodled mountains in his notes on the day one professor discussed the rise of slavery in Virginia. Yet it was true that slavery stayed on the margins in Davis's courses. Stampp was showing him that it actually lay at the heart of American history.

Davis started teaching at Cornell, where he learned that the library held an extensive antislavery collection that few historians had used. By the summer of 1957, he recognized that he could use the Cornell collection to do the antislavery equivalent of Stampp's book: a study of nineteenth-century abolitionism. He suspected that the subject of slavery would allow him to probe what he later called "the extreme limits of dehumanization"—the understanding of which he saw as essential to a proper conception of human nature.[14]

The scope of the project expanded a year later, when Davis learned about the deep transatlantic roots of the antislavery movement while on a Guggenheim Fellowship in England. Then, back in the United States, he encountered Elkins and McKitrick's *Slavery* soon after it was published. It blew him away. The way they used sociology and psychology, the way they related slavery to antislavery within the broader context of American culture, the way they raised fundamental questions about human nature, freedom, and American exceptionalism—this was exactly the kind of thing Davis was working toward, and it served as an inspiration.[15]

Soon Davis's planned book on nineteenth-century abolitionism morphed into something different: its background chapter grew into a five-hundred-page "introductory" volume of its own. He called it *The Problem of Slavery in Western Culture.* For Davis, the "problem of slavery" was that even as enslavers sought to make slaves into pure property, they could never fully deny the humanity of their slaves. He believed that this problem had been a source of tension in Western thought since the Greeks and that the fundamental character of slavery in the Western world had not changed over the course of some three thousand years. Slavery "was a single phenomenon, or *Gestalt,*" he determined, "whose variations were less significant than underlying patterns of unity." It was a problem that "transcended national boundaries."

But if there was nothing especially new about modern British American slavery, then what could explain the rise of the world's first antislavery movement in the British colonies? This was the central question that Davis was trying to answer. The emergence of abolitionism, he wrote, was "less a direct response to a unique evil than a result of particular cultural and religious developments in the English-speaking world." First, Enlightenment thinkers like Hobbes swept away traditional authorities, and then reactions to Hobbes emphasized the basic inner goodness of human beings and recommended a new ethic of benevolence. The rise of evangelical religion reinforced both the burden on humans to do good in the world and the belief that all were capable of spiritual redemption. Africans began to be seen as not only barbarous and beastly but also innocent and potentially virtuous—as in the works of Anthony Benezet. The British imperial crises of the 1760s and 1770s catalyzed these abstract ideals into antislavery protest.[16]

Published in the spring of 1966, *The Problem of Slavery in Western Culture* won the Pulitzer Prize. The book's success opened new opportunities for Davis; he soon joined Vann Woodward at Yale.

Despite his professional accomplishments, Davis was sensitive to reviews, especially from people he respected. One review in particular stuck with him as he started to work on his next *Problem of Slavery* volume. Writing in the *New York Review of Books*, the ancient historian Moses Finley said he found *Western Culture* frustrating on the "decisive question" of why slavery was finally abolished in the West. Davis had outlined the tremendous shift in moral perception that enabled abolitionist thought to emerge, but he stopped just short of showing how those ideas translated into policy. "Nothing is more difficult perhaps than to explain how and why, or why not, a new moral perception becomes effective in action," Finley wrote. "Yet nothing is more urgent if an academic historical exercise is to become a significant investigation of human behavior with direct relevance to the world we now live in."[17]

This was the main question that guided Davis's work over the next few years. Overflowing with notes and ideas, he was constantly writing reminders to himself: "Don't let the material dominate you! Stick to the point!"[18]

Luckily, Davis happened to have a fellowship at the Center for Advanced Study in the Behavioral Sciences in 1972–73, which put him in Palo Alto at the same time as Eugene Genovese was there writing *Roll, Jordan, Roll*. Davis and Genovese were already on good terms, with a mutual respect for each other's work, and their friendship deepened during their year together in California. Genovese had a sharp, logical mind, honed over decades of Marxist dialectics, and it provided the perfect complement to Davis's more diffuse philosophical digressions. The two men spent hours discussing domination and submission, swapped drafts, and even shared a typist. Often, Genovese worked to tighten Davis's prose, and he was especially annoyed by Davis's use of underlined or italicized words for emphasis. "Try underlining your ass," he wrote. "David Davis eats shit!" Yet he could not hide his admiration for what Davis was doing. By the final chapter, he had only half a page of notes, followed by a flourish: "The whole chapter is brilliant——————." Davis later considered it the most productive year of his life. "It's now clearer to me than even before," he told Genovese just before he returned to New Haven, "that our books move along very similar lines of analysis."[19]

The Problem of Slavery in the Age of Revolution was published in the spring of 1975. The Age of Revolution served, Davis wrote, as "a major turning point in the history of New World slavery." Wartime disruptions and Revolutionary ideals meant that slavery was disavowed in principle and in practice in much of the West. In the United States, one function of antislavery ideas was to allow Americans to show that they were virtuous republicans whose revolution had not been about their own self-interest. More generally, abolitionism posited a hard distinction between slavery and other forms of labor. In Britain, entrepreneurial Quakers and others like them needed an outlet for the expression of Christian humanitarian ideals that would not also undercut their own business; the antislavery movement provided that, giving a "certain moral insulation to economic activities less visibly dependent on human suffering and injustice." This was not a simple question of economic interest, according to Davis, but also an unconscious one of ideological function. Antislavery ideology supplied a simplified definition of freedom as the freedom to receive wages for one's labor. Although this view of freedom may have been narrow, it made sense to the men who were developing the new economic order of industrial capitalism. "They unwittingly drew distinctions and boundaries which opened the way," Davis wrote, "under a guise of moral rectitude, for unprecedented forms of oppression."[20]

Age of Revolution won the Bancroft Prize and the National Book Award. Even fifty years later, it continues to influence how historians think about slavery, antislavery, and capitalism. But as responses from readers flowed in, it became clear that what Davis accomplished in *Age of Revolution* was somehow different from an ordinary history book. "I was strangely moved by it," one historian told him, describing the book as "always a moral exercise AND an intellectual exercise as well." The book also marked Davis's transition from an intellectual historian to a slavery scholar—perhaps the top slavery scholar in America—as he began what he called "a substantive study of black slavery."[21]

Davis was far from the only historian thinking about the relationship among slavery, freedom, and democracy in the late 1970s. Two other efforts, in particular, would soon become central to the field of slavery studies, especially in America. The first came from Moses Finley, the ancient historian who reviewed *Western Culture* and spurred Davis to focus on how ideas were translated into action. Finley was interested in seeing how a society went from depending on slavery to ending it—perhaps because, at just that moment, he was confronting a similar question in his own work.

When Finley reviewed *Western Culture* in early 1967, he had just finished writing an entry on "Slavery" for the *International Encyclopedia of the Social Sciences*. In it, he established several of the basic concepts that would structure scholarly understandings of slavery over the next few decades. The usual state of things in world history, according to Finley, was for societies to have a small number of enslaved outsiders as a result of warfare, kidnapping, or piracy. These slaves existed alongside other forms of free and dependent labor. Finley called the societies where this was the case "*slave-owning* societies," which also became known as "societies with slaves."

But according to Finley, there had also been a few times and places in world history where slavery developed into "the main dependent labor force," replacing or supplanting other forms of labor. In places where "the economic and political elite depended primarily on slave labor for basic production," he believed, slavery took on a fundamentally different character and function than it did in places where a smaller number of slaves occupied primarily domestic roles. Finley called these places where slavery assumed a new significance "*genuine* slave societies," or simply "slave societies." He thought they were rare in world history, and in fact he could identify only a handful: Greece and Rome in the ancient world, the American South and the Caribbean in modern times.[22]

This division of the world into "slave societies" and "societies with slaves" would become vastly influential. After his "Slavery" entry was published in the late 1960s, Finley became widely acknowledged as one of the world's chief experts on the subject, and everyone wanted him to write a full book on it. He repeatedly declined, however, and his own scholarship on slavery slowed considerably. In part, this reflected his own success. His clear and engaging style made him a sought-after book reviewer and presenter of public education programs in Britain, where he taught at Cambridge; at the same time, he had to curtail his work schedule because of high blood pressure. Projects started to pile up, many of them uncompleted, and eventually it was only the hard deadline of a public lecture that could force him to put ideas on paper.[23]

Finley's lack of progress on a slavery book also reflected the fact that even though he had defined the characteristics of "societies with slaves" and "slave societies," he didn't know how to explain the transformation from one type of society to the other. Finally, after more than a decade of thinking about the problem, he forced himself to confront it—by agreeing to give a series of four lectures on the subject at the College de France in Paris. He picked a date about eighteen months in the future, at the end of 1978, because even then he still needed plenty of time to prepare, filling blank exam books with notes as he went through all the existing scholarship.[24]

By the time he delivered his lectures, Finley saw the rise and fall of slave societies as depending primarily on changes in the position of the native lower classes. In the case of ancient Greece and Rome, for example, the key turning point occurred when peasants became part of the political community. The rise of a somewhat more democratic and egalitarian society as the peasantry attained landownership and citizenship constituted "something radically new in the world," Finley said, and meant they could no longer be exploited as a dependent labor force. The upper classes had to turn to enslaved outsiders for labor, leading to the rise of a slave society.[25]

Similarly, Finley believed that the decline of ancient slavery several hundred years later was the result of "a gradual erosion in the capacity of the lower classes to resist working for the benefit of others under conditions of less than full 'freedom of contract.'" Peasants lost the political rights of citizenship at the same time as burdensome land taxes made things harder for small farmers and tenants. These once-free people became available again for compulsory labor, rendering it unnecessary for large landowners to seek outside sources. Slaves still existed, but there was no longer a slave society.[26]

Finley turned his lectures into a book called *Ancient Slavery and Modern Ideology*. "To the astonishment of many and the disgust of some," he confided, this relatively brief set of lectures would be "the book on slavery everyone seems to be expecting from me, because the first lecture ends by asserting that one cannot write a history of ancient slavery." What he meant was that ancient slavery was not separable from ancient society. "A genuine 'synthesis' of the history of ancient slavery," as he put it in the book, "can only be a history of Graeco-Roman society."[27]

Just as Finley was finishing *Ancient Slavery and Modern Ideology*, he happened to receive a large manuscript in the mail from a scholar named Orlando Patterson. A Black sociologist who had started his career with a study of slavery in his home country of Jamaica, Patterson sent the draft to Finley because he considered Finley's work "a point of departure" for his own. It turned out that he was also at work on a project to examine slavery's essence across history. Using an anthropological sample of world cultures, he posed a series of forty-three questions about population, slave status, manumission, and so on. The answers went into a large database that he began to analyze in 1975, resulting in one of the first truly global studies of slavery in nearly a century.

Patterson identified three "constituent elements" of slavery. The first was that slavery involved the violent domination of an individual; force was essential in maintaining slavery, which was a relationship of extreme power and powerlessness. The second element was that the slave was "a socially dead person," someone with no formally recognized social relations or cultural heritage. This lack of legally enforceable connections was precisely what made the slave valuable to masters as a human tool. Finally, the third element of slavery was dishonor. Typically, there would be various rituals of enslavement and marks of servitude that would symbolize the dishonor of the slave and mark him or her as socially dead. Patterson memorably described slavery as a form of "parasitism," with the slaveholder leeching the slave of power, honor, and authority.[28]

Even as Finley and Patterson pursued projects that seemed similar on the surface, Finley's response to Patterson's draft revealed the gulf between them. "This is a difficult, and indeed embarrassing, letter for me to write,"

Finley began, difficult and embarrassing because he disagreed so strongly with Patterson on the fundamental questions of how to define slavery and how to assess its historical significance. "I do not accept your global inclusion of all possible forms of involuntary labour under the rubric 'slavery,'" Finley wrote. What really mattered, in his mind, were the handful of instances that were truly different. As he put it to Patterson, "Your method precludes the very possibility of examining and explaining the 'minority,' which happen to be the important slave societies in history."[29]

Patterson went to work on revisions, but he stuck to his main ideas. *Slavery and Social Death* was published in 1982, and "social death" quickly became both a shorthand definition of slavery and an influential concept for analyzing how slavery operated in law and in practice.

Meanwhile, Davis was also at work on his own effort to examine slavery's essence. After publishing *Age of Revolution*, he did not turn directly to the planned final volume of his trilogy, *The Problem of Slavery in the Age of Emancipation*, about which he felt considerable trepidation. Instead, he outlined a separate book called *Slavery and Human Progress*. His goal was to sketch the origins of Black slavery and explore connections between the idea of historical progress and the project of emancipation. He hoped the work would "explode a few mines" before he began *Age of Emancipation* in earnest.[30]

The book took Davis years longer than he thought it would, and it ended up as a bit of a mess. To the extent that the book had a point, it was that there had been a "momentous shift from 'progressive' enslavement to 'progressive' emancipation"—from theories of slavery as a "progressive" institution to theories that slavery was an obstacle to progress. Finley reviewed *Slavery and Human Progress* in the *New York Times* and declared the book "a melancholy waste of immense effort" because of Davis's reluctance to go beyond "a lively but superficial account of the rhetoric" about slavery. Privately he was even harsher: "I wouldn't have accepted this from a Ph.D. dissertation, let alone from a senior historian and Pulitzer prizewinner." He was not alone in his confusion and frustration. Davis became depressed as he saw that his attempt to combine a survey of slavery with a reflection on progress had yielded a book that performed neither task particularly well and pleased almost no one.[31]

By this time, Davis felt tremendous pressure to finish his *Problem of Slavery* trilogy, and to do so in a way that would maintain the high standards of the first two volumes. But in the wake of *Slavery and Human Progress*, he found it impossible to work on what he thought of as "THE Book." His confidence was shot, his enthusiasm for the project at a low ebb. He turned eagerly toward distractions even as he told himself not to, and became embroiled in a yearslong exchange with an impertinent younger historian regarding the relationship between capitalism and moral reform. Some scholars saw it as the most significant historiographical debate in years—it was collected in a book that became widely used in graduate history courses—but it was not how Davis really wanted to be spending his time.[32]

As that debate was grinding away, Davis also found other distractions. One was professional responsibilities: during one especially busy year, he was supervising a dozen senior essays and nearly two dozen dissertations while also teaching, chairing a search committee, and serving on two book-prize committees. Another was religion. His wife was Jewish, and now, after about fifteen years of marriage, he decided to convert. He set aside Shabbat to study the Torah and other works of Judaica, and he and his wife spent their Saturday evenings at a discussion group devoted to each week's parashah. By the fall of 1987, he saw his whole life as "a religious quest," and he completed his conversion a few months later. His older son, Adam, believed that Judaism became "a substitute" for *Age of Emancipation*, a way for Davis to explore moral problems without the pressure of another *Problem of Slavery* book.[33]

By the 1980s, the study of American slavery was becoming broader not only across time and place but in other ways as well. Up until this point, nearly all scholars of slavery were men. At the start of the 1960s, a grand total of four women held professorships in the country's ten highest-ranking graduate history programs, and the numbers were even more disproportionate for Black women.[34]

Partly for that reason, the slave culture and community studies of the late 1960s and 1970s focused largely on proving that enslaved Black men retained their manhood—and, therefore, their potential for political action. Enslaved Black women were sidelined. In all 660 pages of *Roll, Jordan, Roll,* for example, Genovese included precisely one seven-page section on "wives and mothers."[35]

Already in 1971, the Black scholar and activist Angela Davis identified some of the key tensions that would later characterize much of the scholarship on slave women. One was that Black women's work in the slave home, which was the kind of domestic labor that the feminist movement considered oppressive for women, was for slaves the only work not done for the direct benefit of their owners and indeed laid the foundation for whatever degree of autonomy the slave community had. Another was that enslaved Black women didn't benefit from the traditional protections that patriarchal society afforded to women, but they also didn't face the limited roles and expectations of traditional femininity. Although they were forced to work in the fields and were more vulnerable to abuse, they also enjoyed something much closer to equality with their men than was possible in genteel white society at the time.

There was a limit to what Davis could do in that early article—in part because she was doing her research from behind bars, where she was being held for her involvement in a deadly shootout in a Marin County courtroom. She was later released on bail and found not guilty, but it turned out there was not much more she could learn about enslaved women even with access to a better library. Enslaved Black women had produced vanishingly few sources, and scholars had devoted little attention to the particularity of their experiences. "With the sole exceptions of Harriet Tubman and Sojourner Truth," Davis lamented, "black women of the slave era remain more or less enshrouded in unrevealed history."[36]

Around the same time, Gerda Lerner, a European immigrant who was one of the pioneering women's historians in the United States, assembled a documentary collection called *Black Women in White America* that featured more than six hundred pages of primary sources. The collection started with some seventy pages on enslaved women, but Lerner admitted that this section "posed special research problems" owing to the limited and contradictory nature of the sources. She believed that it was still "too early to attempt the writing of a social history of black women," a task that would have to await more detailed research into their lives.[37] This was one reason why many early forays into the history of enslaved women looked a lot like Davis's essay, sketching the outlines of what a full study *could* look like or *should* look for in the future.

Women's position in higher education changed rapidly in the 1970s as a result of the women's movement and new antidiscrimination laws. Harvard, Yale, and Princeton had finally opened their undergraduate colleges to female students in 1969, the same year as the first women's studies program started at San Diego State. Women's studies spread to 270 schools within seven years, mirroring the Black studies boom that was occurring at the same time. Overall, female enrollments increased by more than 50 percent in the 1970s, but male enrollments saw only single-digit growth. By the middle of the decade, more women than men were entering college, and they predictably became a majority of college students just a few years after that. In the field of American history, women were earning 30 percent of the doctorates by 1980.[38]

On the faculty side, a new federal law in 1972 prohibited discrimination by sex in any institution of higher education that received federal funding. Not only that, but universities now had to submit detailed affirmative action plans for the hiring of women and minorities or face the suspension of their federal contracts. The old-boy network for faculty hiring was out, replaced by job ads and standardized protocols. As a direct result of these changes, women made up the bulk of young faculty hires at major universities in 1973. Change came more slowly at the highest levels of the profession; by the end of the 1970s, women still accounted for fewer than 2 percent of full professors across the country's top ten history departments.[39] But this still marked the start of the long-term feminization of the humanities.

As more women, including Black women, went to graduate school and became professors, they expanded slavery studies to include enslaved women, a shift that began in earnest in the early 1980s. This was when the first generation of female historians, those who started college in the late 1960s and attended graduate school during the 1970s, began to enter the profession. Over the next few years, there was a sudden outpouring of historical scholarship by women as these scholars published their first articles and books.

As the first full studies of enslaved women took shape, they fell into the same rough division as the rest of slavery scholarship in this period, with some scholars examining the essence of female slavery through the centuries while others looked closely at the specific experiences of slave women across America. Gerda Lerner, for example, turned to an ambitious global history of patriarchy. Looking at sources such as the Bible, the *Iliad*, the *Odyssey*, and Hammurabi's Code, Lerner saw that most of the earliest slaves in recorded history were women. They were the first group in human history to be marked off as different—as outsiders. This fact had been ignored by most scholars of slavery, Lerner believed, because of their "androcentric focus," which had also prevented them from noticing that women's experiences of slavery were fundamentally different from men's. In 1981, she presented her research at the Berkshire Conference of Women Historians; a revised version was published two years later in the new journal *Slavery & Abolition*, then incorporated into her book *The Creation of Patriarchy* in 1986.

For Lerner, women's experience of slavery was defined by sexual exploitation. Indeed, she believed that the sexual exploitation of captive women represented the very essence and even origin of slavery. Rape dishonored and subdued women, who might then become pregnant and psychologically attached to their master. This resulted in the creation of the concubine, which proved to be a transitional step on the way to enslavement—first of women, then of any other group that could be defined as outsiders. "By experimenting with the enslavement of women and children," Lerner wrote, "men learned to understand that all human beings have the potential for tolerating enslavement, and they developed the techniques and forms of enslavement which would enable them to make of their absolute dominance a social institution."[40]

In the field of American history, the first and also the most important book on slave women in this period was Deborah Gray White's *Ar'n't I a Woman? Female Slaves in the Plantation South*. One sign of the novelty of White's book was that when it arrived at the Library of Congress for cataloging in early 1985, there was not yet a subject heading for it. Confronted with

Ar'n't I a Woman?, a cataloguer suggested a new heading for "women slaves." It was approved that March.

This was not a new experience for White. Working on the subject as her dissertation in the 1970s, she confronted one obstacle after another, with professors questioning her sources and sending her back to do more work. Later, after she got her first job, a joint appointment in history and African American studies, she faced resistance from both sides. Initially, neither department considered a book on Black women significant, or sufficient for tenure.[41]

Similar stories littered the early years of Black women's historical scholarship, which did not fit neatly into any existing boxes—just like Black women's activism more generally. In response, Black feminists who felt neglected by both the (heavily masculine) Black liberation movement and the (mostly white) feminist movement began to form independent groups, such as the National Black Feminist Organization in New York and the Combahee River Collective in Boston. These activists articulated the idea, which they experienced in their own lives, that "the major systems of oppression are interlocking," as the Combahee River Collective Statement put it—that is, it was "difficult to separate race from class from sex oppression because in our lives they are most often experienced simultaneously."[42]

This idea, which later took the name "intersectionality," soon became a keynote of much early scholarship about enslaved Black women, who were seen as occupying the intersection of multiple overlapping forms of oppression. "Black in a white society, slave in a free society, woman in a society ruled by men," as White put it, "female slaves had the least formal power and were perhaps the most vulnerable group of antebellum Americans."

For White, Black women's work under slavery involved not just field or domestic labor but also reproductive labor, the work of bearing and raising the children who represented their own family—and slavery's future. Childbirth functioned as both the literal reproduction of the slave system and, according to White, "an act of defiance" because it served as "a signal to the slave owner that no matter how cruel and inhumane his actions, African-Americans would not be utterly subjugated or destroyed." White suggested that slave women recognized their role as "cogs in the plantation regime's reproductive machine." But her work, and other studies of slave women, also raised a troubling question. What would have been the larger psychological effects of bearing and raising children who were never entirely one's own, some of whom were the product of sexual abuse, and whose role was to reproduce the very system that kept them enslaved?

As early as 1971, Angela Davis had suggested an answer: the surrender of childbirth to the economic interests of slave owners was a "profound trauma." The word *trauma*, from the Greek for "wound," had first been applied in psychoanalysis at the end of the nineteenth century. Only in the 1970s, however, did its use become more widespread, as combat veterans returning from Vietnam and women's movement activists analyzing the effects of rape and domestic abuse observed similar psychological effects among people who had experienced overwhelming events that left them feeling powerless or helpless. In 1980, post-traumatic stress disorder (PTSD) was included for the first time in the American Psychiatric Association's *Diagnostic and Statistical Manual of Mental Disorders*.[43]

The most visceral and memorable exploration of these themes came in the work of Toni Morrison, whose novel *Beloved* was published in 1987. Morrison based the book on the case of Margaret Garner, an enslaved woman who escaped to Cincinnati in the 1850s. Faced with reenslavement, Garner killed one of her daughters rather than see her return to slavery. Garner's story was included in Gerda Lerner's *Black Women in White America* collection, which may be where Morrison first saw it sometime in the 1970s. Morrison was drawn to what the story suggested about the strength of a mother's love, which could also be powerfully destructive, and to the fact that the story provoked deep questions that could never be answered by the few surviving historical sources. She wondered, for example, what it would be like for a mother to be haunted simultaneously by slavery and by the child she'd killed to prevent its enslavement. If such experiences proved impossible for traditional scholarly methods to capture, then perhaps their representation should be ceded to the imaginative arts.

As she worked on the novel, Morrison decided not to do much more research about the Garner case itself because she wanted her imagination to be unencumbered, but she did hire an assistant to help her plow through stacks of research on slavery, Cincinnati, and the abolitionist movement. She read the diaries of slave owners and descriptions of violent punishments; she saw, in the collections of a Brazilian museum, the tools of slave torture. Initially, she envisioned the Garner story as the first part of a larger novel, but it eventually grew two hundred pages too long. When she finally handed it over to her editor, Robert Gottlieb, two years late, she apologized and said she thought she'd never be able to finish the full novel she had in mind. Gottlieb wisely recognized that what she had already written was a novel of its own.

Not only had Morrison written a stand-alone novel, but possibly the greatest novel ever written about American slavery. As with the Garner story on which it was based, *Beloved* centers on a formerly enslaved woman, Sethe, and the ways that slavery warps her relationship with her family and her children. Sethe successfully escapes to freedom in Cincinnati, but when someone from the old plantation comes to reclaim her and her children, she tries to kill her children to prevent their return. She manages to murder one daughter before she is stopped. Years later, after her older sons have fled the family, Sethe's dead daughter returns to life in the form of a young woman named Beloved—the same word that Sethe inscribed on her daughter's tombstone. Beloved proves to have an insatiable hunger for sweets and for stories of Sethe's life in slavery. The details of Sethe's former life emerge gradually in a series of fragments and flashbacks, suggesting something about the haunting effects of enslavement—a haunting that is literally embodied by her resurrected daughter. Sethe is utterly dominated by her desire to satisfy Beloved's many demands—until her other daughter, Denver, finally goes out to seek help.

Despite its dark subject and difficult story, *Beloved* received mostly rave reviews and became a bestseller. The novel won the Pulitzer Prize, and five years later Morrison was awarded the Nobel Prize in Literature. The Black philosopher Christina Sharpe, who was in her early twenties when *Beloved* came out, later reflected that Morrison's novel "completely rewired how one could write and think about slavery."[44]

BELOVED IS ABOUT THE TRAUMA OF SLAVERY, THE WAY IT HAUNTED PEOPLE long after it was gone, but it is also about the possibility of healing. It is no accident that the man who comes to take Sethe back to slavery is named

Schoolteacher, or that when Denver goes to get someone to help her mother escape from Beloved's domination (that is, from the haunting of slavery), the person she turns to is the woman who was once her own teacher. A bad education can enslave, the book suggests, while a better education provides one way, perhaps the only way, to become truly free.

For Morrison, this was not only a symbol or metaphor but also a practical matter. In a speech accepting one of the various awards she received for *Beloved*, she recounted her reason for writing the novel:

> There is no place you or I can go, to think about or not think about, to summon the presences of, or recollect the absences of slaves; nothing that reminds us of the ones who made the journey and of those who did not make it. There is no suitable memorial or plaque or wreath or wall or park or skyscraper lobby. . . . And because such a place doesn't exist (that I know of), the book had to.[45]

Morrison was exaggerating the case, but in the 1980s, she was not far off. Slavery had become central to academic interpretations of American history, but it had yet to be integrated into the public history of the United States, the kind told at museums and historic sites and high schools across the country.

At first, scholars did not see this as a separate problem. Everyone studying slavery in the 1970s came of age during a postwar period when academic scholarship was able to reach a reasonably wide readership. But that situation changed dramatically at precisely the moment when slavery scholarship was beginning to boom. As higher education expanded and funding improved, it became easier for historians and other academics to ignore the public and write only for one another. Not only easier, but in many cases imperative, because hiring and tenure were now based more on scholarly merit than on teaching or sociability. The pursuit of scholarship displaced the provision of a liberal education as the main mission of many institutions, which dropped core courses in favor of a distribution requirement better suited to faculty specialization. Graduate training became more focused, dissertation topics narrower—including in the field of slavery studies.

Then colleges confronted a new crisis. In 1975, enrollments fell for the first time in a generation. At the same time, double-digit inflation rates meant the real value of federal and state appropriations for education also fell, as did the real value of tuition payments. The crunch was felt most keenly at public institutions, but even wealthy private schools were squeezed. The crisis eased in the 1980s, thanks in part to the expansion of medical research and the rise in revenues from university health centers, but its legacy was a decisive shift toward privatization and entrepreneurialism in academic life.[46]

All humanities departments saw steep declines, including history. Under the elective system, the vast majority of colleges didn't require students to take a single history course, and over the course of the 1970s and early 1980s, the percentage of undergraduates majoring in history tumbled by nearly two-thirds. Faculty hiring stalled, and the production of history doctorates quickly fell by half.[47]

With fewer students stepping foot in a college history course and historians increasingly writing specialized studies for one another, a gap opened between academic and popular understandings of US history. This trend accelerated after the Bicentennial, which felt to some scholars like the prostitution of history on a public stage and caused them to retreat from reaching for a popular audience.[48]

It is only a slight simplification to say that this issue—the growing gap between academic and popular understandings of American history—is what caused the culture wars of the 1980s and early 1990s. One book that became a primary touchstone in these debates was Howard Zinn's *A People's History of the United States*, which sold more than two million copies in the decades after its publication, in 1980. Zinn and his publisher positioned *A People's History* as a radical, alternative high school textbook, one that would show students everything their traditional textbooks glossed over or left out. Drawing on Old Left scholarship as well as newer works of social history, Zinn told a story defined largely by "conquest, slavery, [and] death." There was nothing especially new about the way Zinn approached slavery, but he put it all in a framework of relentless class struggle. In his telling, oppressed people were always virtuous, powerful people inevitably corrupt. "Slaves hung on determinedly to their selves, to their love of family, their wholeness," Zinn wrote, while the national government supported slavery and ended it "only when required by the political and economic needs of the business elite of the North."[49]

Zinn's book represented a change in the tone and style of academic scholarship about the United States as some historians focused increasingly on exposing the injustices and sordid deeds of the past. They showed skepticism toward the optimistic narratives that dominated public interpretations and wanted to bring darker stories of dispossession, struggle, and enslavement into the picture. Elite confidence in America was eroding—a process mirrored by, and perhaps related to, the erosion of American confidence in elites.[50]

In public, a conservative reaction against the main trends of academic history took hold: Ronald Reagan's optimistic, entrepreneurial, individualist vision of America as a shining city on a hill. During his 1980 presidential campaign, Reagan gave a speech defending "states' rights" in a town where three civil rights workers were murdered in the summer of 1964. After his election, he followed up by cutting government spending on social programs and reducing enforcement of affirmative action and antidiscrimination regulations. Believing that inequality was either an essential ingredient or a necessary by-product of dynamism and growth, Reagan curtailed the commitment to egalitarianism that had been the defining feature of the federal government's domestic policy since the New Deal.[51]

Perhaps it should come as no surprise, then, that around the time of Reagan's election, an overwhelming two-to-one majority of Black Americans said they felt closer to Black Africans than to white Americans. This sense of pessimism about the possibility of racial progress in America, particularly within the existing system, received a powerful academic expression over the next few years with the rise of critical race theory, which taught that racism was endemic to American life. Developed initially by Derrick Bell, the first Black professor to gain tenure at Harvard Law School, critical race theory rejected the incrementalist vision of the civil rights movement, in which Black advocacy for civil rights would result in both greater Black participation in mainstream American life and the fulfillment of America's egalitarian promise, in favor of a radical view of America's institutions as reflecting the country's foundation in white supremacy, despite their claims to be color-blind. "Racism in America is not a curable aberration—as we all believed it was at some earlier point," Bell wrote. "Rather, it is a key component in this country's stability."[52] The only way to root out racism, in this view, was a wholesale transformation.

It was in the midst of these debates that slavery began to be incorporated into public history. As a result of the tight academic job market of the 1970s, when enrollments and faculty hiring in the humanities began a long-term decline, a growing number of academically trained historians were turning to jobs at museums and historic sites. By the 1980s and 1990s, this new generation of museum administrators and public historians, people who were trained in social history and the new scholarship on slavery, was gaining the authority to implement new interpretations.

They soon changed the landscape of public history by bringing into it the ideas they learned in school. This happened at some of the most prominent places on the American historical landscape because some of the nation's most famous and well-documented historic sites are, in fact, former slave plantations—places like Mount Vernon and Monticello. Hundreds of thousands of people visited the sites every year, and they played an outsized role in defining the national self-image. Uncovering evidence of slavery there, and integrating that evidence into public programming, had the potential to reshape how large numbers of Americans thought about slavery.

At both Mount Vernon and Monticello, new interest in and engagement with the sites' history of slavery started in the 1980s. Developments occurred at both sites in parallel, but Monticello proved more symbolically significant because of Jefferson's association with the Declaration of Independence and because he left a more detailed record of his own reckoning with slavery.

For decades, the Thomas Jefferson Memorial Foundation, which operated Monticello, had used the house, which Jefferson designed himself, to celebrate the man as an architect and inventor as well as an American founder, president, and proponent of political and religious freedom. Enslaved people did not appear in the story except as "servants." That began to change as the Jefferson Foundation realized that its presentation of slavery didn't reflect recent academic interpretations of the institution. Recognizing a unique opportunity for public education, the foundation decided to revamp its presentation of Monticello by focusing on the place's history as a working plantation during Jefferson's time. Slaves would no longer be called "servants," and their role would no longer be ignored.[53]

The study of slavery at Monticello drew on the relatively new field of plantation archaeology, which had emerged in the 1930s and then expanded beyond the big house in the late 1960s, with the rise of Black history and the historic-preservation movement. By the end of the 1970s, plantation archaeology was becoming an established field that focused on the excavation of slave cabins and other sites that could yield information about plantation life. In 1980, the Jefferson Foundation started excavations at a site known as Mulberry Row, a lane near the main house that, during Jefferson's time, was home to the shops and cabins of the mountaintop's enslaved and hired workers. The area turned out to contain thousands of artifacts, providing a detailed picture of slave life at the most granular level. Archaeologists learned, for example, that some slaves used elegant ceramics, which could have been either stolen or cast off from the main house. Garbage areas showed that slaves generally ate poor cuts of meat from pigs and cattle, while people at the main house consumed delicacies such as sheep.[54]

By the early 1990s, all this behind-the-scenes archaeological activity was making its way into public interpretations. At Monticello, some slave artifacts went into a new exhibition at the visitors center, and in 1993, the Jefferson Foundation offered its first guided tours of Mulberry Row. Fewer than 10 percent of visitors took the new tour, but their mostly positive reactions encouraged some guides to integrate more information about slavery into the main-house tour as well. In the same year, Lucia Stanton, a historian at the Jefferson Foundation, wrote her first essay on Jefferson as a slaveholder, marking the start of studies dedicated to the enslaved community at Monticello. The Jefferson Foundation also launched a long-term oral history project called "Getting Word," which collected the stories of descendants of Monticello's enslaved families; over the next twenty-five years, Stanton and a colleague would identify and interview more than two hundred descendants.[55]

As the new style of public history became more widespread, however, it also began to provoke more criticism. Flashpoints occurred at the National

Museum of American Art, where an exhibition on *The West as America* critiqued the traditional romanticization of westward expansion and Native American dispossession, and perhaps most notably at the National Air and Space Museum, where a proposed fiftieth-anniversary exhibition about the atomic bomb ended up being significantly curtailed after veterans' groups and others complained about the exhibition's treatment of the bomb's effects and legacy.

Debates also occurred over the history curriculum in public schools, sparked by a 1986 survey of high school juniors showing that they had no clue about US history. This was not necessarily anything new—but in the late 1980s, amid a growing gap between academic historians and the public, a decline in the popularity of history in higher education, and an increasing number of non-European immigrants, it caused a panic. The survey confirmed what many Americans feared, which was that they no longer had a shared sense of the past.

The response was a flurry of curriculum-reform efforts. New York put out a curriculum that conservatives and even some liberals criticized for its emphasis on oppression, while California developed a plan that gained the support of some conservatives for the way it balanced multiculturalism with a common cause. One of the California curriculum's authors, Charlotte Crabtree, then collaborated with Gary Nash, a historian at UCLA, to lead the development of a set of national history standards that were similar to the California curriculum in their attempt to balance diversity with civic identity. But when the standards were eventually published in the fall of 1994, on the eve of an important midterm election, they provoked an uproar for what some saw as their "grim and gloomy" focus on "greed, racism and corruption . . . [as] the real commonalities of American history." The US Senate voted 99–1 against the proposed standards, the one dissent coming from a senator who thought they needed an even stronger rebuke.[56]

It was only in the late 1980s and early 1990s, when public history exhibits and curriculum reforms based on professional scholarship began to spark major controversies, that scholars fully recognized the gulf that had emerged between their interpretations of US history and public understandings of it. They suddenly realized that if they wanted Americans to know more about slavery, they needed to go out and do the work themselves—at museums and historic sites, in high schools, and in books aimed at a broader audience.

Around that time, David Brion Davis was forcing himself back to work on *The Problem of Slavery in the Age of Emancipation* with a fresh sense of desperation. Davis had become obsessed with the efforts of slaveholders to turn slaves into the equivalent of domesticated animals with tame personalities. These efforts left a legacy among both masters and slaves, he believed, and were one major reason why emancipation proved difficult in a democracy like the United States. References to Elkins and "Sambo" began to pepper his notes. "I'll even venture to predict that Elkins will be re-read some day and reformulated in a more convincing way," he told a fellow historian. But free Black people also began to occupy a larger role in his thinking about emancipation because they always provided the most effective counter to the argument that enslaved Blacks were incapable of full citizenship. "I couldn't be more convinced that I'm on to something new and important," he told his editor in the spring of 1994.[57]

But then, just as Davis thought he was gaining momentum, his attention shifted to a new opportunity. On March 2, 1994, he delivered a lecture at the Morgan Library in New York. The occasion was an exhibition of historical documents called "Seeds of Discord: The Politics of Slavery," drawn largely from the collection of Richard Gilder and Lewis Lehrman, a pair of wealthy philanthropists and history enthusiasts. Gilder and Lehrman had first joined forces in 1990, when they cosponsored a rich new prize for the best book on the Civil War. At the same time, Gilder convinced Lehrman that they should pool their money to build a major collection of American historical documents, the early fruits of which were now on display.[58]

When Davis came to the exhibition in March 1994, he delivered a lecture called "The Origins and Nature of New World Slavery: Seeking the Big Picture." Too often, he thought, slavery as a subject was stuffed into boxes—national borders, chronological periods—that were too small to contain it. He believed that people needed to see it whole, as what he called "a unified historical phenomenon," if they were ever to understand its full significance. Yet he also worried that the subject might be too big to condense into a manageable survey. "Danger," he reminded himself—"if truly 'global,' too much scattered, disconnected material, without context or background—could be totally confusing & incoherent. Yet need some breadth, sense of diversity and of Big Picture."[59]

"The Big Picture" became Davis's shorthand way of talking about how he was trying to reframe the history of slavery. He defined the Big Picture as "the interrelationships that constituted an Atlantic Slave System as well as the place of such racial slavery in the evolution of the Western and modern worlds." The promotion of this Big Picture view, particularly in essays and books aimed at the general public, started to occupy more and more of his time. "I have been advocating such an approach to American slavery for nearly forty years," he lamented at the end of the decade, "and am still disheartened by the minimal effect that the vast scholarship on slavery has had on the job market and the course descriptions in most college catalogs."[60] Not to mention the public understanding of slavery beyond the college quad.

This was the purpose of Davis's "Big Picture" lecture at the Morgan Library. The effect was far beyond anything he could have imagined. Richard Gilder was in the audience, and at one point he heard Davis say that twelve times as many Africans as Europeans arrived in the New World before 1800. This statistic blew him away, giving him—as Davis intended—a sense of slavery's true significance in the modern world. Gilder was immediately convinced that this kind of information needed to be incorporated more fully into high school history courses.[61]

Gilder worked quickly to put his idea into action. About a week later, he hosted a dinner for Davis and several local school administrators and history teachers. A plan emerged to have Davis lead a two-week summer seminar on slavery for about thirty schoolteachers. "During two weeks we could cover in some detail the kind of material I briefly described in my Morgan Library lecture," Davis told Gilder, "with a good bit more attention to the nature of slavery in the U.S., including the testimony of slaves themselves and the points of (legitimate) current historical controversy." The teachers would be drawn from schools around New York City, with the hope that "most [would] become Davis disciples."[62]

Davis hated to put his work on *Age of Emancipation* aside yet again, but he "felt morally obliged" to take on the slavery seminar. "I think it's terribly important, if it can be done, to get the facts about this subject into the public school curriculum," he explained. Meanwhile, Gilder decided to make Davis's course the start of an ongoing program of summer history seminars for schoolteachers, and he established the new Gilder Lehrman Institute of American History to run the whole thing. The institute's freshly hired administrator, Lesley Herrmann, scrambled to find teachers for Davis's seminar on short notice—"[we] basically took them off the street corner," she later recalled—while Davis put together a syllabus.

The seminar ran for two weeks in early July. The teachers were housed, ironically, at Yale's Calhoun College, named for the pro-slavery politician who had attended Yale in the early nineteenth century. Initially, Herrmann, the Gilder Lehrman administrator, worried that Davis would prove too scholarly and detached, but those fears evaporated early in the first week, when she saw him discussing a tribe of cannibalistic slaveholders in Brazil. Suddenly he paused and put his hand on his heart. "Isn't this just horrible?" he said. Tears were in his eyes, and in the eyes of all the teachers, too.

The course provided a full overview of New World slavery, with a special focus on "the particular issues and problems of teaching the history of slavery to younger students in a variety of classroom situations." In addition to absorbing information from Davis, each teacher also prepared a lesson plan on some aspect of New World slavery, which was then distributed to the whole group so they'd all have a bank of ideas for teaching what they'd learned when they got back home. The teachers ended up adoring Davis, and several sent him thank-you notes after the two weeks were over.[63]

Gilder, meanwhile, was so delighted with Davis's seminar that he donated $30,000 to the Yale History Department. Davis was named cochair of the advisory board of the Gilder Lehrman Institute, which began operating out of Lewis Lehrman's large townhouse on the Upper East Side. Before the summer was over, they were already planning to run Davis's slavery seminar again the next year, and he continued to offer it every summer until the end of the decade.[64] By that time, starting from the seed of Davis's slavery lecture and seminar, the Gilder Lehrman Institute had grown to become the leading history-education nonprofit in the country, offering a dozen teacher seminars every summer along with a wide range of other programs and resources.

For Davis, the Gilder Lehrman connection also had other important consequences. He had been trying for years to break out of the traditional boundaries of slavery scholarship, but he knew there was still more to be done. Working with Gilder, he envisioned a permanent university-based program that would offer a regular seminar on slavery as well as fellowships and public talks, all of it designed to promote the study of slavery and bring together slavery scholars from different disciplines. Discussions with Yale's president began in the spring of 1996, leading to the new program's start in the fall of 1998, with Davis as the founding director. Known as the Gilder Lehrman Center for the Study of Slavery, Resistance, and Abolition, it was the first university-based center for the study of slavery in the world.[65]

The Gilder Lehrman Center soon became the central organizing institution for slavery scholarship in the United States. Its fall conference became a major event, which in its early years yielded a steady stream of edited volumes about topics such as the domestic slave trade and the arming of slaves. The Gilder Lehrman Center also started an annual award for the best book on slavery, resistance, or abolition. In 1999, the inaugural prize went to two giant books that served as the capstone of a generation of scholarship about the development of slavery across time and space: Ira Berlin's *Many Thousands Gone* and Philip Morgan's *Slave Counterpoint.*

In addition to these scholarly programs, Davis dreamed that the Gilder Lehrman Center would do more—that it would also promote public understanding of slavery outside the university. "Many historians now see the absolute centrality of slavery and race in our historical heritage," he wrote a few years later. What still needed to happen, however, was for that scholarship on slavery to transform the story of American history. Davis wanted to see a new "'national epic,'" which he described as "an epic filled with paradox, irony, and evil, but also revealing a slow and brave and uncertain struggle to fulfill the ideals of the Founders." He believed that the development of that new epic should be the main public mission of the Gilder Lehrman Center, which soon hired a director of education and public outreach.[66]

In his own work, too, Davis continued to focus on conveying the Big Picture to a broader audience. Eventually this would lead to his book *Inhuman Bondage*, but it was only after his retirement in the early 2000s that he would set down to write that book—and, finally, in his eighties, to finish *The Problem of Slavery in the Age of Emancipation*. In the meantime, the first step he took was to translate his Gilder Lehrman seminar into an undergraduate survey on New World slavery, which he began to offer at Yale in the fall of 1995. As part of the course, he delivered a striking lecture about why the Big Picture mattered. "It was the larger Atlantic slave system, including trade with the West Indies, and the export of southern rice, tobacco, and indigo, that prepared the way for everything America was to become," he told his students. "Thus vital links developed between the profit motive, which led to the dehumanization of African slaves, & a conception of the New World as an environment of white liberation & opportunity. Racial slavery became an *intrinsic* and indispensable part of New World settlement . . . not an accident or an unfortunate shortcoming on the margins of the American experience."

The tragedy, according to Davis, was that white Americans had long been unable to accept that Black people and slavery were integral to the country's history. Now, he continued, "we face a decisive test . . . how long will it be before large numbers of American whites can really imagine what it would have been like to be a black slave?" And because Davis saw slavery as a complex phenomenon with multiple legacies, he also asked another question: "No less important, how long will it be before large numbers of American blacks can acquire the freedom to picture themselves as white overseers or slave owners?"[67]

11

THE GHOST

BY THE LATE 1990S, THE EFFORTS OF SCHOLARS AND PUBLIC HISTORIans to expand awareness of slavery were beginning to bear fruit. Interest in American slavery was surging so rapidly that it was widely considered to be at an all-time high. Even historians who were alive during the civil rights movement and the heyday of 1970s slavery scholarship declared that they'd never seen slavery playing such a prominent role in American life.

One important turning point in this growing public awareness of slavery was the discovery of the African Burial Ground in lower Manhattan. The burial ground was once the largest Black cemetery in the country, the resting place of more than fifteen thousand enslaved and free Blacks, before being sold at the end of the eighteenth century and later developed. In the early 1990s, the federal government planned to build an office tower on the site. Archaeologists knew that the old African Burial Ground had been there, but they figured it had been obliterated by two centuries of development. They were wrong. As they dug, they discovered that the burials still survived, about thirty feet beneath the street, and remained relatively intact. Plans for the tower were revised to retain a portion of the site as an outdoor memorial, and the African Burial Ground was named a National Historic Landmark.[1]

This level of recognition showed that slavery was being acknowledged in public in new ways—perhaps because, a generation after the civil rights movement, its legacy seemed confined so securely to the past. Yet as with the burial ground itself, slavery remained perhaps closer to the surface than many people thought. After all, the burial ground demonstrated in an uncomfortably tangible way that Black lives and labor lay almost literally at the foundation of American wealth and power. Its discovery prompted new public discussions of slavery in New York City and throughout the Northeast, places not usually associated with slave labor, and spurred a growing sense that slavery was a thread that ran throughout the country's history.

At least part of the surge of interest in slavery in the 1990s could also be connected to a new generation of Black scholars, largely women, then entering the academy—people who were born in the early 1960s, who were able to attend integrated schools their whole lives, and who never had formal policies of segregation stand in their way. The most influential scholar of this cohort would be an English professor named Saidiya Hartman.

The daughter of a middle-class civil rights activist from Alabama and an ex-airman whose family came from Curaçao, Hartman grew up in Brooklyn in the 1960s and 1970s. By her childhood, the heroic period of the civil rights movement was over. Yet many Black Americans considered that struggle heartbreakingly incomplete. One major problem was the growing gap between the Black middle class, which had been doing reasonably well since the 1960s, and the Black lower class, which was left behind as wealthier Blacks and whites continued their migration to the suburbs and as the federal government reduced its spending on cities and welfare. With Black poverty and unemployment seemingly stuck, lower-class Black Americans were demonized by some conservative politicians as an underclass of welfare queens and crack addicts.[2]

How much, then, had really changed? Was it worse to live on the far side of the major civil rights laws and know exactly how little difference they made—to no longer have the hope that they represented real freedom or equality? "One of the founding truths of the white republic," Hartman answered in the mid-1990s, was that "black bodies are excluded from the 'we the people' that establishes the citizen subject."[3]

Younger Black Americans, those who didn't live through the civil rights and Black Power movements, felt a pressing need to assert their own humanity and identity in the face of what often seemed like a public stigmatization of Blackness. The rise of hip-hop music was one sign of this search for identity. Another could be found in Black history. Growing up, Hartman learned about slavery mostly from her great-grandfather in Alabama. He told her stories about his mother, who was a young girl at the time of emancipation, but he didn't know many details about her life. Hartman, at age twelve, became obsessed with trying to fill in the gaps. She also delved even deeper into the past, and like others in the 1980s, she tried to answer the question of identity through Afrocentrism, attempting to define Black culture by its African roots. In her sophomore year of college, at Wesleyan, she rebelled against her middle-class mother's assimilationist dreams by changing her name from Valarie to Saidiya, a Swahili word for "help" or "helper," which she found in a book of African names.[4]

A few years later, Hartman started graduate school in English at Yale, at that time the American capital of literary theory and deconstruction. She wanted to write her dissertation on the blues, but soon she realized that she needed to start with the music's background in slavery. She read a stack of recent books: Orlando Patterson's *Slavery and Social Death*, Sterling Stuckey's *Slave Culture*, Toni Morrison's *Beloved*. She was transfixed. "There was no turning back," she later recalled. Her dissertation transformed into a study of slavery and racial subjugation in nineteenth-century America.[5]

As she began her research, Hartman was drawn to other writers in the 1980s who shared her interest in developing what she would later call "a critical language of slavery." From Patterson's *Slavery and Social Death* she learned a vocabulary for discussing the constituent elements of slavery: violent domination, social death, dishonor. From Morrison's *Beloved* she saw how to reimagine a person's story from the barest fragments, and also how to use fragmented storytelling to suggest something about the experience and legacy of slavery. From Hortense Spillers, whom she heard speak at the Yale Humanities Center, she saw a model for applying postmodern thought to the problem of slavery. From Cedric Robinson's *Black Marxism* she picked up the concept of "racial capitalism," which Robinson used to describe the way he saw racialism permeating the social structures that capitalism created.[6]

Robinson's book proved especially inspiring for Hartman. It identified a massive, slavery-sized gap in the intellectual tradition of Marxism. Hartman noticed a similar gap in the works of the French historian and theorist Michel Foucault, whose influential writings on power almost never mentioned slavery or Black people. The same went for other twentieth-century European thinkers such as Hannah Arendt and Walter Benjamin. None of them spent much time on slavery, which appeared to Hartman as a startling silence in writers who were supposedly interested in power and violence.[7]

These theorists were also interested in the making of the modern world—all the transformations, economic and political and technological and intellectual, that created the liberal framework of freedom, rights, and citizenship. Yet in this, too, they ignored slavery, which was often depicted as a premodern throwback rather than a key factor in modernization. Hartman could feel in her bones that this was wrong. "I had an intuitive sense," she later said, "even if I didn't have the language to articulate it, that racial slavery was a constitutive feature of the world I inhabited."[8]

During the 1990s, the mainstream of American life remained committed to a story of racial progress, with slavery as history rather than current events. At home, Hartman would get into big arguments about the subject with her brother Peter. Both siblings agreed that slavery was central to Black American identity and that Black people faced a variety of pressing problems: welfare was being reformed out of existence, affirmative action was being rolled back (California voters outlawed the practice in 1996), and Black men were being rounded into prison at alarming rates. Black people of all classes continued to face discrimination when searching for a job or trying to get a mortgage. But Peter thought Hartman made too much of the connection between the past and the present. "Slavery was a long time ago," he said.[9]

Beneath the color-blind dream there coursed an undercurrent of racial malaise—and a search for some new approach to a problem that seemed to be lingering for an uncomfortably long time. One result was a resurgence of the old damage argument about American slavery. In an influential essay in the mid-1990s, Nell Irvin Painter, a Black historian at Princeton, revived discussion of the trauma of slavery using the psychological concept of "soul murder" to describe its effects. Referring to recent research on the long-term psychological effects of traumatic experiences, she explained that she was interested in examining "the consequences of child abuse and sexual abuse on an entire society in which the beating and raping of enslaved people was neither secret nor metaphorical."

This line of thought stepped straight into an array of controversial questions that had been largely off-limits since the reaction against Stanley Elkins in the late 1960s and early 1970s. As Painter put it, "The Sambo problem was solved through the pretense that black people do not have psyches." But what if slaves were considered as full humans with all the usual psychological faculties? "It is doubtful," she observed, "that slaves possessed an immunity that victims lack today." Elkins and McKitrick were more than a little amused to see the pendulum beginning to swing back in their direction after their retirement. But Painter did not want to revive their ideas without modification. She wondered whether it might be possible to combine their awareness of slavery's devastating effects with the subsequent generation's research into all the ways that slaves found to survive and resist, and to create their own alternative systems of meaning and value.[10]

Hartman was asking a similar question. After finishing graduate school, she got a job in the English Department at Berkeley and turned her dissertation into a book, *Scenes of Subjection*, that appeared in 1997. Dense and difficult, full of dilemmas and double binds, its message of relentless racial subjugation before and after emancipation did not fit in well with the multiracial, cosmopolitan optimism of the late 1990s.

Against the ingrained habit of exposing the horrors of slavery by relating its most shocking incidents, Hartman focused instead on what she called "the terror of the mundane and quotidian," "the violence perpetrated under the rubric of pleasure, paternalism, and property." It was not that these were new subjects in the study of slavery; they'd been discussed, in some form, for decades. But Hartman had a way of framing these problems that felt fresh—and, perhaps more important, a way of answering them that opened new questions about what agency and autonomy could even mean to the enslaved. "Is the scene of slaves dancing and fiddling for their masters any less inhumane than that of slaves sobbing and dancing on the auction block?" she asked. "If so, why? Is the effect of power any less prohibitive? Or coercive? Or does pleasure mitigate coercion?"

The recognition of a slave's humanity didn't entail rights and protections, Hartman claimed. Instead, it was the very recognition of humanity that allowed for even more brutal exercises of power and coercion. She believed that these exercises of power continued after emancipation; the racial regime merely changed form. "From this vantage point," she wrote, "emancipation appears less the grand event of liberation than a point of transition between modes of servitude and racial subjection." She went so far as to call it a "non-event." But what did it mean if the doors of rights and liberties and humanity led not to the exit but straight back into the torture chamber? Were those concepts somehow compromised? Hartman would later say that real emancipation required "dismantling the Western scheme of value and . . . [t]he end of private property—that's what abolition entails."[11]

Over the next two years, in 1998–99, Ira Berlin's *Many Thousands Gone*, Philip Morgan's *Slave Counterpoint*, and the first version of the Trans-Atlantic Slave Trade Database all appeared almost simultaneously. They marked the culmination of a generation of scholarship that studied slavery at the level of statistics and society. By that time, however, younger scholars were starting to rebel against that mode of slavery scholarship. In contrast to aggregation and generalization, broad tendencies and bare numbers, these scholars started to ask different questions—the kinds of questions that cascaded through Hartman's paragraphs and pages. They began to home in on individual stories as a way of exploring deep dilemmas and conveying lived experience. They wanted a more personal connection, more feeling and emotion, not just cold debates.

But the new emphasis on individual stories was also something more. It represented for this generation of scholars a form of redress, of redemption, of reparation.

The idea of providing reparations for slavery was not new. In the United States it could be traced all the way back to the eighteenth century, when some abolitionists asserted that freed slaves were entitled to recompense for their labor, a point that was made most poignantly in the petitions of some enslaved Blacks for their own freedom. Subsequent demands for reparations bubbled up periodically over the next two centuries, particularly at the peak of the Black Power movement in the late 1960s. Then, in the 1990s, the reparations movement gained new life. To some extent this was a straightforward response to the federal government's reduced commitment to affirmative action and antidiscrimination measures during the Reagan era. As the government retreated from its commitment to redress racial injustice, reparations emerged as an alternative strategy.[12]

The conclusion of the Cold War also played an important role in the revival of reparations claims across the globe. The end of ideological conflict between communism and capitalism unleashed a flood of ethnic and national rivalries that had been festering under the surface, with different groups claiming a variety of long-standing grievances. Truth commissions proliferated as authoritarian regimes collapsed and their crimes could be investigated. Somewhat less concretely, the death of the communist dream left many progressives with no clear vision for or even faith in the future. Confronting the past and repairing the mistakes that led to the dismal present became the new and perhaps only path they saw to liberation—a way of thinking that took the therapeutic concept of trauma and applied it to society as a whole.[13]

In the United States, there was also the crucial example of a recent reparations claim that worked. In 1980, in response to demands growing out of the Asian American studies movement, Congress created a committee to investigate the internment of Japanese Americans during World War II. The committee issued a report condemning internment, which then paved the way for a formal apology and monetary reparations under the Civil Liberties Act of 1988.

A few months later, Representative John Conyers Jr., a Black Democrat from Michigan, borrowed language from the internment commission bill to introduce his own legislation calling for a similar commission to study slavery and racial discrimination. The proposal faced steep opposition, especially from white legislators, and never made it out of committee. Polls showed that a small majority of Black Americans supported reparations but that an astounding 95 percent of whites opposed them—a stark racial disparity. Conyers continued to reintroduce his bill every year, but the route to reparations was effectively blocked at the level of national politics, especially after Republicans took control of Congress in the election of 1994.

Advocates soon turned to other options. One was lawsuits, first against the federal government and then against a handful of private companies, following the example of some successful class-action suits against Swiss banks and German corporations that profited from forced labor under the Nazi regime.

The reparations suits took years to work their way through the legal system, but in the meantime advocates began to see success in state and local politics. In 2000, California passed the first slavery-disclosure law, which required any insurance company doing business in the state to look through its records, find any policies written on the lives of slaves, and place them in an online registry. Within two years this resulted in a database of hundreds of policies linking slavery directly to current business concerns. In 2002, Chicago became the first major municipality to enact a similar disclosure law. Banking giant JPMorgan Chase soon found that it had ties to some Louisiana banks that took the title to more than a thousand slaves when borrowers defaulted. As its own form of reparations, JPMorgan set up a website where scholars and genealogists could search the loan records, and the company established a $5 million scholarship fund for Black students in Louisiana.[14]

These revelations, combined with the broader wave of interest in slavery and the growing sense that slavery was connected to many major US institutions, led other organizations and even families to voluntarily investigate their ties to slavery. The most significant place where this happened was at universities. Research universities had long been the most significant site where the study of slavery occurred in America—since Hermann von Holst visited Johns Hopkins in 1883—but in all that time they had never seriously examined their own connections to slavery. Yet once the issue had been raised, universities' foundational commitment to free inquiry and expression ultimately made it difficult for them to turn away—even as the investigation might reveal uncomfortable truths that could call the institutions into question and show their ideals to have been a sham.

The problem of slavery first reared its head at Yale, which was celebrating its three-hundredth anniversary in 2001. The university prepared an official brochure highlighting the institution's antislavery past and its modern scholars who studied slavery, culminating in the establishment of the Gilder Lehrman Center with David Brion Davis at its head. At the same time, the university was about to start a round of negotiations with two graduate-student and employee organizations. Ahead of the negotiations, the organizations decided to embarrass Yale by getting three graduate students to investigate its ties to slavery, ostensibly as a response to what they saw as the university's whitewashed official history, and write a report of what they found. Thousands of copies were mailed out, and a website with the information was set up online.

The report itself was haphazard and disorganized, a mix of truth and errors, but it accomplished its basic goal. It came out in August, typically a sleepy news month, and provided good copy for local and national columnists who were surprised to see slavery tied to higher education—in this case, to one of the country's oldest, wealthiest, and most elite institutions. Several of Yale's early leaders owned slaves, the report showed, and money for the school's first endowed professorship, first scholarship fund, and first library fund all derived from slavery. Later, in 1831, Yale leaders helped kill a proposed "Negro college" in New Haven. Finally, in the twentieth century, Yale repeatedly chose to honor alumni, such as John Calhoun, who held pro-slavery positions, rather than those who worked for abolition and Black rights.

Some commentators criticized Yale for its history, while others condemned what they saw as the "Great Reparations Shakedown." A group of local Black clergy seized on the report to demand changes at Yale, which had long had a troubled relationship with the surrounding community. But within weeks, the terrorist attacks of September 11, 2001, turned national attention away from the report. It continued to be discussed on campus, but there was no longer any momentum for change.[15]

By that time, however, events were unfolding elsewhere that would lead to the first official university investigation of its own ties to slavery. Earlier that year, during Black History Month, the conservative provocateur David Horowitz submitted an anti-reparations ad to dozens of college newspapers around the country. Titled "Ten Reasons Why Reparations for Slavery Is a Bad Idea—and Racist Too," the ad was intentionally inflammatory, asking, "What about the debt blacks owe to America?" Most campus newspapers rejected it, but the Brown *Daily Herald* and several others did not. After the ad ran at Brown in the middle of March, student protesters demanded that the *Daily Herald* donate its proceeds from the ad to a minority group on campus. The editors refused, prompting the protestors to respond by stealing thousands of copies of the next day's paper from distribution sites around campus—a tactic that never fails to draw attention. The incident made national headlines and provoked predictable editorials about Brown's illiberal students.[16]

It happened that Brown had recently announced the appointment of its next president, Ruth Simmons. The great-granddaughter of slaves, Simmons grew up as the youngest of twelve children who lived in a series of sharecroppers' shacks on cotton farms in rural East Texas. Some fifty years later, she became the first Black leader of an Ivy League school. She took over in the fall of 2001, not long after the newspaper incident, and in her first convocation address she made a point of mounting a strong defense of free speech. "I believe that learning at its best is the antithesis of comfort," she declared.[17]

The following spring, Brown was listed, along with Harvard and Yale, as "probable targets" of future reparations lawsuits. Back in the 1920s, the university and Brown family descendants had stonewalled Elizabeth Donnan's and John Franklin Jameson's repeated requests to look through the family's papers for documents relating to the slave trade. Now Simmons saw the slavery question as a clear opportunity to put the university's principles of truth and transparency to work. "I came to university life," she later said, "because it was the one space that I could see in the country where one could begin to tell the truth." In 2003, she formed a faculty-student steering committee to "help the campus and the nation come to a better understanding of the complicated, controversial questions surrounding the issue of reparations for slavery."[18]

Simmons knew that she, as a Black president, could come in for scathing criticism if things went sideways, or even if they didn't. But she forged ahead, focusing on ensuring that the committee's credentials and conduct would be so solid that no one could question the integrity of its work. (The errors and antagonistic tone of the Yale report loomed as an example to avoid.) The group included a few students and administrators, but most of its members were faculty chosen specifically for their fields of expertise: one was a historian of the Holocaust, one a lawyer who worked with victims of abuse, one a scholar of Caribbean history, one a political scientist who studied humanitarian intervention. They devised a name for themselves, the Steering Committee on Slavery and Justice, to reflect what they would be investigating—not just slavery but also broader questions of crimes against humanity and forms of redress.

The committee also chose its own chair. They settled on a historian named James Campbell, whose work looked at African Americans and South Africa. Over the previous two decades, Campbell had spent significant time in South Africa, where he'd attended hearings of the country's postapartheid Truth and Reconciliation Commission. He harbored no illusions about America's history of slavery and racism, but he also held on to an optimistic, liberal faith in America as a land where progress was possible. Perhaps most important, he believed in the power of clear-eyed history to heal old wounds. He would later remember his work with the committee as "one of the most hopeful experiences of my professional life."[19]

Simmons formally announced the committee's existence in the spring of 2004. Over the next two years, it organized more than thirty public programs. But its most influential work would be its research into Brown's historical ties to slavery. Starting in the fall of 2004, about twenty undergraduate students signed up for a research project with Campbell and a younger history professor named Seth Rockman. The students spent time at the university library and the Rhode Island Historical Society digging up whatever they could about slavery's role at Brown and across the state. Campbell thought he knew a lot about American slavery, which he had been studying in some form for more than two decades, but even he was surprised by what his students found about slavery's centrality in the eighteenth-century Rhode Island economy.[20]

The information that the committee uncovered ultimately went into a published report. It was not inevitable that this would be the case. At the same time, several other universities were also starting to investigate their historical connections to slavery, and they all chose somewhat different ways of making the information public. At Yale, the Gilder Lehrman Center held a scholarly conference in the wake of the graduate students' report. At Emory, the university launched a decade-long "Transforming Community Project" to conduct "community dialogues" about racial problems on campus. At the University of Alabama, the faculty senate issued an apology, the first of its kind, for the school's treatment of enslaved people on campus in the antebellum era. (The law professor who led the initiative received death threats.) And at the University of North Carolina, another place where Horowitz had stirred up a controversy about reparations, the next graduating class decided to make its class gift a memorial "honoring men and women of color who helped raise the first buildings on campus." In conjunction with what became known as the Unsung Founders Memorial, which was dedicated on the campus's old quad in the fall of 2005, the university also mounted a library exhibition called "Slavery and the Making of the University."[21]

But at Brown, there was never any question that the committee's work would result in a written document that would lay out all the facts about the school's relationship with slavery as well as information about how other societies had approached similar issues of historical injustice. The faculty involved were teachers at heart, and they, like Simmons, saw the committee's work as teacherly in intent, an attempt to model a specific form of engagement with American history. "How are we, as members of the Brown community, as Rhode Islanders, and as citizens and residents of the United States, to make sense of our complex history?" the report asked. "How do we reconcile those elements of our past that are gracious and honorable with those that provoke grief and horror?"

Released in the fall of 2006, the report offered an account that placed Brown and Rhode Island in the broader context of New World slavery and antislavery. As the report pointed out, "It is hard to imagine any eighteenth-century Rhode Islander whose livelihood was not entangled, directly or indirectly, with slavery." About thirty members of the university's early governing body, including several members of the Brown family, had owned or captained slave ships, and much of the wealth that built the university in its formative years was derived from slavery and the slave trade. Some members of the Brown family later became abolitionists, but Rhode Island continued to rely for at least some of its wealth on the business of turning slave-grown cotton into coarse "Negro cloth" that was sold back south for use as cheap slave clothing.[22]

The report concluded with a series of recommendations for redress, which Brown's governing body endorsed the following year. The university's official histories were rewritten, and the Department of Africana Studies received more support. A new Center for the Study of Slavery and Justice (later named for Ruth Simmons) was established in 2012, and two years later a slavery memorial was unveiled on the Front Green. The university also pledged to raise $10 million to help reduce racial disparities in local schools—although donations to that fund languished, and the university had to reach into its own pockets for the rest.

Around the time the Brown report came out, the last of the major reparations lawsuits was dismissed from federal court because the plaintiffs lacked standing and the statute of limitations had expired. Universities could now rest easy that they would not be held financially liable for anything that an investigation of their ties to slavery might turn up. The Brown Steering Committee's work quickly became a model for these proliferating university studies. Not only did the committee provide a blueprint for the process (an interdisciplinary faculty committee) and the product (an evenhanded report concluding with a set of relatively minor recommendations for redress), but the university's record-breaking fundraising over the next fiscal year also demonstrated that donors would not turn away—indeed, that donations might even increase as wealthy, liberal alumni took pride in the way their alma mater confronted its difficult past.[23]

Brown's slavery report—like most of the scholarship in this book—was based on a bedrock faith that traditional methods of scholarly inquiry were sufficient for the study of slavery. Interests could be put aside, evidence examined, conclusions debated, errors corrected, truths established. For a brief moment in the late 1960s, some radicals rejected those procedures as flawed, little more than a cover for power, and critical theorists kept up a similar critique in the intervening years. Now, around the time of the Brown report, new questions about the adequacy of traditional scholarship emerged again as scholars wondered whether research about slavery could ever correct for the bias, complicity, and erasure that lay where enlightenment and enslavement overlapped.

For Saidiya Hartman, these did not feel like academic questions, or at least not only academic questions, but vitally important personal and political ones. Once, while doing research in the Yale library, she stumbled upon an interview with one of her enslaved ancestors, a woman named Polly. Hartman was overjoyed—but when she read through Polly's testimony, she saw a disappointing answer to the question of what Polly remembered about slavery: "Not a thing." Later, when she tried to go back and read Polly's words again, she couldn't find them. This incident, she remembered, "served as my introduction to the slipperiness and elusiveness of slavery's archive."

After publishing *Scenes of Subjection*, Hartman had a similar experience in Ghana, where she spent a year studying the slave trade. She made regular visits to a slave dungeon, hoping to discover something there, but all she found was her own panic. The people who had been captured left behind no records; they could be known only from the accounts of merchants and traders. These were the kinds of sources that first enabled Anthony Benezet to study slavery in the 1750s, but when Hartman turned to the ship manifests and plantation ledgers, all she saw were rows of graves.

In her next book, *Lose Your Mother*, Hartman started trying to redeem the captives whose presence she had tried to summon in the slave dungeon, to imagine stories for them that would save them from the silencing power of the archive. An accessible combination of travelogue, memoir, and history, *Lose Your Mother* helped make Hartman's work more popular and influential. The book's concepts had been present in her work from the start, but it had taken her several years to find the simple yet resonant phrases—"the time of slavery," "the afterlife of slavery"—that captured what she meant: "If the ghost of slavery still haunts our present, it is because we are still looking for an exit from the prison."[24]

In her research, Hartman had come across an account of one girl who died aboard a slave ship. The girl's name did not survive; no one bothered to write it down, or perhaps even to ask what it was. A small scrap of her story entered the archive because the ship's captain was put on trial for her murder. Hartman already knew, from the field of subaltern studies, how to read sources against the grain, question official narratives, and reconstruct the everyday lives of people whose words had not been preserved. But she took these techniques another step or two further. She went through what each person who left a record in the girl's case might have been thinking, then imagined what could have been going on in the girl's mind as she starved herself to death. Hartman's acts of imagination went beyond what the bare sources said, and also beyond what most historians would have allowed themselves to say. She later described her technique as "attentive reading amplified by speculative narrative," or "critical fabulation."[25]

After writing *Lose Your Mother*, Hartman kept thinking about the story of the slave ship. In addition to the girl whose experience she had tried to reconstruct, there was also another girl on board, a girl named Venus, about whom Hartman knew only that she also passed away on the Middle Passage. Hartman mentioned Venus briefly in *Lose Your Mother* but decided not to write about her. A year later, in an essay called "Venus in Two Acts," she returned to Venus's story and reflected again on the problem of the archive. "The archive of slavery rests upon a founding violence," she wrote, drawing on Foucault's ideas about knowledge and power. The vast majority of what we know about slavery, or claim to know, comes from owners or traders, she explained, and much of it, such as slave-trade statistics, was originally intended to facilitate the trade. The archive, then, was itself an instrument of enslavement. As Hartman put it, "This violence determines, regulates and organizes the kinds of statements that can be made about slavery and as well it creates subjects and objects of power."[26]

In addition to Foucault, Hartman was also building on the work of the Haitian scholar Michel-Rolph Trouillot, who in his influential book *Silencing the Past* (1995) highlighted the fact that archives are not neutral repositories of knowledge but are actively shaped by the process of saving some stories and silencing others. Trouillot's point was that the content of sources, and of the histories that were written from them, was not natural but was created—not just presences and absences but also mentions and silences. An uncritical approach to the archive would inevitably reproduce the inequality that was inherent in that archive's creation (an inequality, he noted, that did not always reflect what its producers intended).[27]

To some extent, these problems are the fundamental problems of all historical work. You rarely have access to all the information you want. Some of it has been lost to time or to more purposeful forces; some of it was never created in the first place, for reasons that can be mundane or malicious. You always have to use some intuition to work your way into the minds and experiences of the people you study, and use some imagination to re-create their world as they saw it. Yet the study of slavery has always brought these problems front and center.

Hartman wanted to rebel against the constraints of the archive, which she saw as full of "rumors, scandals, lies, invented evidence, fabricated confessions, volatile facts, impossible metaphors, chance events, and fantasies." Why should historians be bound to repeat information that was itself a lie? Could stories be told about people like Venus that did not simply recapitulate the violence that had been visited upon them during their lives? Hartman advocated for writing in the subjunctive, in the speculative mode of *woulds* and *mights* and *coulds*, as a way of demonstrating the problems with the archive and "flout[ing] the realist illusion customary in the writing of history." She suggested that such stories might function "as a form of compensation or even as reparations, perhaps the only kind we will ever receive."[28]

In Hartman's work the theoretical and imaginative aspects could sometimes overwhelm the purely historical, to the extent that some historians questioned whether it was really history. But by the 2000s, she was not the only scholar thinking in new ways about the archive of slavery. Indeed, the study of enslaved women in particular raised questions about the archive precisely because enslaved women's voices and experiences and even existence were so rarely recorded—which was one reason, though not the only one, that they had not been the subject of much study. Perhaps the best example of how these related problems could affect and enrich the study of slavery came in the work of the Black legal scholar and historian Annette Gordon-Reed. Deeply committed to rescuing people from what she called "the enforced anonymity of slavery," Gordon-Reed nevertheless developed an approach to the archive, and to the study of slavery, that hewed closer to traditional historical methods than Hartman's.[29]

Growing up in Texas in the 1960s, Gordon-Reed was the first person to integrate her local elementary, and the district now has a school named in her honor. As a young girl, she became interested in Thomas Jefferson because a simple school biography said that he liked books, just as she did. She felt drawn to his curiosity and his contradictions, and she continued to read about him as she grew older. But the other thing that stuck with her from that first Jefferson biography was its narrator, a fictional slave who can't understand why his white companion is always reading.

Later, in college at Dartmouth and in law school at Harvard, Gordon-Reed always found herself as the only Black person in the courses that she took on southern history and Reconstruction. She suspected that other Black students stayed away in part because of concerns about how their ancestors would be depicted.

After working at a law firm in the 1980s, Gordon-Reed became a professor at New York Law School. By that time, she had long been drawn to the problem of how prejudice affected people's perception of history. To her, the paradigmatic case was Jefferson's alleged relationship with Sally Hemings, an enslaved woman who was also the half-sister of Jefferson's deceased wife. Historians had long dismissed rumors of the relationship despite substantial evidence for its reality in the testimony of Hemings's descendants. Using her skills as a lawyer, Gordon-Reed decided to investigate how historians had assessed the evidence on both sides of the issue. In her first book, *Thomas Jefferson and Sally Hemings* (1997), she showed that scholars who rejected the allegations out of hand had been engaging in a "systematic dismissal of the words of the black people who spoke on this matter" by subjecting them to an impossibly high standard and had been privileging the testimony of whites even though there was little corroborating evidence in its favor.

Like Hartman, Gordon-Reed thought it was ridiculous that historians still tended, on the whole—and despite great strides in the use of slave narratives and other sources—to trust the testimony of slaveholders more than that of slaves and their descendants. "It is a strange turn of events," she ruefully noted, "when individuals who held other human beings in bondage are given presumptive moral superiority over their captives."[30]

Gordon-Reed's book proved prescient. A year after its publication, DNA testing of Jefferson and Hemings descendants showed "compelling evidence" that Jefferson fathered at least one child with Hemings. The results were published in the journal *Nature* and made front-page news in the *New York Times* and other newspapers around the country. The Jefferson Foundation then performed its own investigation, came to a similar conclusion, and began to include the information in tours at Monticello.[31]

The public mostly accepted the news without difficulty. At just that moment, Americans were becoming intimately familiar with the sex life of their sitting president; in comparison with secret liaisons in the West Wing, a long-term monogamous relationship, even between an owner and a slave, appeared somewhat less scandalous. It seemed comforting, to some, to imagine Jefferson with a companion for the final three or four decades of his life, not living alone on his mountaintop.[32]

But to think about the relationship in this way was to approach it solely from Jefferson's point of view. Gordon-Reed wanted people to consider it from the perspective of the Hemings family. Because they belonged to one of the most famous figures in American history, a man who was also a prolific writer and detailed record keeper, the Hemingses appeared in the historical archive more than perhaps any other enslaved family in American history. Gordon-Reed took on the challenge of telling their story in *The Hemingses of Monticello*, the most detailed biography of an enslaved family ever written. Starting with Sally Hemings's grandmother in the early eighteenth century, she traced the family over the course of about a hundred years, until their dispersal from Monticello following Jefferson's death in 1826. Successive generations of Hemings women provided the backbone of the book.

Aside from her own interest in the Jefferson-Hemings story, Gordon-Reed had several reasons for focusing narrowly on this particular family. First, she believed that "each story that has survived must be treated as the rare, and thus valuable, artifact that it is." Honoring those stories meant excavating them and telling them in full. Where Hartman, the literary scholar, lamented the lack of sources about slavery and advocated a method of "critical fabulation," Gordon-Reed, working in a more strictly historical mode, believed that the imaginative reconstruction of past lives required an archival record that was particularly rich. "There is some irony here," Gordon-Reed later reflected. "Hartman's method works best with a person about whom much is known."[33]

Focusing on individual lives made it possible for Gordon-Reed to demonstrate that enslaved people could have an influence and exert some power even as their lives were dominated and constrained. The heart of her book dealt with Jefferson's years in Paris in the late 1780s. Several members of the Hemings family accompanied him to France, where they were technically free people. It was there, in those foreign and fraught circumstances, that Jefferson and Sally started their relationship, and Gordon-Reed spent more than one hundred pages analyzing and assessing how it might have happened.

By the early 2000s, the nature of the relationship inevitably raised the question of rape. Under Virginia law, at least, Jefferson owned Hemings and could in theory make her do whatever he wanted. Consent was literally impossible, in a legal sense, and even putting that issue to the side, the power differential between the two was tremendous. For these reasons, Gordon-Reed believed, it made sense to presume rape for the master-slave relationships for which no details survived—the vast majority of them. But when the information was there—as it was in the case of Jefferson and Hemings—she believed that scholars were obligated to examine it and to assess the situation on its merits. "What might make sense for her to think or feel about him from an ideological standpoint," Gordon-Reed wrote, "could be overcome, or even made irrelevant, by the promptings of her inner life that grew out of her own experiences." To assume otherwise, she said, would be to perpetuate in a new guise the old idea that an enslaved person's individuality and humanity didn't matter.

As with all her work, *The Hemingses* was characterized throughout by Gordon-Reed's own humanity—her deep, keen, commonsense understanding of human behavior and emotions. She went through what Sally might have contemplated and calculated as she agreed to become Jefferson's consort—the influence she might have back at Monticello and the opportunities that would open for her children, who would be able to pass as white (as three of them later did) and whose freedom she probably got Jefferson to promise her. Given the world that Sally lived in, Gordon-Reed concluded, this was an incredible outcome.

Even so, their relationship, their emotional attachment to each other, the children they had together—none of it could change the fundamental nature of slavery or the fact that Hemings remained Jefferson's property. "For any who fear the effects of romanticizing the pair," Gordon-Reed wrote, in what became the book's most famous and devastating line, "the romance is not in saying that they may have loved one another. The romance is in thinking that it makes any difference if they did."

Epic in scope yet intimate in detail, *The Hemingses of Monticello* has been rightly recognized as one of the greatest books ever written about American slavery. It won the Pulitzer Prize and the National Book Award, and a few years later Gordon-Reed received a MacArthur "genius" grant as well. What set her work apart was the way she was able to use the archive to tell a multigenerational story of intertwined lives that illuminated the system as a whole, slaveholders as well as enslaved. "The world they shared twisted and perverted practically everything it touched, made entirely human feelings and connections difficult, suspect, and compromised," she concluded. "What could have been in the hearts of any human beings living under the power of that system was inevitably complicated, inevitably tragic."[34]

Even as official slavery investigations spread in the years after the Brown report, discussions of reparations faded after a financial crisis rocked the global economy in 2007, sending the United States into a deep recession. Yet the Great Recession also reshaped the study of slavery—and it did so in a way that would eventually provide more historical ammunition to a revived reparations movement a few years later.

One effect of the crisis was to accelerate a field of study known as the new history of capitalism. The history of capitalism was not itself a new field; it was as old as Adam Smith and Karl Marx. But starting in the 1990s, with capitalism freed from the ideological weight of the Cold War, scholars began to probe its history in new ways, looking at what policies made it possible and how it operated on the ground. The influence of these ideas could be seen in slavery scholarship by the end of the decade, when Ira Berlin and Philip Morgan examined the commodities that slaves produced, while a younger historian, Walter Johnson, studied the commodification of slaves themselves in *Soul by Soul*, his influential book on the domestic slave trade.

The financial crisis and subsequent recession gave this work much greater momentum. These events revealed on a daily basis that markets did not operate according to natural laws, as economics courses often taught, but were political creations defined and structured by particular people at specific moments in time. Whether through bailouts or processes such as "quantitative easing," markets were being exposed as *historical* creations, things whose existence was not handed down by God but was shaped by humans and whose development could be investigated and analyzed. Thanks to this key insight, seemingly abstruse subjects such as insurance, banking, and regulation could be revealed as world changing.

The connection between capitalism and slavery was an old subject that played a prominent role in the work of scholars such as W. E. B. Du Bois in the first half of the twentieth century and then was investigated more fully by economic historians in the 1960s and 1970s. But Eugene Genovese's assertion that slaveholders were a precapitalist or anticapitalist ruling class, along with the controversy that surrounded Robert Fogel and Stanley Engerman's *Time on the Cross* in 1974, led American historians largely to drop economics from the study of slavery, which became equated instead with the social and cultural history of enslaved people.

By the time that the new historians of capitalism were coming of age in the 1990s, however, there was a growing sense that slavery affected more than just the people directly involved in it. It was a national institution whose influence and legacy could be felt in the North as well as the South, in economics as well as in social relations. This was only reinforced by the reparations lawsuits and disclosure ordinances of the early 2000s, which revealed that various northern banks, insurance companies, and other corporations did business in slave property. The slave South and the capitalist North turned out to have more connections than most Americans, even many scholars, thought. A new edition of Cedric Robinson's book *Black Marxism* was published in 2000, and his concept of "racial capitalism" helped scholars make sense of what they were seeing.

Another important factor spurring the study of slavery and capitalism was the start of the first university investigations of slavery. It was no accident that two of the most prominent historians leading the slavery and capitalism movement, Seth Rockman at Brown and Sven Beckert at Harvard, were also studying their own universities' ties to slavery and could see firsthand the deep financial connections between slavery and their wealthy northern institutions. In the spring of 2011, they hosted a "Slavery's Capitalism" conference at Harvard and Brown that was intended in part as an extension of each school's slavery investigation. The conference's keynote was delivered by Brown president Ruth Simmons, and the book of essays that eventually came out of the conference was dedicated to her.[35]

A surge of slavery and capitalism books followed in the early 2010s. The one that garnered the most attention was *The Half Has Never Been Told*, an ambitious book that Edward Baptist, a white historian at Cornell, published in 2014. Baptist had been working on it for more than a dozen years. As he started, he saw himself as building on Walter Johnson's work in *Soul by Soul*, which managed to combine the perspective of the enslaved with visceral descriptions of slavery's brutality and close attention to the commodification and marketing of slave property. But in the early 2000s, relatively few people understood what Baptist was doing when he gave talks on the relationship between slavery and, say, finance capital. It was only during the Great Recession, as more scholars became interested in markets and financial policies, that they started to see the point of a paper connecting the Panic of 1837 to slavery and cotton.

Baptist's book represented a sweeping attempt to weave together politics and economics into a new history of antebellum America with slavery at its center. And it provoked a fierce debate that foreshadowed more contentious disputes over slavery scholarship in the public sphere during the following decade.

Baptist viewed the South's "slave labor camps," as he called them, as the driving force of American expansion. "The returns from cotton monopoly powered the modernization of the rest of the American economy . . . ," he wrote. "In fact, slavery's expansion shaped every crucial aspect of the economy and politics of the new nation." He tied everything important in the country's early development to slavery: the assertion of federal authority over the economy, the extension of national sovereignty to the west, the development of new forms of finance and credit and trade. In a sentence that was probably meant to stand for the whole history of the United States, he wrote that "this modern and modernizing process brought benefits and rights to ever wider groups of people while stripping them, with great violence, ever more radically from others." Not only was slavery at the foundation of American capitalism and modernity, he (and the other new historians of capitalism) suggested, but it turned out that capitalism and modernity had violence and degradation at their heart.[36]

There were multiple controversies over *The Half Has Never Been Told*, one that occurred in public as soon as the book was published, in the late summer of 2014, and another that unfolded more slowly in scholarly conferences and journals. The public controversy began in early September, when *The Economist* posted a brief review of Baptist's book on its website. The review was anonymous, as was standard practice at the magazine. It accused Baptist of dismissing the notion that slaveholders had an incentive to keep their slaves fit and healthy, and of relying too heavily on "the testimony of a few slaves" for his portrayal of slavery's brutality. "Mr Baptist has not written an objective history of slavery," the review concluded. "Almost all the blacks in his book are victims, almost all the whites villains. This is not history; it is advocacy."[37]

The prominent Black author Ta-Nehisi Coates, then a national correspondent for the *Atlantic*, criticized the review on Twitter and offered his own mocking twist on its complaint that Baptist treated Blacks as victims and whites as villains. "Read a book about the Holocaust," Coates tweeted. "Must be unfair because it painted all the Nazis in a bad light." A torrent of similar #economistbookreviews followed: "Sadly, the Bible is biased against Pharaoh, preferring rebels led by a turncoat with no sense of direction." "Nowhere in Dostoevsky's portrayal of Siberia do we find an evenhanded appraisal of the benefits of forced labor." Within a day, *The Economist* withdrew the review. Preserved online for posterity, it now appeared with a headnote specifying that slavery was evil, that most of its victims were Black, and that most of its beneficiaries were white.[38]

Soon the controversy was being covered in outlets that didn't usually pay attention to academic squabbles. *Newsweek* had a story about it, and *Slate*, in full listicle mode, offered "A Few Helpful Rules for Reviewing Books About Slavery." Baptist also wrote two quick columns of his own. "The Economist revealed just how many white people remain reluctant to believe black people about the experience of being black," he lamented.[39]

At first, the public controversy quelled substantive scholarly criticism of Baptist's book; no one was eager to be labeled a racist. But eventually that subsided, and the book became the target of searing critiques, in part because its ambition and its notoriety made it the symbol of slavery and capitalism scholarship. Economic historians, in particular, accused Baptist—and the whole slavery and capitalism movement—of overstating their case, of being unfamiliar with earlier generations of economic research, and of not really understanding elementary economic calculations.

One chapter that caused Baptist considerable trouble dealt with whipping and cotton picking. He claimed that the efficiency of cotton picking in the Old Southwest increased by an astonishing 361 percent over the five decades from 1811 to 1860. He attributed this increase primarily to whipping, which he called an "innovation in violence" intended "to force cotton pickers to figure out how to increase their own productivity." (If you squinted, you might see a worker in a modern Apple factory or Amazon warehouse, their efficiency tracked and optimized down to the second, lurking behind

Baptist's sped-up slaves.) Over time, he claimed, this "technology of the whip, steelyard, and slate" resulted in productivity increases comparable to those achieved by the introduction of new technologies in cotton factories.

What this explanation ignored, according to Baptist's critics, was that the evidence showed wild variations in daily picking owing to all manner of human and environmental variables, not a relentless increase in production. The testimony of some former slaves might corroborate Baptist's account, but their testimony was only one piece of evidence—and, contrary to what Baptist claimed in his spat with *The Economist*, it wasn't necessarily racist to question slave sources. "Good historians question sources," the economic historian Alan Olmstead said. Olmstead and another economist had recently suggested that increased cotton production in the South resulted not from torture, as Baptist claimed, but from technological innovation: new seed varieties that yielded more easily pickable cotton.

The most fundamental criticism of Baptist's book, and of the other slavery and capitalism scholarship that appeared in the 2010s, concerned the crucial question of whether slavery was really the main driver of the country's growth in the antebellum years. Generations of previous scholars studying American economic development had come to something like the opposite conclusion—that slavery, however profitable it may have been for individual slaveholders, was actually a drag on the US economy as a whole and that what actually drove growth in those years was accelerating activity in the free-labor North. What the new historians of capitalism were really showing, according to their critics, was not causation but merely complicity. "If the goal is to expose unclean hands," the historian James Oakes wrote, "the point is well taken and easily made. In the long and sordid history of Atlantic slavery, everybody's hands eventually got dirty." But the fact that northern firms invested in or facilitated the slave economy was far from proof that slavery laid the foundation of the American economy.[40]

The controversies over Baptist's book revealed a rapidly changing landscape for slavery studies in the United States. New slavery scholarship was tapping into a fresh vein of interest in economic inequality, with the slavery and capitalism studies in particular gaining a following for their claim that capitalism and economic markets were fundamentally about coercion rather than freedom. This kind of argument appealed strongly to younger activists and college-educated Americans who came of age during the Great Recession and the Occupy movement.[41]

Racial injustice and reparations had again become major issues in American life. For young Black Americans, Hurricane Katrina's devastation of New Orleans in 2005 served as a potent reminder of the federal government's seeming indifference to Black suffering and death, something over and above the broader sense of American incompetence and even evil that arose around the same time among opponents of the war in Iraq. In stark contrast, the election of Barack Obama three years later as the nation's first Black president, based in part on his opposition to the Iraq War, seemed a beacon of hope. But instead of seeing progress in the years after Obama's election, Black Americans experienced economic stagnation and decline as a result of the Great Recession. And with Obama in office, every new instance of discrimination and brutality against Black Americans, including the Harvard professor Henry Louis Gates Jr.'s arrest for trying to enter his own house, acquired striking resonance. In 2010, Michelle Alexander's book *The New Jim Crow* focused popular attention on racial disparities in American prison populations, which had been growing unabated for decades. Then, in the winter of 2012, a Black teenager named Trayvon Martin was shot dead on a street in Florida, touching off national protests.

After the dream of a postracial future that had accompanied Obama's election, the reality was disillusioning. "Until there was a black Presidency," Jelani Cobb wrote, "it was impossible to conceive of the limitations of one." The killing of Michael Brown in Ferguson, Missouri, in the summer of 2014, just a few weeks before the initial controversy over Baptist's book, became a flashpoint. Over the next year, protests occurred in more than 150 cities across the country. The Black Lives Matter movement became the main channel by which this anger, frustration, and desire for change was expressed. Some 40 percent of Americans said they were sympathetic to the movement, which encouraged a new activist engagement with the history of slavery and racism.[42]

There was also now a whole cohort of Black (and some white) journalists at major media outlets who were not only well-versed in slavery scholarship but also able to write about it in a way that made it interesting, accessible, and relevant. In print, online, and on social media, where such discussions increasingly took place, these journalists could conduct very public conversations about slavery and its legacies, pointing out the connections they saw between past injustices and present inequities.[43]

These writers included Jelani Cobb at the *New Yorker* and Jamelle Bouie at *Slate* (and later the *New York Times*), but the dominant figure among them was Ta-Nehisi Coates at the *Atlantic*, who had criticized *The Economist*'s review of Baptist's book on Twitter. For years, Coates had been conducting a kind of public education in the history of slavery and racism on his blog and in the magazine. In the spring of 2014, he had also published a landmark essay called "The Case for Reparations," which almost single-handedly revived the issue after it had receded in the wake of the financial crisis. Coates focused on the decades of segregation and discrimination that followed the Civil War, but he also included a section on slavery. "America begins in black plunder and white democracy," he wrote. The new slavery and capitalism scholarship dovetailed with the argument for reparations: its whole point was that slavery built white wealth on Black backs. Coates drew on some of this recent scholarship to claim that slavery, especially slave-grown cotton, laid the foundation for American prosperity. This was one reason why he thought reparations were justified.

For Coates, however, reparations meant more than a payment. "What I'm talking about," he wrote, "is a national reckoning that would lead to spiritual renewal." This reckoning would be a reckoning with US history, and it would require what he described as "the full acceptance of our collective biography and its consequences." Coates believed that such a reckoning was necessary because he saw white supremacy as the keynote of US history. White supremacy was "not merely the work of hotheaded demagogues, or a matter of false consciousness," he wrote, "but a force so fundamental to America that it is difficult to imagine the country without it." Confronting that history head-on was the only way to repair American democracy. Books like Baptist's *The Half Has Never Been Told* became essential reading for anyone who wanted to begin the work.[44]

This desire not just to know about but to reckon with US history was also a direct response to the rise of the Tea Party movement, beginning in 2009.

In reaction to the reality of a Black president and a growing immigrant population, the Tea Party turned to a version of the American past that was heavily patriotic and religious, focused largely on Christian whites fighting for freedom from tyrannical government. Oddly enough, however, the Tea Party and Black Lives Matter agreed on certain aspects of American history, in the sense that they both thought the United States rested on a foundation of whiteness and capitalism. Where they differed was that one side saw those things as a source of comfort and strength, while the other side thought they needed to be fundamentally transformed in order to make the country a real multiracial democracy.[45]

A generation earlier, in the previous round of culture wars, the battles over US history ultimately died away because almost everyone involved still agreed that the American story was fundamentally one about the promise of freedom, even as they disagreed over whether and when that promise had been achieved. By the 2010s, however, that had changed. Some maintained that US history was defined by freedom and opportunity, but many others contended that it was nothing but slavery and oppression. It was increasingly difficult to reconcile these different accounts of America's past, which became freighted with an almost unbearable political burden.[46]

The election of Donald Trump, whose successful 2016 presidential campaign was built on a desire to return the United States to a supposedly better past, drew the lines even more sharply. Public debates became pitched battles in which any conscientious objectors were quickly cast as opponents. In this environment, many liberals, including academic historians, felt forced to pick a side, and the side they chose was not Trump's. Instead, they agreed with activists that Trump's victory, and the events that surrounded it—the murders at Charleston's Emanuel AME Church in 2015, the deadly Charlottesville protest in 2017—demonstrated the dire need for a reckoning with the bias that was supposedly endemic in the traditional narrative of American history, and for the development of a new history that would reveal the American past for what it really was.

EPILOGUE
THE WORK

Reckoning with slavery in America has never taken a single form. Most recently, the key debates have concerned the centrality of slavery to the American past and present, the proper means of telling that story to the public, and the extent to which the existence of slavery tarnishes or even discredits the American experiment in free self-government.

The culmination of these debates about slavery and US history came with the publication of the 1619 Project as a special issue of the *New York Times Magazine* in August 2019. The project was the brainchild of a Black writer at the *Times* named Nikole Hannah-Jones. Back in the early 1990s, when she was a high school student in Waterloo, Iowa, Hannah-Jones first encountered the date 1619—the year of the forced arrival of the first Africans in colonial Virginia—in Lerone Bennett Jr.'s popular Black history book *Before the Mayflower*, which grew out of the articles he wrote for *Ebony* magazine in the early 1960s.

In late 2018, the date came to Hannah-Jones's mind again as she wondered how to mark its anniversary the following year. By that time, she was a decorated journalist who'd recently been awarded a MacArthur grant for her work chronicling racial segregation and education reform. She knew that scholarship on slavery and race had been central to academic understandings of America for decades, but she believed that the subject was still sidelined among the broader public and in schools. To correct that perceived problem, she came up with a plan for a special issue of the *Times Magazine* devoted to tracing the influence of slavery on American society. "I wanted people to know the date 1619 and to contemplate what it means that slavery predates nearly every other institution in the United States," she later wrote. "I wanted them to be transformed by this understanding, as I have been." After convincing the magazine's editor, Jake Silverstein, to get on board, Hannah-Jones convened a meeting of nearly two dozen scholars at the *Times* office in midtown Manhattan. When she asked them to list aspects of modern America that had their roots in slavery, she got a whiteboard full of suggestions—article topics that she then spent six months refining, assigning, and editing.[1]

When the *Times* published the 1619 Project in the middle of August, the front cover of the magazine featured a beautiful, haunting image of the ocean off the coast of Point Comfort, Virginia, where the first Africans were unloaded. "On the 400th anniversary of this fateful moment," the teaser read, "it is finally time to tell our story truthfully." This tone of surprising and even shocking revelations characterized much of the project's packaging. The Sunday *Times* that day also included a separate broadsheet section that provided a quick history of slavery in America—including an article claiming that the full history of slavery had never been taught in the United States.[2]

What is the full history of slavery in the United States? That is, as this book has tried to show, a complicated question—one that many generations of Americans have reckoned with in different ways. The 1619 Project addressed it with ten nonfiction essays on slavery's legacy, covering everything from health care and sugar consumption to traffic patterns, interspersed with several short stories and poems. Most of the articles dealt with the latter-day effects of racism rather than with slavery specifically, but the central point of the project was that all modern manifestations of racial inequality could be traced straight back to slavery. As Silverstein wrote in his editor's note, "Out of slavery—and the anti-black racism it required—grew nearly everything that has truly made America exceptional," including its electoral and legal systems, its economy, its diet, and so on.[3]

The 1619 Project accomplished exactly what every work of journalism aims to do: it drove conversation. Ultimately, much of the discussion centered on the project's interpretation of the American founding. "Our founding ideals of liberty and equality were false when they were written," Hannah-Jones declared at the outset of her introductory essay. The radical critique that the country's principles were corrupted from the start by the presence of slavery has always been around, but it is only recently that it could receive such prominent placement in the pages of one of the country's most prestigious publications. Later in the same essay, Hannah-Jones went on to claim that "one of the primary reasons the colonists decided to declare their independence from Britain was because they wanted to protect the institution of slavery."[4] This thrust her squarely into a topic that had become the subject of heated scholarly debate during the previous decade as historians argued over the extent to which American revolutionaries and later writers of the Constitution were motivated by the desire to defend slavery.

When one of those historians, the Princeton scholar Sean Wilentz, first read Hannah-Jones's assertion about slavery's role in the Revolution, he threw his copy of the magazine across the room. He had recently published a whole book, *No Property in Man*, devoted to the contests over slavery at the Constitutional Convention, and his research told him that Hannah-Jones had it backward. He believed that the evidence showed that slaveholders at the convention were soundly defeated in their attempts to inscribe "property in man" in national law, leaving slavery as a local institution and instead enshrining the principle of equality at the country's foundations. In early November he used the occasion of a prominent public lecture, later adapted and published online in the *New York Review of Books*, to criticize portions of the 1619 Project for their factual errors and "easy cynicism" about US history, which he worried would undermine the work of understanding the more complex dynamics of slavery and antislavery in the nation's past.[5]

By that time, criticism was coming from other quarters as well. The World Socialist Web Site, which objected to the 1619 Project on the grounds that it made slavery into an idealist story of racial prejudice rather than a materialist story of labor exploitation, had begun to post interviews with a handful of American historians who disagreed with various aspects of the project. None of them were Trotskyists, but all were happy to talk about what they saw as the project's problems. Not least of these was the way the project dismissed their own efforts by pretending that professional historians had never presented the story of slavery and its legacies to the public—when, in fact, slavery had played a significant role in most college-level American history courses for more than forty years.[6]

Another thing that troubled the 1619 Project's academic critics was the tendency of the essays to present a picture of relentless racial oppression, as if the entire antislavery movement, the Civil War and Reconstruction, and the civil rights movement had never existed, and as if the United States had not experienced its deepest and most violent divisions over precisely the issues of slavery and racism. The problem with the project, in this view, was not that slavery and racism weren't central to American history—they were—but that the project ignored the fact that they had been contested since at least the time of the Revolution, when Anthony Benezet and his allies first began to study slavery to show what it was like and prove to people that it was wrong.

Wilentz soon got all the scholars who did interviews with the World Socialist Web Site on board with a public letter he was writing to ask for corrections. When the letter arrived at the *Times*, however, it was perceived as an attack. To some extent, this was a product of the impoverished Trump-era public discourse in which there were only ever two sides to any issue: with us or against us. The historians' letter attempted to approach the 1619 Project from a more nuanced perspective, one that saw value in the project but also thought it got several important things wrong. "Far from an attempt to discredit the 1619 Project," Wilentz said, "our letter is intended to help it." But Hannah-Jones and her editor, Silverstein, didn't take it that way. Coming from a group that included several older white men who held endowed professorships at Ivy League schools, the letter had the tone of tenured scholars punching down at someone else's attempt to interpret the past. Indeed, several other academics saw the letter as appalling and refused to sign when Wilentz first circulated it to a wider group.[7]

Silverstein issued a long, defensive response in which he name-checked a large group of historical consultants. More letters and essays fired back and forth. The debate popped up in countless conversations at the American Historical Association's annual meeting in January, and many popular publications covered the controversy in their pages. Eventually the *Times* ran a clarification and revised Hannah-Jones's introductory essay to say that the protection of slavery was "one of the primary reasons *some of* the colonists decided to declare their independence from Britain." Nevertheless, Hannah-Jones soon won a Pulitzer Prize for the essay—though for commentary rather than for explanatory reporting or feature writing.[8]

By that time, however, the COVID-19 pandemic had taken over the world, and debates about the 1619 Project largely dropped out of the news. But then Minneapolis police officers knelt on the neck of a Black man named George Floyd for nine minutes as he struggled to breathe. In the wake of Floyd's death, people across the country poured outside to protest racism and police violence—and to release the pent-up tensions of nearly three months of stay-at-home orders and more than three years of the Trump presidency.

The protests and the broader racial reckoning that followed brought the 1619 Project back into the news. The Pulitzer Center, which had collaborated with the *Times* to develop a school curriculum based on the project, announced that it was being used in thousands of classrooms. This did not sit well with conservatives, who decried the new racial justice movement's emphasis on white supremacy and racial oppression rather than freedom and opportunity as the defining characteristics of American history. In July 2020, Senator Tom Cotton, a Republican from Arkansas, proposed a bill (the "Save American History Act") that would strip federal funding from any schools that used the 1619 Project curriculum, claiming that the project's goal was "to indoctrinate our kids to hate America."[9] Similar bills emerged in state legislatures across the country. They all went nowhere, but they represented the opening shot in what became a fresh round of curriculum battles about the teaching of slavery and race in public schools. As always, the public school curriculum, which sits at the dangerous intersection of politics and culture, proved to be a contentious topic among competing groups that, in this case, had fundamentally different ideas about how to frame the story of the United States.

The book version of the 1619 Project appeared the following year. It debuted at the top of the *New York Times* bestseller list and remained there for months, competing with (and often outpacing) celebrity memoirs by the likes of Paul McCartney and Dave Grohl. In a new concluding essay on "Justice," Hannah-Jones made the link between the project and the politics of reparations clear. To close the wealth gap that was opened by generations of slavery, segregation, and discrimination, she wrote, would require "a vast social transformation," the centerpiece of which "must be reparations."[10] By this time, Representative John Conyers Jr. had passed away, but earlier that year his reparations bill finally made it out of committee for the first time. It went no further, but the committee vote still represented a historic step for reparations advocates.

Public controversies can move quickly, but scholarly assessments are slow by design because it often takes time for evidence to emerge, emotions to settle, and ideas to cohere. In December 2022, more than three years after the 1619 Project was originally published, the American Historical Association's flagship journal ran an eighty-page forum about it, featuring contributions from more than a dozen leading scholars. "There is no precedent in the history of the journal for a review forum of this scope and magnitude," the forum's editors noted. But the 1619 Project merited the attention, they believed, because the public debates about it had illuminated so clearly "the work history does in the world."[11]

WHAT IS THAT WORK? IT INVOLVES THE CAREFUL COLLECTION AND INTERpretation of evidence, to be sure, but its more compelling public task is to provide an explanation to a fundamental question: How did we get here?

We have not reached the end of the study of slavery in America, or of debates and controversies about the subject. For centuries, scholars have been trying to make sense of American slavery—its purpose, its nature, its effects, and its meaning. This last issue may be the thorniest. With the 250th anniversary of American independence approaching, what role will slavery play in new accounts of the country's founding? Presumably we will continue to wonder how a country established on the ideals of liberty and equality could have allowed the enslavement of millions of people. Presumably we will continue to debate the extent to which more than two centuries of slavery determined our current moment, where racial discrimination and inequality stubbornly persist.

Ideas about slavery are a mirror image of ideas about freedom, and complicated legacies of slavery and freedom lie at the heart of our country. Even though we might have some idea in our head of how those pieces are supposed to fit together, we still struggle to make sense of them in our own way. Sometimes this is seen as a problem or a defect—why can't we put slavery behind us, or at least come to some agreement about what it was and what it meant? But to some extent this misunderstands the nature of the problem, which has always had a political and even philosophical dimension. It involves not just the evidence about slavery, or its place in American history, but also what it means to be free. This would certainly explain some of the passion that has always surrounded the subject. The fact that we continue to wrestle with it today is a sign that we are still grappling with the meaning of liberty and equality, still figuring out how to put those ideas more fully into practice.

How, then, do we make sense of slavery? Maybe we can only keep trying.

ACKNOWLEDGMENTS

THIS BOOK IS DEDICATED TO MY PARENTS. MY DAD TAUGHT ME HOW TO think, how to write, and how to love America—its history, its literature, its landscape, its people. My mom taught me nearly everything else. She also read every word multiple times in drafts.

I began this project more than fourteen years ago as my dissertation at Stanford University. Caroline Winterer suggested the topic and got me started. James Campbell kept me going; I wouldn't have finished without his support. Richard White helped me understand the nineteenth century, and Allyson Hobbs did the same for the twentieth. James Oakes convinced me that the project had potential as a book, and his characteristically vigorous criticism helped me rework parts 1 and 2. (The two Jims, Campbell and Oakes, appear briefly in the text, and I have tried to do them justice.)

This project could not have been completed without financial assistance from the Stanford University Department of History, Stanford's Graduate Research Opportunities Fund, Stanford's Ric Weiland Graduate Fellowship, a Whiting Dissertation Fellowship, the Anglo-California Foundation, and the Huntington Library. Along the way, librarians at Cambridge University, Columbia, Duke, Harvard, the Huntington, the Library of Congress, Johns Hopkins, Smith, Yale, the University of California at Berkeley, the University of Chicago, the University of North Carolina at Chapel Hill, the Massachusetts Historical Society, and the Wisconsin Historical Society were kind and generous with their time. The Prospector interlibrary loan system and the Denver Public Library (especially Jim, Angel, and the rest of the staff at my local Ford-Warren branch) made my research in published sources possible.

I did not conduct extensive or systematic interviews with contemporary scholars for this book, but several people were kind enough to chat with me about the field. At Stanford, Richard Saller and Walter Scheidel helped me get started on ancient slavery. In Cambridge, Peter Garnsey did the same, while the late Michael O'Brien provided guidance on the antebellum South. In New York, Eric Foner, Jennifer Morgan, and James Oakes reflected on their own careers. And James Campbell shared his memories of the Brown University Steering Committee on Slavery and Justice.

Several good friends looked at bits of this book along the way. Ian Beacock, Sam Bett, Brenda Constan, Jon Kuehler, and Kyle Pietari read the opening chapters and assured me that I was on the right track. Diane Shearer and Leila Watkins read the first two parts and provided valuable feedback. JC Boyle and Andrew Lewis made it through the first three parts and spent a pleasant afternoon alongside Turquoise Lake telling me everything I was doing wrong—as they've been doing since we were all about ten years old.

I finished the manuscript in a spacious corner office at the Gilder Lehrman Center for the Study of Slavery, Resistance, and Abolition, which is under the umbrella of Yale's MacMillan Center for International and Area Studies. Thanks to the GLC's staff—David Blight, Daisha Brabham, Melissa McGrath, Daniel Vieira, and Michelle Zacks—for helping to make my time in New Haven so productive, and to my fellow fellows—Makini Chisolm-Straker, Mishal Khan, Briana Royster, and especially Eric Herschthal and Evan Turiano—for their helpful comments and lunchtime companionship. After I was done, David Bell, James Campbell, Andrew Lewis, Meghan Morris, and Evan Turiano read the long version and offered a series of great suggestions, and Caroline Winterer provided perceptive comments on the preface.

I have always depended on the kindness of editors. Jon Baskin at *The Point* and Leon Wieseltier and Celeste Marcus at *Liberties* allowed me to test out some of this book's ideas in their pages. Jon has always been especially generous with his editorial guidance, and I have learned a great deal over the years from his marginal questions and comments. Another generous editor, Alex Star, showed interest in this project at just the right moment. He also pointed me to the people who would find it a home: Don Fehr at Trident

Media Group and Brian Distelberg at Basic Books. I am grateful to Brian for believing in this book's potential.

At Basic, Brandon Proia showed me how to make my manuscript shorter and sharper, Donald Pharr cleaned up the copy, Chin-Yee Lai designed a wonderful cover, Alex Cullina and Michelle Welsh-Horst shepherded the whole thing to publication, and Angela Messina led the marketing. A great team of fact-checkers—Patience Collier, Jacob Ross, Indira Saha, and Jordan Virtue—made sure that all the dates and details were correct.

Finally, I might have completed this project much sooner without Meghan, Birch, and Bennet. But the book would have been much worse—and, more important, it would not have been worth it. They fill my life with joy.

ABBREVIATIONS

AHR	*American Historical Review*
ASNLH	Association for the Study of Negro Life and History
b	Box
c	Carton
CVW	C. Vann Woodward Papers, Manuscripts & Archives, Yale University
DBD	David Brion Davis Papers, Manuscripts & Archives, Yale University (a2001 = Accession 2001-M-081; a2017 = Accession 2017-M-0002)
DCG	Daniel Coit Gilman Papers, Special Collections, Johns Hopkins University
DRS	Robert L. Brunhouse, ed., "David Ramsay, 1749–1815: Selections from His Writings," *Transactions of the American Philosophical Society* 55, no. 4 (1965): 1–250.
E&M	Stanley Elkins and Eric McKitrick
ELK	Stanley Elkins Papers, Smith College Archives
f	Folder
FBP	Frederic Bancroft Papers, Rare Book & Manuscript Library (RBML), Columbia University
FJT	Frederick Jackson Turner Collection, Huntington Library
FLP	Francis Lieber Papers, Huntington Library
FO	Founders Online, National Archives (founders.archives.gov)
HBA	Herbert Baxter Adams Papers, Special Collections, Johns Hopkins University
JAH	*Journal of American History*

JBP	Jeremy Belknap Papers, Massachusetts Historical Society
JFJ	J. Franklin Jameson Papers, Library of Congress
JFR	James Ford Rhodes Papers, Massachusetts Historical Society
JHR	John Herbert Roper Papers, Southern Historical Collection (SHC), University of North Carolina at Chapel Hill
JHUC	*Johns Hopkins University Circulars*
JHUS	Marvin E. Gettleman, ed., *The Johns Hopkins University Seminary of History and Politics: The Records of an American Educational Institution, 1877–1912*, 5 vols. (Garland, 1987).
JNH	*Journal of Negro History*
JSH	*Journal of Southern History*
KSP	Kenneth M. Stampp Papers, Bancroft Library, University of California at Berkeley
M&R	August Meier and Elliott Rudwick, *Black History and the Historical Profession, 1915–1980* (University of Illinois Press, 1986).
MCK	Eric L. McKitrick Papers, Columbia RBML
MFP	Moses I. Finley Papers, Cambridge University
MOP	Michael O'Brien Papers, SHC
MVHR	*Mississippi Valley Historical Review*
NYRB	*New York Review of Books*
NYT	*New York Times*
PSQ	*Political Science Quarterly*
R&G	Morey Rothberg and Jacqueline Goggin, ed., *John Franklin Jameson and the Development of Humanistic Scholarship in America*, 3 vols. (University of Georgia Press, 1993–2001).
RHP	Richard Hofstadter Papers, Columbia RBML
RPC	Robert Ezra Park Collection, Special Collections Research Center, University of Chicago
SHPS	*Johns Hopkins University Studies in Historical and Political Science*
SLM	*Southern Literary Messenger*
UBP-NC	Ulrich Bonnell Phillips Papers, SHC
UBP-Y	Ulrich Bonnell Phillips Papers, Manuscripts & Archives, Yale University
WAD	William Archibald Dunning Papers, Columbia RBML

NOTES

Prologue: Knowledge Is Power

1. David Brion Davis, *The Problem of Slavery in Western Culture* (1966; Oxford University Press, 1988), 35–46; David Brion Davis, *The Problem of Slavery in the Age of Revolution, 1770–1823* (1975; Oxford University Press, 1999), 45–48.

2. François, Marquis de Barbé-Marbois, quoted in George S. Brookes, *Friend Anthony Benezet* (University of Pennsylvania Press, 1937), 452.

3. Anthony Benezet, *Observations on the Inslaving, Importing and Purchasing of Negroes*, 2nd ed. (Christopher Sower, 1760), 4–8; David L. Crosby, "Anthony Benezet's Transformation of Anti-slavery Rhetoric," *Slavery and Abolition* 23, no. 3 (2002): 42–50; Maurice Jackson, "The Social and Intellectual Origins of Anthony Benezet's Antislavery Radicalism," *Pennsylvania History* 66 (1999): 96–97.

4. The details of Benezet's early life can be found in Maurice Jackson, *Let This Voice Be Heard: Anthony Benezet, Father of Atlantic Abolitionism* (University of Pennsylvania Press, 2009), 5–22; and J. William Frost, "Anthony Benezet: The Emergence of a Weighty Friend," *Quaker History* 103, no. 2 (2014): 1–11.

5. Jackson, *Let This Voice Be Heard*, 20.

6. Jackson, 14, 21–22.

7. Benezet to Franklin, May 5, 1783, FO.

8. Davis, *Problem of Slavery in Western Culture*, 297–306.

9. Jackson, *Let This Voice Be Heard*, 31–53.

10. Anthony Benezet, *The Complete Antislavery Writings of Anthony Benezet, 1754–1783*, ed. David L. Crosby (Louisiana State University Press, 2013), 8–10; Frost, "Anthony Benezet," 10–11.

11. Benezet, *Complete Antislavery Writings*, 12–14.

12. Montesquieu, *The Complete Works of M. de Montesquieu* (T. Evans and W. Davis, 1777), 1:7–8, 310–318; Davis, *Problem of Slavery in Western Culture*, 393–415.

13. Crosby, "Anthony Benezet's Transformation," 40.

14. Margaret T. Hodgen, *Early Anthropology in the Sixteenth and Seventeenth Centuries* (University of Pennsylvania Press, 1964), 8, 123; Joan-Pau Rubiés, *Travellers and Cosmographers: Studies in the History of Early Modern Travel and Ethnology* (Ashgate, 2007), 168–169; P. J. Marshall and Glyndwr Williams, *The Great Map of Mankind: Perceptions of New Worlds in the Age of Enlightenment* (Harvard University Press, 1982), 228–229, 237.

15. Jonathan D. Sassi, "Africans in the Quaker Image: Anthony Benezet, African Travel Narratives, and Revolutionary-Era Antislavery," in *Bringing the World to Early Modern Europe*, ed. Peter Mancall (Brill, 2007), 100–102; Brookes, *Friend Anthony Benezet*, 57; Benezet, *Observations*, 3–7; David L. Crosby, "The Surgeon and the Abolitionist: William Chancellor and Anthony Benezet," *Pennsylvania Magazine of History and Biography* 137, no. 2 (2013): 125–145.

16. Benezet, *Complete Antislavery Writings*, 12–14; Crosby, "Anthony Benezet's Transformation," 47–48; Benezet, *Observations*, 3–4.

17. Benezet, *Complete Antislavery Writings*, 25–27; Anthony Benezet, *A Short Account of That Part of Africa, Inhabited by the Negroes* (Philadelphia, 1762), 8, 9ff; Jackson, "Social and Intellectual Origins," 98.

18. Benezet, *Complete Antislavery Writings*, 104–106; Brookes, *Friend Anthony Benezet*, 273.

19. Benezet to Samuel Fothergill, in Brookes, *Friend Anthony Benezet*, 280–281; Benezet, *Complete Antislavery Writings*, 112–116.

20. Anthony Benezet, *Some Historical Account of Guinea* (Joseph Crukshank, 1771), 40–44, 98. See also Sassi, "Africans in the Quaker Image," 104.

21. Benezet, *Some Historical Account*, 46, 65, 80–93, 129–130, 142.

22. Benjamin Rush to Granville Sharp, May 1, 1773, in John A. Woods, "The Correspondence of Benjamin Rush and Granville Sharp, 1773–1809," *Journal of American Studies* 1, no. 1 (1967): 2; Stephen Fried, *Rush: Revolution, Madness, and the Visionary Doctor Who Became a Founding Father* (Crown, 2018), 94.

23. Jonathan D. Sassi, "Anthony Benezet as Intermediary Between the Transatlantic and Provincial: New Jersey's Antislavery Campaign on the Eve of the American Revolution," in *The Atlantic World of Anthony Benezet (1713–1784): From French Reformation to North American Quaker Antislavery Activism*, ed. Marie-Jeanne Rossignol and Bertrand Van Ruymbeke (Brill, 2017), 132–133.

24. Jackson, *Let This Voice Be Heard*, 118; Nancy Slocum Hornick, "Anthony Benezet and the Africans' School: Toward a Theory of Full Equality," *Pennsylvania Magazine of History and Biography* 99, no. 4 (1975): 404; Donald J. D'Elia, "Dr. Benjamin Rush and the Negro," *Journal of the History of Ideas* 30, no. 3 (1969): 413; Fried, *Rush*, 73.

25. Jackson, *Let This Voice Be Heard*, 120–121; Benjamin Rush, *An Address to the Inhabitants of the British Settlements, on the Slavery of the Negroes in America*, 2nd ed. (John Dunlap, 1773), preface, 2, 11–12, 23.

26. Sassi, "Anthony Benezet as Intermediary," 133–134; Jackson, *Let This Voice Be Heard*, 122.

27. A West-Indian [Richard Nisbet], *Slavery Not Forbidden by Scripture* (Philadelphia, 1773), 4–8, 15, 29, iii.

28. Fried, *Rush*, 95–96; Rush, "A Vindication of the Address," in *Address* (separate pagination), 14–21, 36–44, 53.

29. *A Forensic Dispute on the Legality of Enslaving the Africans, Held at the Public Commencement in Cambridge, New-England, July 21st, 1773* (John Boyle, 1773), 3–4, 23–31.

30. Jackson, *Let This Voice Be Heard*, 141–181.

Chapter 1: National Identity

1. Paul J. Polgar, *Standard-Bearers of Equality: America's First Abolition Movement* (University of North Carolina Press, 2019), 52–53; Jackson, *Let This Voice Be Heard*, 215–216.

2. Benezet, *Complete Antislavery Writings*, 222, 228–229.

3. DRS, 13–14; Arthur H. Shaffer, "Between Two Worlds: David Ramsay and the Politics of Slavery," *JSH* 50, no. 2 (1984): 175; Arthur H. Shaffer, *The Politics of History: Writing the History of the American Revolution, 1783–1815* (Precedent, 1975), 164, 42; Arthur H. Shaffer, *To Be an American: David Ramsay and the Making of the American Consciousness* (University of South Carolina Press, 1991), 104, 252.

4. DRS, 12; Shaffer, *To Be an American*, 9–13.

5. James McLachlan, *Princetonians, 1748–1768: A Biographical Dictionary* (Princeton University Press, 1976), xx, xxiii; Mark A. Noll, *Princeton and the Republic, 1768–1822* (1989; Regent College Publishing, 2004), 16–17, 217.

6. Noll, *Princeton*, 20; Fried, *Rush*, 25; Alexander Leitch, *A Princeton Companion* (Princeton University Press, 1978), 3, 100.

7. Caroline Winterer, *The Culture of Classicism: Ancient Greece and Rome in American Intellectual Life* (Johns Hopkins University Press, 2002), 29–43; William J. Barber, "Political Economy and the Academic Setting Before 1900: An Introduction," in *Economists and Higher Learning in the Nineteenth Century*, ed. Barber (1988; Transaction, 1993), 5–6; George H. Callcott, *History in the United States, 1800–1860: Its Practice and Purpose* (Johns Hopkins Press, 1970), 60–61.

8. R. Isabela Morales, "Slavery at the President's House" and "Princeton's Slaveholding Presidents," Princeton & Slavery Project, slavery.princeton.edu.

9. Shaffer, "Between Two Worlds," 177–178; Shaffer, *To Be an American*, 16, 166; DRS, 13–15, 51.

10. DRS, 15, 188; David Waldstreicher, *In the Midst of Perpetual Fetes: The Making of American Nationalism, 1776–1820* (University of North Carolina Press, 1997), 43.

11. DRS, 16–17, 60; Robert L. Brunhouse, "David Ramsay's Publication Problems, 1784–1808," *Papers of the Bibliographical Society of America* 39, no. 1 (1945): 52–55.

12. David Ramsay, *The History of the Revolution of South-Carolina, from a British Province to an Independent State* (Isaac Collins, 1785), 1:29; 2:5, 64.

13. Ramsay, *History of the Revolution of South-Carolina*, 2:31–33, 122–123.

14. Ramsay, 2:32, 384; DRS, 110.

15. Ramsay, 2:387; DRS, 105.

16. DRS, 92, 99, 105; Adams to Ramsay, February 9, 1786, FO.

17. DRS, 20, 40; Shaffer, *To Be an American*, 1.

18. DRS, 120.

19. DRS, 113.

20. David Ramsay, *The History of the American Revolution* (R. Aitken and Son, 1789), 1:23–25.

21. DRS, 48n37.

22. DRS, 99.

23. DRS, 88, 92, 101, 104; Thomas Jefferson, *Notes on the State of Virginia* (John Stockdale, 1787), 229–239.

24. DRS, 101.

25. Winthrop D. Jordan, *White over Black: American Attitudes Toward the Negro* (University of North Carolina Press, 1968), 287–289.

26. Polgar, *Standard-Bearers of Equality*, 122–134.

27. Jordan, *White over Black*, 216–265; Noll, *Princeton*, 119.

28. Noll, 116, dates this trip to 1785 or 1786. I believe the evidence suggests a date in May 1786. DRS, 101, 103.

29. Noll, *Princeton*, 6, 187, 297; Geneva Smith, "Slavery in the Curriculum," Princeton & Slavery Project, slavery.princeton.edu.

30. Noll, *Princeton*, 13, 62–63, 192–194.

31. DRS, 103; Noll, *Princeton*, 116; Samuel Stanhope Smith, *An Essay on the Causes of the Variety of Complexion and Figure in the Human Species* (Robert Aitken, 1787), 3, 10–11, 20.

32. Smith, *Essay*, 57–59, 77.

33. Jordan, *White over Black*, 505–508, 517; John C. Greene, "The American Debate on the Negro's Place in Nature, 1780–1815," *Journal of the History of Ideas* 15, no. 3 (1954): 384–396.

34. See, generally, Louis Leonard Tucker, *Clio's Consort: Jeremy Belknap and the Founding of the Massachusetts Historical Society* (Massachusetts Historical Society, 1990); DRS, 48, 140.

35. Jeremy Belknap, *The History of New-Hampshire*, vol. 1 (Robert Aitken, 1784), 74–75; Jeremy Belknap, *The History of New-Hampshire*, vol. 3 (Belknap and Young, 1792), 280–281.

36. Philip Hamilton, "Revolutionary Principles and Family Loyalties: Slavery's Transformation in the St. George Tucker Household of Early National Virginia," *William & Mary Quarterly* 55, no. 4 (1998): 533–535, 544; Paul Finkelman, "The Dragon St. George Could Not Slay: Tucker's Plan to End Slavery," *William & Mary Law Review* 47, no. 4 (2006): 1218–1220.

37. Some histories written in the early nineteenth century got the date right, but most had it wrong. The date was corrected for good when Black history emerged as a field of serious study in the decades after the Civil War.

38. Tucker to Jeremy Belknap, April 11, 1795, and June 29, 1795, JBP.

39. St. George Tucker, *A Dissertation on Slavery: With a Proposal for the Gradual Abolition of It, in the State of Virginia* (Mathew Carey, 1796), 34–66.

40. Tucker to Belknap, January 24, 1795, JBP; Finkelman, "Dragon," 1223.

41. Jeremy Belknap, "Queries Respecting the Slavery and Emancipation of Negroes in Massachusetts," *Collections of the Massachusetts Historical Society*, 1st series, vol. 4 (1835): 192, 199, 201–204; Margot Minardi, *Making Slavery History: Abolitionism and the Politics of Memory in Massachusetts* (Oxford University Press, 2010), 13–27, 41–42.

42. Tucker to Belknap, June 29, 1795, and November 27, 1795, JBP.

43. Tucker to Belknap, April 3, 1797, and August 13, 1797, in "Letters and Documents Relating to Slavery in Massachusetts," *Collections of the Massachusetts Historical Society*, 5th series, vol. 3 (1877): 425–428; Hamilton, "Revolutionary Principles and Family Loyalties," 537, 546.

44. Tucker to Belknap, November 27, 1795, JBP; Sylvestris [St. George Tucker], *Reflections on the Cession of Louisiana to the United States* (Samuel Harrison Smith, 1803), 25; Hamilton, "Revolutionary Principles and Family Loyalties," 541–543.

45. Hamilton, 545–553. See also Willie Lee Rose, "The Domestication of Domestic Slavery," in Rose, *Slavery and Freedom*, ed. William W. Freehling (Oxford University Press, 1982), 20–35.

46. Joanna Bowen Gillespie, *The Life and Times of Martha Laurens Ramsay, 1759–1811* (University of South Carolina Press, 2001), 105–107; Shaffer, *To Be an American*, 77.

47. Merrill Jensen and Robert A. Becker, eds., *The Documentary History of the First Federal Elections, 1788–1790* (University of Wisconsin Press, 1976), 147–148, 173–197; Shaffer, *To Be an American*, 179–187.

48. DRS, 123.

49. DRS, 27; Gillespie, *Life and Times*, 117; *Memoirs of the Life of Martha Laurens Ramsay*, 2nd ed., ed. David Ramsay (Samuel Etheridge, 1812), 47; David Ramsay, *History of the United States, from Their First Settlement as English Colonies, in 1607, to the Year 1808* (M. Carey, 1816–1817), 1:221; Peter C. Messer, "From a Revolutionary History to a History of Revolution: David Ramsay and the American Revolution," *Journal of the Early Republic* 22, no. 2 (2002): 228.

50. Finkelman, "Dragon," 1220, 1213; Hudgins v. Wrights, 1 Hening and Munford 134, 139–141, 144 (Supreme Court of Appeals of Virginia, 1806).

51. Finkelman, "Dragon," 1242; Hamilton, "Revolutionary Principles and Family Loyalties," 551–556.

Chapter 2: Land and Labor

1. Jefferson to John Holmes, April 22, 1820, FO.

2. Adam Rothman, *Slave Country: American Expansion and the Origins of the Deep South* (Harvard University Press, 2005), chs. 4–5.

3. Thomas Malthus, *An Essay on the Principle of Population* (J. Johnson, 1798), chs. 1, 5.

4. Dennis Hodgson, "Malthus' Essay on Population and the American Debate over Slavery," *Comparative Studies in Society and History* 51, no. 4 (2009): 743.

5. *Annals of Congress*, 16th Cong., 1 sess., House, 1532–1536, 1581.

6. Jefferson to John Holmes, April 22, 1820, FO.

7. William Clark, *Academic Charisma and the Origins of the Research University* (University of Chicago Press, 2006), ch. 5; Winterer, *Culture of Classicism*, 32–34, 59–60.

8. Lilian Handlin, *George Bancroft: The Intellectual as Democrat* (Harper & Row, 1984), 30, 47, 51; Fred L. Burwick, "The Göttingen Influence on George Bancroft's Idea of Humanity," *Jahrbuch für Amerikastudien* 11 (1966): 194.

9. Handlin, *George Bancroft*, 52–66; Richard Hofstadter and Wilson Smith, eds., *American Higher Education: A Documentary History* (University of Chicago Press, 1961), 1:264–265.

10. Handlin, *George Bancroft*, 68–70.

11. Arnaldo Momigliano, "Niebuhr and the Agrarian Problems of Rome," *History and Theory* 21, no. 4 (1982): 8; Clark, *Academic Charisma*, 225–226; Augustus Böckh, *The Public Economy of Athens* (John Murray, 1828), 2:469, 1:52, 2:474.

12. George Bancroft, "Economy of Athens," *North American Review* 32, no. 71 (1831): 344–346; Burwick, "Göttingen Influence," 196–197; Handlin, *George Bancroft*, 80–90; Edgar Hutchinson Johnson III, "George Bancroft, Slavery, and the American Union" (PhD diss., Auburn University, 1983), 30, 33.

13. Handlin, *George Bancroft*, 89–100.

14. Daniel Kilbride, "Slavery and Utilitarianism: Thomas Cooper and the Mind of the Old South," *JSH* 59, no. 3 (1993): 470–471; Thomas Cooper, *Two Essays* (1826; Da Capo, 1970), 37–38; John K. Whitaker, "Early Flowering in the Old Dominion: Political Economy at the College of William and Mary and the University of Virginia," in *Economists and Higher Learning in the Nineteenth Century*, ed. William J. Barber (1988; Transaction, 1993), 23–25; M. Frederick Lochemes, *Robert Walsh: His Story* (American Irish Historical Society, 1941), 79–80.

15. Michael D. Bordo and William H. Phillips, "Faithful Index to the Ambitions and Fortunes of the State: The Development of Political Economy at South Carolina College," in *Economists and Higher Learning in the Nineteenth Century*, ed. William J. Barber (1988; Transaction, 1993), 49–50.

16. Adam Smith, *The Wealth of Nations, Books I–III*, ed. Andrew Skinner (Penguin, 1999), 488.

17. Thomas Cooper, *Lectures on the Elements of Political Economy* (Doyle E. Sweeny, 1826), 94–96.

18. Hofstadter and Smith, eds., *American Higher Education*, 1:406, 416–417.

19. Bordo and Phillips, "Faithful Index," 57–59.

20. Whitaker, "Early Flowering in the Old Dominion," 32–37; Alfred L. Brophy, *University, Court, and Slave: Pro-Slavery Thought in Southern Colleges and Courts and the Coming of Civil War* (Oxford University Press, 2016), 35.

21. David Walker, *Walker's Appeal, in Four Articles; Together with a Preamble, to the Coloured Citizens of the World*, 3rd ed. (David Walker, 1830), 4–5, 33–34; Manisha Sinha, *The Slave's Cause: A History of Abolition* (Yale University Press, 2016), 205–207.

22. Crosby, "Anthony Benezet's Transformation," 41; Sinha, *Slave's Cause*, 214–227; Daniel Walker Howe, *What Hath God Wrought: The Transformation of America, 1815–1848* (Oxford University Press, 2007), 424–427.

23. Edward Bartlett Rugemer, *The Problem of Emancipation: The Caribbean Roots of the American Civil War* (Louisiana State University Press, 2008), 43, 52–53, 66–67.

24. Howe, *What Hath God Wrought*, 325–327.

25. Thomas R. Dew, *Review of the Debate in the Virginia Legislature of 1831 and 1832* (T. W. White, 1832), 5–10, 28.

26. On southern pro-slavery thought, see Drew Gilpin Faust, "A Southern Stewardship: The Intellectual and the Proslavery Argument," *American Quarterly* 31, no. 1 (1979): 63–80; Drew Gilpin Faust, "Introduction: The Proslavery Argument in History," in *The Ideology of Slavery: Proslavery Thought in the Antebellum South, 1830–1860*, ed. Faust (Louisiana State University Press, 1981), 1–20; Larry E. Tise, *Proslavery: A History of the Defense of Slavery in America, 1701–1840* (University of Georgia Press, 1987), 33–36.

27. Hodgson, "Malthus' Essay," 742–747.

28. Handlin, *George Bancroft*, 115.

29. Bancroft, "Economy of Athens," 352–353, 360, 356–357.

30. Gordon S. Wood, *The Radicalism of the American Revolution* (1992; Vintage, 1993), 276–286; Gordon S. Wood, *Empire of Liberty: A History of the Early Republic, 1789–1815* (Oxford University Press, 2009), 702–703; M. L. Weems, *A History of the Life and Death, Virtues and Exploits, of General George Washington*, 3rd ed. (John Bioren, [1800]), 48.

31. George Bancroft, "Slavery in Rome," *North American Review* 39, no. 85 (1834): 415, 421, 433, 437, 417.

32. Benjamin Franklin, "Observations Concerning the Increase of Mankind" (1751), FO.

33. Edward Gibbon Wakefield, *A Letter from Sydney, the Principal Town of Australasia*, ed. Robert Gouger (Joseph Cross, 1829), 34.

34. Edward Gibbon Wakefield, *England and America: A Comparison of the Social and Political State of Both Nations* (Richard Bentley, 1833), 2:22, 46.

35. Karl Marx, *Capital: A Critical Analysis of Capitalist Production*, ed. Frederick Engels, trans. Samuel Moore and Edward Aveling (1887; George Allen & Unwin, 1946), 1:791.

36. Handlin, *George Bancroft*, 144, 166, 169.

37. George Bancroft, *A History of the United States* (Charles Bowen, 1834), 1:v; Handlin, *George Bancroft*, 126; *The Life and Letters of George Bancroft*, ed. M. A. DeWolfe Howe (Charles Scribner's Sons, 1908), 1:209–210.

38. George Bancroft, *Literary and Historical Miscellanies* (Harper and Brothers, 1855), 487.

39. Handlin, *George Bancroft*, 172–173.

40. Bancroft, *History*, 1:177.

41. Bancroft, 1:190.

42. George Bancroft, *History of the United States* (Charles C. Little and James Brown, 1840), 3:402, 233, 412.

43. Rugemer, *Problem of Emancipation*, 2–3.

44. Rugemer, 133–136; Lydia Moland, *Lydia Maria Child: A Radical American Life* (University of Chicago Press, 2022), 93–104; Carolyn L. Karcher, *The First Woman in the Republic: A Cultural Biography of Lydia Maria Child* (Duke University Press, 1994), xiv–xxi, 173–205.

45. Lydia Maria Child, *An Appeal in Favor of That Class of Americans Called Africans* (Allen and Ticknor, 1833), 38, 35, 66, 86, 97, 99.

46. James A. Thome and J. Horace Kimball, *Emancipation in the West Indies* (American Anti-Slavery Society, 1838), v, 7, 15, 19, 72, 108, 114; Rugemer, *Problem of Emancipation*, 156–175, William Ellery Channing quoted on 170.

47. Rugemer, *Problem of Emancipation*, 261–262.

48. Bancroft, *Literary and Historical Miscellanies*, 462; Handlin, *George Bancroft*, 185–222, 241.

Chapter 3: Laws of Nature and Nations

1. *Trial of Thomas Sims, on an Issue of Personal Liberty, on the Claim of James Potter, of Georgia, Against Him, as an Alleged Fugitive from Service* (William S. Damrell, 1851), 47; Andrew Delbanco, *The War Before the War: Fugitive Slaves and the Struggle for America's Soul from the Revolution to the Civil War* (Penguin, 2018), 267–282, 303, 305; David S.

Reynolds, *Mightier Than the Sword: Uncle Tom's Cabin and the Battle for America* (Norton, 2011), 14, 20–35, 88, 128, 169.

2. Harriet Beecher Stowe, *Uncle Tom's Cabin: Or, Life Among the Lowly* (John P. Jewett, 1852), 1:23, 2:310.

3. Theodore Dwight Weld, *American Slavery as It Is: Testimony of a Thousand Witnesses* (American Anti-Slavery Society, 1839), iv, iii, 62, 32–34, 40.

4. Reynolds, *Mightier Than the Sword*, 92–93; Delbanco, *War Before the War*, 142–154; Ann Fabian, *The Unvarnished Truth: Personal Narratives in Nineteenth-Century America* (University of California Press, 2000), 79–89. See also Jesse Olsavsky, *The Most Absolute Abolition: Runaways, Vigilance Committees, and the Rise of Revolutionary Abolitionism, 1835–1861* (Louisiana State University Press, 2022), esp. 17–33, 110–121.

5. Harriet Beecher Stowe, *A Key to Uncle Tom's Cabin; Presenting the Original Facts and Documents upon Which the Story Is Founded* (John P. Jewett, 1853), 5.

6. Brophy, *University, Court, and Slave*, 169; Robert M. Cover, *Justice Accused: Antislavery and the Judicial Process* (Yale University Press, 1975), 160–161; Delbanco, *War Before the War*, 314.

7. George M. Stroud, *A Sketch of the Laws Relating to Slavery in the Several States of the United States of America* (Kimber and Sharpless, 1827), 46, 50–51.

8. Stowe, *Key to Uncle Tom's Cabin*, iii, 70, 72–77; Jacob D. Wheeler, *A Practical Treatise on the Law of Slavery* (Allan Pollock Jr., 1837).

9. William Goodell, *The American Slave Code in Theory and Practice: Its Distinctive Features Shown by Its Statutes, Judicial Decisions, and Illustrative Facts*, 2nd ed. (American and Foreign Anti-Slavery Society, 1853), 43, 372–373.

10. George Frederick Holmes, "Uncle Tom's Cabin," *SLM* 18, no. 12 (1852): 721–729.

11. George Frederick Holmes, "Observations on a Passage in the Politics of Aristotle Relative to Slavery," *SLM* 16, no. 4 (1850): 195.

12. Neal C. Gillespie, *The Collapse of Orthodoxy: The Intellectual Ordeal of George Frederick Holmes* (University of Virginia Press, 1972), 3–38.

13. Gillespie, *Collapse of Orthodoxy*, 81; Eugene D. Genovese and Elizabeth Fox-Genovese, "Slavery, Economic Development, and the Law: The Dilemma of the Southern Political Economists, 1800–1860," *Washington and Lee Review* 41, no. 1 (1984): 9–10, 19–21; David Christy, "Cotton Is King: Or, Slavery in the Light of Political Economy," in *Cotton Is King, and Pro-Slavery Arguments*, ed. E. N. Elliott (Pritchard, Abbott and Loomis, 1860), 127.

14. Olmsted's articles were collected in multiple books, including *The Cotton Kingdom: A Traveller's Observations on Cotton and Slavery in the American Slave States*, 2 vols. (Mason Brothers, 1861). Hinton Rowan Helper, *The Impending Crisis of the South: How to Meet It* (Burdick Brothers, 1857), 329–330, 155–156.

15. Louisa McCord, "Slavery and Political Economy, Part 1," *De Bow's Review* 21, no. 4 (1856): 335; Holmes to John R. Thompson, November 20, 1850, f: "Correspondence and Papers, 1848–1859," b1, George Frederick Holmes Papers, Rubenstein Library, Duke University.

16. Holmes, "Observations," 193–198; Harvey Wish, "Aristotle, Plato, and the Mason-Dixon Line," *Journal of the History of Ideas* 10, no. 2 (1949): 254–266.

17. George Frederick Holmes, "The History of the Working Classes," *SLM* 21, no. 4 (1855): 203; George Frederick Holmes, "Slavery and Freedom," *Southern Quarterly Review* 1, no. 1 (1856): 95.

18. Genovese and Fox-Genovese, "Slavery, Economic Development, and the Law," 21.

19. Henry Hughes, *Treatise on Sociology, Theoretical and Practical* (Lippincott, Grambo, 1854), esp. 79–83.

20. George Fitzhugh, *Sociology for the South, or the Failure of Free Society* (A. Morris, 1854), 69, 72, 48.

21. Eugene D. Genovese, *The World the Slaveholders Made: Two Essays in Interpretation* (Pantheon, 1969), 130; Harvey Wish, "George Frederick Holmes and Southern Periodical Literature of the Mid-Nineteenth Century," *JSH* 7, no. 3 (1941): 352; George Frederick Holmes, "Failure of Free Societies," *SLM* 21 (March 1855): 132.

22. George Fitzhugh, "Southern Thought," in *The Ideology of Slavery: Proslavery Thought in the Antebellum South, 1830–1860*, ed. Drew Gilpin Faust (Louisiana State University Press, 1981), 276–277, 285–286.

23. Holmes, "Observations," 200.

24. Arthur P. Hayne to Francis Lieber, January 6, 1843, b10, FLP; Faust, "Introduction," 15.

25. Ann Fabian, *The Skull Collectors: Race, Science, and America's Unburied Dead* (University of Chicago Press, 2010), 1, 14–15, 17–20; William Stanton, *The Leopard's Spots: Scientific Attitudes Toward Race in America, 1815–59* (University of Chicago Press, 1960), 26–27, 45; Mia Bay, *The White Image in the Black Mind: African-American Ideas About White People, 1830–1925* (Oxford University Press, 2000), 35.

26. Samuel George Morton, *Crania Americana: Or, a Comparative View of the Skulls of Various Aboriginal Nations of North and South America* (John Penington, 1839), 88.

27. Stanton, *Leopard's Spots*, 46–50.

28. Samuel George Morton, *Crania Aegyptiaca; Or, Observations on Egyptian Ethnography, Derived from Anatomy, History and the Monuments* (John Penington, 1844), 59, 60, 66.

29. Stanton, *Leopard's Spots*, 58–66, 212; Edward Jarvis, "Statistics of Insanity in the United States," *Boston Medical and Surgical Journal* 27, no. 7 (September 21, 1842): 119; Edward Jarvis, "Statistics of Insanity in the United States," *Boston Medical and Surgical Journal* 27, no. 17 (November 30, 1842): 281–282.

30. *The Works of James McCune Smith*, ed. John Stauffer (Oxford University Press, 2006), xiv, xix–xxiii, 53, 61.

31. Stanton, *Leopard's Spots*, 65–68, 118–119; Josiah C. Nott, *Two Lectures on the Connection Between the Biblical and Physical History of Man* (Bartlett and Welford, 1849), 14, 17.

32. Anemona Hartocollis, "Who Should Own Photos of Slaves?," *NYT*, March 20, 2019; Samuel A. Cartwright, "Diseases and Peculiarities of the Negro Race," *De Bow's Review* 11, no. 1 (July 1851): 66.

33. Benjamin Quarles, *Black Mosaic: Essays in Afro-American History and Historiography* (University of Massachusetts Press, 1988), 110–125; Bay, *White Image in the Black Mind*, 14–35; Minardi, *Making Slavery History*, 139–149.

34. Martin Robinson Delany, *The Condition, Elevation, Emigration, and Destiny of the Colored People of the United States* (self-pub., 1852), 47–48, 14, 171ff.

35. Stanton, *Leopard's Spots*, 159–165; Bay, *White Image in the Black Mind*, 43; J. C. Nott and George R. Gliddon, *Types of Mankind: Or, Ethnological Researches* (Lippincott, Grambo, 1854), 255.

36. Bay, *White Image in the Black Mind*, 67–68.

37. J. C. Nott and George R. Gliddon, *Indigenous Races of the Earth; Or, New Chapters of Ethnological Inquiry* (J. B. Lippincott, 1857), ch. 4, 431.

38. Stanton, *Leopard's Spots*, 176–185.

39. Sean Wilentz, *No Property in Man: Slavery and Antislavery at the Nation's Founding* (Harvard University Press, 2018), 190–201, 219–220.

40. James M. McPherson, *Battle Cry of Freedom: The Civil War Era* (1988; Ballantine, 1989), 170–181; Sean Wilentz, *The Rise of American Democracy: Jefferson to Lincoln* (Norton, 2005), 707–715.

41. Scott v. Sandford, 60 US 393, 403, 407, 410–411, 450–452, 624, 621. On Taney in the 1830s, see Paul Finkelman, *Supreme Injustice: Slavery in the Nation's Highest Court* (Harvard University Press, 2018), 8.

42. Johnson, "George Bancroft, Slavery, and the American Union," 152; George Bancroft, *History of the United States* (Little, Brown, 1852), 4:12; Peter Wirzbicki, *Fighting for the Higher Law: Black and White Transcendentalists Against Slavery* (University of Pennsylvania Press, 2021), 197; *Life and Correspondence of Theodore Parker*, ed. John Weiss (D. Appleton, 1864), 2:234–235; George Bancroft, *History of the United States* (Little, Brown, 1858), 7:421.

43. William B. McCash, *Thomas R. R. Cobb: The Making of a Southern Nationalist* (Mercer University Press, 1983), 5–54, 91–95, 137, 166–167, 155–156.

44. Thomas R. R. Cobb, *An Inquiry into the Law of Negro Slavery in the United States of America* (T. & J. W. Johnson, 1858), cxxxiv, 221.

45. McCash, *Thomas R. R. Cobb*, 109, 119, 111.

46. Hurd to Francis Lieber, October 15, 1858, b12, FLP; John Codman Hurd, *The Law of Freedom and Bondage in the United States* (Little, Brown, 1858–1862), 1:xiii–xiv.

47. Hurd, *Law of Freedom*, 1:569, 2:234–235, 575, x.

48. Wilentz, *No Property in Man*, 249–252.

49. *The Portable Abraham Lincoln*, ed. Andrew Delbanco (Viking, 1992), 182–183, 176, 185.

50. McCash, *Thomas R. R. Cobb*, 185–188.

51. "Declaration of the Immediate Causes Which Induce and Justify the Secession of South Carolina from the Federal Union," Avalon Project, Yale Law School, https://avalon.law.yale.edu/19th_century/csa_scarsec.asp; McCash, *Thomas R. R. Cobb*, 197; *Portable Abraham Lincoln*, 197, 201.

52. McCash, *Thomas R. R. Cobb*, 205–228, 248, 254, 317–327; Wilentz, *No Property in Man*, 261–262.

53. James Oakes, *Freedom National: The Destruction of Slavery in the United States, 1861–1865* (Norton, 2013), ch. 4.

54. Lieber to Sumner, April 29, 1862, b42, FLP; Lieber to Sumner, December 19, 1861, b42, FLP; Oakes, *Freedom National*, 201.

55. For Lieber, see Frank Freidel, *Francis Lieber: Nineteenth-Century Liberal* (Louisiana State University Press, 1947); and John Fabian Witt, *Lincoln's Code: The Laws of War in American History* (Free Press, 2012).

56. Harmut Keil, "Francis Lieber's Attitudes on Race, Slavery, and Abolition," *Journal of American Ethnic History* 28, no. 1 (2008): 13–14, 20–21; Freidel, *Francis Lieber*, 325–326; Lieber to George S. Hillard, December 8–13, 1850, b30, FLP.

57. Lieber, "Is there any implied insult to the South in Slavery being excluded from California?" (1849), b19, FLP.

58. Freidel, *Francis Lieber*, 324–331; Witt, *Lincoln's Code*, 228.

59. Francis Lieber to Norman Lieber, March 23, 1862, b32, FLP; *Collected Works of Abraham Lincoln* (Rutgers University Press, 1953), 5:434; Lieber to Charles Sumner, November 28, 1862, b42, FLP.

60. Oakes, *Freedom National*, 350; Witt, *Lincoln's Code*, 229, 240, 246; *The Miscellaneous Writings of Francis Lieber* (J. B. Lippincott, 1881), 2:255–256, 259.

61. Witt, *Lincoln's Code*, 245, 248; Lieber to Charles Sumner, June 8, 1863, b43, FLP.

62. Lieber to Sumner, February 14, March 5, March 12, and March 20, 1864, b44, FLP.

63. Oakes, *Freedom National*, 440–441, ch. 12.

64. Lieber to Sumner, April 15, 1865, b46, FLP.

65. Eric Foner, *Reconstruction: America's Unfinished Revolution, 1863–1877* (1988; Perennial, 2002), 199; Oakes, *Freedom National*, 489–491; Francis Lieber to Matilda Lieber, April 19, 1866, b36, FLP.

66. Freidel, *Francis Lieber*, 370–375; Lieber to Andrew Dickson White, July 28, 1871, b53, FLP.

Chapter 4: Still Fighting It

1. Eric Foner, *The Second Founding: How the Civil War and Reconstruction Remade the Constitution* (Norton, 2019), 40–41, 52–53, 112; Ezra Greenspan, *William Wells Brown: An African American Life* (Norton, 2014), 410–411.

2. Kirk Savage, *Standing Soldiers, Kneeling Slaves: Race, War, and Monument in Nineteenth-Century America* (Princeton University Press, 1997), 17.

3. William Wells Brown, *Clotel and Other Writings*, ed. Ezra Greenspan (Library of America, 2014), 925.

4. Brown, *Clotel and Other Writings*, 9–53, 973–984.

5. Greenspan, *William Wells Brown*, 370, 382–388, 423–424.

6. William Wells Brown, *The Negro in the American Rebellion: His Heroism and His Fidelity* (Lee and Shepard, 1867), v.

7. Dena J. Epstein, *Sinful Tunes and Spirituals: Black Folk Music to the Civil War* (University of Illinois Press, 1977), 241–243, 303, 329.

8. *The Magnificent Activist: The Writings of Thomas Wentworth Higginson*, ed. Howard N. Meyer (Da Capo, 2000), 178.

9. McPherson, *Battle Cry of Freedom*, 371. See also Willie Lee Rose, *Rehearsal for Reconstruction: The Port Royal Experiment* (1964; University of Georgia Press, 1999).

10. Samuel Charters, *Songs of Sorrow: Lucy McKim Garrison and* Slave Songs of the United States (University Press of Mississippi, 2015), 57–59, 89, 95, 27–28, 40–49, 103.

11. Charters, *Songs of Sorrow*, 10, 91, 104, 117–129; Epstein, *Sinful Tunes and Spirituals*, 244–248, 260–270; Lucy McKim, "Songs of the Port Royal 'Contrabands,'" *Dwight's Journal of Music* 22, no. 6 (November 8, 1862): 254–255.

12. Charters, *Songs of Sorrow*, 144, 150–151; Epstein, *Sinful Tunes and Spirituals*, 317–318.

13. *Magnificent Activist*, 12–16, 69.

14. *Magnificent Activist*, 18–19; *The Complete Civil War Journal and Selected Letters of Thomas Wentworth Higginson*, ed. Christopher Looby (University of Chicago Press, 2000), 16, 42; William Wells Brown, *The Black Man: His Antecedents, His Genius, and His Achievements* (Thomas Hamilton, 1863), 148; Thomas Wentworth Higginson, *Army Life in a Black Regiment* (Fields, Osgood, 1870), 4.

15. Higginson, *Army Life*, 62–63, 86–87, 249.

16. *Complete Civil War Journal*, 56–57, 78; Thomas Wentworth Higginson, "Negro Spirituals," *Atlantic*, June 1867.

17. *Complete Civil War Journal*, 13; *Magnificent Activist*, 36, 27–29.

18. *Complete Civil War Journal*, 375; Higginson, "Negro Spirituals." See also Higginson, *Army Life*, 253.

19. *A Yankee Scholar in Coastal South Carolina: William Francis Allen's Civil War Journals*, ed. James Robert Hester (University of South Carolina Press, 2015), 1–3; Ray Allen Billington, *Frederick Jackson Turner: Historian, Scholar, Teacher* (Oxford University Press, 1973), 31.

20. *Yankee Scholar in Coastal South Carolina*, 28–29, 34, 62, 37; William Francis Allen, "The Negro Dialect," *Nation*, December 14, 1865, 744–745.

21. Epstein, *Sinful Tunes and Spirituals*, 308–309; *Yankee Scholar in Coastal South Carolina*, 32–33.

22. Epstein, *Sinful Tunes and Spirituals*, 318–336; Charters, *Songs of Sorrow*, 183–186, 194–213; *Yankee Scholar in Coastal South Carolina*, 215.

23. Charters, *Songs of Sorrow*, 255–257; William Francis Allen, Charles Pickard Ware, and Lucy McKim Garrison, *Slave Songs of the United States* (A. Simpson, 1867), vi–xii, xxiii.

24. Allen, Ware, and Garrison, *Slave Songs*, x, xx; David W. Blight, *Race and Reunion: The Civil War in American Memory* (Harvard University Press, 2001), 313–319; Andrew Ward, *Dark Midnight When I Rise: The Story of the Jubilee Singers Who Introduced the World to the Music of Black America* (Farrar, Straus and Giroux, 2000), 404.

25. Charters, *Songs of Sorrow*, 216, 252–253; Epstein, *Sinful Tunes and Spirituals*, 340.

26. David Levering Lewis, *W. E. B. Du Bois: Biography of a Race, 1868–1919* (Henry Holt, 1993), 58; Ward, *Dark Midnight When I Rise*, 404–405.

27. Horace Greeley, *The American Conflict: A History of the Great Rebellion in the United States of America, 1860–'65* (O. D. Case, 1864–1866), 2:7; 1:9, 406; 2:237, 242, 528.

28. Greeley, *American Conflict*, 1:11; Jack P. Maddex Jr., *The Reconstruction of Edward A. Pollard: A Rebel's Conversion to Postbellum Unionism* (University of North Carolina Press, 1974).

29. Edward Pollard, *The Southern Spy; Or, Curiosities of Negro Slavery in the South* (Henry Polkinhorn, 1859), 8–9, 25.

30. Maddex, *Reconstruction of Edward A. Pollard*, 5, 16–22.

31. Edward A. Pollard, *The Lost Cause; A New Southern History of the War of the Confederates* (E. B. Treat, 1866), 47–49, 746–752; Rollin G. Osterweis, *The Myth of the Lost Cause, 1865–1900* (Archon, 1973), 11.

32. Maddex, *Reconstruction of Edward A. Pollard*, 6, 44–46.

33. Edward A. Pollard, *The Lost Cause Regained* (G. W. Carleton, 1868), 13–14.

34. Richard White, *The Republic for Which It Stands: The United States During Reconstruction and the Gilded Age, 1865–1896* (Oxford University Press, 2017), 202–212; Greeley, *American Conflict*, 1:12; Blight, *Race and Reunion*, 59–61.

35. Edward A. Pollard, *A Southern Historian's Appeal for Horace Greeley* (Daily Republican Book and Job Printing Establishment, 1872), 2, 4, 9, 28, 31.

36. Edward A. Pollard, "The Anti-Slavery Men of the South," *Galaxy* 16, no. 3 (1873): 329, 339–341.

37. Gaines M. Foster, *Ghosts of the Confederacy: Defeat, the Lost Cause, and the Emergence of the New South, 1865–1913* (Oxford University Press, 1987), 49; Keith S. Hébert, *Cornerstone of the Confederacy: Alexander Stephens and the Speech That Defined the Lost Cause* (University of Tennessee Press, 2021), 72.

38. Richard H. Abbott, *Cobbler in Congress: The Life of Henry Wilson, 1812–1875* (University Press of Kentucky, 1972), 162; Hébert, *Cornerstone of the Confederacy*, 68–71.

39. Alexander H. Stephens, *A Constitutional View of the Late War Between the States: Its Causes, Character, Conduct and Results* (National Publishing Company, 1868–1870), 1:28–29, 539; 2:652.

40. George H. Moore, *Notes on the History of Slavery in Massachusetts* (D. Appleton, 1866), 68, 9, 11; John David Smith, *Slavery, Race, and American History: Historical Conflict, Trends, and Method, 1866–1953* (M. E. Sharpe, 1999), 3–15.

41. Alexander H. Stephens, *A Compendium of the History of the United States from the Earliest Settlements to 1872* (E. J. Hale and Son, 1872), 59–61, 257, 326–329, 398, 419, 471–472.

42. Gregory P. Downs, *After Appomattox: Military Occupation and the Ends of War* (Harvard University Press, 2015), 7–8; White, *Republic for Which It Stands*, 211; Foner, *Reconstruction*, 533.

43. For Wilson, see Abbott, *Cobbler in Congress*, and John L. Myers, *Henry Wilson and the Era of Reconstruction* (University Press of America, 2009), 195–205; quotation from Henry Wilson, *History of the Rise and Fall of the Slave Power in America* (James R. Osgood, 1873–1877), 3:740.

44. Blight, *Race and Reunion*, 258–259.

45. John Hope Franklin, *George Washington Williams: A Biography* (1985; Duke University Press, 1998), 236, 2–21.

46. George W. Williams, *History of the Negro Race in America from 1619 to 1880* (G. P. Putnam's Sons, 1882), 1:v–vi, ix; Franklin, *George Washington Williams*, 33–39, 101–106.

47. Williams, *History of the Negro Race*, 1:116–118, 172, 252, 411, viii; 2:545.

48. Franklin, *George Washington Williams*, 164–165, 178–231.

Chapter 5: Look Away

1. Michael Kammen, "Moses Coit Tyler: The First Professor of American History in the United States," *History Teacher* 17, no. 1 (1983): 66, 70–71.

2. Deborah L. Haines, "Scientific History as a Teaching Method: The Formative Years," *JAH* 63, no. 4 (1977): 896–897; Joseph J. Mathews, "The Study of History in the South," *JSH* 31, no. 1 (1965): 8.

3. Scrapbook in b62, HBA; "Reminiscences," f3, b68, HBA.

4. Carl Diehl, *Americans and German Scholarship, 1770–1870* (Yale University Press, 1978), 50–51, 155; Clark, *Academic Charisma*, 162; Adams notes in f9, b30, HBA.

5. Hugh Hawkins, *Pioneer: A History of the Johns Hopkins University, 1874–1889* (Cornell University Press, 1960), 3, 9–22, 50–56. For Allen at Hopkins, see *JHUC* 2, no. 2 (February 1878): 2.

6. Adams to JHU Trustees, 1876?, f19, b6, HBA; Hawkins, *Pioneer*, 80–81, 225–229.

7. Adams to JHU Trustees, April 26, 1877, f19, b6, HBA; "An Autobiography," f3, b68, HBA; Adams to Austin Scott, May 11, 1878, f19, b14, HBA; "Instruction in History, Political Economy, Logic, and Ethics, 1878–9," *JHUC* 2 (1878): 3–4; Hawkins, *Pioneer*, 170–173.

8. Von Holst to Adams, October 4, 1883, f20, b8, HBA.

9. Eric F. Goldman, "Hermann Eduard von Holst: Plumed Knight of American Historiography," *MVHR* 23, no. 4 (1937): 511–514, 520.

10. Hermann von Holst and Ira Hutchinson Brainerd, *Constitutional and Political History of the United States: Index and List of Authorities* (Callaghan, 1892), 269–282.

11. Hermann von Holst, *The Constitutional and Political History of the United States*, trans. John J. Lalor and Alfred B. Mason (Callaghan, 1877), 1:340, 351; Hermann von Holst, *The Constitutional and Political History of the United States*, trans. John J. Lalor and Paul Shorey (Callaghan, 1881), 3:320.

12. Von Holst, *Constitutional and Political History*, 3:iii; Eric F. Goldman, "Importing a Historian: Von Holst and American Universities," *MVHR* 27, no. 2 (1940): 267; minutes, January 24, 1879, in *JHUS*, 29–31.

13. Goldman, "Importing a Historian," 268–269; Hawkins, *Pioneer*, 170; George William Brown to Gilman, June 30, 1879, and July 7, 1879, and von Holst to Gilman, August 12, 1879, f18, b1.23, DCG.

14. Goldman, "Hermann Eduard von Holst," 514; Hermann von Holst, *The Constitutional and Political History of the United States*, trans. John J. Lalor (Callaghan, 1885), 4:iii–iv.

15. Von Holst to Adams, October 4, 1883, f20, b8, HBA.

16. "Dr. von Holst's Lectures," *JHUC* 3, no. 28 (January 1884): 43; Jameson diary entry for October 12, 1883, b3, JFJ.

17. R&G, 1:xxix; Herbert B. Adams, "Methods of Historical Study," *SHPS* 2, nos. 1–2 (1884): 97–109.

18. Foner, *Reconstruction*, 532, 556.

19. Civil Rights Cases, 109 US 3, 34, 35, 37, 4, 22, 24.

20. Albert Bushnell Hart, who had just returned from studying with von Holst in Freiburg, was also beginning to have his undergraduates at Harvard investigate topics including "Slave Insurrections; Fugitive Slave Cases; Slavery in the Free States; the Slave Trade." Adams, "Methods of Historical Study," 62.

21. Minutes, April 18, 1884, and October 10, 1884, in *JHUS*, 86, 104; "Proceedings of Societies," *JHUC* 4, no. 35 (December 1884): 28; Birney to Adams, October 23, 1884, f18, b2, HBA.

22. "Proceedings of Societies," *JHUC* 4, no. 38 (March 1885): 66; Adams to Bancroft, March 5, 1885, b143, FBP; "Proceedings of Societies," *JHUC* 4, no. 41 (July 1885): 122; *Men of Mark in Maryland* (B. F. Johnson, 1910), 2:239–240 (Leigh Bonsal).

23. Jeffrey R. Brackett, "Report of Certain Studies in the Institution of African Slavery in the United States," *Papers of the American Historical Association* 1, no. 6 (1886): 436–437.

24. Minutes, April 29, 1887, and December 14, 1888, in *JHUS*, 361, 551; Jeffrey R. Brackett, *The Negro in Maryland: A Study of the Institution of Slavery* (N. Murray, 1889), 1.

25. Brackett, *Negro in Maryland*, 2, 130, 139–144.

26. Brackett to Adams, June 13, 1889, f38, b2, HBA.

27. Tyson R. Meekins to Adams, April 10, 1893, f22, b11, HBA.

28. Birney to Adams, January 14, 1891, and January 29, 1891, f18, b2, HBA; John David Smith, *An Old Creed for the New South: Proslavery Ideology and Historiography, 1865–1918* (Greenwood, 1985), 139; Scharf to Adams, February 20, 1892, f16, b14, HBA; Gilman memo, February 22, 1896, f16, b1.61, DCG.

29. Gilman memo, February 22, 1896, f16, b1.61, DCG; Haines, "Scientific History as a Teaching Method," 901; minutes, October 10, 1889, in *JHUS*, 611–612.

30. Minutes, June 1, 1900, in *JHUS*, 542.

31. Blight, *Race and Reunion*, 216–217, 222, 264; Osterweis, *Myth of the Lost Cause*, 34–52, 113; Foster, *Ghosts of the Confederacy*, 6–7; Thomas Nelson Page, *The Old South: Essays Social and Political* (Charles Scribner's Sons, 1892), 289.

32. Jackson Lears, *Rebirth of a Nation: The Making of Modern America, 1877–1920* (Harper, 2009), 104; George M. Fredrickson, *The Black Image in the White Mind: The Debate on Afro-American Character and Destiny, 1817–1914* (Harper & Row, 1971), 198–255.

33. White, *Republic for Which It Stands*, 628–635; Lewis, *W. E. B. Du Bois: Biography of a Race*, 260.

34. Edward Ingle, "The Negro in the District of Columbia," *SHPS* 11, nos. 3–4 (1893): 99, 104.

35. Marion Gleason McDougall, *Fugitive Slaves (1619–1865)* (Ginn, 1891), 53–54.

36. W. E. B. Du Bois, *Writings*, ed. Nathan Huggins (Library of America, 1986), 193.

37. Rhodes autobiographical document, and Rhodes to Bancroft, March 26, 1892, b143, FBP.

38. James Ford Rhodes, *History of the United States from the Compromise of 1850* (1892; Harper and Brothers, 1896), 1:1; John T. Morse to Rhodes, May 4, 1893, c1, JFR.

39. Rhodes, *History*, 1:303–304; Smith, *Slavery, Race, and American History*, 17.

40. Witold Rybczynski, *A Clearing in the Distance: Frederick Law Olmsted and America in the 19th Century* (Scribner, 1999), 117.

41. Rhodes, *History*, 1:305–316, 323, 333.

42. Rhodes, 1:359, 348, 367, 380.

43. J. W. Burgess, review of *History of the United States, from the Compromise of 1850* by James Ford Rhodes, *PSQ* 8, no. 2 (1893): 346, 342; John W. Burgess, *The Middle Period, 1817–1858* (Charles Scribner's Sons, 1897), xii.

44. John W. Burgess, *Reminiscences of an American Scholar: The Beginnings of Columbia University* (Columbia University Press, 1934), 3, 11, 16–25; and John W. Burgess, "How I Found Amherst College and What I Found," *Amherst Graduates' Quarterly* 17, no. 1 (1927): 7.

45. John W. Burgess, "The Ideal of the American Commonwealth," *PSQ* 10, no. 3 (1895): 406, 407.

46. Burgess, review of *History of the United States*, 343.

47. [Woodrow Wilson], "Anti-Slavery History and Biography," *Atlantic*, August 1893, 272, 273; Henry Wilkinson Bragdon, *Woodrow Wilson: The Academic Years* (Harvard University Press, 1967), 190, 110, 237.

48. Rhodes to Bancroft, August 12, 1893, b143, FBP.

49. Billington, *Frederick Jackson Turner*, 125; Turner to Constance Lindsay Skinner, March 15, 1922, bTU31, and Turner to Carl Becker, December 16, 1925, bTU34A, FJT.

50. Turner, "Tribute to William Francis Allen," f24, bTU56, and Turner to Merle Curti, August 8, 1928, bTU39, FJT; Billington, *Frederick Jackson Turner*, 25–31.

51. Billington, *Frederick Jackson Turner*, 36–38, 56, 58, 67; Turner to Allen, October 31, 1888, bTU1, FJT.

52. Billington, *Frederick Jackson Turner*, 58–59, 70, 75; Turner to William E. Dodd, October 7, 1919, bTU29, FJT.

53. Billington, *Frederick Jackson Turner*, 82–88; Bragdon, *Woodrow Wilson*, 233–240; Frederick Jackson Turner, *The Early Writings of Frederick Jackson Turner* (University of Wisconsin Press, 1938), 71.

54. Billington, *Frederick Jackson Turner*, 125–127; Frederick Jackson Turner, *The Frontier in American History* (Henry Holt, 1920), 2–3.

55. Billington, *Frederick Jackson Turner*, 129–130; Roosevelt to Turner, February 10, 1894, bTU1, FJT.

56. Turner, *Frontier*, 29.

57. Charles A. Beard, *An Economic Interpretation of the Constitution of the United States* (Macmillan, 1913), 17, 30; Charles A. Beard and William C. Bagley, *The History of the American People* (Macmillan, 1918), vi–vii.

58. A. M. Simons, *Social Forces in American History* (Macmillan, 1911), 268; John R. Commons et al., *History of Labour in the United States*, vols. 1–2 (Macmillan, 1918).

59. Frederick Rudolph, *Curriculum: A History of the American Undergraduate Course of Study Since 1636* (Jossey-Bass, 1977), 135–137, 177–179.

Chapter 6: Dixie Land

1. Du Bois, *Writings*, 439; Smith, *Old Creed for the New South*, 240; John Herbert Roper, *U. B. Phillips: A Southern Mind* (Mercer University Press, 1984), 5–19, 26–30; John Herbert Roper interview with Ellis Merton Coulter, June 9, 1976, f7, UBP-NC.

2. Phillips to Turner, February 20, 1899, bTU2, FJT; Roper, *U. B. Phillips*, 51–54; Robert B. Townsend, *History's Babel: Scholarship, Professionalization, and the Historical Enterprise in the United States, 1880–1940* (University of Chicago Press, 2013), 22.

3. Dunning to Bancroft, September 9, 1909, b41, FBP.

4. William Dunning to Charlotte Dunning, December 1913, b1, WAD; William A. Dunning, "Truth in History," *AHR* 19, no. 2 (1914): 227–228.

5. Dunning, diary entry for April 19, 1884, b3, WAD; Dunning to Bancroft, July 30, 1909, b41, FBP. For Dunning's grades, see the folder on Columbia in b7, WAD. On Dunning's expulsion, see the folder on Dartmouth in b5, WAD.

6. William Archibald Dunning, *Essays on the Civil War and Reconstruction* (1897; Macmillan, 1898), 250, 175, 247.

7. William Archibald Dunning, *Essays on the Civil War and Reconstruction*, rev. ed. (1904; Macmillan, 1910), 383–385.

8. Dunning to Bancroft, May 16, 1907, b40, FBP; John David Smith, "Introduction," in *The Dunning School: Historians, Race, and the Meaning of Reconstruction*, ed. Smith and J. Vincent Lowery (University Press of Kentucky, 2013), 8.

9. John Herbert Roper interview with Thomas E. Drake, June 12, 1975, f7, UBP-NC; Roper, *U. B. Phillips*, 52–55.

10. Phillips to George J. Baldwin, May 2, 1903, and Phillips to Lucien Boggs, February 23, 1903, f1, UBP-NC.

11. William E. Dodd, "The Status of History in Southern Education," *Nation*, August 7, 1902, 110.

12. John R. Thelin, *A History of American Higher Education*, 3rd ed. (Johns Hopkins University Press, 2019), 140; Dodd, "Status of History," 110–111; Erik Larson, *In the Garden of Beasts: Love, Terror, and an American Family in Hitler's Berlin* (Crown, 2011), 12.

13. Karen L. Cox, *Dixie's Daughters: The United Daughters of the Confederacy and the Preservation of Confederate Culture* (University Press of Florida, 2003), 2–5, 19–20, 29, 49–50, 94–129, 160; Foster, *Ghosts of the Confederacy*, 180–190; Blight, *Race and Reunion*, 255–296.

14. Phillips to Carl Russell Fish, May 19, 1922, f4, UBP-NC; Roper, *U. B. Phillips*, 81–84.

15. Ulrich B. Phillips, "Documentary Collections and Publication in the Older States of the South," *Annual Report of the American Historical Association for the Year 1905* (Government Printing Office, 1906), 1:204; Ulrich Bonnell Phillips, "The Public Archives of Georgia," *Annual Report of the American Historical Association for the Year 1903* (Government Printing Office, 1904), 1:454–455.

16. Phillips to Carnegie Institution, March 23, 1903, f75, b4, UBP-Y.

17. Postcards are in f1, b1, and f1, b2, UBP-Y. Folders are in b27–29, UBP-Y. For Georgia law firms, see Sibley & McWhorter to Phillips, October 1, 1904, f268, b29, UBP-Y. Office described in John Herbert Roper interview with Bell I. Wiley, September 13, 1974, f7, UBP-NC.

18. Phillips to Jameson, November 20, 1905, b119, JFJ; Phillips, "Documentary Collections," 203–204.

19. Ulrich Bonnell Phillips, *The Slave Economy of the Old South: Selected Essays in Economic and Social History*, ed. Eugene D. Genovese (Louisiana State University Press, 1968), 83, 78, 73.

20. Ulrich B. Phillips, "The Economics of Slave Labor in the South," in *The South in the Building of the Nation*, ed. James Curtis Ballagh (Southern Publication Society, 1909), 5:121.

21. Peter Daniel, "The Metamorphosis of Slavery, 1865–1900," *JAH* 66, no. 1 (1979): 89; Du Bois, *Writings*, 467.

22. Phillips to A. C. McLaughlin, April 27, July 28, and November 5, 1904, b119, JFJ.

23. Ulrich B. Phillips, "The Economics of the Slave Trade, Foreign and Domestic," in *The South in the Building of the Nation*, ed. James Curtis Ballagh (Southern Publication Society, 1909), 5:124–129.

24. Phillips, *Slave Economy*, 124–134.

25. Phillips, 196, 197, 214.

26. Billington, *Frederick Jackson Turner*, 245–246; Roper, *U. B. Phillips*, 59–60, 81.

27. Ulrich Bonnell Phillips, *A History of Transportation in the Eastern Cotton Belt to 1860* (Columbia University Press, 1908), v; William Carpenter to Phillips, October 16, 1907, f2, UBP-NC.

28. Lewis, *W. E. B. Du Bois: Biography of a Race*, 11–69.

29. Albert Bushnell Hart, *Slavery and Abolition, 1831–1841* (Harper and Brothers, 1906), xv; Lewis, *W. E. B. Du Bois: Biography of a Race*, 79–101; Smith, *Old Creed for the New South*, 126–129; Carol F. Baird, "Albert Bushnell Hart: The Rise of the Professional Historian," in *Social Sciences at Harvard, 1860–1920: From Inculcation to the Open Mind*, ed. Paul Buck (Harvard University Press, 1965), 150–154.

30. Lewis, *W. E. B. Du Bois: Biography of a Race*, 102–114.

31. Lewis, 126–143; Aldon D. Morris, *The Scholar Denied: W. E. B. Du Bois and the Birth of Modern Sociology* (University of California Press, 2015), 19–22, 151.

32. Lewis, *W. E. B. Du Bois: Biography of a Race*, 144–160.

33. Du Bois, *Writings*, 197; Lewis, *W. E. B. Du Bois: Biography of a Race*, 156–159.

34. Du Bois, *Writings*, 582; Fred H. Matthews, *Quest for an American Sociology: Robert E. Park and the Chicago School* (McGill-Queen's University Press, 1977), 89–91; Morris, *Scholar Denied*, 45–56.

35. Francille Rusan Wilson, *The Segregated Scholars: Black Social Scientists and the Creation of Black Labor Studies, 1890–1950* (University of Virginia Press, 2006), 23; W. E. Burghardt Du Bois, "The Study of the Negro Problems," *Annals of the American Academy of Political and Social Science* 11 (January 1898): 12, 14, 21.

36. Wilson, *Segregated Scholars*, 27; Morris, *Scholar Denied*, 57–79.

37. W. E. Burghardt Du Bois, ed., *The Negro American Family* (Atlanta University Press, 1908), 47.

38. Du Bois, *Writings*, 359, 363, 364; Lewis, *W. E. B. Du Bois: Biography of a Race*, 291–294.

39. Du Bois, *Writings*, 495.

40. Du Bois, 494; Charters, *Songs of Sorrow*, 252–253.

41. Du Bois, *Writings*, 538–544.

42. Lewis, *W. E. B. Du Bois: Biography of a Race*, 226–228, 333–337; Wilson, *Segregated Scholars*, 81; Morris, *Scholar Denied*, 98.

43. Smith, *Slavery, Race, and American History*, 55–58.

44. Alfred Holt Stone, "Is Race Friction Between Blacks and Whites in the United States Growing and Inevitable?," *American Journal of Sociology* 13, no. 5 (1908): 677, 684, 686; Lewis, *W. E. B. Du Bois: Biography of a Race*, 366–368; Wilson, *Segregated Scholars*, 79–80.

45. Lewis, *W. E. B. Du Bois: Biography of a Race*, 383–386; M&R, 5–6; *Annual Report of the American Historical Association for the Year 1909* (Government Printing Office, 1911), 36–37; W. E. Burghardt Du Bois, "Reconstruction and Its Benefits," *AHR* 15, no. 4 (1910): 788, 795, 799; Du Bois, *Writings*, 786–787.

46. Roper, *U. B. Phillips*, 82–85, 34, 37; Phillips, "A History of American Negro Slavery," f247, b27, UBP-Y.

47. Ray Billington to Roper, November 14, 1975, f33, JHR; *Catalogue of the University of Michigan for 1914–1915* (University of Michigan, 1915), 186–188; John Herbert Roper interview with Thomas E. Drake, June 12, 1975, f7, UBP-NC.

48. John David Smith, "Finding '*Pax Plantation*' at Camp Gordon, Georgia: Historian Ulrich Bonnell Phillips and World War I," *Journal of the Gilded Age and Progressive Era* 13, no. 4 (2014), 574, 576, 580–582; Roper, *U. B. Phillips*, 88.

49. Phillips, *Slave Economy*, 270–271; Smith, "Finding '*Pax Plantation*,'" 584.

50. Ulrich Bonnell Phillips, *American Negro Slavery: A Survey of the Supply, Employment and Control of Negro Labor as Determined by the Plantation Regime* (1918; Louisiana State University Press, 1966), 52, 307, 323, 343, 401, 514.

51. David Brion Davis, "Slavery and the Post–World War II Historians," *Daedalus* 103, no. 2 (1974): 2.

52. W. E. Burghardt Du Bois, review of *American Negro Slavery* by Ulrich Bonnell Phillips, *American Political Science Review* 12, no. 4 (1918): 722, 725, 723.

Chapter 7: New Foundations

1. Thelin, *History of American Higher Education*, 205; Peter Novick, *That Noble Dream: The "Objectivity Question" and the American Historical Profession* (Cambridge University Press, 1988), 174–175.

2. Lewis, *W. E. B. Du Bois: Biography of a Race*, 421, 424, 510.

3. Charles R. Beard and Mary R. Beard, *The Rise of American Civilization* (Macmillan, 1927), 1:710, 632; 2:6; Nina Silber, *This War Ain't Over: Fighting the Civil War in New Deal America* (University of North Carolina Press, 2018), 136–143; Michael O'Brien, *The Idea of the American South, 1920–1941* (Johns Hopkins University Press, 1979), 169–171.

4. Michael Rogin, "'The Sword Became a Flashing Vision': D. W. Griffith's *The Birth of a Nation*," *Representations* no. 9 (1985): 150–157, 184; Nick Sacco, "Outrageous Inaccuracies: The Grand Army of the Republic Protests *The Birth of a Nation*," *Muster*, November 14, 2017; Lewis, *W. E. B. Du Bois: Biography of a Race*, 506–510.

5. Jacqueline Goggin, *Carter G. Woodson: A Life in Black History* (Louisiana State University Press, 1993), 1–32; Carter G. Woodson, "Ten Years of Collecting and Publishing the Records of the Negro," *JNH* 10, no. 4 (1925): 598.

6. Robert E. Park, review of *The Education of the Negro Prior to 1861* by Carter Goodwin Woodson, *American Journal of Sociology* 21, no. 1 (1915): 119–120; Jeffrey Aaron Snyder, *Making Black History: The Color Line, Culture, and Race in the Age of Jim Crow* (University of Georgia Press, 2018), 30.

7. *Annual Register of the University of Chicago, Covering the Academic Year Ending June 30, 1914* (University of Chicago Press, 1914), 163; Matthews, *Quest for an American Sociology*, 83–85; Park, "The Negro in America" notes, f7, b1, RPC. Winifred Raushenbush dates the course to 1914 in *Robert E. Park: Biography of a Sociologist* (Duke University Press, 1979), 77.

8. Goggin, *Carter G. Woodson*, 32–35; M&R, 1–2.

9. Brenda E. Stevenson, "'Out of the Mouths of Ex-Slaves': Carter G. Woodson's *Journal of Negro History* 'Invents' the Study of Slavery," *Journal of African American History* 100, no. 4 (2015): 701; Snyder, *Making Black History*, 48.

10. R&G, 1:xxxvii–xxxviii; Jameson to Woodson, April 8, 1916, f: ASNLH, b57, JFJ.

11. R&G, 1:xxvii–xxix, 160–161; 2: 3–4, 6, 9, 131, 203–205; Novick, *That Noble Dream*, 48, 88.

12. *Annual Register of the University of Chicago, July, 1900–July, 1901* (University of Chicago Press, 1901), 196–197; *Annual Register of the University of Chicago, July, 1902–July, 1903* (University of Chicago Press, 1903), 237.

13. R&G, 3:5; Charles H. Haskins, "Report of the Proceedings of the Nineteenth Annual Meeting of the American Historical Association," *Annual Report of the American Historical Association for the Year 1903* (Government Printing Office, 1904), 1:29.

14. Jameson to George A. Plimpton, September 24, 1919, f: "Slave Trade Documents," b128; and Robert S. Woodward to Jameson, October 13, 1915, b132, JFJ.

15. Goggin, *Carter G. Woodson*, 37; M&R, 30; Jameson to Woodson, May 17, 1916, and June 24, 1916, f: ASNLH, b57, JFJ.

16. Jameson to Catterall, June 27, 1918, and November 21, 1918, b69, JFJ.

17. Jameson to Donnan, March 8, 1923, and Donnan to Jameson, March 24, 1923, b78, JFJ. Catterall's illness is mentioned in letters from November 1919 to March 1920, f: Helen T. Catterall, b69, JFJ.

18. August Meier and Elliott Rudwick, "J. Franklin Jameson, Carter G. Woodson, and the Foundations of Black Historiography," *AHR* 89, no. 4 (1984): 1006, 1010. See also Woodson, "Ten Years," 599.

19. Goggin, *Carter G. Woodson*, 45–53.

20. David M. Kennedy, *Over Here: The First World War and American Society* (1980; Oxford University Press, 2004), 55–59, 113–114, 187–189, 279–283; Goggin, *Carter G. Woodson*, 147.

21. Matthews, *Quest for an American Sociology*, 176; Goggin, *Carter G. Woodson*, 148; John H. Stanfield, *Philanthropy and Jim Crow in American Social Science* (Greenwood, 1985), 119–120.

22. Martin Bulmer and Joan Bulmer, "Philanthropy and Social Science in the 1920s: Beardsley Ruml and the Laura Spelman Rockefeller Memorial, 1922–29," *Minerva* 19, no. 3 (1981): 349–350; Thelin, *History of American Higher Education*, 239.

23. Meier and Rudwick, "J. Franklin Jameson, Carter G. Woodson," 1011–1013; M&R, 32–35.

24. Jacqueline Goggin, "Carter G. Woodson and the Collection of Source Materials for Afro-American History," *American Archivist* 48, no. 3 (1985): 265; Goggin, *Carter G. Woodson*, 84.

25. William S. Willis Jr., "Franz Boas and the Study of Black Folklore," in *The New Ethnicity: Perspectives from Ethnology*, ed. John W. Bennett (West, 1975), 313–320; Keith S. Chambers, "The Indefatigable Elsie Clews Parsons—Folklorist," *Western Folklore* 32, no. 3 (1973): 185.

26. Lee D. Baker, *From Savage to Negro: Anthropology and the Construction of Race, 1896–1954* (University of California Press, 1998), 150; Chambers, "Indefatigable Elsie Clews Parsons," 185–187; Willis, "Franz Boas," 320–322.

27. Baker, *From Savage to Negro*, 152; Willis, "Franz Boas," 321; Goggin, *Carter G. Woodson*, 72; Zora Neale Hurston, "Cudjo's Own Story of the Last African Slavery," *JNH* 12, no. 4 (1927): 649.

28. Baker, *From Savage to Negro*, 128, 140–144; Arthur A. Schomburg, "The Negro Digs Up His Past," in *The New Negro: An Interpretation*, ed. Alain Locke (Albert and Charles Boni, 1925), 237, 232; M&R, 47.

29. Scott Spillman, "Institutional Limits: Christine Ladd-Franklin, Fellowships, and American Women's Academic Careers, 1880–1920," *History of Education Quarterly* 52, no. 2 (2012): 200–210, 217, 220n104. For pay, see, e.g., Catterall to Jameson, May 5, 1922, b69, JFJ.

30. "Historical Summary of Faculty, Enrollment, Degrees Conferred, and Finances in Degree-Granting Postsecondary Institutions," Digest of Education Statistics (2022), National Center for Education Statistics, https://nces.ed.gov/programs/digest/d22/tables/dt22_301.20.asp.

31. Jameson to Nathaniel W. Stephenson, February 28, 1919; Lawrence C. Wroth to Jameson, September 10, 1927, f: "Slave Trade Documents," b128, JFJ.

32. R&G, 3:141–142; Jameson to Catterall, December 15, 1927, and March 27, 1928, b69, JFJ.

33. *Carnegie Institution of Washington Year Book* no. 28 (1929), 91. Annual reports were often stitched together from memos written by individual researchers.

34. Ulrich B. Phillips, review of *Judicial Cases Concerning American Slavery and the Negro* by Helen Tunnicliff Catterall, *AHR* 32, no. 2 (1927): 332.

35. See f: "Catterall—Judicial Cases," b70, JFJ; and *Carnegie Institution of Washington Year Book* no. 34 (1935), 146, and no. 35 (1936), 147.

36. R&G, 3:311.

37. Wendell Holmes Stephenson, *The South Lives in History: Southern Historians and Their Legacy* (Louisiana State University Press, 1955), 1, 22; Jameson to Charles Moore, January 15, 1930, b113, JFJ.

38. John Herbert Roper Sr., "Ransack Roulhac and Racism: Joseph Grégoire de Roulhac Hamilton and Dunning's Questions of Institution Building and Jim Crow," in *The Dunning School: Historians, Race, and the Meaning of Reconstruction*, ed. John David Smith and J. Vincent Lowery (University Press of Kentucky, 2013), 187; Matisha H. Wiggs, "Ransacking the South: J. G. de Roulhac Hamilton and the Founding of the Southern Historical Collection" (master's thesis, University of North Carolina at Chapel Hill, 2012), 37; J. G. de Roulhac Hamilton, "On the Importance of Unimportant Documents," *Library Quarterly* 12, no. 3 (1942): 514.

39. O'Brien, *Idea of the American South*, 44–46; Wiggs, "Ransacking the South," 2, 25–28, 39–44.

40. Hamilton, "On the Importance," 514.

41. Alex H. Poole, "The Strange Career of Jim Crow Archives: Race, Space, and History in the Mid-Twentieth-Century American South," *American Archivist* 77, no. 1 (2014): 26–31, 37–45; Roper, "Ransack Roulhac and Racism," 195.

42. R&G, 3:274, 1:xlvi, 3:289.

43. Goggin, "Woodson and the Collection," 263–267.

44. Goggin, *Carter G. Woodson*, 89–90; Goggin, "Woodson and the Collection," 262–269.

45. R&G, 3:290; Goggin, *Carter G. Woodson*, 89–92. Meier and Rudwick report that the 1930 grant came from the Rockefeller-funded General Education Board. M&R, 53.

46. David Levering Lewis, *W. E. B. Du Bois: The Fight for Equality and the American Century, 1919–1963* (Henry Holt, 2000), 286; Goggin, *Carter G. Woodson*, 62–63, 81, 93–94.

47. Raymond B. Fosdick, *The Story of the Rockefeller Foundation* (Harper and Brothers, 1952), 140, 207–208.

48. Woodson to Jameson, April 29, 1935, and Jameson to John D. Rockefeller Jr., April 30, 1935, f: "Negro History," b115, JFJ.

49. Goggin, "Woodson and the Collection," 262–269.

50. R&G, 3:283–284; Meier and Rudwick, "J. Franklin Jameson, Carter G. Woodson," 1015.

51. "Slavery," notes by L. R. Creutz on Phillips' lectures at Wisconsin, 1903–1904, f386, b36, UBP-Y; Ulrich Bonnell Phillips, *Life and Labor in the Old South* (1929; Little, Brown, 1963), 219; Norman R. Yetman, *Life Under the "Peculiar Institution": Selections from the Slave Narrative Collection* (Holt, Rinehart and Winston, 1970), 2.

52. Stanfield, *Philanthropy and Jim Crow*, 87, 121; Wilson, *Segregated Scholars*, 162; Norman R. Yetman, "The Background of the Slave Narrative Collection," *American Quarterly* 19, no. 3 (1967): 538–543; E. Franklin Frazier, "The Negro Slave Family," *JNH* 15, no. 2 (1930): 205.

53. Yetman, "Background," 540; John B. Cade, "Out of the Mouths of Ex-Slaves," *JNH* 20, no. 3 (1935): 295, 302.

54. B. A. Botkin, *Lay My Burden Down: A Folk History of Slavery* (University of Chicago Press, 1945), x; Yetman, "Background," 541–542; Stevenson, "'Out of the Mouths of Ex-Slaves,'" 702; Goggin, *Carter G. Woodson*, 121; L. D. Reddick, "A New Interpretation for Negro History," *JNH* 22, no. 1 (1937): 20.

55. Jerre Mangione, *The Dream and the Deal: The Federal Writers' Project, 1935–1943* (Little, Brown, 1972), 45–46, 9, 257; Yetman, "Background," 548–549.

56. Nolan Porterfield, *Last Cavalier: The Life and Times of John A. Lomax, 1867–1948* (University of Illinois Press, 1996), 114, 161–171, 304, 340–343, 383. Questionnaire in George P. Rawick, *From Sundown to Sunup: The Making of the Black Community* (Greenwood, 1972), 174–176; and quoted with slight differences in Porterfield, *Last Cavalier*, 388.

57. Yetman, "Background," 552; Yetman, *Life Under the "Peculiar Institution,"* 1; Mangione, *Dream and the Deal*, 263.

58. Botkin, *Lay My Burden Down*, xiii, 59, 137, 138, ix; Mangione, *Dream and the Deal*, 265; Yetman, "The Limitations of the Slave Narrative Collection" and "The Importance of the Slave Narrative Collection," in "An Introduction to the WPA Slave Narratives," Library of Congress.

Chapter 8: The Problem of Slavery

1. Elazar Barkan, *The Retreat of Scientific Racism: Changing Concepts of Race in Britain and the United States Between the World Wars* (Cambridge University Press, 1992), 336–345; Snyder, *Making Black History*, 129.

2. Lewis, *W. E. B. Du Bois: Fight for Equality*, 435–436; Maribel Morey, *White Philanthropy: Carnegie Corporation's* An American Dilemma *and the Making of a White World Order* (University of North Carolina Press, 2021), 16, 134–141.

3. Morey, *White Philanthropy*, 141–152, 186; Jerry Gershenhorn, *Melville Herskovits and the Racial Politics of Knowledge* (University of Nebraska Press, 2004), 94–96; Stanfield, *Philanthropy and Jim Crow*, 139–163; Lewis, *W. E. B. Du Bois: Fight for Equality*, 435–436, 447–449.

4. E. Franklin Frazier, *The Negro Family in the United States* (University of Chicago Press, 1939), xix; Robert E. Park, "The Conflict and Fusion of Cultures with Special Reference to the Negro," *JNH* 4, no. 2 (1919): 116–118.

5. Frazier, "Negro Slave Family," 205; E. Franklin Frazier, "The Status of the Negro in the American Social Order," *Journal of Negro Education* 4, no. 3 (1935): 294–295; Frazier, *Negro Family*, 40–43.

6. Gunnar Myrdal, *An American Dilemma: The Negro Problem and Modern Democracy* (1944; Transaction, 1996), 930–931; Melville J. Herskovits, "The American Negro Family," *Nation*, January 27, 1940, 104–105.

7. Gershenhorn, *Melville Herskovits*, 97–108; Richard H. King, *Race, Culture, and the Intellectuals, 1940–1970* (Woodrow Wilson Center Press, 2004), 133; Morey, *White Philanthropy*, 193.

8. Melville J. Herskovits, *The Myth of the Negro Past* (Harper and Brothers, 1941), 1, 31–32, 293, 78, 136–139, chs. 6–8.

9. Gershenhorn, *Melville Herskovits*, 111–116; E. Franklin Frazier, "The Negro's 'Cultural Past,'" *Nation*, February 14, 1942, 196.

10. Morey, *White Philanthropy*, 194–197; Myrdal, *American Dilemma*, lxxix–lxxxiii, 4, 84–89, 441.

11. Myrdal, 999–1022; Thomas J. Sugrue, *Sweet Land of Liberty: The Forgotten Struggle for Civil Rights in the North* (Random House, 2008), 50–57, 64, 68.

12. Morey, *White Philanthropy*, 2; Glenda Elizabeth Gilmore, *Defying Dixie: The Radical Roots of Civil Rights, 1919–1950* (Norton, 2008), 394–411; Ellen Herman, *The Romance of American Psychology: Political Culture in the Age of Experts* (University of California Press, 1995), 178–180; Sugrue, *Sweet Land of Liberty*, 99.

13. Jonathan Zimmerman, "*Brown*-ing the American Textbook: History, Psychology, and the Origins of Modern Multiculturalism," *History of Education Quarterly* 44, no. 1 (2004): 51–54.

14. Nick Witham, *Popularizing the Past: Historians, Publishers, and Readers in Postwar America* (University of Chicago Press, 2023), 81–83; M&R, 116–121; Goggin, *Carter G. Woodson*, 73; Wilson, *Segregated Scholars*, 141–142; John Hope Franklin, *Mirror to America: The Autobiography of John Hope Franklin* (Farrar, Straus and Giroux, 2005), 12, 55–95, 167–169.

15. Franklin, *George Washington Williams*, xiv–xix; Franklin, *Mirror to America*, 122–136; Poole, "Strange Career of Jim Crow Archives," 32; Witham, *Popularizing the Past*, 83–91; M&R, 121.

16. Franklin to Woodward, January 8, 1948, b19, CVW; John Hope Franklin, *From Slavery to Freedom: A History of American Negroes* (Alfred A. Knopf, 1947), 596, 599, 49, 184, 197, 205, 198, 266.

17. M&R, 124–125; August Meier, "Introduction: Benjamin Quarles and the Historiography of Black America," in Benjamin Quarles, *Black Mosaic: Essays in Afro-American*

History and Historiography (University of Massachusetts Press, 1988), 8; Thelin, *History of American Higher Education*, 267.

18. M&R, 126–128, 131, 134; Charles P. Henry, *Black Studies and the Democratization of American Higher Education* (Palgrave Macmillan, 2017), 42; Martha Biondi, *The Black Revolution on Campus* (University of California Press, 2012), 30; Neil Jumonville, *Henry Steele Commager: Midcentury Liberalism and the History of the Present* (University of North Carolina Press, 1999), 149.

19. Thelin, *History of American Higher Education*, 205–206, 232, 247; Baker, *From Savage to Negro*, 198; Novick, *That Noble Dream*, 348–349.

20. Gilmore, *Defying Dixie*, 301, 306.

21. Woodward to O'Brien, June 14, 1972, b12, MOP; James C. Cobb, *C. Vann Woodward: America's Historian* (University of North Carolina Press, 2022), 9, 18, 23, 27–30.

22. Cobb, *C. Vann Woodward*, 32, 39–43, 51; Novick, *That Noble Dream*, 228.

23. Silber, *This War Ain't Over*, 15; Margaret Mitchell, *Gone with the Wind* (Macmillan, 1936), 4, 23, 589, 654, 674, 985, 1037.

24. Cobb, *C. Vann Woodward*, 46; Silber, *This War Ain't Over*, 129–130.

25. Cobb, *C. Vann Woodward*, 67, 114–122.

26. Kenneth M. Stampp, "Historian of Slavery, the Civil War, and Reconstruction, University of California, Berkeley, 1946–1983," oral history conducted in 1996 by Ann Lage, Regional Oral History Office, Bancroft Library, University of California, Berkeley, 100, 103–104; David S. Brown, *Richard Hofstadter: An Intellectual Biography* (University of Chicago Press, 2006), 3, 11, 38–40.

27. Stampp, "Historian," 1, 3–4, 23–33.

28. Stampp, 93–94; Brown, *Richard Hofstadter*, 9, 11–12, 24–25.

29. Stampp, "Historian," 95–105, 113.

30. Felice Swados, "Negro Health on the Ante Bellum Plantations," *Bulletin of the History of Medicine* 10, no. 3 (1941): 460–472.

31. Herbert Aptheker, *American Negro Slave Revolts* (Columbia University Press, 1943), 7; Herbert Aptheker, "*S&S*: Some Memories," *Science & Society* 50, no. 3 (1986): 330; Phillips, *Life and Labor*, 196; Benjamin P. Bowser and Louis Kushnick, eds., *Against the Odds: Scholars Who Challenged Racism in the Twentieth Century* (University of Massachusetts Press, 2002), 193–200.

32. Raymond A. Bauer and Alice H. Bauer, "Day to Day Resistance to Slavery," *JNH* 27, no. 4 (1942): 389–390, 418.

33. Kenneth M. Stampp, "Our Historians and Slavery," *politics*, March 1944, 58.

34. Richard Hofstadter, "U. B. Phillips and the Plantation Legend," *JNH* 29, no. 2 (1944): 122, 124.

35. Arthur Schlesinger Sr. to Hofstadter, May 11, 1944, bCC1, RHP.

36. Richard Shryock to Hofstadter, May 9, 1944, bUC8, RHP.

37. Brown, *Richard Hofstadter*, 9, 41–50. In the early 1940s, Hofstadter started an article called "Some Psychological Aspects of the Pro-Slavery Argument" but never published it. Hofstadter to Stampp, October 11, 1967, bUC8, RHP.

38. Stampp, "Historian," 113, 120–127, 130–132, 180; Kenneth M. Stampp, *And the War Came: The North and the Secession Crisis, 1860–1861* (Louisiana State University Press, 1950), 165.

39. Stampp, "Historian," 171; Kenneth M. Stampp, "The Historian and Southern Negro Slavery," *AHR* 57, no. 3 (1952): 613, 620, 621; Hofstadter to Stampp, April 3, 1951, c1, KSP.

40. Stampp, "Historian," 171–178, 181–182, 188; Stampp to Merle Curti, [fall] 1952, b39, Merle Curti Papers, Wisconsin Historical Society.

41. James T. Patterson, *Brown v. Board of Education: A Civil Rights Milestone and Its Troubled Legacy* (Oxford University Press, 2001), 39–40; Franklin, *Mirror to America*, 156–157.

42. Woodward to Franklin, September 3, 1954, and Franklin to Woodward, September 7, 1954, b19, CVW; Cobb, *C. Vann Woodward*, 154–156, 162.

43. Cobb, 160–161, 203.

44. Stampp, "Historian," 185.

45. Hofstadter to Stampp, March 2, 1954, c1, KSP.

46. Hofstadter to Stampp, December 4, 1954, c1, KSP.

47. Hofstadter to Stampp, December 16, 1954, c1, KSP.

48. Kenneth M. Stampp, *The Peculiar Institution: Slavery in the Ante-Bellum South* (1956; Vintage, 1989), vii.

49. Stampp, *Peculiar Institution*, 28, 422, 86, 340, 364, vii, 430; Phillips, *Life and Labor*, 366.

50. C. Vann Woodward, "A Plain-Speaking Study of Slavery in the Old South," *New York Herald Tribune*, October 21, 1956, E6; Stampp, "Historian," 189.

51. Hofstadter to Stampp, October 1956, c1, KSP; Stampp, "Historian," 193; Leon Litwack, "Historian of the American People and the African American Experience, Professor at Berkeley, 1964–2007," oral history conducted in 2001–2002 by Ann Lage, Regional Oral History Office, Bancroft Library, University of California, Berkeley, 170.

Chapter 9: Culture and Consciousness

1. Hofstadter to Stampp, summer/fall 1954, c1, KSP; McKitrick to Frank Thistlethwaite, June 5, 1954, f10, b19, MCK.

2. Hofstadter to Professor Schlatter, March 3, 1960, f: "PhD Candidates—General," bUC7, RHP.

3. Woodward to McKitrick, April 9, 1959, b75, CVW.

4. E&M, introduction, f8, b46, MCK.

5. E&M, "Essays in American History," introduction and p. 38, in f5, b46, MCK; Stanley Elkins, "Opening Remarks, Conference on Slavery, St. Petersburg, Fla., Feb. 2000," f8, b28, MCK.

6. McKitrick to Riesman, May 28, 1954, b31, MCK; Elkins, "Why Does the Past Keep Changing" (1992), b2, ELK; Elkins, "Opening Remarks, Conference on Slavery, St. Petersburg, Fla., Feb. 2000," f8, b28, MCK; E&M, "Essays in American History," pp. 38–41, f5, b46, MCK.

7. Riesman to McKitrick, July 12, [1953], b31; Elkins to McKitrick, July 13, 1953, and July 19, 1953, b28; Knopf contract in f1, b22, all in MCK.

8. Trilling to McKitrick, March 1, 1954, b33, MCK.

9. Woodward to E&M, June 10, 1955, b75, CVW.

10. McKitrick to Woodward, August 1, 1955, b75, CVW.

11. McKitrick to Jack Hawes, July 19, 1957, Alfred Knopf to E&M, June 25, 1958, and McKitrick to Knopf, January 23, 1961, f1, b22; and McKitrick to Chadbourne Gilpatric, July 31, 1958, f7, b19, all in MCK.

12. William Palmer, *From Gentleman's Club to Professional Body: The Evolution of the History Department in the United States, 1940–1980* (Charleston, SC, 2008), 204; Witham, *Popularizing the Past*, 44–45; Daniel Boorstin, *America and the Image of Europe: Reflections on American Thought* (Meridian, 1960), 66; McKitrick to Hofstadter, October 17, [1957], b29, MCK.

13. Hofstadter to Elkins, January 2, 1957 [1958]; and Woodward to Elkins, January 26, 1958, b75, CVW.

14. McKitrick to Woodward, October 11, 1958, b75; Woodward to Elkins, June 16, 1958, b75; Hofstadter to Woodward, May 1958, b26; and Woodward to Roger Shugg, September 12, 1958, f650, b54, all in CVW.

15. Elkins to Woodward, April 13, 1959, b75, CVW; Stanley M. Elkins, *Slavery: A Problem in American Institutional and Intellectual Life* (University of Chicago Press, 1959), 223–230.

16. McKitrick to Elkins, November 7, 1959, b28, MCK.

17. McKitrick to Elkins, August 24, 1961, and Elkins to McKitrick, August 26, 1961, b28, MCK.

18. James T. Patterson, *Grand Expectations: The United States, 1945–1974* (Oxford University Press, 1996), 478–485; Sugrue, *Sweet Land of Liberty*, 302–305.

19. Howard Fertig to Elkins, February 4, 1964, and September 4, 1964, f: "Correspondence In—1964," b1, ELK; M&R, 250.

20. William L. Van Deburg, *New Day in Babylon: The Black Power Movement and American Culture, 1965–1975* (University of Chicago Press, 1992), 5.

21. E. James West, Ebony *Magazine and Lerone Bennett Jr.: Popular Black History in Postwar America* (University of Illinois Press, 2020), 24–39; Lerone Bennett Jr., *Before the Mayflower: A History of the Negro in America, 1619–1964*, rev. ed. (Johnson, 1964), vii–viii.

22. Jonathan Zimmerman, *Whose America? Culture Wars in the Public Schools*, 2nd ed. (University of Chicago Press, 2022), 104; Van Deburg, *New Day in Babylon*, 192–193; Manning Marable, *Race, Reform, and Rebellion: The Second Reconstruction and Beyond in Black America, 1945–2006*, 3rd ed. (University Press of Mississippi, 2007), 86, 73; Joe Street, *The Culture War in the Civil Rights Movement* (University Press of Florida, 2007), 81.

23. Van Deburg, *New Day in Babylon*, 58–60; Marable, *Race, Reform, and Rebellion*, 105.

24. Ralph Ellison, *Shadow and Act* (Random House, 1964), 112; Ralph Ellison, "'A Very Stern Discipline,'" *Harper's*, March 1967, 83–84.

25. Street, *Culture War*, 81–100; Van Deburg, *New Day in Babylon*, 51–53.

26. Lee Rainwater and William L. Yancey, eds., *The Moynihan Report and the Politics of Controversy* (MIT Press, 1967), 11–12, 22–25; James T. Patterson, *Freedom Is Not Enough: The Moynihan Report and America's Struggle over Black Life—from LBJ to Obama* (Basic Books, 2010), 1, 35; Godfrey Hodgson, *The Gentleman from New York: Daniel Patrick Moynihan* (Houghton Mifflin, 2000), 90.

27. Patterson, *Freedom Is Not Enough*, 42–43, 45; Rainwater and Yancey, *Moynihan Report*, 61–62, 75–76, 94, 126–130.

28. Patterson, *Freedom Is Not Enough*, xi–xv, 65–90; Rainwater and Yancey, *Moynihan Report*, 458, 271–272; Novick, *That Noble Dream*, 482.

29. Elkins to Fritz Stern, February 5, 1982, f: Foner, b1, ELK; J. William Harris, "Eugene Genovese's Old South: A Review Essay," *JSH* 80, no. 2 (2014): 346 (quoting Michael O'Brien).

30. On Genovese, see James Surowiecki, "Genovese's March: The Radical Reconstructions of a Southern Historian," in *Quick Studies: The Best of* Lingua Franca, ed. Alexander Star (Farrar, Straus and Giroux, 2002), 247–268; and Harris, "Eugene Genovese's Old South." Eugene D. Genovese, *The Southern Front: History and Politics in the Cultural War* (University of Missouri Press, 1995), 297n5.

31. Eugene D. Genovese, "Problems in the Study of Nineteenth-Century American History," *Science & Society* 25, no. 1 (1961): 43; Eugene D. Genovese, "Marxian Interpretations of the Slave South," in *Towards a New Past: Dissenting Essays in American History*, ed. Barton J. Bernstein (1968; Vintage, 1969), 92.

32. Genovese, "Problems in the Study," 47, 42–43.

33. Eugene D. Genovese, "The Slave South: An Interpretation," *Science & Society* 25, no. 4 (1961): 333, 337; Eugene D. Genovese, *The Political Economy of Slavery: Studies in the Economy and Society of the Slave South* (1965; Vintage, 1967), 3, 254.

34. Surowiecki, "Genovese's March," 253.

35. Genovese to Woodward, January 25, 1967, b21, CVW.

36. Genovese, "Problems in the Study," 46n8.

37. Daniel T. Rodgers, *Age of Fracture* (Harvard University Press, 2011), 91–94; Novick, *That Noble Dream*, 440; Jonathan M. Wiener, "Radical Historians and the Crisis in American History, 1959–1980," *JAH* 76, no. 2 (1989): 431.

38. Eugene D. Genovese, "Rebelliousness and Docility in the Negro Slave: A Critique of the Elkins Thesis," in *The Debate over Slavery: Stanley Elkins and His Critics*, ed. Ann J. Lane (University of Illinois Press, 1971), 49, 71.

39. Eugene D. Genovese, "The Legacy of Slavery and the Roots of Black Nationalism," *Studies on the Left* 6, no. 6 (1966): 7, 8, 19, 22; Genovese to Woodward, August 3, 1966, b21, CVW.

40. Sterling Stuckey, "Through the Prism of Folklore: The Black Ethos in Slavery," *Massachusetts Review* 9, no. 3 (1968): 418, 436–437; M&R, 261–262.

41. Genovese, "Rebelliousness and Docility in the Negro Slave," 73–74; Eugene D. Genovese, *Roll, Jordan, Roll: The World the Slaves Made* (1974; Vintage, 1976), 669–674.

42. Genovese to Elkins, January 8, 1967 [1968], f: "Correspondence, 1968"; Genovese to Elkins, October 20, 1967, f: 1967; Genovese to Elkins, August 25, 1969, f: "General," all in b1, ELK.

43. Zimmerman, "*Brown*-ing the American Textbook," 48, 63; Zimmerman, *Whose America?*, 98, 105; ASNLH to Woodward, December 10, 1967 (with Woodward's handwritten "yes"), b5, CVW; Litwack, "Historian," 154.

44. Jonathan Holloway, "The Price of Recognition: Race and the Making of the Modern University," in *American Labyrinth: Intellectual History for Complicated Times*, ed. Raymond Haberski Jr. and Andrew Hartman (Cornell University Press, 2018), 76–77; Biondi, *Black Revolution*, 17, 30; Henry, *Black Studies*, 32.

45. Biondi, *Black Revolution*, 1, 41, 81–101; M&R, 303.

46. Robert L. Harris Jr., "Coming of Age: The Transformation of Afro-American Historiography," *JNH* 67, no. 2 (1982): 108; Biondi, *Black Revolution*, 201–203, 188; M&R, 303, 306; David Brion Davis to Woodward, November 11, 1968, and Woodward to Davis, November 19, 1968, b15, CVW; Litwack, "Historian," 147.

47. Van Deburg, *New Day in Babylon*, 273; West, Ebony *Magazine and Lerone Bennett Jr.*, 74–75; Vincent Harding, "Beyond Chaos: Black History and the Search for the New Land," in *Amistad 1*, ed. John A. Williams and Charles F. Harris (Random House, 1970), 288, 284.

48. Van Deburg, *New Day in Babylon*, 69–75; Biondi, *Black Revolution*, 175, 177–178; Hofstadter to Melvin Drimmer, January 31, 1969, bUC3, RHP.

49. Eugene D. Genovese, *In Red and Black: Marxian Explorations in Southern and Afro-American History* (Pantheon, 1971), 10; Eugene D. Genovese, "Black Studies: Trouble Ahead," *Atlantic*, June 1969.

50. Marable, *Race, Reform, and Rebellion*, 109–110, 132–134; Van Deburg, *New Day in Babylon*, 302–303.

51. Witham, *Popularizing the Past*, 89; M&R, 178; Gershenhorn, *Melville Herskovits*, 234.

52. Eugene D. Genovese, "The Influence of the Black Power Movement on Historical Scholarship: Reflections of a White Historian," *Daedalus* 99, no. 2 (1970): 483.

53. Eugene D. Genovese, "The Nat Turner Case," *NYRB*, September 12, 1968; Genovese to Woodward, August 4, 1969, b21, CVW.

54. Lawrence Levine, *Black Culture and Black Consciousness: Afro-American Folk Thought from Slavery to Freedom*, 30th anniversary ed. (Oxford University Press, 2007), ix–xvi; Lawrence Levine, *The Unpredictable Past: Explorations in American Cultural History* (Oxford University Press, 1993), 35.

55. M&R, 266; Woodward to Blassingame, July 23, 1970, and Blassingame to Woodward, October 25, 1969, b8, CVW; John W. Blassingame, *The Slave Community: Plantation Life in the Antebellum South* (Oxford University Press, 1972), 237.

56. Blassingame, *Slave Community*, 154, 76.

57. Woodward to Blassingame, September 18, 1972, b8, CVW; Cobb, *C. Vann Woodward*, 250–252.

58. Stampp to Woodward, January 29, 1973, b52; Woodward to Blassingame, February 5, 1973, and Blassingame to Woodward, February 7, 1973, b8, all in CVW.

59. M&R, 267. On demography, see Philip D. Curtin, *The Atlantic Slave Trade: A Census* (University of Wisconsin Press, 1969), and C. Vann Woodward, *American Counterpoint: Slavery and Racism in the North-South Dialogue* (Little, Brown, 1971), 78–106.

60. Bruce J. Schulman, *The Seventies: The Great Shift in American Culture, Society, and Politics* (2001; Da Capo, 2002), 13–15.

61. McKitrick to Levine, May 17, 1972, f: "Larry Levine (Hofstadter Memorial Volume)," b2, ELK.

62. Eugene D. Genovese, *Miss Betsey: A Memoir of Marriage* (Intercollegiate Studies Institute, 2009), 9; Genovese, *World the Slaveholders Made*, xii; Eugene D. Genovese et al., "An Exchange on 'Nat Turner,'" *NYRB*, November 7, 1968.

63. Ira Berlin, "Introduction: Herbert G. Gutman and the American Working Class," in Herbert G. Gutman, *Power and Culture: Essays on the American Working Class* (Pantheon, 1987), 46–47; Gutman to Woodward, February 26, 1969, b22, CVW.

64. Thomas L. Haskell, "The True & Tragical History of 'Time on the Cross,'" *NYRB*, October 2, 1975.

65. Gutman to Woodward, February 2, 1971, b22, CVW; Berlin, "Introduction," 47–56.

66. See, e.g., Woodward to Fogel, February 6, 1973, b18, CVW.

67. Robert William Fogel and Stanley L. Engerman, *Time on the Cross* (Little, Brown, 1974), 1:192, 84–85, 263; Davis, "Slavery and the Post–World War II Historians," 12.

68. Gutman to Woodward, August 1, 1973, b22, CVW; Herbert G. Gutman, "The World Two Cliometricians Made: A Review-Essay of F+E=T/C," *JNH* 60, no. 1 (1975): 216.

69. Fogel and Engerman, *Time on the Cross*, 145; Gutman, "World Two Cliometricians Made," 69–72.

70. Richard C. Sutch, "The Economics of African American Slavery: The Cliometrics Debate," Working Paper 25197, National Bureau of Economic Research (October 2018), 40–41.

71. Genovese, "Black Studies"; Genovese to Woodward, October 11, 1972, b21, CVW.

72. Genovese to Allan and Stan, January 16, 1973, f: "Personal Correspondence, 1973," b1, ELK.

73. Woodward to Genovese, April 2, 1973, b21, CVW. See Genovese, *Roll, Jordan, Roll*, 134–137.

74. Woodward to Genovese, April 9, 1973, b21, CVW.

75. Woodward to Genovese, July 2, 1973, and Genovese to Woodward, October 11, 1972, b21, CVW; Genovese, *Roll, Jordan, Roll*, 3.

76. Genovese, 147–148, 273, 283–284, 594.

77. Davis to Betty Zirnite, December 3, 1974, and Davis to George Bauer, February 4, 1975, f6, b58, a2017, DBD; Gutman to Woodward, [October 1974?], b22, CVW; Peter H. Wood, "Phillips Upside Down: Dialectic or Equivocation?," *Journal of Interdisciplinary History* 6, no. 2 (1975): 289, 293; Surowiecki, "Genovese's March," 248.

Chapter 10: The Big Picture

1. Schulman, *Seventies*, 54–55; Marable, *Race, Reform, and Rebellion*, 131, 143–156, 167–168; West, Ebony *Magazine and Lerone Bennett Jr.*, 107.

2. Matthew F. Delmont, *Making* Roots: *A Nation Captivated* (University of California Press, 2016), 25–27.

3. Delmont, *Making* Roots, 4–5, 37–47, 54, 72–79, 169; Alex Haley, *Roots* (Doubleday, 1976), 1, 124–126, 206, 225, 274–275, 291, 358–360, 362.

4. Delmont, *Making* Roots, 129, 145, 175, 190–193; Henry Louis Gates Jr., "Foreword," in *Reconsidering* Roots: *Race, Politics, and Memory*, ed. Erica L. Ball and Kellie Carter Jackson (University of Georgia Press, 2017), xi; "'Roots' Gets Emmy as a Show; Takes 8 Other Awards," *NYT*, September 12, 1977, 65; Erica L. Ball and Kellie Carter Jackson, "Introduction: Reconsidering *Roots*," in *Reconsidering* Roots: *Race, Politics, and Memory*, ed. Ball and Jackson (University of Georgia Press, 2017), 2; Elkins to Edwin Yoder, March 1, 1977, Elkins to Jill Butterfield, October 14, 1977, and Elkins to Bertram Wyatt-Brown, February 6, 1977, f: "General Correspondence," b1, ELK.

5. Delmont, *Making* Roots, 180, 200, 112.

6. Delmont, 125; Zimmerman, *Whose America?*, 196.

7. C. Vann Woodward, "What Became of the 1960s?," *New Republic*, November 9, 1974, 20; Schulman, *Seventies*, 8–16.

8. Rose, *Slavery and Freedom*, 172.

9. Herbert G. Gutman, *The Black Family in Slavery and Freedom, 1750–1925* (Pantheon, 1976), 304, 260, 194–199, 465.

10. Gutman to Woodward, January 1, 1973, b22, CVW; Gutman, *Black Family*, 327, 145, 152.

11. Gutman, *Power and Culture*, ix; Berlin, "Introduction," 62–63.

12. Ira Berlin, "Time, Space, and the Evolution of Afro-American Society on British Mainland North America," *AHR* 85, no. 1 (1980): 44, 78.

13. David Brion Davis, "Intellectual Trajectories: Why People Study What They Do," *Reviews in American History* 37, no. 1 (2009): 149–151; David Brion Davis, "The Americanized Mannheim of 1945–1946," in *American Places: Encounters with History*, ed. William E. Leuchtenburg (Oxford University Press, 2000), 89.

14. David Brion Davis, *In the Image of God: Religion, Moral Values, and Our Heritage of Slavery* (Yale University Press, 2001), 3; Davis, "Intellectual Trajectories," 152–154; Davis's Harvard courses are in f5, b71, a2017, DBD; Davis, introduction to "Session on Kenneth Stampp's The Peculiar Institution" (1996), f16, b10, a2017, DBD; David Brion Davis, *The Problem of Slavery in the Age of Emancipation* (Alfred A. Knopf, 2014), xii; "Outline of Proposed Project—Aug. 24, 1957," f6, b22, a2017, DBD; David Brion Davis, *From Homicide to Slavery: Studies in American Culture* (Oxford University Press, 1986), vii.

15. Davis, "A History of Antislavery," in f11, b61, a2017, DBD; on Elkins, see f8 and f18, b39, a2017, DBD.

16. Davis to Seymour Drescher, September 25, 2008, f4, b19, a2017, DBD; Davis, *Problem of Slavery in the Age of Emancipation*, 339; Davis, *Western Culture*, vii–viii, 62, 226–229, 443.

17. M. I. Finley, "The Idea of Slavery," *NYRB*, January 26, 1967.

18. Davis to Bernhard Kendler, January 7, 1971, enclosed in Davis to Woodward, January 7, 1971, b15, CVW.

19. Davis to Woodward, March 16, 1973, b15, CVW; Genovese's handwritten comments in f9, b23, a2017, DBD; Genovese notes on "Ch. X The Good Book," f5, b58, a2017, DBD; Davis to C. Peter Ripley, August 21, 1991, f: "Correspondence, 1989–May 1992," b2, a2001, DBD; Davis to Genovese, August 13, 1973, f5 b58, a2017, DBD.

20. Davis, *Problem of Slavery in the Age of Revolution*, 71, 251–253, 350.

21. Warren Susman to Davis, December 3, 1973, f6, b58, a2017, DBD. For "substantive study," see syllabi in f: "Grad. Reading Seminar," b5, a2001, DBD.

22. Finley was sending around the article by 1966; see f: "Slavery (En SS)," b13, MFP. M. I. Finley, "Slavery," in *International Encyclopedia of the Social Sciences*, ed. David L. Sills (Macmillan, 1968), 14:307–310.

23. Lynn White Jr. to Peter Schwed, May 1, 1967, f: Publishers, b5, MFP; Finley to G. E. M. de Ste Croix, August 21, 1971, f: Ste Croix, b5, MFP.

24. See f: "Slavery—Paris," b13, and bluebooks in fH15, b20, MFP.

25. Moses I. Finley, *Ancient Slavery and Modern Ideology*, ed. Brent D. Shaw (Markus Wiener, 1998), 157–158.

26. Finley, *Ancient Slavery*, 200–217.

27. Finley to "Jan," February 3, 1979, fD32, b20, MFP; Finley, *Ancient Slavery*, 134.

28. Patterson to Finley, July 16, 1980, f: "Slavery—Paris—Reviews and Correspondence," b13, MFP; Orlando Patterson, *Slavery and Social Death: A Comparative Study* (Harvard University Press, 1982), x, 345–347, 1–13, 335.

29. Finley to Patterson, July 6, 1980, f: "Slavery—Paris—Reviews and Correspondence," b13, MFP.

30. Davis to Willie Lee Rose, January 22, 1978, f: "Correspondence, Jan–June 1978," b1, a2001, DBD.

31. David Brion Davis, *Slavery and Human Progress* (Oxford University Press, 1984), xvi–xvii; M. I. Finley, "Suddenly, Owning People Was Wrong," *NYT*, February 3, 1985, 26; Finley to Robert Fogel, February 23, 1985, f: "NY Review, etc, 1960–," b15, MFP; Davis to Rebecca Scott, April 19, 1985, f: "Correspondence, Sept. 1984–," b2, a2001, and Davis to Robert Abzug, August 3, 1989, f2, b59, a2017, DBD.

32. Davis notes, July 24, 2007, f4, b19, a2017, DBD; Thomas Bender, ed., *The Antislavery Debate: Capitalism and Abolitionism as a Problem in Historical Interpretation* (University of California Press, 1992).

33. Davis to "Bill," [May 31, 1990], f1, b57, a2017, DBD; Davis, *In the Image of God*, 1; Davis notes, July 24, 2007, f4, b19, a2017, DBD.

34. Novick, *That Noble Dream*, 367, 491–492; Biondi, *Black Revolution*, 258.

35. Genovese, *Roll, Jordan, Roll*, 494–501.

36. Angela Davis, "Reflections on the Black Woman's Role in the Community of Slaves," *Massachusetts Review* 13, nos. 1/2 (1972): 81–90.

37. Gerda Lerner, ed., *Black Women in White America: A Documentary History* (1972; Vintage, 1973), xxxi, xx.

38. Roger L. Geiger, *American Higher Education Since World War II: A History* (Princeton University Press, 2019), 131, 232–241; Novick, *That Noble Dream*, 493.

39. Biondi, *Black Revolution*, 259; Rosalind Rosenberg, "Women in the Humanities: Taking Their Place," in *The Humanities and the Dynamics of Inclusion Since World War II*, ed. David A. Hollinger (Johns Hopkins University Press, 2006), 255; Geiger, *American Higher Education*, 226; Novick, *That Noble Dream*, 493.

40. Gerda Lerner, *The Creation of Patriarchy* (Oxford University Press, 1986), vii–viii, 80–89.

41. Deborah Gray White, "'Matter Out of Place': *Ar'n't I a Woman?* Black Female Scholars and the Academy," *Journal of African American History* 92, no. 1 (2007): 9–10; Biondi, *Black Revolution*, 263.

42. Keeanga-Yamahtta Taylor, introduction to *How We Get Free: Black Feminism and the Combahee River Collective* (Haymarket, 2017); Combahee River Collective Statement (1978), https://web.archive.org/web/20170224021117/http://circuitous.org/scraps/combahee.html.

43. Deborah Gray White, *Ar'n't I a Woman? Female Slaves in the Plantation South* (Norton, 1985), 15, 110, 103; Davis, "Reflections," 84; Judith L. Herman, *Trauma and Recovery: The Aftermath of Violence—From Domestic Abuse to Political Terror* (1992; Basic Books, 2022), 5, 46–48.

44. Elizabeth Kastor, "Toni Morrison's 'Beloved' Country: The Writer and Her Haunting Tale of Slavery," *Washington Post*, October 5, 1987; Jenna Wortham, "The Woman Shaping a Generation of Black Thought," *NYT Magazine*, April 26, 2023.

45. Delmont, *Making Roots*, 199.

46. Novick, *That Noble Dream*, 362–364, 372–373, 581–583; Palmer, *From Gentleman's Club to Professional Body*, xii; Geiger, *American Higher Education*, 165–171, 251–269, 284–294; Thelin, *History of American Higher Education*, 320–327.

47. Roger L. Geiger, "Demography and Curriculum: The Humanities in American Higher Education from the 1950s Through the 1980s," in *The Humanities and the Dynamics of Inclusion Since World War II*, ed. David A. Hollinger (Johns Hopkins University Press, 2006), 51–55; Geiger, *American Higher Education*, 244; James Oliver Horton, "Slavery in American History: An Uncomfortable National Dialogue," in *Slavery and Public History: The Tough Stuff of American Memory*, ed. James Oliver Horton and Lois E. Horton (New Press, 2006), 42; Novick, *That Noble Dream*, 574–576.

48. Jill Lepore, *The Whites of Their Eyes: The Tea Party's Revolution and the Battle over American History*, paperback ed. (Princeton University Press, 2011), 68–69.

49. Witham, *Popularizing the Past*, 105, 114–116; Howard Zinn, *A People's History of the United States* (Harper & Row, 1980), 7, 174, 182.

50. Andrew Hartman, *A War for the Soul of America: A History of the Culture Wars* (University of Chicago Press, 2015), 256–257; Geiger, *American Higher Education*, 299, 353–354.

51. Lepore, *Whites of Their Eyes*, 68–69; Marable, *Race, Reform, and Rebellion*, 176–179, 203.

52. Schulman, *Seventies*, 58; Hartman, *War for the Soul of America*, 109–111.

53. Peter S. Onuf and Annette Gordon-Reed, "Introduction," in Lucia Stanton, *"Those Who Labor for My Happiness": Slavery at Thomas Jefferson's Monticello* (University of Virginia Press, 2012), viii–ix; Lois E. Horton, "Avoiding History: Thomas Jefferson, Sally Hemings, and the Uncomfortable Public Conversation on Slavery," in *Slavery and Public History: The Tough Stuff of American Memory*, ed. James Oliver Horton and Lois E. Horton (New Press, 2006), 138.

54. William M. Kelso, "Mulberry Row: Slave Life at Thomas Jefferson's Monticello," *Archaeology* 39, no. 5 (1986): 29–35.

55. Kelso, "Mulberry Row," 35; Horton, "Avoiding History," 138; Onuf and Gordon-Reed, "Introduction," ix; Gardiner Hallock, "Mulberry Row: Telling the Story of Slavery at Monticello," *SiteLINES* 14, no. 2 (2019): 5; Clint Smith, *How the Word Is Passed: A Reckoning with the History of Slavery Across America* (Little, Brown, 2021), 42.

56. Hartman, *War for the Soul of America*, 261–284, quoting Lynne Cheney ("grim") and Diane Ravitch ("greed"); Sean Wilentz, "The 1619 Project and Living in Truth," *Opera Historica* 22, no. 1 (2021): 87n1.

57. Davis to Stanley Engerman, August 17, 1994, f3, b59; and Davis to Sheldon Meyer, May 30, 1994, f4, b19, a2017, DBD.

58. Harold Holzer, "Prizing History," *American Heritage* 51, no. 3 (May/June 2000); Herbert Mitgang, "On Paper, the Evolution of the United States," *NYT*, July 6, 1992.

59. Davis, "New Course Form" ("unified historical phenomenon") and "Slavery and Antislavery in Global Perspective" syllabus from 1989 or 1990 ("Danger"), f9, b4, a2017, DBD.

60. David Brion Davis, "Looking at Slavery from Broader Perspectives," *AHR* 105, no. 2 (2000): 454.

61. Myron Magnet, "The Growth Investor," *Philanthropy*, July 1, 2010.

62. Davis to Richard Gilder, March 13, 1994, and Davis notes, March 19, 1994, f11, b10, a2017, DBD.

63. Davis to Sheldon Meyer, May 30, 1994, f4, b19, a2017, DBD; Magnet, "The Growth Investor"; Lesley Herrmann to Davis, May 2, 1994, f11, b10, a2017, DBD; "The Origins and Nature of New World Slavery," July 1994, f: "Summer Slavery Course—Syllabus," b4, a2001, DBD; "Report on Slavery Seminar at Yale" and thank-you notes in f11, b10, a2017, DBD.

64. Lesley Herrmann to Richard Levin, August 28, 1994; and Herrmann to Davis, August 30, 1994, f11, b10, a2017, DBD.

65. Davis to Paul Freedman, April 25, 1996, f: "Slavery Correspondence, 1996–2000," b58, a2017, DBD; David W. Blight, *Yale and Slavery: A History* (Yale University Press, 2024), 2–3.

66. Davis to Robert Forbes, [January 14 or 15, 2000], f5, b57, a2017, DBD.

67. Davis, "Intellectual Trajectories," 159; David Brion Davis, *Inhuman Bondage: The Rise and Fall of Slavery in the New World* (Oxford University Press, 2006), 4; Davis to John Mack Faragher, April 17, 1995, f: "US History Faculty," b5, a2001; Davis, "The Origins and Nature of New World Slavery: Seeking the Big Picture," Spring 2000, f3, b2, a2017, DBD.

Chapter 11: The Ghost

1. Smith, *How the Word Is Passed*, 228–230; "African Burial Ground: History & Culture," National Park Service, www.nps.gov/afbg/learn/historyculture/index.htm.

2. Alexis Okeowo, "Secret Histories," *New Yorker*, October 26, 2020; Sugrue, *Sweet Land of Liberty*, 507–537.

3. Saidiya Hartman, "The Territory Between Us: A Report on 'Black Women in the Academy: Defending Our Name: 1894–1994,'" *Callaloo* 17, no. 2 (1994): 441.

4. Marable, *Race, Reform, and Rebellion*, 225–226; Saidiya Hartman, *Lose Your Mother: A Journey Along the Atlantic Slave Route* (Farrar, Straus and Giroux, 2007), 8–12; Hartman, *War for the Soul of America*, 126.

5. Saidiya Hartman, "The Tragic Mode," *NYRB*, November 19, 2022.

6. Elias Rodriques, "How Saidiya Hartman Changed the Study of Black Life," *Nation*, November 3, 2022.

7. Okeowo, "Secret Histories"; Saidiya Hartman, *Scenes of Subjection: Terror, Slavery, and Self-Making in Nineteenth-Century America*, rev. ed. (Norton, 2022), xxxvi.

8. Rodriques, "How Saidiya Hartman."

9. Hartman, *Lose Your Mother*, 74; Marable, *Race, Reform, and Rebellion*, 220–221.

10. Nell Irvin Painter, "Soul Murder and Slavery: Toward a Fully Loaded Cost Accounting," in *U.S. History as Women's History: New Feminist Essays*, ed. Linda K. Kerber, Alice Kessler-Harris, and Kathryn Kish Sklar (University of North Carolina Press, 1995), 130–138; McKitrick to Elkins, February 8, 1996, b28, MCK.

11. Saidiya Hartman, *Scenes of Subjection: Terror, Slavery, and Self-Making in Nineteenth-Century America* (Oxford University Press, 1997), 4–6, 42, 116; Rodriques, "How Saidiya Hartman."

12. Marable, *Race, Reform, and Rebellion*, 234–235.

13. John Torpey, *Making Whole What Has Been Smashed: On Reparations Politics* (Harvard University Press, 2006), 24.

14. James T. Campbell, "Settling Accounts? An Americanist Perspective on Historical Reconciliation," *AHR* 114, no. 4 (2009): 967–973.

15. Jia Lynn Yang, "Yale Slavery Report Questioned by Experts," *Yale Daily News*, December 12, 2001; Mark Alden Branch, "The Slavery Legacy," *Yale Alumni Magazine*, February 2002; Antony Dugdale, J. J. Fueser, and J. Celso de Castro Alves, *Yale, Slavery and Abolition* (Amistad Committee, 2001).

16. David Horowitz, "Ten Reasons Why Reparations for Slavery Is a Bad Idea—and Racist Too," Brown *Daily Herald*, March 13, 2001, 6; Kira Lesley, "Paying for Controversy," Brown *Daily Herald*, September 21, 2004; Diana Jean Schemo, "Ad Intended to Stir Up Campuses More Than Succeeds in Its Mission," *NYT*, March 28, 2001; James T. Campbell, "Slavery and Justice at Brown—A Personal Reflection," in *Brown University's Slavery and Justice Report with Commentary on Context and Impact*, 2nd ed., ed. Anthony Bogues, Cass Cliatt, and Allison Levy (Brown University, 2021), 14.

17. Ruth J. Simmons, *Up Home: One Girl's Journey* (Random House, 2023), 18–19; Ruth J. Simmons, "Opening Convocation Address," September 4, 2001, www.brown.edu/Administration/News_Bureau/2001-02/01-014t.html.

18. Campbell, "Slavery and Justice at Brown," 13; Anthony Bogues interview with Ruth J. Simmons in *Brown University's Slavery and Justice Report with Commentary on Context and Impact*, 2nd ed., ed. Anthony Bogues, Cass Cliatt, and Allison Levy (Brown University, 2021), 9; Simmons letter to prospective committee members, April 30, 2003, https://slaveryandjustice.brown.edu/committee-communications/president-ruth-j-simmons-letter-prospective-committee-members-april-2003.

19. Campbell, "Slavery and Justice at Brown," 12.

20. Bogues, Cliatt, and Levy, eds., *Slavery and Justice Report*, 59, 63–64; Campbell, "Slavery and Justice at Brown," 20.

21. Leslie M. Harris, "Higher Education's Reckoning with Slavery," *Academe*, Winter 2020; Renée Ater, "The Challenge of Memorializing Slavery in North Carolina: The Unsung Founders Memorial and the North Carolina Freedom Monument Project," in *Politics of Memory: Making Slavery Visible in the Public Space*, ed. Ana Lucia Araujo (Routledge, 2012), 145–150.

22. Bogues, Cliatt, and Levy, eds., *Slavery and Justice Report*, 111, 126, 155–157.

23. Harris, "Higher Education's Reckoning"; Campbell, "Settling Accounts?," 972; James T. Campbell, Leslie M. Harris, and Alfred L. Brophy, "Introduction," in *Slavery and the University: Histories and Legacies*, ed. Harris, Campbell, and Brophy (University of Georgia Press, 2019), 13; "Donors and Dollars Set New Fund-Raising Records in FY 2007," *News from Brown*, July 23, 2007, https://news.brown.edu/articles/2007/07/new-fund-raising-record.

24. Hartman, *Lose Your Mother*, 6, 15–17, 118–121, 133; Saidiya Hartman, "The Time of Slavery," *South Atlantic Quarterly* 101, no. 4 (2002): 762.

25. Hartman, *Lose Your Mother*, 136–151; Saidiya Hartman, "The Dead Book Revisited," *History of the Present* 6, no. 2 (2016): 211; Saidiya Hartman, "Venus in Two Acts," *Small Axe* 12, no. 2 (2008): 11.

26. Hartman, "Venus," 9–10.

27. Michel-Rolph Trouillot, *Silencing the Past: Power and the Production of History* (Beacon, 1995), 26, 48.

28. Hartman, "Venus," 9, 11–12, 4.

29. Annette Gordon-Reed, *The Hemingses of Monticello: An American Family* (Norton, 2008), 23.

30. John Jeremiah Sullivan, "Annette Gordon-Reed, The Art of Nonfiction No. 11," *Paris Review* 238 (Winter 2021); Annette Gordon-Reed, *Thomas Jefferson and Sally Hemings: An American Controversy* (University Press of Virginia, 1997), xi–xviii, 95.

31. Dinitia Smith and Nicholas Wade, "DNA Test Finds Evidence of Jefferson Child by Slave," *NYT*, November 1, 1998, 1; Smith, *How the Word Is Passed*, 38.

32. Gordon-Reed, *Thomas Jefferson and Sally Hemings*, 231–234.

33. Annette Gordon-Reed, "Celia's Case," in *Race on Trial: Law and Justice in American History*, ed. Gordon-Reed (Oxford University Press, 2002), 48; Annette Gordon-Reed, "Rebellious History," *NYRB*, October 22, 2020.

34. Gordon-Reed, *Hemingses of Monticello*, 265, 291–303, 312–342, 361–365, 651.

35. Bogues, Cliatt, and Levy, eds., *Slavery and Justice Report*, 63–64; Sven Beckert and Katherine Stevens, *Harvard and Slavery: Seeking a Forgotten History* (Harvard and Slavery Research Seminar, 2011), 3–4; Sven Beckert and Seth Rockman, eds., *Slavery's Capitalism: A New History of American Economic Development* (University of Pennsylvania Press, 2016), 405–406.

36. Edward E. Baptist, *The Half Has Never Been Told: Slavery and the Making of American Capitalism*, paperback ed. (Basic Books, 2016), 421–427, xxi–xxii, 73.

37. "Our Withdrawn Review 'Blood Cotton,'" *Economist*, September 5, 2014.

38. Zach Schonfeld, "The Economist Retracts a Book Review Complaining That a Historical Account of Slavery Depicted Slaves as 'Victims,'" *Newsweek*, September 5, 2014; Fred Barbash, "'Slavery Wasn't All That Bad' Book Review Spawns #economistbookreviews Satire," *Washington Post*, September 8, 2014.

39. See previous note for *Newsweek* article. Jamelle Bouie, "A Few Helpful Rules for Reviewing Books About Slavery," *Slate*, September 5, 2014; Edward E. Baptist, "The Economist's Review of My Book Reveals How White People Still Refuse to Believe Black People About Being Black," *Guardian*, September 7, 2014; Edward Baptist, "What the Economist Doesn't Get About Slavery—and My Book," *Politico*, September 7, 2014.

40. Baptist, *Half Has Never Been Told*, 116–117, 126–130, 142; James Oakes, "A Few Random Thoughts on Capitalism and Slavery," *Economic Historian*, May 23, 2021; Alan L. Olmstead in "Roundtable of Reviews for *The Half Has Never Been Told*," *Journal of Economic History* 75, no. 3 (2015): 922; James Oakes, "Capitalism and Slavery and the Civil War," *International Labor and Working-Class History* 89 (Spring 2016): 216.

41. Ari Kelman, "Slaving for Profits," *Times Literary Supplement*, April 3, 2015, 7; Marc Parry, "Shackles and Dollars," *Chronicle of Higher Education*, December 8, 2016.

42. Rodriques, "How Saidiya Hartman"; Keeanga-Yamahtta Taylor, *From #BlackLivesMatter to Black Liberation* (Haymarket, 2016), 10–12, 151; Gary Gerstle, *The Rise and Fall of the Neoliberal Order: America and the World in the Free Market Era* (Oxford University Press, 2022), 202–204; Barbara Ransby, *Making All Black Lives Matter: Reimagining Freedom in the Twenty-First Century* (University of California Press, 2018), 1, 22.

43. Baptist, *Half Has Never Been Told*, 431.

44. Ta-Nehisi Coates, "The Case for Reparations," *Atlantic*, June 2014; Kelman, "Slaving for Profits," 8.

45. Peniel E. Joseph, *The Third Reconstruction: America's Struggle for Racial Justice in the Twenty-First Century* (Basic Books, 2022), 108, 128.

46. Zimmerman, *Whose America?*, 196.

Epilogue: The Work

1. Nikole Hannah-Jones, "Origins," in *The 1619 Project: A New Origin Story*, ed. Hannah-Jones et al. (One World, 2021), xvii–xxiii; details about the 1619 Project can be found in Sarah Ellison, "How the 1619 Project Took Over 2020," *Washington Post*, October 13, 2020.

2. Ellison, "How 1619"; *NYT Magazine*, August 18, 2019; Nikita Stewart, "Why Can't We Teach This?," *NYT*, August 18, 2019, MC3.

3. Jake Silverstein, "Editor's Note," *NYT Magazine*, August 18, 2019, 4.

4. Nikole Hannah-Jones, "The Idea of America," *NYT Magazine*, August 18, 2019, 18.

5. Ellison, "How 1619"; Wilentz, "1619 Project," 89–92; Sean Wilentz, "American Slavery and 'the Relentless Unforeseen,'" *NYRB*, November 19, 2019.

6. James Oakes, "What the 1619 Project Got Wrong," *Catalyst* 5, no. 3 (2021).

7. Adam Serwer, "The Fight over the 1619 Project Is Not About the Facts," *Atlantic*, December 23, 2019; Ellison, "How 1619."

8. Alex Lichtenstein, "1619 and All That," *AHR* 125, no. 1 (2020): xv–xvi; Jake Silverstein, "An Update to the 1619 Project," *NYT Magazine*, March 11, 2020, www.nytimes.com/2020/03/11/magazine/an-update-to-the-1619-project.html.

9. Ellison, "How 1619."

10. Nikole Hannah-Jones, "Justice," in *The 1619 Project: A New Origin Story*, ed. Hannah-Jones et al. (One World, 2021), 472–473.

11. Mark Philip Bradley and Fei-Hsien Wang, "Introduction" to The 1619 Project Forum, *AHR* 127, no. 4 (2022): 1793.

INDEX

INDEX

Photo credit: Melanie Stengel

SCOTT SPILLMAN RECEIVED HIS PHD IN HISTORY FROM STANFORD UNIversity. His writing has appeared in the *New Republic*, the *Los Angeles Review of Books*, *n+1*, and *The Point*. He lives in Denver, Colorado.